BETWEEN the BRANCHES

PITT SERIES IN POLICY
AND INSTITUTIONAL STUDIES

Bert A. Rockman, *Editor*

BETWEEN THE BRANCHES

THE WHITE HOUSE OFFICE
OF LEGISLATIVE AFFAIRS

Kenneth E. Collier

University of Pittsburgh Press

Published by the University of Pittsburgh Press, Pittsburgh, Pa. 15261
Copyright © 1997, University of Pittsburgh Press

Manufactured in the United States of America
Printed on acid-free paper

10 9 8 7 6 5 4 3 2 1

Collier, Kenneth E., 1959–
Between the branches : the White House Office of Legislative
Affairs / Kenneth Collier.
p.   cm. — (Pitt series in policy and institutional studies)
Includes bibliographical references and index.
ISBN 0-8229-3978-9 (cloth : acid-free paper). — ISBN
0-8229-5629-2 (pbk. : acid-free paper)
1. Executive power—United States. 2. Legislation—United States.
3. Separation of powers—United States. 4. United States. White
House Office. Office of Legislative Affairs. I. Title.
II. Series.
JK585.C58   1997
320.473—dc21   96-51293

A CIP catalog record for this book is available from the
British Library.

This book is dedicated to my parents,
Joe and Betty Lyn Collier

CONTENTS

	Preface	ix
	Acknowledgments	xi
1	Introduction	1
2	The Eisenhower Administration	29
3	The Kennedy Administration	57
4	The Johnson Administration	79
5	The Nixon Administration	109
6	The Ford Administration	138
7	The Carter Administration	163
8	The Reagan Administration	197
9	The Bush Administration	231
10	The Clinton Administration	260
11	Conclusion	279
	Appendix A	291
	Appendix B	292
	Notes	293
	Index	327

PREFACE

This book is about how the two great branches of United States government interact. My research took me repeatedly to Washington D.C. so that I could learn from "insiders" how the game was played. I learned that, although the game of influence is played out within the Beltway, these insiders always keep a cautious eye toward their constituents outside Washington. This is very much an outside-in process and winning legislative battles inside the Capitol requires winning battles back in congressional districts. The workings of the machine are within Washington, but the dynamics of the process originate beyond the District's boundary. Citizens' imperfect information about legislative issues leaves them open to presidential influence; this in turn leaves legislators open to presidential influence because they are unable to anticipate citizen response to legislative activity. Thus, presidential influence in Congress turns upon the White House's ability to capitalize on congressional uncertainty and to shape—or at least appear to shape—citizen opinions on legislation.

Sources

The research presented here makes use of material from the Truman, Eisenhower, Kennedy, Johnson, and Carter presidential libraries as well as documents from the Nixon Project in the National Archives and the Everett Dirksen Congressional Center. This includes memos and other internal communications from these administrations as well as oral histories maintained by the libraries.

In addition, personal interviews were conducted with a range of actors involved in the process. In order to provide a perspective from both branches, interviews were conducted with White House and departmental liaison staff as well as members of Congress, primarily those in leadership positions or more senior legislators who had worked with several presidents. Almost all of these interviews were confidential and not for attribution in order to facilitate an open discussion. Fifty-seven people were interviewed, some on several occasions, totaling seventy-five interviews. A more detailed discussion of the interviews and subjects can be found in Appendix A. *All quotations without citations are drawn from these interviews.*

The Structure of This Study

The manuscript is organized historically to examine the ebb and flow of presidential power in Congress and to explore the impact of changes in political context on White House resources. Chapters 2 through 10 each examine an administration, from Eisenhower to Clinton. Each of these chapters highlights one or two legislative tools relied upon by that administration and explores those strategies and techniques in depth as well as discusses how these tools were necessitated by the political context. This approach permits an examination of the resources that presidents draw upon in attempting to lead Congress and helps us understand the historical development of these resources in response to changes in context and the functioning of each administration.

Each chapter also includes a discussion of the president's personal approach to Congress. Although it is dangerous to ascribe too much to the personality of a president, in congressional–White House relations Clark Clifford's adage that government takes its "color from the character and personality of the president" is especially true.[1] Members of Congress interviewed for this book often stressed that relations between the White House and Congress began with the person in the Oval Office, and the liaison staff from every administration inevitably mentioned that the president was their best lobbyist. As tempting as it would be to offer an electoral explanation for all of what the White House does, the personality of the person at the heart of this process presents the greatest challenge. It is hard to imagine a theory of the presidency that could predict all the differences between the proximate cases of Lyndon Johnson and Richard Nixon. Johnson's staff had to struggle to keep him off of Capitol Hill while Nixon's staff struggled to get him to have even the briefest meetings with members, and even then he usually refused to ask for their votes. The differences between presidents make the study of the presidency interesting, but the general forces behind the relationship between the branches make the topic important beyond the particular cases presented. Fortunately, the White House staff and members of Congress interviewed were witnesses to both, permitting both an exploration of the contributions of the rich diversity of the officeholder and the broad political forces behind the office.

ACKNOWLEDGMENTS

This project has left me with a great debt to many people. The promises of anonymity that led to frank discussions with White House staff and members of Congress preclude me from thanking specific individuals, but the generous gift of their time made my work possible. An equal debt is owed to their assistants who suffered through a barrage of letters and phone calls as well as numerous bouts of rescheduling. Without their patience this book would not be possible.

Bob Whittaker introduced me around Washington and arranged some of my initial interviews there. Without his enthusiastic support I likely never would have gained the level of access I did. I owe a similar debt to Larry Harlow, son of Bryce Harlow, for introducing me to several generations of White House veterans. I also would like to thank these men, and the staff of Senator Kassebaum's office, for their guidance on area scafood restaurants and numerous other small acts of hospitality that made my time in Washington filling as well as fulfilling.

When I was not in Washington, I found myself in a variety of archives where numerous archivists labored to guide me through the mounds of White House and congressional memoranda. While the list of every archivist who assisted me in some way is too long to give here, I would like to acknowledge a particular debt to Dwight Strandberg at the Eisenhower library.

While back home in Kansas I was assisted in the research for this project with the energies and enthusiasm of David Boggs, Ginger Klemme, and Jason Burritt. These research assistants helped track down a bewildering variety of newspaper and other sources. I should also thank my Eisenhower's Presidency Seminar students, who looked at the earliest bits of this research and dared to criticize the work of their professor. I have also benefited from the insights of the graduate students in my Presidency Seminar.

Intellectually, this book has a number of debts to acknowledge. My interest in the White House Office of Legislative Affairs was inspired by Steve Wayne's *The Legislative Presidency*. This fueled my work with Terry Sullivan, who guided me into graduate school and introduced me to the possibilities of work in presidential archives. Readers will immediately note my heavy reliance on Samuel Kernell's distinctions of institutionalized and individualized pluralism and my appropriation of Richard Neustadt's labeling of prestige, merchandising, and special publics. The writings of both men guided me, but they bear no responsibility for what I have done with these terms.

Jeff Cohen and Mike Towle waded through various versions of this project and lent their time and insights without hesitation. Elaine Sharp, Burdett Loomis, Al Cigler, and Bruce Buchanan also pitched in to help repair various bits and pieces of the manuscript. Of course, I owe much to Bert Rockman, who cheerfully shepherded this book into print. Cynthia Miller and the staff at the University of Pittsburgh Press graciously accepted the burden of working with an inexperienced author.

This research was supported by the General Research Fund at the University of Kansas, as well as travel grants from the Gerald R. Ford Foundation and the Everett Dirksen Congressional Center.

I owe a great debt to my wife, Sandy, my most overworked reader, who too often was left to change too many of our daughter Nicole's diapers as I finished this book.

BETWEEN THE BRANCHES

1

INTRODUCTION

Through his White House staff, through his cabinet, and
through his supporters in Congress, presidential influence
must weld policy despite the separation of powers.

Pendleton Herring, *Presidential Leadership*

OVER FIFTY YEARS AGO, PENDLETON HERRING[1] OBSERVED
that presidents must exercise leadership in the policy process through others and that this leadership must come in spite of the separation of powers
specified in the Constitution. Richard Neustadt suggested that the Constitution created a government of "separated institutions *sharing* powers,"[2] yet
how the two great branches of American government share power may be
one of the most misunderstood issues in politics—ironically, because it seems
to be one of the most visible. One prevalent image is that of President Johnson, physically towering over a smaller member of Congress, prodding him
with an outstretched index finger and extracting support with a barrage of
horse trading, back slapping, and desk pounding. Another image is of
Ronald Reagan going on national television to rally citizens to his cause
through fervent rhetoric and poignant stories. These instances of presidential influence make for high drama, although neither provides a realistic picture of how the president works with Congress.

Presidential leadership of Congress is inherently difficult because of the
separation of powers and the system of checks and balances put in place over
two hundred years ago. Bryce Harlow, who along with Wilton Persons set up
the first formal lobbying operation in the White House, described his career

as "a lifetime of building bridges across the yawning constitutional chasm, a chasm fashioned by our power-fearing Fathers to keep the Congress and the President at a safe distance from one another in the interest of human liberty."[3] He reminded his audience that the president and his assistants must work against the system, to give the president some control over Congress, in Harlow's words to "uncheck the checks and imbalance the balances."[4] Despite the barriers, citizens and members of Congress expect the president to exercise legislative leadership successfully. As Richard Nixon pointed out in 1980, "We choose Presidents to make things happen."[5]

This book explores how the White House tries to overcome the institutional barriers to legislative influence and how Congress has resisted presidential leadership. This process of mutual adaptation or emulation has produced significant changes in how the president attempts to lead Congress and the periodic shifts in the balance of power between the branches. As Richard Neustadt suggested, presidents derive their power from the dependence of others,[6] but Congress has little reason to accept a subordinate role and constitutional resources to resist becoming dependent on the president for resources they need to get reelected.

I argue that the shifting balance between the branches has been motivated by the electoral concerns of members of Congress and the president. The president needs a compliant Congress to advance his legislative agenda, but legislators need independence so that they can pursue the local interests essential to their reelection. The conflict between the constituency pressures of the two branches creates an intragovernmental lobby where local and national interests collide and the system of checks and balances is vigorously exercised.

The Myth of "Presidential" Influence

Researchers have often overpersonalized and oversimplified the relationship between the executive branch and Congress. Journalists often portray presidential leadership of Congress as a simple process in which a president negotiates for his bill as the final vote approaches, but the contemporary presidency is represented before Congress by a large corps of full-time, professional lobbyists that work for the White House, cabinet departments,[7] and the Office of Management and Budget. By focusing so much attention on the role of the president personally, we have overlooked the efforts of the legions of officials who labor to push administration legislation at every step in the process. The president's personal involvement represents only a small portion of the total energy expended on behalf of the administration, and the president's time is a closely guarded resource, used only in extreme situations after all other efforts have failed. As one thirty-year veteran member of the House put it, "Congress usually has more of a relationship with the White House staff than with the president."

This study examines the broad picture of the interaction between the executive branch and Congress. The command center of this effort is the White House Office of Legislative Affairs.[8] This office is responsible for coordinating the lobbying of the president, cabinet departments, the Office of Management and Budget, and the rest of the White House staff. Every day these administration lobbyists fan out over Capitol Hill to work quietly behind the scenes, providing members with information about legislation, counting votes, persuading reluctant members, and then returning to the executive branch to share the information they have gathered during the day. Most legislation involves no direct participation by the president, while some bills do not even receive serious attention from the White House staff and are guided through the process by the legislative relations operations of the relevant cabinet departments.

Thus, a study that includes the White House Office of Legislative Affairs brings together the full range of actors involved in lobbying Congress on behalf of the president. Stephen Wayne's *The Legislative Presidency* is the only book to examine the function of the Office of Legislative Affairs across several administrations,[9] although several other books and dissertations have examined the liaison staffs of specific administrations.[10]

A study of the White House Office of Legislative Affairs and departmental liaison offices presents the best perspective for understanding the entire process. The experiences of staff members provide insights into the motives of both branches, because the legislative liaison staff of the White House carries the national agenda of the president to Congress and then returns to the White House with the more localized concerns of members of Congress. By examining the role of the president's many agents in Congress we can better see the impact that the administration has throughout the process, and by including the congressional perspective we can better understand the nature of resistance to presidential leadership.

Current Perspectives in the Literature

In the 1980s and early 1990s a number of books and articles examined the president's influence in Congress. Inspired by the early research of Stephen Wayne and George Edwards,[11] the primary motivation of these works has been to measure the impact of the president on the legislative process. Each of these works contributed something to our understanding of the limits of presidential influence in Congress. However, in the flood of empirical studies much of the emphasis on how the relationship is conducted has often been put aside. Although the contribution of these studies has been important, some of the processes that have been overlooked can contribute to our understanding. I hope that this book will complement that literature and resolve some of the dilemmas produced by differences in their findings. Despite differences in the approach employed, the research here is motivated by the same two questions posed by George Edwards at the beginning of his most recent book: "what do presidents do to try to lead Congress, and how reliably can they use each source of influence?"[12]

IN SEARCH OF PRESIDENTIAL INFLUENCE

One disagreement in the literature is over the standard of presidential performance in Congress. Some studies have chosen to focus on *success,* which evaluates presidential performance in terms of the passage of legislation supported by the president. Others have examined *influence,* which emphasizes the president's ability to alter the actions of others.

Bond and Fleisher believe that the emphasis on presidential influence is too narrow and choose instead to study the broader concept of success: "The problem of government responsiveness in a system of separate institutions sharing power makes it important to analyze the conditions that might lead to presidential success, regardless of whether success results from the president's influence or from forces beyond his control."[13] Their choice reflects a desire to examine the process as a whole, rather than to highlight the role of the president. Because my intention is to examine the forces under the White House's control and highlight the potential for presidential leadership, the focus of this research is *influence.* Even if the president is a marginal player, as George Edwards and others contend, the ability of a president to lead, despite the separation of power and the decentralized American system, merits study.

Finding evidence of presidential influence through quantitative analysis has produced a wide range of measures and results. While the empirical research on the topic has proven to be valuable, the research presented here suggests that there are some elements of presidential influence that have not been captured by current measures. It is unlikely that any measure of influence will ever capture every nuance of presidential efforts; however, by exploring the process in depth we can better understand the potential sources of bias in our measures.

One of the most important limitations of most measures of presidential success or influence is that such studies typically rely upon roll call votes or some other analysis of floor action. This overlooks an important goal of presidential influence: stopping legislation, preferably before it reaches the floor of Congress. Often, the most impressive victory the White House can win is for objectionable legislation to die quietly in committee. Of course, it is difficult to measure the influence of the president in votes never taken, but often the success of an administration lies in the failure of congressional opponents to get legislation out of committee. Similarly, while the sustaining of a presidential veto at the end of the legislative process appears to be a victory, it reflects a failure to stop legislation earlier in the process.

The importance of stopping legislation is most evident in the administrations of conservative presidents like Dwight Eisenhower, who see their role as much in preventing the expansion of government as in their own contribution to statutes. Charles O. Jones noted that when the Clinton administration cited its ability to stop Republican legislation as evidence of its success, "It's never been the case . . . that a president can do well by preventing things from happening. Nobody ever argued that with Republican presidents."[14] However, Bryce Harlow, who worked for both Eisenhower and Nixon, described the function of the liaison staff in both positive and negative terms: "The role of the liaison staff is to lobby for the president's program and to keep Congress from doing something different."[15] Eisenhower, Nixon, Ford, Reagan, and Bush were all conservative presidents who hoped to slow the growth of government and a standard that fully recognizes their motives is needed to understand adequately presidential influence during this period. While political scientists' measures of presidential influence in the past have always been based upon the ability to advance legislation, it is evident that presidents often may define their legislative goals in other terms.

The White House's inability to get legislation to the floor provides another example of the limitations of roll call analysis. Richard Reeves points out that Kennedy was winning on most floor votes, but that more often than not his legislation failed to make it out of committee.[16] Substantial effort is often required for the executive branch to get its legislation considered, and congressional opponents have many different means of foiling presidential wishes before a roll call vote is taken.

The content of legislation poses an additional challenge for evaluating presidential influence. Passage of legislation is assumed to represent success, but it is often the case that the bill the president signs bears little resemblance to what the president originally requested. Quite often, presidential accomplishment cannot be measured by asking if a bill passed; rather, the most telling fact often is what version of the bill passed. Legislation can be watered down or dramatically altered by amendments that may change the bill while leaving the title of the bill the same. Presidents may see much desired legislation altered beyond recognition and yet still claim political victory after the bill passes.

Strategic behavior on the part of a member of Congress or the president makes the task of gauging presidential clout difficult. Most measures of presidential success rely on public statements by the president to derive presidential intent. However, as Stephen Wayne points out, "a high score may indicate that Congress is persuading the president to support, or at least not to oppose its most popular bills."[17] Presidents may attempt to inflate their success rates by claiming a role on a winning issue after the fact or by avoiding taking a position when polls of members indicate that defeat is likely.

The impact of executive branch lobbying is hard to gauge because it is an ongoing process with no clear beginning. Since the executive branch is often involved in drafting legislation, influence (in both directions) begins before a piece of legislation is drafted. It is widely held that smart presidents consult with Congress before introducing legislation. When presidents modify their proposals or negotiate with legislators before legislation is officially introduced, the degree and even direction of influence may not be evident. Presidents may alter their legislative agenda to fit what they believe can pass Congress so that presidents with high levels of public approval or large congressional majorities may push an ambitious legislative agenda, while presidents in weak strategic positions may limit their agenda and make substantive concessions to congressional opposition. The decision about how aggressive an agenda the White House can hope to achieve is often based upon the political intelligence gathered by the congressional liaison staff. Bryce Harlow would often tell others in the White House, "you can't come running in here and give us a lead weight and tell us to float it across a pond."[18] Clinton's head lobbyist, Howard Paster, described this function as part of the job. "Your job is to listen to everybody, and talk to everybody and feed information back. You shape the policy around the edges by determining what flies and what won't fly."[19]

One crucial issue in measuring influence revolves around the principle of presidential involvement. Both Cary Covington and Barbara Kellerman dispute the validity of some aggregate measures of presidential success because they may include issues of little interest to the president.[20] A similar criticism of such scores was volunteered by several White House veterans, who complained that these measures were virtually useless because they included issues that never received the attention of the president and should therefore not be used to measure their impact on the process. One veteran of two administrations argued that presidents only get involved in "cosmic issues" and that a president will work seriously on only ten to twelve issues each year. Therefore, researchers must be cautious when saying that a vote offers an opportunity to measure a president's influence unless there is clear evidence of presidential effort.

At the same time, the number of issues that a president chooses to involve the administration in may be an important aspect of presidential influence. It is tempting to measure the ambitiousness of an agenda in the number of bills the president proposes, but policy goals cannot be measured by the volume of legislation, since many issues can be contained in a single piece of legislation, while other bills may carry little more than symbolic meaning and face little opposition.

Some authors have refined their measures by including only "key" votes and by excluding near-unanimous votes.[21] While this approach improves the validity of the measure, it still does not insure that those issues selected by scholars are the same as those selected by the president. Some studies have used White House records to identify those issues most important to the president and this may provide the best foundation for including presidential involvement.[22]

White House veterans object to the exclusion of "noncontroversial" votes (those with very few opposing votes) from measures of influence,[23] because stripping the White House of large victories underestimates their impact. At the same time, measures that rely too heavily on the size of the coalition may be misleading. The assumption of simple vote maximization is problematic because the utility of a large winning coalition is unclear. If we assume that presidents are interested in gaining passage of legislation, either for policy or credit claiming, votes beyond a minimum winning coalition are of limited value. Presidents would obviously prefer lopsided victories, but there are often costs to members supporting the president on controversial issues and the support of some members may be held in reserve. One account from the Nixon administration's struggle to extend the 10 percent income tax surcharge dramatically illustrates the process of calling upon reserve support to cast difficult votes.

> After the second call of the roll, the nays had it, 201–194. Then the Administration began committing its surprise reserves—conservative Republicans who had promised their votes only if absolutely necessary. Behind the House rail, a small knot of congressmen hud-

dled together drawing straws. Shortstraw men trudged disconsolately down to the well to switch sides or withdraw their nays. The final tally: 210 ayes, 205 nays.[24]

Even when empirical measures provide an indicator of an overall level of influence, they are not well suited to uncovering statistical relationships with strategies that are used selectively. If, for example, presidents alternate between public appeals and personal bargaining, then a measure that tests for the impact of these continuously across time is less likely to find a statistical relationship. The challenge of presidential leadership of Congress is to know what will win votes at a particular moment, and any study of presidential influence that expects to find the same mix of strategies across administrations will likely produce disappointing results.

Advantages and disadvantages aside, roll call votes are used in quantitative studies because there are few alternatives. The challenge for researchers is to understand the limitations of their use and to accommodate them.[25] While the research presented here cannot replace the results of quantitative studies, I hope that it can help better explain some of the findings in the current literature and refine the hypotheses tested in future studies.

WHAT IS THE PRESIDENT'S ROLE?

Recently, the most visible debate in the literature on presidential-congressional relations has been between "presidency-centered" and "Congress-centered" perspectives. Richard Neustadt is often cited as being a prominent representative of the presidency-centered perspective, although this perspective has been attributed to the work of many well-regarded scholars, including James McGregor Burns, Edward S. Corwin, Thomas Cronin, Samuel Huntington, Barbara Kellerman, Harold Laski, and Clinton Rossiter.[26] Some scholars regard Neustadt's classic work on presidential power as presidency-centered because it describes presidential leadership of Congress in terms of the president's bargaining skill, public prestige (or public support), and professional reputation.[27] However, implicit in Neustadt's description of two branches sharing power is a recognition of the limitations of the president, and his emphasis on the powers of the presidency results from his selection of the president as a subject of study. Jeffrey Tulis has described the tendency of presidency scholars to view the political process from the perspective of the presidency as "institutional partisanship."[28] While Neustadt may be criticized for demonstrating institutional partisanship, given the goals of his study this is completely understandable. The label *presidency-centered* results more from Neustadt's desire to illuminate the resources and strategies of the president specifically than his arguments about the balance of power in the government.

The presidency-centered perspective has recently come under attack with two similar alternatives being offered. The Congress-centered perspective has been represented recently by several prominent works in the field. Jon Bond and Richard Fleisher attempt to shift the emphasis away from presidential bargaining skills and offer the makeup of Congress as a predictor of presidential success. They do not deny the significance of leadership skills, but they argue that the partisan balance and political ideology of Congress is much more important in understanding presidential success in Congress.[29] George Edwards made his perspective clear with his title: *At the Margin*. Edwards finds that presidential resources like public approval, electoral strength, and legislative skill have a marginal effect on Congress and that researchers should "focus less exclusively on the president and devote more attention to the context in which the president seeks to lead Congress."[30] Like Bond and Fleisher, Edwards used aggregate data sets to test predictors of presidential victories and finds that factors beyond the control of the president, like the ideology and partisanship of members, predict much better than presidency-centered variables such as bargaining skills.

The presidency-centered and Congress-centered labels have outlived their utility and may now detract from a more constructive debate. No scholar expects the legislative process to be "centered" around anything other than Congress and even the most enthusiastic believers in executive power do not expect to find the work of Congress centered around the presidency. While the Congress- versus presidency-centered labels were clearly intended to serve as end points for a spectrum of beliefs, one extreme remains so clearly beyond the terms of the actual debate within political science that describing scholars as subscribing to that camp is to do an injustice to the subtlety of their work. For example, even though he has been identified as a presidency-centered scholar, James McGregor Burns's remedy for the Clinton administration's problems with Congress was to seek out a larger Democratic majority—a clearly Congress-centered view.[31]

Mark Peterson, in *Legislating Together,* offers a promising alternative. He proposes a "tandem institution" perspective in which the president and Congress compose a partnership in the policy process.[32] The tandem institution perspective describes a symbiotic rather than hostile relationship between the branches. Leadership by one branch can be included under this perspective by "the placement of one member behind another, as on a tandem bicycle," but overall the emphasis is the need for cooperation.[33]

Peterson's model represents a significant step forward and we can learn much from the balancing of tension between the branches with the need for cooperation, although my findings emphasize the tension more than Peterson's. It is true that the two branches must cooperate in order to make policy; however, underlying this cooperation are serious institutional conflicts arising from differences in the electoral needs of the two branches. Walter Mondale, after serving in both Congress and the vice presidency, emphasized the distance placed between the president and lawmakers by the differing demands of their constituencies.

> When the time comes for heavy lifting, a president finds just how lonely it gets at the top. Only one person—the president—is elected to watch out for the interests of the whole country. Regardless of party, members of Congress are elected, first of all, to represent their state or district. If it comes down to a question of what is good for the nation as described by the president and what is good for the district, a Congressman might wish to stick with the president—and he might actually take a day or two, praying for guidance—but in the end he will probably vote for his district.[34]

The two branches are joined together in a partnership in the policy process and the two branches have mutual needs, but they are often reluctant partners who must share power even when they do not share interests. As Charles O. Jones points out, these are separated institutions that must often compete for shared powers and "for how credits are shared for a race well run."[35] Richard Cook, a legislative assistant for Richard Nixon, described a close relationship between Congress and the president as an unnatural state. "The only time in 30 years that it occurred was during the 89th Congress, following the Kennedy mourning period and we had a President who literally ran the Congress from the Oval Office. That was unnatural."[36] In the 1920s, Congressman Robert Luce argued that "Something is to be said for the benefits of hostility in moderate degree. Friction has its advantages in state craft as well as in mechanics. The rivalries encouraged by the present system, the antagonism, yes, even the controversies, invigorate and stimulate."[37] The founders created separation of powers to make difficult the possibility of such a close relationship between the president and the Congress, and history demonstrates that they were successful. As Jones declares, "Institutional competition is an expected outcome of the constitutional arrangements that facilitate mixed representation and variable electoral horizons."[38]

The debate between Congress- and presidency-centered perspectives—if it still exists—is no longer instructive. Scholars who have been labeled presidency-centered brought close scrutiny to the role of the president in the process. Congress-centered scholars have demonstrated that there is much more to the legislative process than the president. Likewise, Mark Peterson's tandem institution perspective has demonstrated convincingly that presidential relations with Congress involve cooperation as well as conflict and that we have forgotten Neustadt's claim that the institutions do share power.[39]

There seems to be little utility left for scholars to continue to line up according to whether they cast their lot with the powers of the president or the institutional forces in Congress. The most compelling reason to abandon the existing debate is that the advocates of the Congress-centered and tandem institution perspective have offered up a compelling case and it is time to focus our debates on the deeper causes of the president's influence or lack thereof. Previous research has raised these issues, but the debate has not been organized along these particular lines and the energies of researchers have not been directed toward the most important questions.

Rather than engaging in the existing debate, I would offer terms for a new one. I argue that the relationship between the president and Congress is guided by electoral concerns. The question becomes: do elections guide the policy-making process in a direct way to past elections or in an indirect way to future elections?

Of course, any democratic system is driven by electoral forces. Here I am concerned whether the most important linkage is direct or indirect.[40] Bond and Fleisher, for example, see a very direct, mechanical linkage between the previous election and a president's success in Congress. They argue that "presidential success is determined in large measure by the results of the last election. If the last election brings individuals to Congress whose local interests and preferences coincide with the president's, then he will enjoy greater success."[41] When Bond and Fleisher point out that ideology and party are at the core of congressional decision making they are arguing that representation is the dominant force in the relationship between the president and Congress. An argument that the preferences of constituents are excluded from influencing the process would be disturbing. The president's bargaining skills should not be expected to overwhelm the representative link between lawmaker and constituent in order to be significant. We should expect to find evidence of a direct linkage to presidential success because it determines the level of support for the president. What is unclear is how much presidential success results from shared interests and how much results from the powers of the presidency. This issue distinguishes presidential support in Congress from presidential influence.[42]

An emphasis on the direct linkage may not be satisfying to many readers who wish to consider what the president's ability is to construct coalitions in the Congress created by the last congressional election. I do not deny the importance of the partisan balance of Congress or the ideology of individual members. Rather, I suggest that the last election is only one barometer of a more important concern to lawmakers: the next election.

Indirect linkages involve electoral dynamics that are potentially within the grasp of the president as he works to build a coalition. Indirect linkages are connections to future elections, whereas direct linkages connect the process to past elections. The indirect linkage speaks to the level of influence the president has that enables him to go beyond the environment created by the last election. Indirect linkages are the product of concerns about future elections, and congressional uncertainty about the future provides opportunities for presidential influence. Members are always looking to the next election and it would seem that this is where the president can find influence. Such an impact may be marginal, but I argue that it is significant, or at least perceived as significant by members of Congress. The study of indirect linkages, while drawing attention to sources of presidential influence, does not require that this impact is large. Rather, a study of the indirect linkage acknowledges that presidential influence is inherently limited, given that it is indirect. This new perspective should not preclude the discussion of the balance between the branches; it should place this debate in the context of explanations.

A Theory of Electoral Expectations

The central argument of this book is that presidential influence in Congress is the product of the White House's ability to shape the electoral expectations of members of Congress. This theory of presidential influence resembles both the presidency- and Congress-centered perspectives because it deals with presidential ability to shape expectations about the Congress-centered variable of election outcomes. However, it is most similar to Mark Peterson's tandem institution perspective, which defines the relationship in terms of the needs of both branches.[43] The role of electoral forces is not entirely new to the study of the presidency, but it has seldom enjoyed a prominent position in theories of presidential power. David Mayhew's classic *Congress: The Electoral Connection* has played a central role in the congressional literature for twenty-five years, but his contribution is seldom incorporated in models of presidential influence.[44] Congressional interest in elections was not lost even on the least political president studied here. President Eisenhower, in a letter to a close friend, commented that "Each congressman thinks of himself as intensely patriotic; but it does not take the average member long to conclude that his first duty to his country is to get himself re-elected."[45]

Presidents, like members of Congress, are concerned with winning re-election and, in the face of the two-term limit, the broader goals of gaining public approval or standing in history. Richard Reeves describes history as a "goddess" that John Kennedy pursued.[46] Presidents understand that voters will judge them for a second term and scholars for history in part on the basis of the policy changes they produce and their ability to get Congress to co-operate. George Edwards points out that while the president's position in the constitutional system is weak, the public fails to recognize this, and when they do, they fail to incorporate it into their evaluations of presidential suc-cess.[47] This motivation has drawn the presidency further and further into the legislative process as expectations increased. William Leuchtenburg has de-scribed the extent to which modern presidents operate in the shadow of Franklin Roosevelt,[48] and the expectations of the legislative presidency has been an important force in the modern presidency. Dwight Eisenhower was judged harshly by contemporaries and historians for his lack of activism, and even Eisenhower revisionism has relied on the "hidden-hand" argument of Fred Greenstein, who argued that Eisenhower was more activist than he ap-peared.[49] Paul Light quotes a Kennedy aide who noted, "We looked at the legislative program as a major weapon in our struggle for both reelection and national influence."[50]

My model of influence incorporates "expectations" because of the prospective concerns of both branches. The uncertainties of prospective evaluations in a volatile political world are important because they create presidential opportunities. The president will enjoy influence when lawmak-ers believe that the White House might be able to influence the next con-gressional election. Thus, a theory of electoral expectations only requires that legislators believe that the president might be able to play a pivotal role in the next election, not that this influence be demonstrated by previous electoral performance. One senior Republican congressional staff person suggested that "Congress is a very human institution, complete with insecu-rities." These insecurities, he reflected, helped Ronald Reagan create more fear among members than was fully justified. Members of Congress may un-derstand that the president's influence on the next congressional election likely will be small, but there is often little reason to risk incurring the wrath of the White House, especially for lawmakers who feel their next election may be close.

Congressional scholars have debated how to best describe electoral se-curity.[51] A large margin of victory in one election is no guarantee of a similar victory in the next, and a strong challenger or voter dissatisfaction can quickly change the climate of the next campaign. In his study of lawmakers' behavior in their districts, Fenno observed that "knowing or sensing or fearing these several unhappy electoral possibilities, House members will continue to be a lot more uncertain than the statistics of their last election would warrant."[52] Lawmakers may believe that while the potential risk in opposing a president is likely low, there may be little point in taking that risk. The president, while perhaps a small player in a congressional campaign, can motivate contributors and challengers, making reelection more difficult.

Thus, the prospective element of the theory adds a subtle yet significant opportunity to gain influence. Clearly, congressional expectations of the president's impact on the next election are closely tied to his impact in the last election. However, if Congress only looks back in judging presidential clout, we would expect to see little change in presidential influence between elections. The prospective view of Washington is also evident in the lame-duck status that befalls presidents fortunate enough to win a second term. The second-term victories of Dwight Eisenhower, Richard Nixon, and Ronald Reagan failed to produce a receptive Congress, despite the declaration of Nixon's and Reagan's reelection victories as "landslides" and the fact that both second-term victories were larger than the initial victories. Both presidents saw less success in their second term, despite a stronger showing at the polls.

Means of Influence

How then does the president influence congressional elections, or at least convince members that the White House may influence the next election? The answer to this question varies with the political environment within which the presidency must lead. The broad political context shapes presidential attempts to manipulate electoral expectations. Presidential influence over future elections in the period described by Samuel Kernell as "institutionalized pluralism" requires a different set of leadership techniques than the context labeled as "individualized pluralism." Kernell described how members of the Washington community moved from relying upon the bargaining powers found in political institutions like party to a system in which individuals in the bargaining community have few loyalties.[53] In 1989, looking back over the twenty years of change since its first publication, the *National Journal* described the change in remarkably similar terms: "Under the influence of the TV camera and the journalistic pack, the cult of the individual has replaced that of the institution."[54]

In response to the shifting contexts of Washington politics, presidents developed new resources for leading Congress. In response, Congress protected itself from presidential control over election-related resources by capturing or copying these tools of persuasion. Senator Daniel Patrick Moynihan has suggested that Congress is driven by "the iron law of emulation." Moynihan observed, "Whenever any branch of government acquires a new technique which enhances its power in relation to the other branches, that technique will soon be adopted by those other branches as well."[55] As soon as a president develops a tool for legislative leadership, Congress will adapt that tool for its own use to protect its independence from the executive branch. Thus, presidential success produces a perception of increased presidential power that triggers a congressional adaptation that will, in turn, spur further presidential innovation.

The White House Office of Legislative Affairs is the best focal point for a study of relations between the executive and legislative branches because it has come to serve the needs of Congress as well as those of the president. The dilemma of the modern White House legislative shop was made clear to me by the comment of one White House legislative assistant, who described the staff of the White House Office of Legislative Affairs as members of one branch but answerable to another: "The job is positioned about Eighth street, one-half way between the two great institutions." In order to conduct relations between the president and Congress, the congressional liaison staff must be able to understand the electoral concerns of the Oval Office and Capitol Hill.

As Joseph Pika has pointed out, these White House lobbyists are, by the nature of their jobs, outsiders within the White House.[56] Their days are spent trying to bargain with members of Congress, while some in the White House staff think they should be less concerned with congressional needs. The policy people in the White House become very attached to their policy proposals and expect the liaison staff to protect their policy initiatives from compromise. At the same time, members of Congress often need compromises to avoid electoral problems at home. One journalist described the job of Max Friedersdorf, the first head of Ronald Reagan's Office of Legislative Affairs:

> Friedersdorf's position makes him a high-tension conductor in the alternating current of information between the Hill and the White House, the pro in the quid-pro-quo symbiosis of government: The executive branch wants congressional compliance; and the legisla-

tors need a bewildering range of services and favors from the executive.[57]

It is the White House legislative affairs staff that must construct a harmony of purposes between the two branches with their different electoral needs. They are the managers of an uneasy alliance that must constantly be maintained, and their dilemma becomes an opportunity for research because they are witnesses to both sides of the struggle.

PRESIDENTIAL LEADERSHIP UNDER INSTITUTIONALIZED PLURALISM

As Samuel Kernell has pointed out, for many years Washington operated under a system in which individuals functioned through a set of institutions in Washington.[58] This arrangement facilitated bargaining within Washington by providing a stable community with institutional norms that regulate behavior and reduce uncertainty. Public opinion and elections represent disruptions to this stable system, and presidential attempts to bring them into bargaining were not welcome. This left the president to bargain with the resources he could access through Washington institutions. While these resources were accessed through Washington, their significance to legislators was decidedly electoral. For example, because the national committees of the two parties were able to control a significant amount of money flowing into congressional campaigns, presidents could attempt to influence elections through institutions like national parties and Washington-based interest groups.

Although the techniques below were most important in the period of individualized pluralism, they remain today, just as some evidence of the tools associated with individualized pluralism can be found throughout both periods. While each period is dominated by a particular form of politics, elements of the other exist. These different periods of pluralism only suggest what the most prevalent form of bargaining was and should not be interpreted to completely exclude the other.

The Office of Legislative Affairs and the Autopilot Approach

One of the first adaptations that the president made in order to manage congressional leadership was to create a specialized lobbying unit within the White House. This was necessitated both by the proliferating demands from Congress as the president became more involved in legislative business and by the increase in other demands on the presidency. The creation of what would become the Office of Congressional Relations and then the Office of Legislative Affairs granted Eisenhower some freedom from the growing demands of bargaining with Congress so that he could pursue goals he saw as crucial to his reelection and his place in history: foreign policy goals.

I have labeled the use of delegation originated by Eisenhower the *autopilot approach*.[59] As we see in the next chapter, Eisenhower worked primarily through the congressional leadership and left much of the routine interaction with Congress in the hands of his congressional liaison staff. While Eisenhower created the office and may be the most obvious example of an autopilot approach, every president has needed some degree of protection from the constant demands of congressional politics in order to manage the other duties of the office.

At the same time, the growing White House staff gave presidents an ability to become involved in more aspects of the legislative process and oversee bargaining on the increasing number of issues expected to be managed by the White House. By creating a White House office dedicated to working with Congress, Eisenhower and future presidents were better able to gather information and political intelligence and more effectively direct presidential resources like district spending. While the Office of Congressional Relations can be regarded as a tool of White House influence, it must also direct the resources of the rest of the executive branch. Thus, an autopilot approach is both a means of maximizing the president's use of time as he attempts to balance the many duties of the office, and a way of coordinating the growing resources of the executive branch.

Hidden-hand Leadership

Hidden-hand leadership was a technique used by Dwight Eisenhower and other presidents to indirectly influence members of Congress through threatening the election prospects of a legislator by going to important constituents or contributors. While the use of "hidden-hand leadership" here is narrower than Fred Greenstein's original explication, one of his primary examples is President Eisenhower's use of a wealthy supporter to influence Senator Lyndon Johnson. In this case, Eisenhower planted the suggestion that Johnson's rival, Texas Governor Allen Shivers, might be encouraged to challenge Johnson in the Democratic primary.[60]

During the Eisenhower administration, such manipulation was concealed because it would have been inconsistent with Eisenhower's image as an outsider who was above partisan politics. More generally, such efforts to circumvent or undermine bargaining within the Washington community would have violated the norms of institutionalized pluralism and been interpreted as a lack of respect for the legitimacy of the representational role of lawmakers and an affront to the bargaining community.

Granting Favors

One way that presidents can bargain with members under institutionalized pluralism and make election easier for lawmakers is to help them bring federal dollars to their district or state. Lyndon Johnson proved to be a master of this approach and he traded a wide array of favors, most of which were designed to make the next election a little easier for friendly lawmakers. While favors like these continue to be dispensed, they were more plentiful and better suited to political needs in the period of institutionalized pluralism.

The use of presidential favors is described here as "granting" rather than "trading" favors because individual favors were seldom explicitly traded in return for a lawmaker's vote. As we see in the chapter on Lyndon Johnson, this had more to do with logistical concerns of propriety. It is hard for the White House to keep enough key appointments or federal grants pending to provide enough favors to trade for votes on pivotal issues. Instead, the White House is most likely to dispense favors to members who are generally considered friends or likely friends, who have helped the administration in the past or who might be expected to help the administration in the future. In either case, favors represent means for the president to hand out benefits that can be passed along to grateful constituents. Further, the ability to win small favors from the White House was seen as a way for congressmen to demonstrate to constituents their importance within Washington.

Maintaining Favor

Maintaining favor involves remaining on friendly terms with members of Congress in order to facilitate the kind of one-on-one bargaining within Washington that typifies institutionalized pluralism.[61] Because the process of granting favors described above often requires that some time pass between when a vote is needed and when a favor is provided, both sides need some assurance that the other side will reciprocate when the time comes.

While maintaining favor does not directly translate into electoral expectations, it is a necessary component of effective bargaining with members of Congress. Because the signing of written contracts for the exchange of favors would not be wise, members of Congress need to have some level of understanding and a sense of trust that the White House will follow up on its commitments. Without the level of certainty provided by a formal contract, bargaining in this environment requires some means of providing a guarantee.

Party Leadership

Working through the congressional leadership within Congress was essential under institutionalized pluralism because the leadership was the conduit for bargaining within Congress as well as the channel for lawmakers getting party resources like campaign funds. Under institutionalized pluralism, presidents dealt almost exclusively with Congress through its leadership; the White House staff worked hand in hand with congressional leaders on vote counts, and the leadership often set up meetings between members of Congress and White House staff. In fact, presidents during this period did not deal directly with rank-and-file party members without upsetting congressional leadership, because this would have been seen as undermining the norms of Congress at the time.

The importance of working with party leadership is reflected in Eisenhower's secret meetings with Speaker Sam Rayburn and Senate Majority Leader Lyndon Johnson. Despite differences in party affiliation, Eisenhower realized that unless he was able to work with these leaders, he would not be able to work with Congress.

Interest Groups

Among the institutions through which presidents could exercise some influence in Congress without going through party leaders were interest groups, specifically the leadership of Washington-based interest groups who worked frequently with members of Congress and contributed to their campaigns. In the system of institutionalized pluralism, the White House often worked hand in hand with interest group lobbyists, occasionally on issues beyond the natural interests of the groups. The Johnson administration could co-opt the electoral clout of the AFL-CIO to press reluctant members of Congress on civil rights issues because Johnson would link his support for labor initiatives to their support of his agenda. Many lawmakers felt heavily dependent on groups like organized labor to finance and volunteer for their election campaigns, and presidents could attempt to use these groups to threaten members of Congress at the core of their electoral support.

Departmental Liaison

The congressional relations offices of the various cabinet departments and agencies that developed after World War II played a significant role under institutionalized pluralism. Because lawmakers relied on the cabinet departments to draft legislation or amendments and to provide information on the impact of legislation on their constituency, departments could play a significant but largely invisible role in bargaining. Before congressional personal and committee staff expanded and offices like the Congressional Budget Office emerged, Congress often found itself heavily dependent on the executive branch for information and expertise.

Presidential Leadership Under Individualized Pluralism

Eventually, Congress became uneasy with the president's power after Johnson and Nixon and moved to regain control of the political resources that had been used as leverage against them. This change, coupled with the dispersion of power in Congress, reflected the decline of the system of institutionalized pluralism. In its place a system of individualized pluralism developed in which members of Congress had few group or institutional loyalties. While the techniques of the old system would linger, just as elements of institutionalized pluralism would, the new context of individualized pluralism required that lawmakers find new ways of insuring reelection and that presidents find new ways to raise congressional fears of the next election. Because Congress would regain control of so many of the electoral resources in Washington, the president was forced to look outside the Beltway, to the public, in order to regain the upper hand. This spawned three related public relations strategies. While these might be considered part of what Kernell has defined as "going public," each involves different linkages among citizen, president, and Congress and thus they constitute different strategies.

Merchandising

The president's ability to define issues and shape the agenda is given the label *merchandising*.[62] Presidential merchandising can raise congressional concerns about reelection in several ways. The most obvious is for the president to define issues in such a way as to generate voter reaction to congressional votes. A skilled president's ability to define an issue in terms that make opposition hard to defend introduces a new challenge into reelection. Because of the visibility of the office, presidents are often able to define issues in a way that is greater than the ability of members of Congress, even within their own district.

The president's general ability to raise issues and shape the public agenda is in itself a potential threat to congressional reelection.[63] Members of Congress prefer to selectively focus their campaigns on the issues that work in their favor. Challengers may have some success in raising issues, but the president has the ability to go into a district and make an issue a defining one. Legislators prefer to select issues that will generate little opposition, like federal spending in the district, but a president, even speaking from far away in Washington, has the ability to lead voters to raise disruptive issues at election time. This can also work against a president. The election of 1994 saw candidates once again running from a president of their party. Bill Clinton's health care proposal and stimulus package were defined by Clinton (and redefined by opponents) in a way that made support of these issues a liability.

Prestige

Richard Neustadt describes the link between the public standing or "prestige" of the president and his success or influence in Congress.[64] The strategy of building public prestige emphasizes enhancing the public's opinion of the president and using presidential popularity to prod reluctant members of Congress. Popular presidents hope that opposition to them will translate into trouble for members of Congress. One senior Democratic senator commented during the early days of the Clinton administration, "It's an absolute rule up here: popular Presidents get what they want; unpopular ones don't."[65]

A prestige strategy often resembles an attempt to rebuild an electoral mandate or create an electoral mandate that never existed. Richard Nixon sought to overcome a Democratic Congress, and his lack of a strong mandate in 1968, through a public prestige strategy that used public relations to build Nixon's personal popularity rather than support for individual legislative proposals. While every White House is anxious to build the popularity of its president, none seems to have as systematically placed general popularity ahead of support for specific legislation as the Nixon White House.

The difference between prestige and merchandising is significant in several ways. While a generally popular president can attempt to use prestige to intimidate members of Congress without ever addressing the public on an issue, merchandising requires that presidents actively demonstrate their connection to the public and direct citizen energy toward Congress. Prestige is a general force that challenges congressional representation with the claim of presidential representation, while merchandising involves issue representation, which places constituent preferences for issues ahead of support for the president personally.

Because prestige is less specific, its impact is less predictable. Paul Light quotes one presidential aide as noting that "Congress is fairly suspicious of polls as a bargaining tool, and public approval ratings are too general to be of much good."[66] As we see in the chapters ahead, Nixon's dramatic drop in popularity during the Watergate crisis and George Bush's amazing surge in popularity after the Gulf War had little to do with the policy process and therefore had little affect on legislative matters. By contrast, the Reagan administration attempted to build its prestige during the first administration upon Reagan's ability to master Congress and get things done. Because the different sources of popularity represent different linkages to the policy process and congressional elections, we should expect that its impact will vary from case to case.

Special Publics

A special publics strategy involves presidential influence of key constituents or contributors in an attempt to affect the votes of a lawmaker. Rather than talking with one or two individuals from a district already acquainted with the president, as Eisenhower did with his hidden-hand style of leadership, the Carter White House turned to a broader selection of citizens who would be brought to Washington in hopes of turning them into lobbyists for the president's cause. This approach, here labeled "special publics,"[67] uses the public, but only a select portion. It differs from the use of interest groups by earlier presidents in that, rather than working through the institutions of national interest group leaders, the White House went to local leaders or elites who may not have been members of an organized interest group. It differs from merchandising in that the segment of a constituency activated is very narrow. A special publics strategy is the descendant of hidden-hand leadership in that it is a selective strategy; however, under individualized pluralism some tinkering with constituencies is accepted and presidents are more free to wield political power openly. This technique also reflects the shifting of power from Washington interest group lobbyists to grassroots influence.

The chapters to come discuss the ways in which presidents use these leadership tools to influence future elections, or at least to create concerns among members of Congress that they may be able to influence a future election, within the changing environment of Washington. While the president's tools of leadership are unlikely to prove overwhelming, they may collectively provide the president with enough leverage to exert significant influence over the process.

This study begins with the Eisenhower administration since it was the first administration to establish an office designated to maintain relations with Congress. Chapter 2 examines congressional relations during the Eisenhower administration. Eisenhower created the Office of Legislative Affairs to handle day-to-day interaction with members of Congress, with presidential involvement reserved for critical moments. In delegating this responsibility Eisenhower was attempting to balance the growing demands on the president's time. The Eisenhower administration relied heavily upon congressional leaders of both parties to reach out to rank-and-file members and build coalitions. Eisenhower's service with powerful congressional leaders like Sam Rayburn and Lyndon Johnson makes his administration an example of how presidents can make use of congressional leadership. Eisenhower's uneven relationship with the various Republican leaders demonstrates some of the limitations of this strategy.

The creation of the congressional liaison operation and the use of party leaders is related to Fred Greenstein's concept of "hidden-hand leadership," through which presidents attempt to lead by working behind the scenes. In the case of Eisenhower and Congress, the White House often contacted prominent constituents and had them pressure members of Congress. I take exception with Greenstein and suggest that the delegation of responsibility is not leadership in a meaningful sense. I offer evidence that while "hidden-hand" leadership can be used to describe Eisenhower, such methods have also been used by every president since. Chapter 2 also features an examination of the use of the liaison resources of the cabinet departments. Because many of these offices predated the White House liaison operation, they were valuable sources of personnel and expertise.

Chapter 3 examines the Kennedy administration's institutionalization of the White House lobbying corps. Although Kennedy had initially shunned the kind of structured White House favored by Eisenhower, the administration learned the value of organization from the fight to expand the Rules Committee. The administration put the lobbying efforts of cabinet members under the direction of the White House legislative affairs office and aggressively used patronage and grants. Kennedy's close working relationship with Larry O'Brien who headed congressional relations transformed the White House lobbying team into a significant player on Capitol Hill and demonstrated the potential of the office to become an active force in bargaining with Congress.

The White House's use of interest groups is emphasized in the Kennedy chapter. The Kennedy administration began the practice of using interest group lobbyists to reach members not persuaded by other means. The Kennedy administration used interest group lobbyists to broaden the perceived base of support for legislation and bring constituency pressure, as exercised through Washington-based interest groups, to bear on reluctant legislators.

Chapter 4 describes Lyndon Johnson's intense personal involvement and the use of every possible executive branch resource in the legislative process. Johnson committed his personal energies to a much greater degree than any president before or since. While most administrations have used the president sparingly, Johnson became actively engaged in a large number of issues. Johnson's commitment helped bring the presidency to a high point in legislative influence, but this surge in presidential influence triggered concern in Congress about its independence from the executive branch.

The use of trading favors is featured in chapter 4. While every president has traded favors to gain congressional support, Johnson did so aggressively and kept detailed written records. Johnson dispensed favors to gain members' support on a particular bill, but also as part of a long-term strategy of building a relationship between members and the White House. By making members of Congress electoral beneficiaries of a Johnson presidency, the White House gave members of Congress incentive to support presidential legislation whenever possible. While Johnson's favor trading provided a valuable resource in the short run, members of Congress began to resent presidential use of resources that were drawn from budgets written by Congress. They began to limit presidential discretionary spending that could be used as bargaining tools. In a sense, Congress began to capture (or recapture) presidential discretionary spending.

The Nixon administration is examined in chapter 5. Because of the minority status of Republicans in Congress and his weak mandate from the 1968 election, the Nixon White House adopted an aggressive public relations strategy that was designed to promote Nixon personally in hopes of providing him with leverage with Congress. This contrasts with other presidents' manipulation of public opinion to gain legislative support for particular pieces of legislation and can be used to explore the distinction between merchandising and prestige. In the end, the weak link between presidential popularity and Nixon's inability to generate widespread public support limited his influence over Congress.

Nixon's approach to Congress provides an opportunity to reexamine the role of the president's personal involvement since Nixon's distance from Congress stands in sharp contrast to Johnson's style. In attempting to protect the aura of the presidency, Nixon may have missed opportunities to persuade members of Congress, and his lack of personal contact with members of Congress may have contributed to distrust between the branches. As Nixon's personal and political conflicts with Congress became more intense, Congress sought ways of protecting its political interests from presidential manipulation. The Nixon administration witnessed further congressional capture of resources that the White House could use for bargaining. The personal and political animosity between the White House and Congress continued the congressional move to greater independence from the White House that began under Johnson.

The Nixon chapter also examines the use of departmental lobbyists. The Nixon White House relied heavily on lobbyists from the cabinet departments and elevated these positions to make them more significant forces on the Hill. The Office of Management and Budget was also used to increase the effectiveness of central clearance.

Chapter 6 focuses on Gerald Ford's attempt to return congressional relations to friendly but respectable terms. Ford inherited the weakened party leadership that had resulted from the reorganization of Congress and the resurgence of congressional power that had been triggered by the excesses of the Johnson and Nixon presidencies. The new members brought in after Watergate were unresponsive to the wishes of party leaders and, emboldened by the fall of Nixon, were willing to challenge the presidency at every turn. One of the most significant ways in which Congress sought to reclaim resources was the creation of the Congressional Budget Office (CBO) in 1974. The CBO provided independent budget information and enabled Congress to challenge presidential budget initiatives much more effectively. Congress used the Budget and Impoundment Act to place additional limits on presidential budget tools like impoundment.

This chapter also emphasizes the use of "maintaining favor" to create a friendly environment for bargaining between the branches. Ford attempted to open the doors of the White House to members of Congress and tried to create a friendly environment for bargaining. Facing a Congress determined to resist presidential influence, Ford's efforts reflect an attempt to reverse the direction that the relationship was heading.

Chapter 7 describes the continued souring of congressional relations under Jimmy Carter. Although Carter contributed to the tensions between the branches, by the time he took office, Congress had developed the institutional resources that made presidential leadership difficult. Carter and his liaison staff were harshly criticized, but these complaints were greatly exaggerated and reflected the increased sensitivity of Congress as much as any clumsiness on the part of the White House.

Many observers expected a Democratic president to have an easy time with a Democratic Congress. However, the decentralization of power within Congress had made Democrats more independent from their president and their own leaders in Congress. Facing a limitation on some of the president's resources, the Carter administration attempted the most ambitious use of interest groups of any previous administration. However, given the lack of clout of Washington-based interest groups in the evolving system of individualized pluralism, the Carter White House was forced to look outside Washington for support. As the president's resources inside the government were diminished, Carter turned to outside forces to gain influence in Congress, but given his inability to communicate with the general public, the White House, through the Office of Public Liaison, reached into legislators' districts to draw upon the power of political interests.

The Carter administration provides a clear case of the important role that the congressional relations staff plays within the White House. Especially in the case of presidents with little experience in Washington, the congressional liaison staff must educate the president and the rest of the White House on the functioning and needs of Congress. This role is especially crucial in the kind of shifting political context the White House found itself in. The shift from institutionalized to individualized pluralism was rewriting the rules of presidential influence and an effective connection to Congress was needed to follow and respond to these changes.

Chapter 8 discusses Ronald Reagan's frequent attempts to go "over the heads" of Congress as a response to his strategic situation and to capitalize on his personal skills. While previous administrations had used going public only as a last resort, the Reagan administration considered it a core element of the legislative strategy. Just as Carter had looked outside the government to interest groups because of a lack of institutional resources, the Reagan administration turned to the public to replace institutional tools that had been reclaimed by Congress. The administration's early success demonstrates the potential of making appeals on behalf of specific pieces of legislation.

While highlighting Reagan's very visible appeals to the public, this chapter makes clear that behind Reagan's addresses to the nation, the president and the liaison staff were working individually with members of Congress. Even as the political environment was demanding new tools of influence from the presidency, enough of the old system of bargaining remained to require that the same tools utilized by Lyndon Johnson had to be used by the Reagan White House. Reagan's Legislative Strategy Group contributed to the president's success on the Hill by effectively coordinating for the White House this new mix of resources.

During the second Reagan term members of Congress, frustrated by Reagan's ability to reach their constituents, began to develop more elaborate public relations resources. Members' ability to reach constituencies through C-SPAN and the television resources developed by the congressional parties represent how Congress copied Reagan's techniques to counter the influence he had gained. This permitted members to challenge the president's message and to insulate themselves from the electoral impact of opposing a president.

Chapter 9 discusses George Bush's trouble in establishing leadership in Congress. Bush had served in the House of Representatives and had many personal friends in Congress, giving him an understanding of the process and a source of political intelligence. Despite this, the Bush administration frequently found itself unable to gain congressional cooperation.

The administration made some use of departmental liaison. However, it failed to fully gain control over the inherent divisions between the cabinet departments and the White House. This chapter explores how departmental resources can make numerous contributions to winning legislative victory, but also the limits of this resource.

The Bush administration was most successful at stopping legislation, as evident in its ability to sustain all but one of Bush's vetoes. In addition, the administration's early system for signaling the president's intent to veto legislation gave the White House leverage in the legislative process.

While some of the blame is attributed to Bush's lack of a clear agenda in domestic politics, some also lies with the diminished resources for presidential influence in Congress. The Bush administration became involved in the traditional types of bargaining found under the fading system of institutionalized pluralism, but it failed to develop the new resources demanded of the new environment. The Bush presidency was, in many ways, an attempt to manage congressional relations with a president better suited for the old system of institutionalized pluralism. Bush was known and liked by members of Congress and was the kind of stable bargaining partner that might have thrived in the political world before changes in communication and in Congress created a new order. The Bush administration is also typical of relations between the White House and Congress and its limited success with Congress demonstrates that presidents have little influence except under unusual circumstances.

Chapter 10 offers a preliminary analysis of the Clinton administration and demonstrates that the problems experienced by Clinton represent a continuation of the return to congressional independence in the process. Certainly some early missteps by the Clinton administration account for some of its problems in pushing its legislative agenda, but when these problems are put next to historical examples, like Ford's pardon of Nixon, it appears that Clinton's early problems are more common than contemporary critics acknowledge. Chapter 10 also examines the return of divided government, this time with a Democratic president and Republican Congress.

House Speaker Newt Gingrich and his associates devised a strategy for nationalizing elections that they hoped would generate a Republican majority and create expectations that elections could again be influenced by congressional leadership. Gingrich's fund-raising and public relations efforts represent another way in which the presidency's rivals have learned from the power of the office and developed their own means for influencing members of Congress in the most recent battle over electoral expectations.

The final chapter examines our expectations for presidential leadership of Congress, and suggests that our standards of presidential success have been based upon exceptional circumstances, and argues that our expectations far exceed what is likely under the Constitution. This chapter also discusses the decline of presidential resources and considers the future of presidential leadership of Congress.

2

THE EISENHOWER
ADMINISTRATION

DWIGHT EISENHOWER ENTERED THE PRESIDENCY WITH
a reputation as an outsider to Washington politics. Although his admirers are
anxious to point out that he had worked with Congress while in the army and
counted members of Congress among his friends in Washington, this reputation predominated. Eisenhower's limited Washington experience appeared even more limited when he was compared to the congressional leaders of the time. Sam Rayburn, Lyndon Johnson, and Robert Taft represented
some of the most savvy and powerful men ever to lead Congress, and congressional committees were controlled by senior southern Democrats. Next
to the decades of experience he faced in members of Congress, Eisenhower
surely looked the political novice.

As a candidate Eisenhower's distance from the political process was an
asset. Eisenhower encouraged his reputation as a newcomer to Washington
by referring to himself as a "simple soldier" or "just a farm boy from Kansas."[1]
As president, Eisenhower could have jeopardized his appeal had he engaged
in the same kind of vigorous political exercises as Roosevelt and Truman. Instead, Eisenhower benefited from being above the political fray.

Eisenhower worked with Congress primarily through the first White
House congressional liaison office, departmental liaison operations, and
congressional leadership. Eisenhower's respect for the principal of separa-

tion of powers, his lack of interest in bargaining and confrontation, and his reputation as a Washington novice led him to rely upon a quiet form of legislative leadership. Just as important as Eisenhower's expectations of the proper role of the president, the political context of the time dictated that presidential leadership operate through, rather than in competition with, party leaders in Congress who remained a potent force in shaping the electoral expectations of lawmakers.

Further, the extensive use of delegation, labeled here as an "autopilot approach," not only protected Eisenhower's image, it permitted the president to more fully devote his energies to foreign policy where he saw much of his duty. The focus on foreign policy is not surprising coming from a president who had promised "I will go to Korea" and who devoted his first inaugural address to foreign policy and titled the first volume of his presidential memoirs *Waging Peace*.[2]

The Eisenhower Staff

Dwight Eisenhower formally brought congressional relations to the presidency with the establishment of the first office in the White House dedicated specifically to congressional relations. Eisenhower did not so much create an office for legislative affairs as import it from the War Department. Eisenhower chose General Wilton B. Persons to head White House Congressional Affairs (Persons was officially listed as an assistant to Chief of Staff Sherman Adams) in part because he had served as the first head of the Legislative Liaison Division in the army when it was created in 1942. The War Department office had been involved in a broad range of routine functions in dealing with Congress, and the bipartisan nature of liaison during wartime gave Persons trusted friends from both parties; the shared mission of the war created a bipartisan bond that would carry beyond the war. Equally important, Persons also had a close working relationship with Eisenhower developed while Persons had served as Eisenhower's chief of staff and supreme commander of NATO. Persons had earned the president's trust and shared Eisenhower's sense of the proper relationship between the White House and Congress. Both men shared a respect for the authority and autonomy of Congress.[3]

Persons began assembling his staff by calling on Bryce N. Harlow who had served under him in the War Department's congressional liaison office during the war. Before joining the War Department Harlow had served on the staff of several congressional committees and on the staff of Democratic Senator Carl Vinson. Harlow took over as head of the legislative operation when Persons became chief of staff after Sherman Adams' departure in 1958. After the Eisenhower administration Harlow would go on to become the preeminent corporate lobbyist in Washington, and he served as a close advisor to Presidents Nixon and Ford and occasionally was called in to consult with Presidents Johnson and Reagan.

Persons and Harlow typified the legislative liaison staff's exceptional level of experience and ability to work with both parties. The staff as a whole had accumulated almost one hundred years of Washington service in a variety of roles within the executive and legislative branches. Persons also brought in former California Congressman I. Jack Anderson as well as Ed McCabe who had been the chief clerk of the House Labor Committee. Gerald T. Morgan had served as a legislative counsel for the House. After the death of Senator Robert Taft, Jack Martin, who had been Taft's chief legislative assistant, joined the staff. The staff was rounded out by Homer H. Gruenther and Earl D. Chesney.

Based on his years of experience in dealing with Congress and the trust that Eisenhower had in him, Persons was free to create and run the office as he pleased. Persons felt that Eisenhower "took it for granted that I knew the job and it was mine to go ahead and handle, and that I would take up with him anything that I thought needed to be taken up with him."[4] The president and his liaison staff were linked by Persons, whose daily briefings seem to have focused on broad policy concerns rather than the specific tactics of the staff. Jack Anderson commented that "I don't believe the President knew how I operated or how other members of the staff operated. He assumed, of course, that we were doing our job and we were left free to do it."[5] Eisenhower spent very little time with the liaison staff and rarely sat in on the liaison staff meetings. Although staff members were confident of their access to the president, they seldom visited the Oval Office.

The president's trust has been essential for the success of the head of every congressional relations office, but it was especially important for Persons as he sought to establish the office with lawmakers. Without the trust of the president, it is difficult, if not impossible, for the liaison staff to credibly negotiate with Congress. Eisenhower's use of delegation made access even more important if his liaison office were to be adequately equipped to deal with Congress. If members of Congress or the cabinet believed that the liaison staff could not speak for the president they would seek out Eisenhower or other White House staff members directly. This would not only diminish the ability of the liaison staff to operate on the Hill, it would also shift work back to the president, a result contrary to his intentions in delegating responsibility. Eisenhower, however, was careful to back up his staff, saying, "I believe in decentralizing—that's why I took so much care in picking this gang."[6]

Persons and Harlow have been characterized as not holding the same stature that Larry O'Brien would hold during the Kennedy and Johnson administrations, and it is asserted that the placement of Chief of Staff Sherman Adams between the congressional relations shop and the president limited the effectiveness of the lobbying team.[7] While Persons did not have the round-the-clock access that O'Brien enjoyed with LBJ, as an assistant to the chief of staff Persons was assured access to the president and had scheduled daily meetings with him on legislative matters. Persons and Adams shared adjoining offices in the West Wing of the White House and remained closely in contact throughout the day. Undoubtedly, Adams was an important figure in Washington, but he did relatively little work with Congress and was no more involved in congressional relations than later chiefs of staff. Adams, like everyone who has served as chief of staff, did have meetings with members of Congress, but he kept the rest of the liaison staff well informed of his dealings with Congress. Most of his meetings with members of Congress were informal meetings designed to build goodwill, and he avoided becoming engaged in bargaining with members. While Adams had a reputation for being difficult, no liaison staff criticism of Adams was found in the archival research or interviews conducted for this book and, in fact, the regard for Adams was quite high.[8]

Eisenhower was committed to strengthening the White House staff by giving aides the stature of department secretaries.[9] While future heads of congressional relations would be given even more status and authority to direct the legislative activities of cabinet members, giving such status to a new White House position seems improbable. Nonetheless, Persons's position in the administration and his relationship with the president put him in a strong position.

In the end, Eisenhower's close relationship with the Congressional Liaison Office produced its intended results. With a high level of credibility, the liaison staff was able to represent the president effectively. In return, Eisenhower found that the staff protected him from day-to-day legislative matters, permitting him to focus his energies on other affairs.

The congressional relations organization created under Eisenhower resembles the office today. Jack Martin, Gerald Morgan, and later Ed McCabe operated primarily on the Senate side. Bryce Harlow, Earl Chesney, and Homer Gruenther had responsibility for the House of Representatives, with Jerry Morgan available on occasion. Jack Anderson joined the White House staff in 1955 and worked in the House where he had served. Persons (and then later Harlow) was in charge of the overall operation and briefing the president. The division of labor based on chamber has generally remained the standard in the White House liaison office.

The White House liaison office staff met at least once a day, usually in the morning, and kept in close contact throughout the day. Extensive book-keeping was done to ensure that an ongoing connection with members of Congress was maintained through phone calls, regular visits to congressional offices, and lunches with members.

While a clear chain of command was a central feature of the Eisenhower style of organization, narrow specialization was not. One example of the kind of flexibility that Eisenhower sought was that while Bryce Harlow's official role was in the liaison office, he spent much of his first two years in the White House writing speeches for Eisenhower and working on civil rights issues. Other staff members were often drawn into areas where they had policy expertise or close relationships with committees with jurisdiction. While assignments were flexible there was, according to one member of the staff, "a general sense of orderliness" that prevented people from intruding into the assignments of others, and they were not free to improvise. Flexibility under Eisenhower did not mean that staff tasks were competitive or that work assignments were duplicated.

Just as the liaison staff was drawn into other functions, occasionally the rest of the White House staff was drawn into the legislative process. White House staff members from outside the liaison office were advised to report "hints they gather in casual conversation" to members of the liaison staff.[10] In addition, the White House was not reluctant about using senior White House staff or cabinet members to lobby members of Congress.

Eisenhower believed that congenial personal relations with members of Congress were not merely convenient but indispensable to effective leadership. He hoped that "personal acquaintance would help smooth out difficulties inherent in partisanship."[11] He believed that if members felt hostile toward the president, leadership would be impossible. He explained his approach saying, "If you're going to do anything, you've got to make Congressmen your personal friends; that's really what I tried to do."[12]

Over time, the staff developed complementary methods for maintaining friendly relations with members of Congress, keeping careful records to make sure that this goodwill was spread as evenly as possible throughout Congress. White House staff arranged meetings with members of Congress, to build goodwill and to obtain information. Staffers usually circulated memos to Persons and the rest of the liaison office that reported their conversations in these meetings. The liaison office also sent letters to members from both parties after each election, congratulating the winners and commiserating with the losers. While generally form letters that varied little from member to member (for example, references to "the little lady" who helped them win election were omitted for single members), these letters often brought warm, personalized responses from members of both parties.[13] This technique, referred to here as "gaining favor," is discussed more in the chapters on Kennedy and Ford.

Eisenhower and Congress: The Autopilot Approach and Hidden-Hand Leadership

Eisenhower's indirect approach to Congress was shaped by his personality, the expectations of the time, and his own view of the proper relationship between the branches. Eisenhower preferred to do his legislative business through White House liaison staff. He generally disliked using the phone to call members of Congress. Even when Eisenhower talked with members face to face, he did not confront them nose to nose as Lyndon Johnson would. Eisenhower, according to one associate, held "a great regard for the other fellow's point of view" and was adverse to pressuring members of Congress.[14] Likewise, Eisenhower avoided using the traditional inducement of patronage to move Congress.[15]

Eisenhower's desire to work through his staff was necessitated by the political norms of the time. Previous presidents had worked largely through party leadership, and although as president Lyndon Johnson would develop a more intimate working relationship with Congress, he did so based on years of experience and with a heavily Democratic Congress. An attempt by Eisenhower to work more closely with Congress might have created a relationship more intimate than many in Congress would accept, and any attempt to work with lawmakers without consulting party leaders would have violated the norms of institutionalized pluralism.

Eisenhower himself believed that the principle of separation of powers required that congressional independence be protected.[16] He saw presidential leadership as constrained by a need to maintain the dignity of the office and restore some power to the Congress.[17] According to one aide, "it was almost a reverence for the notion of separation of powers."

I have labeled Eisenhower's style of working primarily through the congressional leadership and leaving much of the remaining interaction with Congress in the hands of his liaison staff "the autopilot approach."[18] An autopilot approach features presidential creation of a mechanism to manage contact with Congress. Eisenhower used his congressional relations staff, departmental liaison operations, and congressional party leaders to work with members of Congress. As discussed later in this chapter, the autopilot label is not an attempt to portray Eisenhower as passive or out of touch; rather, the autopilot approach is a device for managing the growing presidential workload that enables the president to focus on priorities that could help him win reelection and a place in history. In fact, the continuation and expansion of the congressional liaison operation by other administrations shows that while Eisenhower might have been the first president to leave much of the work with Congress in the hands of a liaison staff, he was not the last. And, as discussed later, this approach helped the Eisenhower administration make the best use of its most important resource: Dwight Eisenhower.

Delegation

Eisenhower, in part because of his experience with similar techniques in the military, advocated delegation.[19] Preparing for the legislative proposals and strategies in the fall of 1953, the president warned his staff of a "need for effective decentralization within each department." Eisenhower went on to outline his rationale for decentralization.

> My own interest in this matter arises not merely from the hope of saving wear and tear on principal assistants—it is essential to me that the group, both individually and collectively, preserves to itself the maximum time for *thinking and for study*. This can be done only through skillful delegation of authority and responsibility to subordinates. . . . I am sure we all understand that the marks of a good executive are courage in delegating work to subordinates, and his own skill in coordinating and directing their efforts. [20] (emphasis in original)

One day earlier, the president had attended a staff meeting and emphasized that ideas should not be given to him but directed to the proper departments.[21] While many of the staffing and organizational decisions were left to Sherman Adams, Eisenhower was specific and adamant in his desire to decentralize the administration. According to Bryce Harlow, the organization of the White House was specifically designed to make sure that the president could dedicate his efforts to the most important issues before him and prevent him from "being nibbled to death by small things while the world's going to hell in a handbasket."[22] The creation of the first White House office designed solely for dealing with Congress was a logical extension of this decentralization philosophy. Cabinet departments were likewise encouraged to maintain their own liaison operations.

While the free rein that Eisenhower granted his staff generally served him well, it occasionally left the staff unaware of his preferences and left him surprised by the staff's efforts. The push for Alaskan statehood provides an example of the confusion that could be created at both ends of Pennsylvania Avenue.

The status of Alaska had been an issue for years; the Republicans had included statehood in their platform since 1916. During the campaign Eisenhower had supported the plank of the Republican platform in favor of Alaskan statehood. After taking office, the president reminded his staff of his commitment to the Republican platform in its entirety and they believed this included statehood for Alaska. This position, however, clashed with that of congressional Republicans who opposed statehood on the grounds that Alaska could become a Democratic stronghold. While Eisenhower called for statehood for Hawaii in his 1953 State of the Union address and repeated this request throughout his first term, he would not publicly endorse statehood for Alaska until 1957.[23]

Jack Anderson believed that Eisenhower wanted to implement Alaskan statehood based on the president's expressed desire to implement the Republican platform. Even as Anderson and the Interior Department began working on statehood legislation, Eisenhower continued to express opposition to statehood in his meetings with congressional leaders. As late as January 1954 he privately assured the Republican leadership that statehood was "crazy" and that he would veto Alaskan statehood legislation.[24] Eisenhower and the Republican leadership had been counting on Speaker Rayburn to keep any statehood legislation from reaching the floor. When a bill found its way out of committee in the spring of 1958, Jack Anderson, working from a list provided by Representative John Sayer, the ranking minority member of the House Interior Committee, began calling up twenty-six Republicans whose votes were considered key to passage of the bill. Some of those whom Anderson contacted were surprised that the White House was interested in the bill. The legislation passed the House by a slim margin with the votes of members from Anderson's list proving to be pivotal. After the passage of the bill Republican leaders were shocked to learn that they had been beaten, in part, by White House efforts. In the next leadership meeting Minority Leader Joe Martin complained to Eisenhower in Anderson's presence that "we had the thing pretty well under control until we had this blitz." The president too seemed surprised, asking, "What do you mean by the blitz?" Eisenhower invited Martin to a private meeting in the Oval Office to discuss the matter and Anderson assumed he was about to be fired. Later, Wilton Persons met with the president to explain Anderson's action. Eisenhower declared, "Well, forget it. Jack was doing his job and that's good enough for me."[25]

The case of Alaskan statehood demonstrates the potential confusion over the White House agenda when communication between the liaison staff and the president breaks down. Republicans were unaware of the president's position on legislation and the president was unaware of his own staff's efforts on his behalf. Such communication problems were rare during the Eisenhower administration, but as the White House grows, recurrences could plague a future autopilot presidency.

Another consequence of delegation is that lawmakers may come to doubt the president's commitment to issues, unless they hear directly from the president. Duane Tananbaum has suggested that Eisenhower's failure to make clear that he personally opposed the Bricker amendment permitted it to linger on the legislative agenda and almost gain passage.[26] Because Eisenhower seemed to attribute administration opposition to the amendment to Secretary of State John Foster Dulles in order to avoid an open confrontation with Senate Republicans, Senate Republicans interpreted Eisenhower's response to mean that they might gain Eisenhower's support and continued to press for passage of the amendment. Eventually, Eisenhower was forced to more openly oppose the Bricker amendment in order to prevent its passage.

CONGRESSIONAL LEADERSHIP

Eisenhower's closest contact with the legislative branch came in his weekly meetings with the Republican congressional leadership. Despite his disagreements with Republican congressional leaders, Eisenhower told the cabinet that "our long-term good requires that leadership on the Hill be exercised through the party organization there."[27]

The president was frequently criticized by less senior members of Congress for ignoring them. While every member of Congress had been invited to the White House during the year, very few had been invited for anything other than social functions attended by twenty to thirty members at a time. In 1957, Ed McCabe suggested that the president see more Republican members of Congress for "business" meetings. The purpose of these meetings was to "draw Congressional Republicans closer to our program—and in the process try to eliminate criticism about Presidential aloofness."[28]

Eisenhower insisted on leaving as much as possible in the hands of congressional leaders. In a draft of a letter to House Majority Leader Charles

Halleck in 1953, Eisenhower discussed complaints he had received from rank-and-file members of the House who felt detached from the White House. After several members of the House told Eisenhower that freshmen members were never consulted on issues, his response was to suggest to Halleck that the Republican Leadership try to find ways to overcome these objections.[29]

Eisenhower generally assumed that congressional leaders were consulting with rank-and-file members and that they could speak for average members. This was not always the case, especially under Speaker Martin. Some members found that they would not be involved in White House meetings even on policies they themselves had taken a leading role in developing. Eventually the White House staff had to begin sending its own invitations to the White House to members involved in the development of a policy.[30]

Eisenhower's reliance on congressional leadership left his work with Congress heavily dependent on those who occupied leadership positions. The relationship between Eisenhower and Congress took an early, dramatic turn with the death of Senate Majority Leader Taft. After having defeated him at the Republican convention, Eisenhower and many of his advisors had been concerned that Taft would be difficult to deal with. They found that this was not true. After Taft's death, Eisenhower found himself working with Senator William Knowland, whom he cared little for.

Eisenhower showed little interest in the details of politics and held little regard for those who focused on such concerns. For example, Eisenhower seemed indifferent to Senate Republicans' efforts to appoint Mark Trice as comptroller general, a candidate whom the president felt was slightly less qualified than one backed by House members.

> In any event, Knowland, Millikin and Ferguson are coming to have breakfast with me tomorrow morning to plead the case for Trice. I feel that the three Republican leaders of Congress (if they have any comprehension whatsoever of leadership) would have something better to do than to spend their time in petty patronage problems.[31]

While Eisenhower seemed unhappy with the Senate leadership, he seemed to enjoy dealing with House Republican Leader Charles Halleck, whom the president and his staff considered an articulate, dynamic leader. Halleck's stock in the White House was so high that he was included in the congressional leadership meetings even after the Republicans lost control of the House and Halleck lost his leadership position there, as Joe Martin moved down from Speaker to Minority Leader.

Congressional relations were affected noticeably by changes in the Republican congressional leadership in 1959. Just before the 1958 election, Senate Minority Leader William Knowland retired from the Senate to pursue an unsuccessful bid for the governorship of California. Republicans selected Everett Dirksen—whom Fred Greenstein has described as shadow leader for Eisenhower's middle-of-the-road position—as the new Minority Leader.[32]

In the House, the Republican leadership changed when Minority Leader Joe Martin was deposed and replaced by Charles Halleck in 1959. While some members accused Eisenhower and his White House staff of playing a role in the ousting of Martin, Martin's defeat was more closely tied to Republican frustration with their losses in the midterm election. It appears that Eisenhower's role was not so much a direct attempt to undermine Martin as it was the result of Eisenhower no longer asking Halleck to avoid a challenge to Martin.[33] This is consistent with the administration's approach of not tampering with internal congressional politics. Eisenhower and his staff avoided any involvement in the selection of committee chairs or leadership positions within Congress.

The final two years of Eisenhower's presidency composed the most enjoyable and dynamic period of his relationship with the Congress.[34] This was especially evident in the weekly leadership meetings. Ironically, just as the Republicans with whom Eisenhower was most politically and personally compatible vaulted to leadership positions, the Republican party's electoral misfortunes provided only enough votes to barely sustain a veto.

Eisenhower utilized congressional leadership for several reasons. Logistically, it was impossible for the small White House liaison staff to cover every member of Congress. One staffer commented, "you'd wear your shoes out running the halls" if the staff attempted to contact each member. Philosophically, Eisenhower preferred using the structures that were in place. He saw the congressional leadership as a natural conduit for contact with members of Congress and was reluctant to circumvent those leaders. Pragmatically, the administration realized that the parties' leaders held great power in Congress and could effectively deliver votes. Generally, the White House worked in concert with congressional leaders in approaching members. Rank-and-file members might receive phone calls from the president, but such calls were rare.

The administration's reliance on congressional leaders was based on Eisenhower's respect for congressional autonomy and the stature of the congressional leaders of the day. Eisenhower insisted that the separation between the branches be honored, and any attempt to work with Congress without extensive consultation with its leaders would have reflected a lack of respect for congressional prerogatives. The need to work with congressional leaders was further necessitated by the power of the leaders he faced. Eisenhower was faced with two of the strongest congressional leaders of the century, Sam Rayburn and Lyndon Johnson. Their power directly shaped how Eisenhower could work with members of Congress, especially Democrats.

LEADERSHIP MEETINGS

Eisenhower considered his weekly meeting with the Republican congressional leadership his most effective tool for dealing with Congress.[35] These meetings included the president and vice president, the White House liaison staff, and Republican congressional leaders. During 1953–1954, when Republicans controlled the committees, committee chairs with jurisdiction over bills on the agenda for the meeting also attended. Occasionally, the president would invite a cabinet secretary from a department with important legislation pending to sit in and explain the department's legislation. Over time, the number of White House staff members at the meeting grew to around twenty, but this number was reduced slightly after congressional leaders complained about the number of staffers "auditing" the discussion.[36]

An hour before each leadership meeting Harlow or Persons would bring two members from the congressional leadership in for a private breakfast with Eisenhower. Each week they invited one member from the House and one from the Senate on a rotating basis so that the president would have a private breakfast with all the members of the leadership on a regular basis.

While the agenda for these meetings were drawn up by the liaison staff, Persons always consulted Eisenhower, who occasionally added items that he considered important. The meetings would usually begin with members of the congressional leadership reviewing the status of legislation. The president, his staff, and any involved cabinet officials would then outline the administration's position on major legislative issues. From there, the discussion moved to matters of strategy. These meetings were held in the cabinet room, usually lasted about one hour, and were followed by a press conference of the two leading members of the House and Senate delegation.

On December 17 through 19, 1953, the White House hosted a three-day legislative conference with Republican congressional leaders and committee chairs. These eight-hour meetings were designed to unify the party in Congress and map out a plan for the coming session. Despite this effort, Eisenhower was not able to repeat the level of success he enjoyed in 1953.

Ironically, while Eisenhower relied heavily on Republican leadership to help with his legislative program, for much of his presidency his personal relationship with the Republican leadership was weak, while that with Democratic leaders was strong. Although Eisenhower met primarily with Republican leaders, from time to time he held formal meetings with the leaders of both parties. These meetings were usually on foreign policy matters and were used as a way of keeping congressional leaders apprised of actions the president had already taken. While these meetings played some role in building support for foreign policy, they were seldom used to deal with issues that could be resolved with legislation and rarely aimed to solicit the advice of members of Congress.

Beyond these formal meetings, Eisenhower hosted informal evening meetings at the White House with Speaker Sam Rayburn and Democratic Senate Leader Lyndon Johnson about every six weeks. The three enjoyed a friendly relationship; the only thing the Democratic leaders disliked about the president was that he had chosen to be a Republican.[37] These meetings were a closely guarded secret. Not only would publicizing these meetings run contrary to Eisenhower's preference for quiet leadership, news of such meetings with Democrats would undermine and irritate congressional Republican leaders.

PARTISANSHIP

The lack of clear partisanship may have contributed to the image of Eisenhower as a weak leader. Eisenhower backed legislation that often could not be easily classified as part of the Republican or Democratic agenda. Failing to conform in this way to the partisan framework of Capitol Hill, the Eisenhower administration could easily, if mistakenly, be accused of being directionless. Further, since neither side saw the president consistently pushing legislation in their direction, neither side gave him full credit for his efforts.

Strong, consistent partisanship was not a hallmark of Eisenhower's relations with the Congress, in part because he often found much of his support among moderate and conservative Democrats and his most stubborn opposition among Republicans. Eisenhower believed that most congressional Republicans were no longer familiar with "either the techniques or the need for cooperating with the Executive," since only 15 of the 221 Republican members of the House had served with a Republican president.[38]

I had hoped that the first Republican national victory in twenty years would provide a strong, unifying influence within the party and among its representatives in the Senate and the House. But my hope for unanimity was quickly shattered.

It was clear that habitual, almost instinctive opposition to the Chief Executive, as well as differences in political convictions, would create difficulties in Executive-Legislative relations.[39]

Eisenhower differed with fellow Republicans on specific legislative issues and on the scope of executive authority. In part as a response to Franklin Roosevelt's long tenure, and in part as a response to their concerns about Yalta, the Republicans wanted to cut back on the size and the scope of the presidency. These changes took the form of limits on presidential terms and constraints on presidential power like the Bricker amendment. This left Eisenhower in the uneasy position of defending the presidency from his own party. Republicans also consistently questioned Eisenhower's requests for foreign aid.

Eisenhower had hoped to see the Republican party strengthened, but on his own terms. While he did campaign on behalf of congressional Republican candidates, the president did so reluctantly and focused his speeches on the general progress of his administration.[40] Sherman Adams believed that "Eisenhower felt that as President of all the people he should not become personally involved in state and Congressional district issues."[41] Stephen Ambrose suggests that Eisenhower became involved in campaigning for congressional candidates in order to preclude the right wing of the party from taking over the Republican party.[42] When told that his participation in congressional campaigns could help the Republicans regain control of Congress, Eisenhower replied, "Why should I help such people as [Knowland] to get chairmanships—it becomes a terrible thing to do to our country almost."[43]

Eisenhower's conservatism should not be judged by his adherence to the party politics found in Congress. Eisenhower was firmly committed to conservative principals in domestic policy. However, given his clashes with Republicans in Congress on foreign policy and the conservatism of southern Democrats, pursuing a narrowly partisan path would not serve his political goals as neatly as some critics would suggest.

Eisenhower explained his reluctance to involve himself in a partisan campaign to Thomas Dewey by telling him that "there was nothing that Mr. Truman did that so shocked my sense of the fitting and the appropriate as did his barnstorming activities while he was actually the president of the United States." He went on to explain that "no president, regardless of his popularity, can pass that popularity on to a Party or to an individual."[44] He blamed congressional Republicans for failing to follow his leadership despite his popularity and therefore held them responsible for the party's failure to gain seats in Congress. In particular, he blamed Dick Simpson and Barry Goldwater and said that "there were 'too many leaders' running in too many directions at once."[45] In a letter to Thomas Dewey Eisenhower warned, "I do believe that intelligent candidates can participate in a President's popularity by asking only the opportunity to put their shoulders to the wheel in pushing forward the program for which the popular individual may stand. Instead of doing this, they too often ask for a Presidential arm to be cast protectively around them."[46] The criticism that he received from some Republicans for not doing more did little to change Eisenhower's view of the party. "What we need is less headline hunters and more Eisenhower supporters."[47]

At the same time, Eisenhower's political skills were questioned even by some of his strongest congressional friends. House Minority Leader Halleck commented: "Eisenhower wasn't worth a damn as a politician. He was a great President, but he wasn't a politician."[48]

Eisenhower's ability to work with members of both parties may have partly been the result of his limited Washington experience. Eisenhower had made many visits to Capitol Hill as a highly visible and highly respected general rather than as a partisan. He was known to Democrats apart from partisan politics. At least initially, many Democrats may have been thinking more of Eisenhower the General, rather than Eisenhower the Republican. Since Eisenhower's party label was relatively new, his Washington friendships were built purely on his personality and personal accomplishments. Presidents like Johnson or Truman were known on Capitol Hill through years of working with fellow Democrats. Eisenhower had neither reason nor occasion to have spent more time with Republicans than with Democrats. Consequently, Democratic leaders would have been unable to convincingly portray the political process in "us versus them" terms, even if they had been inclined to.

Eisenhower campaigned—though not always enthusiastically—for the election of congressional Republicans. Between elections he was even less the partisan.

> It is astonishing how infrequently anything of a partisan character is mentioned in the Cabinet; problems are discussed objectively and argument proceeds on the basis of bringing to bear every viewpoint on the specific project. Two of my most trusted advisors were, up until a few years ago, dyed-in-the-wool Southern Democrats. Yet this fact is one that I believe rarely occurs to any of the members of the Cabinet as we try to work out composite solutions for specific problems.[49]

Eisenhower valued ability over partisanship, and applied such criteria in his appointments throughout the executive branch. In fact, he avoided consulting with Republican congressional leaders or the Republican National Committee before making appointments.[50] In one meeting Speaker Martin "ruefully" noted that while Democratic administrations had let a Republican member of Congress be the first to know of any action taken in a district, they were not getting similar treatment from a Republican administration.[51]

Eisenhower was fond of many of the southern Democrats in Congress. Beyond his meetings with Rayburn and Johnson, Eisenhower expressed a fondness for Robert Anderson of Texas, whom the president considered an excellent choice to succeed him.[52] The liaison staff, like Eisenhower himself, was not partisan. Some members of the staff had been Democrats and maintained friendships on both sides of the aisle. Bryce Harlow believed that if the White House's lobbyists were too partisan, they would hesitate to approach members of the other party.[53] Democratic Representative L. Mendel Rivers told Homer Gruenther: "You are still my favorite of all the occupants of the White House, both present, past and future. Regardless of politics, I will always be in your corner. So far as I am concerned there are no political parties between you and me."[54]

Eisenhower's popularity with voters made him an unlikely target for partisan attacks. However, it became apparent to Democrats that Eisenhower's popularity did not carry over to Republicans in Congress. The disparity between his own popularity and voter support for congressional Republicans perplexed the president. While he wanted to create a Republican majority in Congress, much to his dismay the public failed to see a clear connection between him and the party.[55] The Republican majority vanished while Eisenhower remained popular. Democrats realized that they could attack Republicans without attacking Eisenhower, and by avoiding open warfare with the popular Eisenhower, congressional Democrats were able to deny voters a reason to toss them out. According to Bryce Harlow, Democrats in Congress realized that openly resisting the president was counterproductive and that by appearing to work with him they could keep getting Democrats reelected.[56] Richard Neustadt concluded, "Eisenhower did not get the Congresses he wanted, but the Democrats he got instead were pledged to treat him well."[57]

Hidden-Hand Leadership and the Autopilot Presidency

Eisenhower's critics portrayed his low-key approach, his agenda of restraining government growth, and his time spent on the golf course as evidence of an inactive presidency. However, the description of Eisenhower as completely passive was a product of contemporary political rhetoric. Fred Greenstein has described Eisenhower's style as "hidden-hand leadership." In Greenstein's view, Eisenhower was an activist who avoided the appearance of involvement in day-to-day politics in order to protect his reputation and maintain public support.[58] Eisenhower was clearly more involved than many critics acknowledge. One of Eisenhower's assistants enthusiastically agreed with Greenstein's descriptions.

> He had his hand into everything but the hand was hidden, and not out there for the public to see. . . .
>
> There was never any question in my mind and I don't think that there was any question in any one else's mind who worked on that staff that the president was the boss, he was actively involved in everything, he was meeting with individual cabinet officers, and so it was always puzzling to me at that time to read newspaper stories and columnists that would treat him as a detached, sort of an amiable fellow, who spent a lot of time playing golf and waving at people and who somehow wasn't involved in the role of government.

As he did in other realms, the president would use intermediaries in his relations with Congress. An important part of hidden-hand leadership in Congress involved going to key constituents. Fred Greenstein cites the case of Eisenhower's use of a wealthy Texas constituent to influence Senate Democratic Leader Lyndon Johnson.[59] Eisenhower's use of an old friend represents only part of the administration's broader strategy to influence members. A lawmaker's closest friend from the administration might call to see if the member could help the president out on a vote. The White House would often have the cabinet member closest to a reluctant lawmaker deliver a message, offer inducements like appointments, or threaten federal spending in the district. This was referred to by one veteran of the White House as "a kind of unspoken arm twisting." As he described it, the White House would use the Republican National Committee to track down important people in the district to push on tough votes.

> If you were wavering on that particular vote, and your district was pretty well divided and you had a lot of people for it and a lot of people against it, which made it tougher for you to vote, we were not averse to getting in touch with your events chairman—the guy who raised the money for your campaign. Provided we knew that he was on our side on that issue, we'd get the word to him and say, your con-

gressman is wavering on this thing, we don't know, you might want
to lay in with him and let him know how you feel.

Eisenhower's hand was not always hidden or gentle.[60] One alumnus of
the Nixon and Reagan White House observed, "I'm not so sure the hidden
hand didn't have a brass knuckle on it." With the Constitution clearly supporting him, Eisenhower's willingness to assert his role grew. While Eisenhower's hidden hand may have nudged legislators as they considered legislation, he openly used the back of his hand to stop legislation with vetoes.
Eisenhower set no records in his use of the veto, but he did use it frequently
and was overridden only twice.[61] His use of the veto power suggests that
Eisenhower was willing to act but was more comfortable doing so within
channels clearly sanctioned by the Constitution.

At times, Eisenhower could be quite direct with members of Congress.
One aide reported that the president ran into Senator Case (Republican-
South Dakota) at a social event. "The senator said something to the president to the effect that, well, 'Mr. President, sorry I couldn't vote with our
leader,' and the president's eyes flashed a little bit, and he said, 'Cliff, what
I'd like to know is when in the hell are you going to line up and start voting
with your party.' It was a strong comment coming from him and everybody
was taken aback."

Still, hardball politics in the Eisenhower White House were relatively
mild by comparison to most other administrations. As one legislative assistant explained to me,

> You come from a congressional district where there are great pres-
> sures both ways, you may have a lot of labor union activity in the dis-
> trict, so it is difficult for you, politically, to vote against the interests
> of the labor unions. Hence, you would rather avoid the burden if
> you could. We were anxious to get that program across, we were not
> anxious to let you off the hook that easily. We were going to put your
> toes to the fire and make you face up to it. We were not adverse to
> calling on other people.

The administration was reluctant to trade for votes. One liaison staffer
described the administration's reluctance to engage in trading as coming
from Eisenhower.

> The one thing we didn't do and others have done it, but, just some-
> how we felt it was not compatible with Eisenhower's way of govern-
> ing. That is, if you, in your congressional district, were very anxious

to have, let's say, a water project approved, a dam of some significance, you know, on again, off again, and the government hadn't
made up its mind whether they were going to put it here, or five
hundred miles away. We would not ever be comfortable, and we
wouldn't do it, because we knew the president wouldn't do it. We
wouldn't ever go to the member and say, "Gosh darn it, you know, if
we lose your vote on this, you might as well kiss that rivers and har-
bors project good-bye." That is real hardball—it was too rough for
us, we wouldn't do it.

Greenstein's hidden-hand analysis has helped scholars better appreciate
Eisenhower's style of governing and provided a more meaningful standard
for judging his presidency. At the same time, in attempting to reestablish the
credibility of Eisenhower, Greenstein may have overstated the degree of direct control that Eisenhower exercised. While the image of Eisenhower as a
passive president was unfairly earned on the golf course, this reputation does
have some legitimate roots. Eisenhower did delegate, although his decentralized style is a credible means of directing the White House. It is inaccu-
rate to conclude that Eisenhower was an activist on the basis of the performance of others in the White House. Given the extensive delegation in the
White House, should Eisenhower's activism be judged on the basis of his actions or those of the people who worked under him? In his relations with
Congress, Eisenhower left much of the work in the hands of congressional
leaders and the staff of his White House and cabinet departments; they seem
to have earned much of the credit.

Eisenhower was not the first or last president to take this approach to
Congress. Harry Truman used his White House to contact constituents of
members who were unlikely to respond to direct appeals from the president.[62] As later chapters show, presidents since Eisenhower have used some
variation of the hidden-hand technique, and its use has gradually been institutionalized in the White House.

An adaptation of Adam Smith's "invisible hand" suggests another analogy for understanding one aspect of Eisenhower's success in Congress, because legislative battles often were guided as much by the presence of Dwight
Eisenhower as by his specific activities. Eisenhower's popularity provided the
White House and its congressional allies with the natural reserve of power
they needed to win legislative victories. However, the relationship between
public and congressional support for Eisenhower is the story of a potential
strength not exploited. The president's personal popularity was an asset in
general terms but was seldom directed at accomplishing specific policy goals.
Jacob Javits commented that "Eisenhower had all kinds of credit with the

American people. He could have done some very extraordinary things in government terms."[63] While there was a significant effort to manage public relations from the White House, Eisenhower resisted pressure to use his personal popularity to move Congress.[64] Eisenhower avoided giving his State of the Union address during prime time because he considered it a message to Congress, not to the people,[65] and he considered making a personal appeal to the public "only with reticence, if not repugnance."[66] When Eisenhower did yield to pressure from his staff, the president avoided a direct address to the public and instead staged an informal discussion with a cabinet member.[67] He repeatedly told them: "I keep telling you fellows I don't like to do this sort of thing. I can think of nothing more boring for the American public, than to have to sit in their living rooms for a whole half hour looking at my face on their television screens."[68] Instead, Eisenhower continually encouraged House Minority Leader Charlie Halleck and Senate Minority Leader Everett Dirksen to continue their regular press conferences.[69]

Eisenhower did not always conceal his leadership. Rather, many activities occurred without his specific direction. Just as the invisible market forces of capitalism were to guide the marketplace, the electoral success and personal popularity of Dwight Eisenhower needed only the effective mechanism of the White House staff to carry his priorities into law. One testament to the power of the political forces that Eisenhower generated is the success of Alaskan statehood even without Eisenhower's direct involvement. This is not to say that Eisenhower was passive or does not deserve credit; only that his activism was focused at a different level and that he deserves credit for the strategy rather than the tactics.

In the case of congressional relations, a better analogy for the Eisenhower style is that of an autopilot. Eisenhower's method was to create a mechanism for maintaining friendly relations with Congress, set the correct course, and then let things run, taking personal control only during critical moments. Eisenhower's autopilot was his liaison staff, which he equipped with the mandate of electoral success and provided with little personal additional involvement. The lack of ongoing attention to legislative details is evident in White House correspondence. The few memoranda by Eisenhower on congressional relations generally take one of two forms: directives on decentralization and on other issues relating to staff organization, and memos on minor matters. In one memo entitled, "And on such things is the government run," the president points out, "All the Congressmen's wives bought new dresses for the Congressional Reception that was canceled. They put pressure on husbands. So the Leaders said we must have a Congressional Reception this year."[70]

Memoranda between liaison staff seldom mention Eisenhower by name. Staffers were assumed to know the president's wishes and focus on staying the course and maintaining the machinery of the liaison operation. He set out to create a liaison operation that "will not be too dependent upon the mere presence, words, or even counsel of the chief, but which will, because of its complete solidarity of faith in ideas and ideals, be capable of functioning both collectively and in all of its parts."[71]

Pilots use an autopilot system to keep the plane on course while they tend to other duties. They must check the functioning of the plane, ensure that they have charted the correct course, and monitor passenger safety and comfort. This does not mean that pilots are not in control of the plane while it is on autopilot, since they can take the controls of the plane if it strays off course. Presidents, like pilots, need some mechanism to permit them to pursue whatever functions most demand attention at critical moments and, at the same time, they must be able to oversee the functions of the entire crew.

My autopilot label intentionally avoids the word *leadership* since Eisenhower did lead, but not in every phase of the legislative process. Instead, he focused his efforts on those parts of the process in which his energies were most effective, leaving inertia and staff to carry his goals through other parts of the process.

The idea of leadership is also avoided since Eisenhower himself seemed unclear as to what makes leadership. He was clearly not looking to provide the same kind of leadership as Franklin Roosevelt and Harry Truman. In fact, Eisenhower repeatedly denounced "desk pounding" as a type of leadership. In a letter to his brother Milton he attacked

> the false but prevalent notion that bullying and leadership are synonymous; that desk-pounding is more effective than is persistent adherence to a purpose and winning to that purpose sufficient for its achievement. For this particular kind of person there is greater satisfaction, possibly sadistic, in seeing their opponents reviled and cursed in the public prints than there is in the knowledge that the causes for which they themselves stand are being constructively advanced.[72]

At the same time, Eisenhower was appalled by the "amount of caution approaching fright that seems to govern the action of most politicians."[73] He seemed to expect more aggressive leadership from congressional Republicans.

They do not seem to realize when there arrives that moment at which soft speaking should be abandoned and a fight to the end undertaken. Any man who hopes to exercise leadership must be ready to meet this requirement face to face when it arises; unless he is ready to fight when necessary, people will finally begin to ignore him.[74]

The "autopilot" label is not a criticism of the Eisenhower administration's dealings with Congress. Given the Democratic majority that he faced six of his eight years in office and the natural momentum of New Deal programs, Eisenhower probably considered slowing down the growth of government to be more realistic than dismantling existing programs or proposing his own. Knowing the odds against passage of his own legislative package, Eisenhower may have been content to dedicate his efforts to obstructing the most objectionable portions of Democratic legislation.

In fact, Eisenhower considered this kind of organization as fundamental to success. In a letter to Emmet Hughes, Eisenhower argues that, "in our complicated political system, even with such an individual standing, success is going to be measured, *over the long term,* by the skill with which the leader builds a strong team around him"[75] (emphasis in original). Eisenhower, in judging how to conduct his own administration, viewed leadership as something closer to management than many political scientists would prefer.

Eisenhower was not passive; however, he was not as active as those who would follow in his footsteps. It is not my intention to imply that Eisenhower was generally unaware of relations with Congress or that he was disengaged from his liaison staff. In fact, Eisenhower's contact with the legislative process was not dramatically different from most presidents. And, far from suggesting that Eisenhower was unduly disengaged, it can be argued that he made more efficient use of his time and energy than most. An autopilot approach does not involve relinquishing "control" in any except the most trivial sense of the word. It is true that Eisenhower did not become involved in a large number of minor decisions, but at the same time by delegating these decisions he freed himself to become involved in a broader range of decisions.

The greatest strength of the autopilot approach to Congress was that it gave Eisenhower the time to deal with foreign affairs. Sherman Adams reported that Eisenhower wanted to see more delegation of authority in the White House so that the president could be freed from routine matters and commit his energies to bigger problems of "world peace and disarmament, national security and domestic welfare."[76] Eisenhower was committed to pursuing the goals of world peace. He entered the race for the presidency, in part, to keep isolationists from taking control of foreign policy. Eisenhower devoted his first inaugural address almost exclusively to foreign policy. Knowing that he had little that he could accomplish in Congress on domestic affairs, Eisenhower left the details of those matters largely in the hands of his staff and the Republican congressional leadership, freeing him to focus on foreign relations.

DEPARTMENTAL RELATIONS

As soon as there were executive departments, there was lobbying by the executive branch. Alexander Hamilton in his service as the first secretary of the treasury used the lack of congressional organization and staff to draft and push legislation. One senator complained that "Nothing was done without him [Hamilton]."[77] By the Third Congress the Democratic-Republicans had rejected the leadership of the departments and instead had to rely on the use of the Committee of the Whole for much of its work. However, by the twentieth century, the complexity and number of issues were beginning to overload congressional resources and Congress found itself turning to the executive branch for information and other favors. As G. Russell Pipes wrote in the mid-1960s, "I heard a lot about lobbyists before I came to Washington and expected to be besieged when I arrived. I was. To my amazement the first ten lobbyists who came to see me were from the ten Executive Departments, offering assistance, literature and advice on their legislative programs."[78]

The Institutionalization of Departmental Liaison

As the administrative demands of the cabinet secretaries grew, they found an increasing need for assistance in maintaining their relationships with Congress. One cabinet member noted that even though he initially had put aside time during each week for maintaining contact with members, "as time went on this was pushed further and further into the background."[79] A legislative liaison system gradually evolved to serve this need and the expanding legislative agenda of a growing bureaucracy. Despite some initial reservations the departments developed specialized organs for dealing with Congress. Some cabinet officers continued to use the prestige of a department head in dealing with Congress on major issues, but a system was needed to permit some less essential liaison functions to be conducted at lower levels.

The institutionalization of executive branch lobbying began in the War

Department. Each branch of the service dealt with the Congress independently: the navy through several bureaus, while the army and air force used public information offices. As the services had more interaction with Congress, they began to develop a system for handling contacts. In the 1920s the army, for example, did not have a spelled-out relationship with Congress except that they assigned one person to deal exclusively with the appropriations committees in the House and Senate. Staff members were initially assigned to duties associated with Congress on an ad hoc basis, but eventually staff members gained enough experience to develop expertise in dealing with congressional matters. The experience of Wilton Persons as a major serving in the War Department in the 1920s is typical.

> I got into this stuff I think by accident. I was in the Assistant Secretary of War's office, and Congress started an investigation in the House on procurement. It was procurement of saddles and bridles for World War I, if I remember correctly, and the disposal of them and some question as to whether or not there was any hanky panky in their disposal. . . . So we went up, and we didn't do well at all. But the next time we went up we did a damned sight better. . . . And from there on I got more and more of it. . . . And I found myself stuck with it.[80]

The high level of interaction between the War Department and Congress generated by the Second World War and following demobilization helped to expand relations with Congress, and by the late 1940s all the service branches had set up liaison offices on the Hill.[81] Today, each of the service branches has its own offices actually located on Capitol Hill. Persons would serve a similar function for Generals Marshall and Eisenhower during their times as chief of staff. His work with Eisenhower during the mobilization helped convince the future president of the value of effective congressional liaison.

Eisenhower's Use of Departmental Liaison

While Persons and his assistant Bryce Harlow brought a congressional relations office into the White House, they understood that the departmental lobbyists would continue to play an important role. In the view of the White House, cabinet officials and their assistants were too valuable a resource to lay idle. Many departments had been pursuing similar activities before the White House formally took on the task and had personnel experienced at liaison. Many of the individuals involved in lobbying Congress on

behalf of the administration were career officials whose experience was valuable.

The use of liaison personnel from the cabinet departments was a natural
extension both of Eisenhower's desire to decentralize decision making and
of his belief in cabinet government. The president wanted to see individual
cabinet departments take more of a role in maintaining good relations with
members of Congress, especially with the leadership and members of related
committees.[82] Cabinet secretaries were advised to set aside time on a regular
basis to meet with the eighty or so members who were key to their departments' concerns. The departments were warned that if good personal relations were not maintained, "needless Congressional troubles will develop
that will take far more time in the long run, and with disappointing results."[83]
The White House was particularly concerned about the failure of cabinet
secretaries to appear at legislative hearings.[84]

To coordinate the efforts of the White House and departmental liaison
staff, the Legislative Council was created.[85] The council met on Saturday
mornings for several years and provided an opportunity for information
sharing and strategic planning. These meetings let the White House staff
brief the departments on the president's priorities and let the departments
provide status reports on their own legislation. A member of the liaison described these meetings as "A chance for people to rub elbows with one another who were in this business, across the administration in congressional
relations in all the departments—you know, have some coffee and dough-
nuts. We developed kind of a fellowship of people."

The Legislative Council was originally composed of the White House liaison staff and assistant secretaries or general councils of the departments.
The departments began to send substitutes to the meetings. Later, they
began sending substitutes for the substitutes. The ability of the departments'
representatives to speak for their departments declined in direct relation to
the bureaucratic authority they possessed. Beyond that, the career bureaucrats who eventually came as substitutes were suspected by some of Eisenhower's people of being New Deal loyalists. Eventually, the council was abandoned after information leaks attributed to New Deal holdovers began to
compromise the administration's legislation.

One researcher has suggested that "The White House team served as a
back-up when help was needed, otherwise it tended to steer clear of Congress."[86] The Eisenhower White House did leave most issues in the hands of
the departments, becoming involved in only selective cases, but they acted
more as a supervisor than a backup. The White House still had a relatively
small staff and the congressional relations team was not able to manage all

of the legislation coming from the departments. Even as the liaison staff grew in later White Houses, their size did not keep pace with the demands generated by the flood of legislation passing through Congress. According to Bryce Harlow, "One of the problems you have with this kind of system is to keep the departments doing that which they ought to do themselves and stop bothering the White House with their bric-a-brac."[87] Also, this distance was maintained to prevent the White House staff from wearing out its welcome. Bryce Harlow felt that the best way to maximize the impact of White House lobbying was to reserve it for only the most important votes.

The system, as described by one member of the liaison staff, used the White House liaison staff to play a significant role in working on "presidential" items, legislation of significant importance to the president, while lesser matters were left to the departments.

> A great many other subjects, a whole range of things across government, would not rise to that level of presidential importance, in the eyes of that president. Thus, they became departmental issues. The Agriculture Department would have bone-breaking problems with farm-price reports, interior department with mineral rights matters, and so on. But, in the bigger scheme of things, if they were not of such a magnitude to be presidential, then they became departmental matters. We were available to consult and work here and there with departments and things like that. But, in general, we tried and pretty much succeeded in not having the White House involved along with departments in a matter that was of somewhat lesser consequence.

The use of departmental lobbying by the Eisenhower White House resembles its successors. While the liaison offices would go through a gradual upgrading over the next twenty years, their relationship remained largely the same. One difference is that the White House would not fully take control of the use of cabinet secretaries until the Kennedy administration. During the Kennedy administration it would become clear that the White House staff directed the lobbying of everyone in the cabinet departments, up to and including the heads of the departments. In part because of the new status of the White House lobbyists and in part out of Eisenhower's view of how the executive branch should operate, the White House staff members were considered more staff functionaries, and their ability to command the resources of the cabinet departments was limited. The control of the Eisenhower White House did not extend as far as it would in future administrations, but it nonetheless had significant control over the day-to-day efforts of the departments' liaison offices.

Conclusion

While Eisenhower has been portrayed as isolated and passive, to the degree that he was, it was deliberate and reflected his fundamental approach to leadership:

> In war and in peace I've had no respect for the desk-pounder, and have despised the loud and slick talker. If my own ideas and practices in this matter have sprung from weakness, I do not know. But they were and are deliberate or, rather, natural to me. They are not accidental.[88]

According to Chief of Staff Sherman Adams, "Eisenhower believes that the stature and authority of the President's immediate assistants must be raised so that they can free him of routine government management and give him time to concentrate on the bigger problems of world peace, disarmament, national security and domestic security."[89] Some researchers have suggested that Eisenhower used his congressional relations staff as a buffer between himself and members of Congress.[90] Eisenhower did distance himself from Congress, but not dramatically differently from most recent presidents. Eisenhower certainly sought a degree of insulation from congressional politics.

Perhaps Eisenhower was the first president to respond institutionally to the press of congressional demands upon his time, but the continuation of virtually all of the institutions he created suggests that he is not out of step with his successors. Eisenhower's respect for Congress as an institution (not necessarily for its members) and the principal of separation of powers coupled with the need to protect his image as someone above partisan politics dictated that Eisenhower not become too intimate with congressional politics. The president felt that he was more valuable rising above the political process than diving into it.

Eisenhower's use of delegation or an autopilot approach was also necessitated by the system of institutional pluralism. Eisenhower dealt primarily with congressional leaders because, under the structure of Congress in the 1950s, doing so permitted him to tap into the major sources of power. For Eisenhower to not work through the powerful party leaders of the time would have been a direct challenge to the power structure of Washington.

Given the priorities of the administration and the political realities of their situation, there is little fault to be found in the legislative strategy they employed. The legislative staff accomplished much of what Eisenhower wanted it to accomplish. Eisenhower may be criticized for not wanting to accomplish more, but given his policy goals, the White House staff provided handsomely. The liaison staff, while not as prominent as it would become during later administrations, was probably as influential as practical given the expectations of the time. Eisenhower's congressional relations staff established a White House presence on Capitol Hill and won legislative victories in tough battles of great interest to the president, but did so in a manner that left Eisenhower time to focus on his primary goal of "waging peace."

3

THE KENNEDY
ADMINISTRATION

THE ELECTION OF 1960 GAVE JOHN KENNEDY THE NARROWEST of victories, and according to Arthur Schlesinger, "he could never escape the political arithmetic."[1] The Democrats lost 21 seats in the House and although they still held a 263-174 majority on paper, serious divisions between southern and northern Democrats made coalition-building problematic, especially on civil rights. Along with 174 House Republicans, Kennedy faced 99 southern Democrats who opposed much of his legislative agenda. In the Senate, the Democrats held a more comfortable 64 to 36 margin, with fewer southern Democrats dividing the party's coalition.

Kennedy had spent fourteen years in Congress, eight in the House and six in the Senate, but had never been part of the leadership on the Hill. Many members believed that Kennedy was "in Congress, but not of Congress," and one Republican liaison staffer delighted in recalling a political cartoon that depicted the new president calling Senator Harry Byrd (Democrat-Virginia), with Kennedy explaining to the senator, "This is Jack . . . Jack Kennedy . . . President Kennedy . . . President of the United States."

While Larry O'Brien would eventually become a respected figure in Washington, Kennedy's liaison chief was new to Washington. This, on top of Kennedy's reputation in Congress, could have led to a cautious approach to

Congress. The transforming event of the Kennedy administration's congressional relations was the struggle to expand the House Rules Committee, transforming the White House's congressional relations much as the Bay of Pigs impacted foreign policy. The battle to expand the Rules Committee taught the novice White House the importance of staying on top of every detail of the process, and their success gave them confidence to expand their activities beyond the limited role of the Eisenhower liaison staff. According to O'Brien, "If we had no hesitancy in 1961 to engage in head counts and work with the House Democratic leadership to bring about the increase in membership of the Rules Committee, why in 1965 not express an interest and state a position?"[2]

Kennedy and his staff had to work with a system with which they were relatively unfamiliar and with people they did not know well. While a lack of familiarity with Congress initially proved to be a disadvantage, O'Brien's understanding of elections provided a foundation for later success.

The Kennedy and Johnson administrations transformed the Office of Congressional Relations into an aggressive lobbying unit. One magazine article described the strength of the Kennedy administration's approach to politics as resting on the "four P's: Pressure, Patronage, Prestige and Personal Contact," of which Kennedy's chief lobbyist ranked personal contact the most important "on the proved theory that successful politics is a matter of personal relations."[3] The Kennedy administration worked to build a friendly relationship, in part because its expansive use of White House powers would seem more palatable coming from friends rather than strangers.

The Kennedy Staff

After the 1960 election the core of what would become the senior White House staff sat down to select White House positions. One researcher concluded that "Kennedy's transition team carefully planned the shape, size and purpose of the OCR."[4] In reality, there was little planning as to who would be on the staff and what their responsibilities would be. O'Brien, like many others in the administration, had never been inside the White House, even as a tourist.[5] Years later O'Brien admitted, "After I was designated as the fellow who was going to deal with the Congress I didn't devote one hour to planning it."[6] While Larry O'Brien later enjoyed a reputation as an experienced political operator, when he began his new job in the White House his experience was primarily in campaigning, and he had little working knowledge of Washington D.C. He had worked for two years as an administrative assistant to Congressman Foster Furcolo but left that job as soon as possible to return to election work.[7] O'Brien later reflected on his experience and Kennedy's understanding of the office: "Thank goodness the President-elect at that time and I had no real understanding of the job. If he had or I had, we probably would have concluded that I didn't have the experience to take on a post of that nature."[8]

Kennedy had suggested to Larry O'Brien that the positions of special assistant for legislative affairs and administrative assistant for personnel be combined so that patronage could be more effectively coordinated with legislative needs.[9] O'Brien did not realize what being in charge of personnel administration entailed until one day in February 1961 when he was called upon to decide whether or not the federal offices should be closed on account of a snowstorm. Later, he noted that "there were half a dozen telegrams laying on my desk inviting me to various functions, get-acquainted functions, of federal unions, employee unions. It hit: personnel wasn't what the President and I had envisioned at all. This was the job of maintaining liaison with the various elements of the federal employee establishment, which was of no interest to me whatsoever. I then had Phyllis check with the printing office; it was too late to eliminate 'and personnel' from my title in the Congressional Directory, so it stayed there for a year."[10]

While Eisenhower's chief legislative aid, Bryce Harlow, offered to sit down and brief his successor, O'Brien initially did not find time to meet with him and instead sent his secretary to meet with Harlow. During her visit to the White House, Bryce Harlow discovered that his successor intended to handle congressional relations and appointments with only the assistance of his secretary. Harlow was amazed by O'Brien's lack of understanding for what was involved and decided that "He needs to be talked to." When he finally got O'Brien into his office he explained the amount of work involved:

> Even now, at the end of the administration—this is our last few days here—even now I average a hundred and twenty-five incoming calls a day. Average. And I'm not mentioning mail. I'm not mentioning visits by people coming in. I'm not mentioning trips I have to make to the Hill. I'm not mentioning my trips to see the President or other people in the White House, or meetings. I'm not taking time out to go to the john, have breakfast, have lunch, have dinner. That's just me working on Congress.[11]

When O'Brien finally began to assemble his staff just a week before inauguration, he attempted to find a balance between sound political judgment and experience with Congress. The Eisenhower White House had emphasized experience, but O'Brien worried that while veterans of the Hill would have some useful experience, they would also be carrying baggage from their service. Staff who had served on the Hill would have political friends that might be of use, but having political friends usually means having political enemies and O'Brien wanted staff who could work effectively with all members. In the end, O'Brien selected men like himself and more emphasis was placed on general political savvy than on legislative experience because he considered the experience not particularly useful and he worried that liaison drawn from congressional staff would continue to feel subordinate to their old bosses.[12]

Henry Hall Wilson Jr. was formally assigned to deal with the House of Representatives, but his primary responsibility was dealing with southern House members. Wilson had served in the North Carolina legislature as president of the state's Young Democrats and most recently as a member of the Democratic National Committee. Richard Donahue, a veteran of several of Kennedy's campaigns, was put in charge of Democrats from the east and northeastern cities. Charles Daly had served on Kennedy's Senate staff doing research and writing. Daly dealt with members from western and midwestern states.

O'Brien picked Mike Manatos to cover the Senate. Having worked in Washington since 1937, Manatos was the most experienced member of the Kennedy liaison team. He had learned about the Senate while working for four different senators from Wyoming and had been elected president of the administrative assistants association on the Hill. He had worked with Johnson and Kennedy during their years in the Senate and had met Larry O'Brien during the campaign. While the staff assigned to handle the House expanded during the administration, Manatos preferred to work the Senate on his own and did so throughout the eight years of the Kennedy and Johnson administrations.

Claude Desautels, a twelve-year veteran of the staff of Rep. Wayne Aspinall (Democrat-Colorado) served as O'Brien's assistant, helping with the organization of the staff and other matters internal to the White House. Desautels supervised the handling of congressional mail addressed to the president. He checked incoming mail for problems that the staff could deal with before these letters were handed over to Jean Lewis, who handled the president's correspondence in general. Desautels handled status reports from the departments, legislative briefs for the president, and the preparation of the agenda for Kennedy's meetings with legislative leaders each week. He also helped coordinate congressional invitations to formal and informal meetings, social events in the White House, and bill signing ceremonies.

The staff organization that O'Brien created remained in place throughout the Kennedy and Johnson administrations, and although there have been some changes since in the name of the office and the titles of the positions, this organization became the model for future administrations. The head of the office usually holds a high rank and reports directly to the president or chief of staff, and lobbyists are assigned to particular members based on House or Senate membership. There is also an "internal assistant" who helps with administrative functions and relations within the White House.

The liaison staff's lack of familiarity with Congress, coupled with their aggressive lobbying style, would occasionally generate considerable congressional criticism.[13] One departmental liaison agent noted the lack of experience: "Remember: The legislative-liaison branch at the White House is inexperienced. Some of its members had never dealt with Congress before. . . . Quite a few of the new men had never worked at the congressional level. Senators and Representatives have been shocked by tactics that the White House often knew nothing about."[14] Some in Congress referred to the Kennedy staff, without affection, as "the young men."[15] Reporter Meg Greenfield summed up the reaction of many on Capitol Hill.

> Congressmen don't like being told how to vote by cabinet members. Much less do they enjoy receiving their instructions from emissaries sometimes forty years their junior against whom they have a bad chemical reaction to begin with, and whose bad manners and lack of sensitivity have reached spectacular proportions.[16]

The Kennedy White House continued the practice of integrating departmental lobbying efforts with their own. Each Monday every department and agency would prepare detailed reports of what had transpired between their department and the Congress in the previous week as well as explaining what they expected from the coming weeks. Departments also had to explain any failures to make progress on legislation. These reports were due at noon on Monday and were reviewed and summarized by the White House staff for the president's reading on Monday night. These reports were used by the staff to develop the agenda for the president's Tuesday morning meetings with congressional leaders and by the president to prepare for discussions in the meeting. Departmental liaison officials also regularly met with the White House staff to review the legislative program and coordinate strategy. Most routine contact with congressional staff was left to departmental liaison offices. Because they dealt with related committees frequently, departments had developed relationships with committee staff. In addition, since departmental liaison officers generally get involved much earlier in the process, they are involved in the research and bill drafting that is often left to congressional staff. Since legislation generally does not get the attention of lawmakers or the White House staff until it reaches the floor, departmental staff found themselves doing a great deal of the work with congressional staff.

Lyndon Johnson found himself stuck in limbo somewhere between the status of the president and that of cabinet members or White house staff. Johnson clearly understood that he had to take a back seat to Kennedy and could do nothing to upstage or undermine the president, but the vice presidency did not give Johnson the prestige to lobby Congress on his own behalf. At the same time, Johnson held a prestige beyond the White House staff or cabinet secretaries. While O'Brien felt comfortable telling cabinet secretaries who to lobby, he did not feel comfortable directing the efforts of the vice president.[17] This left Johnson with no one to work with. He did not fit into the Oval Office, the Office of Congressional Relations, the cabinet, or Congress.

Johnson never had the ability to negotiate on behalf of the president and therefore had little impact as a liaison operative. Kennedy clearly signaled that Larry O'Brien was to be his chief emissary to Congress and any role for Johnson might be seen as undermining O'Brien's status on the Hill. Johnson's exclusion was further necessitated by the Senate's refusal to let their recently departed Majority Leader maintain a leadership role in the Senate. Johnson stepped back from his aggressive lobbying style and focused more on providing the administration team with information and insight. While he was invited to the administration's legislative strategy meetings, he did not always attend. He did attend the weekly congressional breakfasts at the White House but rarely spoke. His clout in the Senate deteriorated to the point that when O'Brien asked him to contact senators on a bill Johnson replied, "Larry, I'll talk to them, but Claude Desautels has more muscle with those fellows than I do."[18]

Although the Kennedy liaison staff represents another step in the development of the office, the differences between the Eisenhower and Kennedy staffs have been overstated. O'Brien saw the Eisenhower administration as a model that he built upon.[19] Bryce Harlow noted that O'Brien was operating much as he had: "This was using the same system that Larry O'Brien, he inherited from us, and he duplicated it. Same system precisely."[20] For example, although Harlow and Persons may have seldom visited Capitol Hill when they were in command of the liaison office, the same can be said of Larry O'Brien, who spent more time in his White House office coordinating legislative strategy. While he did visit Capitol Hill on a regular basis, this was usually to see congressional leaders. Before most members would see Larry O'Brien the matter would have to be pretty serious and the efforts of the department's lobbyists and lesser White House staff would have to have failed.[21]

O'BRIEN AND KENNEDY

Larry O'Brien's greatest tool was his closeness to the presidents he served. O'Brien held the complete confidence of Kennedy, and the president was careful not to undermine him. Early on Kennedy made clear to Congress that O'Brien spoke for him: "Senators and Representatives calling Kennedy with political proposal invariably were asked: 'Have you checked that with Larry O'Brien?' They soon got the idea."[22] Not only did Kennedy make sure that members of Congress heard this from him, there were numerous press accounts of O'Brien's frequent meetings with Kennedy. Whether these stories were planted by the administration or not, they made clear that O'Brien was Kennedy's voice on the Hill.[23]

The ability of White House staff to speak for the president, rather than simply serving as presidential messengers, is a significant step, not only in theoretical distinctions but also in the ability of the staff to operate effectively on the Hill. Once liaison officers acquired the ability to negotiate and speak for the president they became an active part of the process, rather than simply another neutral device for communication. The ability to speak for the president elevates the position to a high level, and failure of the president to place this trust in his congressional assistants can render the staff useless. Once members of Congress sense that the liaison staff does not speak for the president, then members will insist on speaking directly to the president themselves. O'Brien carried a broad mandate from Kennedy. According to one story, Kennedy's direction to O'Brien was, "You know what I want, come as close as you can."[24]

While O'Brien's lack of familiarity with Congress and its members led to some early criticism, his understanding and appreciation of elections would become an important component of the success of the administration. As Neil McNeil points out in his account of the Kennedy lobbying effort, O'Brien's offer of electoral assistance was clear and appreciated by the members he met with.

> There O'Brien spelled out for these members the sort of services they could get from the White House, everything from patronage to autographed pictures of President Kennedy. And he told them

bluntly that President Kennedy would not be at all reluctant to help them win re-election in their next campaign. "The White House certainly remembers who its friends are," O'Brien said, "and can be counted on to apply significant assistance in the campaign." No word could be more welcome to Representatives from marginal Congressional districts.[25]

O'Brien and his staff repeatedly spoke about the importance of understanding the constituency concerns of Congress. As O'Brien often said, "We had the cardinal overriding rule: you never, never suggest remotely to a member that he should commit political hara-kiri to support the President."[26] This meant always looking for a way to frame presidential needs in terms that would highlight how they complemented constituent concerns. Over time, the administration learned to frame issues like foreign aid in terms of local politics.

> Ultimately, and it took a long time to get into this, [we would] do an analysis of the expenditures of foreign aid money district by district. People disliked foreign aid but if you could point out to them over in Missouri that X number of dollars flowed into companies and to employees in Missouri of foreign aid money as part of that foreign aid budget, that could be helpful in suggesting to the members' constituents that it wasn't a giveaway program, that they got a piece of the action.[27]

This kind of information not only could be used to persuade a reluctant member, it could also be used by members who wanted to support the president but worried about how the vote would play out in the district. Armed with this kind of information, members could return to their district and explain their vote on foreign aid to citizens or the media in terms of benefits to the district.[28]

The liaison staff also became involved in helping members make short films that they could use in the districts and developing statements for use in printed materials.[29] The White House was thus acting as an extension of members' campaign staffs, providing film clips, putting together material for speeches or campaign brochures, arranging campaign events with the president, vice president, or cabinet members, and providing advice about how best to explain congressional roll call votes. This resembled the kinds of campaign support often provided by the national parties.

While the administration did not assist nonsupportive members, this was in part due to the fact that members who had not been supportive did not ask for assistance from the administration, either because they felt it would be counterproductive or because they did not want to ask. The attitude of the administration was to not oppose a Democratic incumbent, and it generally stayed out of primaries because dislodging an incumbent during a primary was impossible and involvement would only generate animosity.[30]

Expanding the Rules Committee

The Rules Committee, under the control of a conservative chairman, Judge Howard Smith, had been a formidable barrier to progressive legislation for years.[31] Because every bill that came to the floor required a rule drafted by the committee, the Rules Committee was able to block legislation on every topic. Not only was its chair considered likely to oppose much of the New Frontier, a majority of its members were expected to be hostile as well. The expansion of the Rules Committee would permit Speaker Rayburn to create a majority on the committee that would be more hospitable to the Kennedy legislative agenda by appointing progressive members to offset entrenched conservatives on the committee.

President Kennedy had established weekly Tuesday morning breakfast meetings with the congressional Democratic leadership, and during the first leadership meeting, held four days after the inauguration, Speaker Sam Rayburn warned Kennedy that there might not be enough votes to expand the Rules Committee. Rayburn noted that the vote was scheduled for the next day and that the prospects of passage did not look good. During the meeting Kennedy failed to fully recognize that unless the committee was changed then it would become a major barrier to getting most of his legislation onto the floor of the House. Years later, O'Brien himself could barely believe their oversight.

Well, it's probably difficult to understand—I guess it's difficult for me in reflection—that a president-elect and a new administration would engage in all the activities inherent in moving to president— inauguration day, cabinet appointments, establishing [or] possibly contemplating relationships in the whole foreign policy area, to have a concept of a New Frontier program, that basically would be advocacy of the elements of a party platform—and not focus completely on day one, recognizing that the Rules Committee tradition-

ally had been the bottleneck for all liberal proposals, had successfully for years blocked every movement of a liberal nature, had to be
altered in some way somehow or you were not going to be in business. And [you] get with your designated congressional relations assistant to the first leadership breakfast, now that you are president,
and for the first time recognize that this change in the Rules Committee, which you are aware of, is not going to succeed. You are sitting there with a whole New Frontier program that's just gone down
the drain and you can sit and twiddle your thumbs for at least two
years.[32]

Kennedy and O'Brien had taken for granted that the Rules Committee
would be taken care of, but suddenly realized that without their intervention
much of the president's legislative agenda would be precluded before it
could be proposed. After the meeting had broken up they had to call
Speaker Rayburn back to the White House to request that he delay the vote
for a week.[33] During this week the White House scrambled to take head
counts of members and build a winning coalition. While the vote to change
the Rules Committee sounded like a procedural matter, the administration's
opponents throughout the country realized its significance and responded.
Those southern Democrats willing to support Kennedy's civil rights agenda
were quickly brought under a great deal of pressure in their districts. Congressman Overton Brooks of Louisiana was attacked by local papers and had
a cross burned in his yard.[34] Eventually the administration prevailed by five
votes, gaining the support of twenty-two Republicans and thirty-four southern Democrats.

The battle to create a Rules Committee that was friendly to the administration demonstrated the weakness of their strategic position and the determination of their opposition. Losing the Rules Committee vote could have
been a legislative "Bay of Pigs" for the new administration.[35] Further, this
near-death experience for the New Frontier led the Kennedy White House
to reevaluate its approach. The Kennedy administration entered the White
House distrustful of the rigid organization of the Eisenhower White House,
but after their experience with the expansion of the Rules Committee, Larry
O'Brien became a great believer in organization.

It was a lesson, and that lesson brought me to the realization that I'd
better move as quickly and as vigorously as possible to put together
an organized congressional relations entity in the executive branch

of government. And so we proceeded posthaste. And that, as it un-
folded, took the form of weekly, written, detailed reports that had to
be submitted by noontime every Monday from every department
and agency, reviewing what had transpired between their department or agency and the Congress the prior week, projecting what
they anticipated the next week and beyond, and explaining to the
best of their ability any failure of movement, and [they were] to be
as specific and detailed as possible.[36]

Winning the Rules Committee fight emboldened the White House.
Kennedy's chief House lobbyist, Henry Hall Wilson, reported to O'Brien that
he had been heavily involved in committee appointments during the
Kennedy administration and that "word was all over the Hill that appointments had to clear with us, and I was totally involved."[37] By January 1962,
when Representative John Riley of South Carolina died, the White House
would feel comfortable both lobbying to place an administration supporter
in his vacancy on the Appropriations Committee and actively looking for
someone to run for his seat. According to O'Brien, "I don't think by that
time we had any hesitancy in becoming involved in matters of this nature,
and we certainly didn't feel that we should be inhibited in any political activity we might engage in."[38] This represents a far more aggressive approach
to Congress than Eisenhower's.

Kennedy and Congress

According to James Giglio, Kennedy possessed wit and charm but was
unable to form a deeper bond with members of Congress. Giglio concludes,
"Congressmen liked Kennedy, but they did not feel close—or personally ob-
ligated—to him."[39] Kennedy's education and wealth contributed to the personal barriers between him and Congress. One congressman told David
Brinkley, "All that Mozart string music and ballet dancing down there and all
that fox hunting and London clothes. He's too elegant for me. I can't talk to
him."[40] Larry O'Brien noted that Kennedy was not completely comfortable
with legislators and that it limited the president's effectiveness in meetings.

Jack Kennedy could not bring himself to strong-arm, members of
Congress to secure their vote. He'd make his presentation and he
was relaxed in that regard. He knew his subject, they liked him, and
he had a great asset there. But you would finish one of these sessions

with twenty or thirty members of Congress, and everything was fine except that you couldn't take a head count when they departed. There was one line you didn't cross and that was to say, "Now, let's go around this room, and where are we, and where are you?"[41]

The president's personal contact with members of Congress came in a wide variety of forms. In 1961, for example, he presided over thirty-two leadership breakfasts and ninety group meetings in which he met with select groups of members. Kennedy's meetings with congressional leaders were important because he had not been part of the congressional leadership and was not generally well known by the members. Arthur Schlesinger conceded that Kennedy, despite his service in Congress, was not "one of the cloakroom boys" and "had always been something of an alien on the Hill."[42] In one meeting with O'Brien, Speaker Rayburn admitted that he had little recollection of Kennedy's service in the House.[43]

While the Kennedy administration encountered a divided Democratic party in Congress, he initially benefited from a strong and friendly Democratic leadership. Because Kennedy's legislative staff was relatively inexperienced, the role of educating the president on dealings with Congress fell to congressional leaders.[44] Rayburn began guiding the president with the Rules Committee struggle. The quality of Democratic leadership, however, was depleted by Kennedy's selection of Johnson as vice president and compounded by Sam Rayburn's death in 1961. According to one liaison staff person, "The leadership team of Lyndon Johnson and Sam Rayburn were sorely missed."[45]

Mike Mansfield became Senate Majority Leader after Johnson's departure and reached out to the new administration, offering O'Brien and Manatos a room in his office suite to work out of and hold meetings. The White House's relationship with Majority Leader Mansfield was so close that he shared copies of notes from meetings held in his office with the White House staff. Mansfield would call senators in from the floor to meet with O'Brien and Mansfield, or he would host lunches with key senators and essentially turn the meeting over to O'Brien or Manatos. Hubert Humphrey became the Majority Whip, giving the administration another close ally in the leadership.

Sam Rayburn, while in declining health, still held sway in the House, particularly with southern Democrats. The White House worked to establish a friendly relationship with Rayburn, and the Speaker in return always found time to talk with the administration staff. When Speaker Rayburn died, he was replaced by John McCormack, who lacked Rayburn's impressive experience and clout. Although Kennedy and O'Brien had frequently been at odds with McCormack in the past, the most serious conflict being when they challenged McCormack for control of the Massachusetts Democratic Committee in 1956, McCormack became a trusted ally of the administration.[46] This alliance was tested again in 1962 when McCormack's nephew ran against Teddy Kennedy in the Massachusetts Senate primary.

Occasionally, Republican leaders were brought into the process. Everett Dirksen was dealt with regularly. In the House, Charlie Halleck and Jerry Ford would work with the administration from time to time and William Mc-Culloch, the senior Republican on the Judiciary Committee, assisted the administration on civil rights issues. When support was needed for the legislation that eventually would become the Civil Rights Act of 1964, Kennedy turned to Charlie Halleck "in desperation" and was happily surprised when he eventually helped provide enough Republican support to get it out of the House Judiciary Committee.[47]

Kennedy was reluctant to appeal to the public for support for his agenda because he felt that it creates more resistance within Congress than support among the public. According to one presidential aide, "You can go to the well just so often. The President cannot take every important case to the country. . . . The President did make some speeches and plug for his problems in press conferences. But he felt he could not keep asking the people for support on every item on his legislative program."[48] Kennedy spoke on behalf of his Medicare bill at a large outdoor rally. The speech was carried to thirty-two other rallies and into millions of homes on television. The *New York Times,* which had been editorializing for Medicare, attacked Kennedy's speech, calling it "hippodrome tactics."[49] According to Larry O'Brien, future rallies were canceled because they would have produced more resistance than support.

> The rally made little or no impact but antagonized Wilbur Mills. Subsequent rallies were dropped. The fact of the matter is that you were not going to sway Wilbur Mills, a congressman from Arkansas in a locked-in congressional district, by publicly attacking him.[50]

Kennedy was thus constrained by the system of institutionalized pluralism that continued to dominate Washington. Kennedy needed the support of the powerful committee chairs, which were in the hands of senior southern Democrats who could not be undermined electorally by any number of public appeals from the Oval Office. Kennedy had little choice but to deal directly with the powers in Washington because their secure electoral bases in the solidly Democratic south made them the least vulnerable members at election time.

"The Friendly Lobbies"

Larry O'Brien began to transform the small operation created by Persons and Harlow into what Rowland Evans and Robert Novak would later call "a service agency devoted to the care and feeding of Congressmen—arranging White House tours for constituents, helping to handle constituent problems with governmental agencies, and providing Congressmen with autographed photos of the President."[51] Kennedy and his liaison staff became heavily involved in the activities of what *Time* magazine dubbed "The Friendly Lobbies."[52] While Eisenhower's dealings with Congress had been amicable but businesslike, Kennedy was committed to laying a foundation for an even friendlier relationship so that lawmakers would feel comfortable bringing their concerns to someone on the White House staff and so that members would not be surprised when the staff made contact with them.[53] Eisenhower had met socially with Speaker Rayburn and Majority Leader Lyndon Johnson, but these meetings had been kept secret. Beginning with the Kennedy administration, social contact between lawmakers and the president and White House staff would become the norm. Because the Kennedy administration became much more involved in the day-to-day activities of Congress, their interaction with legislators naturally increased. In addition, as White House staff lost their anonymity and became prominent players in Washington politics, it became more appropriate for them to mix socially with members of Congress.

One of the reasons that the White House lobbyists had to be friendly was that their role was still new. The congressional liaison office had been in place for the entire Eisenhower administration, but the Eisenhower administration had been very cautious in its approach and Congress remained resistant to any intrusion into their domain. The Kennedy administration needed a pool of goodwill because it was suddenly working more intimately with Congress than it had in the past. Building support for the extensive New Frontier agenda required more interaction with Capitol Hill than Eisenhower's more limited agenda. O'Brien, while continuing to work closely with Congress, understood the source of members' sensitivity.

It was unheard of, I'm sure unprecedented, to have a joint head count, [between the White House staff and the congressional leadership], House and Senate—to sit down, actually in a room on the Hill, compare notes on the members of the House and the members of the Senate, with the leadership of the House and Senate, the Democratic leadership, and work out a joint head count. Now you're getting perilously close to violating the separation of powers, and there was a little flak on the House side in that regard.[54]

The friendly approach was not a Kennedy innovation. Eisenhower also understood that members respond favorably to requests from people that they like. "If you're going to do anything, you've got to make Congressmen your personal friends; that's really what I tried to do."[55] The Kennedy White House attempted to expand and institutionalize this approach.

Kennedy understood that good personal relationships can serve good political relationships.[56] He set out to make friends on Capitol Hill using a wide variety of resources. Kennedy frequently had groups of ten to twelve senators to the residence at the White House for informal meetings. While socializing was part of these meetings, the president would often state his views on a pending issue. During the Eisenhower administration only members of the Senate Foreign Relations and House Foreign Affairs Committees were invited to state dinners, but under Kennedy, invitations became another tool for rewarding friends of the administration. The liaison staff would attend in order to get another chance to talk with members.[57]

Every member of Congress was invited at one time or another to informal White House coffees with the president. Key congressional supporters were invited to the numerous bill-signing ceremonies that were held. In addition, administration supporters received letters of thanks after key votes, and every member received a personal letter from the president on their birthday.[58] O'Brien and the liaison staff used similar techniques to meet with members. "We were trying in every conceivable way to get to know these people."[59]

The presidential yacht *Sequoia* became a prime tool for building relationships between the staff and members of Congress. As often as two or three times a week O'Brien and his staff would invite thirty members along with their wives for a three-hour trip down the Potomac to Mount Vernon. The trip featured a buffet dinner and occasionally an accordion player and a sing-along. These trips gave members of Congress and the White House staff time to mingle and become better acquainted. The time was generally passed in social conversation with some friendly conversation about legislation that would be coming before Congress; hard sells were avoided. Still, O'Brien usually had two or three "targets" on each trip and he found that he could often secure agreements that he could not get in an office.[60] Some of these trips were organized to coincide with particular legislative issues but most were designed to build general goodwill. These trips were very popular among members of Congress and invitations were seldom declined. O'Brien regarded the *Sequoia* as "the most effective lobbying device I ever found" and claimed, "There was nothing approaching it."[61] O'Brien and his wife also brought together members of Congress, cabinet members, and journalists at Sunday brunches at the O'Briens' home in Georgetown.

Even when converting members seemed unlikely, the White House hoped that friendly gestures would take some of the steam out of their attacks. Senator Harry Byrd remained a problem to the administration, but Larry O'Brien made annual trips to the apple festival in West Virginia out of the hope that it might someday soften Byrd's opposition. In 1961 Kennedy made a "surprise" visit to a luncheon the senator was hosting at his country estate, much to Byrd's delight. However, one senator later commented, "Don't jump to conclusions. Harry Byrd still opposes us. We'll never get his vote. But he's not sitting up nights figuring out how to be mean."[62]

Early in the administration the congressional liaison staff discovered the importance of grant notification when a senior Democrat found that a Republican from his state had received notification of an eight-million-dollar military contract before him. After being told to go to hell (literally) the staff launched an investigation and discovered that the military was still notifying Republicans as it had under Eisenhower. The Kennedy administration developed a system by which departmental announcements of contracts and grants were first given to the congressional liaison staff, who notified "friendly" members twenty-four hours in advance of the departmental announcements so the member's office could prepare press releases for local media. This process was refined until it became automatic.[63]

Occasionally the liaison staff grew weary of providing favors to members who were troublesome to the administration. After Representative D. S. Saund (Democrat-California) retaliated against the administration's closing of a Veterans Administration hospital in his district by introducing a needless amendment to a Kennedy foreign aid bill, the White House staff found a small way to exact its revenge. Saund had sent a picture of his grandson with the president to have it signed by Kennedy. The staff hid the photo and pretended that it was lost, sending Saund into a frenzy. Eventually the staff retrieved the photo and had it signed but enjoyed the process of tormenting their tormentor.[64] Such incidents were very rare, but probably provided the staff with a much-needed outlet for frustration.

Kennedy needed the "friendly lobbies" to facilitate bargaining under institutionalized pluralism and because White House intrusion into congressional business was more likely to be tolerated coming from a friendly and familiar White House. The social gatherings of the White House staff and members of Congress helped them become more acquainted, and during these meetings the administration could conduct some business without appearing too involved in congressional matters or violating legislators' views of the separation of powers.

ARM TWISTING

While O'Brien admitted in later interviews that arms were twisted,[65] he argued that it occurred within the framework of a friendly relationship and insisted that the administration never pushed to the point of hurting members back in their district. Still, O'Brien insists that the administration twisted arms because it was essential.

> There was an acceptance of vigorous arm-twisting, I guess, in general. But to suggest that we ever let go, no. We couldn't let go. [Congressman] Otis [Passman] could ultimately say no, but he'd have to say no a dozen times perhaps before we'd accepted it finally as no because we couldn't afford the luxury of doing otherwise.[66]

While the administration could be quite aggressive, the president himself was personally uncomfortable applying pressure to members. Arthur Schlesinger believed that Kennedy "spent more of his time than people realized working with Congress. But it cannot be said that this was the part of the Presidency which gave him the greatest pleasure or satisfaction."[67] Because Kennedy had not been part of the leadership of Congress and had not been a part of the backroom dealing in Congress, he was never comfortable aggressively lobbying members of Congress, particularly the leaders under whom he had served. According to O'Brien, Kennedy could not bring himself to press members of Congress to secure their vote: "Kennedy rarely asked a member for his vote on a specific piece of legislation. That was not his style. If there were arms to be twisted, that was our job."[68] Kennedy's avoidance of personal appeals reflects a matter of personal style and a cautious approach to the use of presidential powers with Congress. Kennedy would engage in a vigorous exchange of ideas in his meetings with members but he was always reluctant to press for commitments or to force members into line.[69] This contrasts sharply with Johnson, who would seek a commitment from every member present. Kennedy may also have doubted his ability to get votes with his appeal and felt that members' rejection of a direct personal appeal from the president would diminish the office.

PATRONAGE

Unable to systematically use public opinion to his advantage, Kennedy was forced to work through his party. One of the few resources available to the White House was the dispensing of jobs in the federal government. While Kennedy's use of public opinion could do little to shape the next election of members who were comfortably established in party machines, the White House could use patronage to help maintain parties at the local level. O'Brien was compared to Jim Farley, who moved from winning elections to pushing legislation for Franklin Roosevelt. While Farley never became a full-time lobbyist for the president, he served as postmaster and dispensed patronage with an eye toward winning votes in Congress. Both Farley and O'Brien were credited with being able to be aggressively partisan while still remaining friends with their opponents.

While the use of political patronage has often been a consideration, its impact is much smaller and its use more problematic than legend would suggest. The administration faced widespread complaints about the lack of patronage and the way O'Brien handled it.[70] Bryce Harlow had warned O'Brien to divorce the congressional relations operation from patronage because the two functions clashed. Harlow believed that, "With patronage, you have to turn down ten men for every one you say yes to. You make people unhappy instead of happy."[71] O'Brien later commented, "How in God's name do you ever name a postmaster in Yanktown, Ohio, without creating a bunch of enemies?"[72]

The cost of failing to reward members of Congress is high but the benefits are usually small. Patronage seems to present more problems to be avoided than any real advantage in winning votes, and the process becomes concerned with avoiding major problems rather than gaining significant advantages. After serving in the White House, Larry O'Brien believed that the impact of patronage was overstated: "They talked about patronage, you know, as though you could control the Congress through some patronage device. And it was just not realistic; it never has been and never will be."[73] O'Brien later concluded: "To summarize, any president would prefer that there is no such thing as patronage. It's an overall pain in the neck; it may have an occasional plus factor but there's a lot of negative in it. You have to remember the old saying in politics: every time you make an appointment, you've made one ingrate and created at least ten enemies."[74]

Members do not always expect to have their nominee selected and often are acting out of obligation. However, even in those cases in which the member really doesn't care whether their candidate gets the position, they do need to have their recommendation taken seriously. Often all that members need is a letter of explanation for a decision so that they can send a copy of this letter to the constituent showing that they had made a plea for them. At the same time, anything that appears to be less than careful consideration of a member's wishes can create problems in their district. One of Kennedy's legislative aides described the damage that could be done back in a member's district:

> It's a hell of a damaging blow to a Congressman to have to confess to a constituent with a pet project or a bothersome brother-in-law wanting a job that he hasn't enough influence even to get 1600 Pennsylvania Avenue to place it under advisement. But if he can honestly report it's "under active consideration," it may ease him off the hook.[75]

While patronage is usually a partisan matter, there are appointments of value to the minority, and early on the Kennedy administration discovered Senator Everett Dirksen's (Republican-Illinois) interest in them. Dirksen wanted to place people on regulatory agencies and commissions that, by law, must include members of both parties. Being able to select the Republican members of these commissions helped insure that Dirksen could call up any regulatory commission and have his concerns dealt with.[76]

The Kennedy administration discovered that patronage plays a larger role in those issues in which a member has no compelling interest one way or the other. One example of this was when the administration was pushing for a one-year extension of an emergency feed grain program. Eastern Democrats found little constituent interest in that bill, and the administration turned to them to support the president out of loyalty. While loyalty to Kennedy was sufficient for many members, others saw this as an opportunity to ask for patronage. O'Brien noted later that, "Lord knows, there might have been a few people tucked into positions somewhere as a result of those votes. Or maybe we reopened some old files that we'd put on hold."[77]

After O'Brien untangled himself from the demands of patronage, he handed over day-to-day responsibility for overseeing patronage to Richard Donahue. Donahue worked out of O'Brien's legislative affairs office and became proficient at interpreting letters of recommendation from members of Congress, sorting out routine letters that showed little real interest in getting the candidate the job from more heartfelt recommendations that could lead to fallout if not followed up.

The Democratic National Committee and Chairman John Bailey publicly took much of the heat for the distribution of jobs but they, in fact, played little role. Such decisions came from the White House with the DNC providing some political cover for the White House's tough choices.[78] This effort really provided the White House much protection, since by September 1961 *Time* magazine declared that, "All Congressmen now know that, although John Bailey is the nominal dangler of political plums, O'Brien is really the man to see when they have a patronage problem."[79]

Practitioners no doubt disclaim the use of patronage in gaining legislative votes, and its use may be significantly overestimated. Still, it seems that patronage is not the kind of tool that political mythology would suggest. This is not to say that patronage is not an issue that the White House has to deal with on a daily basis, only that it produces relatively few advantages for the president.

Interest Groups

The Kennedy administration occasionally used the assistance of lobbyists from interest groups. Lobbyists from the AFL-CIO or other groups would be brought in to assist with headcounts and as supplemental lobbyists. In fact, Andy Biemiller of the AFL-CIO helped the Kennedy White House assemble its first headcount on the expansion of the Rules Committee.[80]

The administration's effort to gain passage of the Trade Expansion Act of 1962 represents the extent the White House was willing to involve interest groups in passing legislation. The White House realized that there was a great deal of potential support from key business leaders throughout the country, but because this issue cut across traditional party lines mobilization would not occur if the administration relied on existing political organizations. Working directly or through the Chamber of Commerce and organized labor, the task force built a strong media consensus behind the bill. In August 1961 the administration brought in Howard C. Peterson, a Philadelphia banker and an expert on international economics, as a special assistant to the president for trade policy and put him in charge of a ten-person task force on the bill. Included in his staff was Tom Finney, who had served in

Senator Mike Monroney's (Democrat-Oklahoma) office. The task force was created, in part, to avoid the rivalries among the State, Commerce, Agriculture, Labor, and other departments who shared some jurisdiction in the area of trade. Finney's job was to work with O'Brien as a special assistant. Finney's office was used to coordinate congressional requests for information and to provide public education. This led to the creation of a "citizens group" that brought together many diverse business and political interests. While this group did have the support of the administration, they were semi-autonomous. The administration used its influence to bring these groups together, but their day-to-day activities were out of O'Brien's control. Peterson used this group to lobby the Senate until Majority Leader Mansfield became resentful and sent word, through O'Brien, that their presence on the Hill could be counterproductive.[81]

Conclusion

Researchers have suggested that the Kennedy administration succeeded in transforming the Office of Congressional Relations from buffer device into an important tool of presidential leadership.[82] However, much of what O'Brien did was an extension of the practices established by Eisenhower, and congressional complaints about the Kennedy administration's aggressive style and "arm-twisting" suggest that Eisenhower's concern about respecting Congress was well founded. Congress jealously guarded its independence and White House intrusions into congressional turf would only create setbacks if not pursued cautiously.

While Larry O'Brien's lack of experience in Washington limited his success in the legislative process, he shared congressional interest in elections. O'Brien didn't need a detailed understanding of the legislative process or a long list of congressional friendships to tell him that members of Congress were thinking about their next election as they cast their votes. Unfortunately for the administration, the White House had very few resources that could be used to shape future elections and O'Brien's political trading skills had to await a president with a stronger electoral potential.

Despite the aggressive use of personal lobbying and patronage, Congress proved resistant to Kennedy's legislative agendas. By the time of Kennedy's assassination his legislative program had ground to a halt. Bryce Harlow described it as "The worst I have ever seen in Washington, in all of my years." Harlow, however, did not blame Kennedy's liaison staff and instead explained that southern Democrats and Republicans opposed to Kennedy's civil rights efforts created the resistance.[83] Kennedy's victory in the 1960 elec-

tion had provided only the shakiest foundation for leadership. *Time* magazine asserted, "Kennedy won his way to the White House by such a perilous
plurality (118,000 votes out of a national total of 68 million) that he could in
no sense be considered to have a mandate that might compel Congressmen
to go along with him."[84] Kennedy was aware of how little his electoral clout
influenced his congressional opponents, especially the southern Democrats
who were giving him the most trouble. Kennedy was also limited because he
lacked the intimacy with the legislative process and the legislators themselves
that Johnson would utilize. As Richard Reeves and others have pointed out,
Kennedy lacked Lyndon Johnson's strong commitment to domestic policy.[85]
With little to be gained by attempting to force change on his slim margin,
Kennedy turned his energies toward foreign policy, much as Eisenhower
had.

4

THE JOHNSON
ADMINISTRATION

LYNDON JOHNSON INHERITED MANY ADVANTAGES AS HE entered the White House. He inherited a Congress controlled by his party and, after the 1964 election, he saw Democratic control grow. He inherited the political legacy of John Kennedy and the wave of sympathy following his death. Along with Kennedy's political legacy, Johnson inherited an experienced congressional relations staff. While much of the Kennedy White House staff would leave, Larry O'Brien and his congressional relations operation stayed on. This brought together the unusual combination of an experienced legislative team and a fresh political mandate without the lame-duck status of beginning a second full term. Paul Light has described a cycle of decreasing influence that is somewhat offset by a cycle of increasing effectiveness.[1] In the case of Johnson, the surge of influence shortly after his election was complemented by an effective and experienced White House staff and produced impressive legislative victories.

After the election of 1964 expanded the Democratic majority, Johnson found that even with the geographic divisions within the party, he still had a solid foundation for a winning coalition on most of the issues that he wanted to push. Johnson realized that the election had created a liberal as well as a Democratic majority in Congress, but he understood that this liberal majority would likely not last.[2] When the 89th Congress convened in January 1965,

Democrats held a 68 to 32 advantage in the Senate and a 295 to 140 majority in the House. As legislation began moving through Congress at an incredible pace, Majority Leader Carl Albert suggested, "The explanation lies in the last election."[3] Others have given more credit to Johnson himself. Charles Halleck, who served as House Minority Leader through 1964, until being replaced by Gerald Ford, attributed the passage of these programs to the abilities of Johnson: "I don't think they'd have gone anywhere but for Lyndon Johnson's big push as President."[4] The truth lies somewhere in between. The Democratic Congress provided Johnson with a solid foundation for legislative success, but he knew that he needed to build upon the advantages provided by the 1964 election and he placed the full weight of his office behind his legislative agenda.

The Johnson Staff

By the time Larry O'Brien came to serve Johnson, he was an experienced and trusted political operator. While Johnson was anxious to transform the White House into his own operation, he realized that O'Brien's skills and his strong connections to Kennedy's supporters in the party made him an irreplaceable resource. Johnson began his effort to keep O'Brien before *Air Force One* left Dallas after the assassination by bringing O'Brien into the stateroom on the plane and telling him, "I want to urge you to stay and stand shoulder to shoulder with me. I need you more than you need me—and more than Jack Kennedy needed you."[5]

Johnson put his complete confidence in O'Brien, who would enjoy a privileged position in the Johnson White House. O'Brien enjoyed unlimited access to the president, and he had the ability to direct White House and cabinet resources. He became the first congressional liaison chief elevated to cabinet-level status. In one interview O'Brien described the priority that legislative affairs took.

> In the White House, there isn't a member of the staff that isn't available immediately—regardless of what the individual may be doing, including presidential assignment—if, in our determination, his services are needed in congressional relations. He drops what he is doing and immediately takes on the task assigned to him in congressional relations.[6]

The president told the cabinet that no one in a department could ever be more important than the head of the White House Office of Congressional Relations.[7] Johnson demonstrated his commitment to congressional relations and his respect for Kennedy's people by making O'Brien the high-est-paid member of the White House staff, paying him $29,500 a year, $2,000 more than anyone else.[8]

The personnel and workings of the congressional relations staff changed very little with the new president.[9] Henry Hall Wilson and Mike Manatos continued in their roles in charge of liaison with the House and Senate respectively. Harold Barefoot Sanders came to the White House from the liaison operation in the Justice Department in May 1967 to take over work on the House for Henry Hall Wilson, who became president of the Chicago Board of Trade.

Under Johnson the organization was slightly less hierarchical and the president was much more directly available to everyone on the liaison staff. While Kennedy had always been available to talk with the staff, Johnson was available to individuals beyond O'Brien day and night, regardless of the reason.[10] Staff contact with the president was frequent and Johnson tended to call liaison staff more often than they called him.[11] These calls usually involved Johnson inquiring about the status of a bill, how the headcounts looked and who was being talked to. One member of the staff claimed that "President Johnson wasn't just accessible to his liaison staff; if he didn't hear from his liaison people daily when Congress was in session, he wanted to know why."[12] The staff was permitted to "red tag" memos on legislation that indicated that the president should read the memo immediately. Johnson had "hot lines" that connected him directly to several members of the White House staff. Once Johnson called Joe Califano who failed to answer because he was in the private bathroom next to his office. Later, when Califano had to explain to Johnson why he failed to answer the phone, Johnson replied "We'll have no more of that." Soon thereafter a phone was placed in Califano's bathroom.[13]

O'Brien had agreed to stay on after the 1964 election only with assurances that he would be able to leave the White House in a few years. O'Brien was weary from the long days of work and was determined to leave the White House. In 1965 Johnson appointed O'Brien postmaster general in a desperate bid to keep him within easy reach of the Oval Office. Johnson's reluctance to give up O'Brien became clear when at the press conference announcing his nomination to postmaster general Johnson was asked who would replace O'Brien in the White House and the president replied, "O'Brien."[14] O'Brien remained involved in legislative strategy and key meetings with members of Congress while Sanders and Wilson stepped into many routine duties such as preparing agendas for legislative leadership meetings and writing briefing memos on the status of legislation. Johnson did not let anyone move into O'Brien's office in the West Wing and O'Brien would come in for an hour or so every couple of days, but as time passed he became increasingly interested and involved in running the postal service. Barefoot Sanders became acting head of congressional liaison but Johnson still refused to officially replace O'Brien until O'Brien left the administration to run Bobby Kennedy's campaign.[15]

Many on the Hill saw Johnson's refusal to replace O'Brien as a lack of confidence in the staff that remained. While Sanders and Wilson were competent, O'Brien's reputation on the Hill and his strong position in the White House were difficult to replace, especially without a clear endorsement from the president. No one else in the White House could speak authoritatively for the president in Capitol Hill meetings. In addition, without a powerful head of congressional relations, it was difficult to keep the White House's efforts focused on legislative goals. O'Brien had clearly been in a position to command cabinet officials and the most senior White House staff, but Sanders and Wilson were never able to do so. Ultimately, Sanders lost control over the departmental liaison offices and found that the Treasury Department had undermined his efforts on behalf of the president's Income Tax Surcharge bill.[16]

Sanders even had trouble keeping the White House liaison staff in line. In July 1967 Sanders complained to Johnson that he was not able to keep track of some supporters because the liaison staffer assigned to them was not staying in touch with members of Congress. Sanders complained to the president, "Since Chuck [Roche] does not believe in Daily Reports, as you know, we now have no systematic way of finding that out."[17] In confidential interviews with a senior member of the Johnson staff, Nigel Bowles heard complaints that Roche was spending too much time drinking with a few members of Congress and was generally "worse than useless."[18]

The decline in the quality of the OCR paralleled the decline of the Johnson legislative program. However, given the general decline in influence that all presidents seem to experience, on top of Johnson's growing trouble with the war in Vietnam, it seems unlikely that Johnson could have maintained his early level of success.

Although the active participation of a president in the legislative process might seem to reduce the role of White House lobbyists, Johnson managed to play an increased role in legislative politics without diminishing the role of his staff. Johnson prevented this by placing a high degree of responsibility in the hands of his liaison operatives. According to a member of his staff:

Johnson expected everyone around him to work just as hard as he did (although that was rarely the case—almost no one worked as hard as he did). It disturbed him when his staff was not on top of every detail of government, particularly of legislation, and he arranged for all of us to have radios in our offices so we could catch the hourly news broadcasts to hear what the wire services were saying about us.[19]

Lyndon Johnson and Congress: The Johnson "Treatment"

The biggest change from the Kennedy legislative liaison operation was the activation of Lyndon Johnson. While Kennedy could not be called passive, Johnson's round-the-clock involvement in congressional relations made JFK look passive by comparison. O'Brien commented, "You want presidential support for your efforts? Boy, you had it coming out of your ears."[20] While other presidents may have been interested in legislation or policy, Johnson was obsessed with the legislative process.[21] His liaison staff brought news into Johnson as he awoke in the morning and consulted with him as he went to bed. O'Brien reflected, "It was almost like he didn't want to have any sleep because he'd miss something."[22] Perhaps the best example of Johnson's interest in following the legislative process is an account of losing a battle on Capitol Hill:

> I had been up all night, and we had lost a battle in the House. But anyway we lost in the early hours of the morning in a very tough struggle, and Charlie Halleck [the Republican leader in the House] had prevailed. And you're depressed and you leave the Hill, it's four or four-thirty in the morning, and you're heading home and then you decide not to go to bed at all. But you owe it to the President to advise him of the negative as well as the positive, and so you wait dutifully till six-thirty, a quarter of seven, whatever it was, and you call the President and advise him. Then President Johnson said, "When did this happen?" I said, "It was the early hours of the morning." And he said, "Why didn't you call me? You should have called me and told me about it." Then I'll never forget, he said, "You know, when you're up there bleeding, I want to bleed with you. We have to share these things." I never got over that.[23]

Johnson had much more day-to-day contact with lawmakers than Kennedy had. Kennedy, like most other presidents, had always been willing to make calls to members, but only at the urging of the liaison staff. Kennedy, like Eisenhower, had also been more interested in foreign policy. In contrast,

Johnson saw governing as occurring mostly through the legislative process and sought out ways to help the process along. After years of working one-on-one with members and being intimately involved in the details of policy and the process, Johnson was not shy about diving into the process. Johnson loved using the phone to call up members. According to John Connally, "Television was never to be Lyndon Johnson's medium. The telephone was."[24] While this could have become a problem, with Johnson making deals on the side, he always briefed his liaison staff on each call.[25] A call from Johnson could come at any time, with Johnson asking, "What are you doing?" Congressman Wayne Hays, when woken once in the middle of the night, replied, "Well, Mr. President, I've been lying here hoping you would call."[26]

Other presidents used their legislative liaison staff to keep themselves from having to spend too much time with members of Congress. With Johnson the task became protecting legislators from overexposure to the president. At times, the staff had to argue with Johnson to keep him from making calls.[27] One night Senator Richard Russell, a longtime friend of the president, warned a staff member that Johnson was spending too much time with members. "Since the late President died, Ev Dirksen, Mike Mansfield and I haven't bought a bag of groceries since last November. We're here every week! He's overdoing it!"[28]

The congressional liaison staff saw the risks of the overuse of the president. One problem was that such individual attention could become too demanding even for Johnson. Henry Hall Wilson warned O'Brien, "We just can't forget that there are 324 Democratic members of the Congress and the President can't personally wet nurse them all daily." The staff also noted that attention to some members and not others was often counterproductive. Wilson told O'Brien, "Five out of six Democrats will vote right on everything anyway. He won't change the sixth one, and it's wheel spinning to see the first five. And the first five will be outraged if he sees only the wrong one."[29] While Kennedy may have been reluctant to pressure members of Congress, since he had never been an inside player there, Johnson knew Congress and its members better than anyone and had no reluctance to push them for support. Perhaps Johnson never fully realized that he was no longer a member of Congress and therefore never saw the need to honor the principal of separation of powers. One member described Johnson's intense approach to lawmakers that came to be known as "the treatment."

> "I'm pleading with you. You've got to help me. You can't walk away from this. Come on, you've just—" And that would get to the arm

around the shoulder, the close proximity and the pitch could be lengthy at times. A member would be pretty exhausted.[30]

Johnson drew on a broad range of emotions. For example, as urban unrest in Washington grew, Johnson suggested to Barefoot Sanders that he seek House Minority Leader Gerald Ford's support: "Please go and press Ford— We are playing with fire here in the District. Try to get him to see it and help on the basis he loves our Capitol."[31] Tip O'Neill reflected on how Johnson had approached him on a rent subsidy bill by playing on party and personal loyalty:

> He made me feel a little guilty and cheap for letting him down, but he wasn't rough and he didn't twist my arm. He persuaded me to take a couple of steps back and put myself in his position. And the next time he sees me don't think he won't remember that vote. He damn well will.[32]

A Republican who experienced the Johnson treatment as a freshman recalls it as effective but not arm twisting.

> Johnson used the power of persuasion. He knew everyone. He'd call up and say look I know you want this program for your state and I want something too. . . . He was kind of a horse trader. . . . Lyndon was a master at that. He didn't threaten.

Johnson's lobbying was also personal in the sense that he often took support for his legislation personally. Larry O'Brien commented, "Legislation was intensely personal with Johnson. A vote against one of his bills was a personal rebuff."[33] He often dwelt on these perceived affronts, particularly in the case of Vietnam.[34] At the same time, Johnson did not hold grudges for long and he quickly put losses behind him and looked to the next issue. House Minority Leader Charles Halleck summed up his assessment of Johnson's style and his feelings for the president: "A guy may be hard driving, but he can be a real helpful, gentle person, too; and I would say Lyndon was that; those are the sort of things you never forget"; and "I'd like to believe that he's a good friend of mine as I am of his, because I'm devoted to the guy."[35] Halleck's declaration of friendship and devotion to a Democratic president reflects Johnson's focus on building long-range relationships.

While the Johnson treatment could include intense pressure, it also involved generous thanks and sharing credit to lay a foundation for future support. He understood that the last thing a member of Congress wanted to see after a tough battle in the halls of Congress was the White House taking all the credit. As Tip O'Neill pointed out, "One thing I like about him: he'll ask you to do something but he'll thank you for it."[36] The White House understood that the president should not receive too much credit and that the image of members of Congress being forced into submission by a president would not go over well with voters electing lawmakers to represent their interests.[37] While the relationship between White House and Congress is not a zero-sum game, there likely is a point at which presidential success begins to undermine the image of congressional independence.

The White House staff often went out of its way to give credit to Congress.[38] Even before the chair of one Senate committee could complete hearings on an administration bill he was called out of the room to receive a phone call from Mike Manatos conveying the president's appreciation for his quick action on the bill.[39] Senator Abraham Ribicoff (Democrat-Connecticut) remarked, "The genius of Lyndon Johnson is that he not only calls you when he wants something, but he remembers to call you back and thank you for what you've done."[40]

Johnson hosted several "Salute to Congress" receptions to thank Congress publicly for its effort. These receptions are still warmly remembered by some members of Congress. During one congressional reception Johnson reminded members of his connection to Congress.

> I have spent the better part of my working life in the Congress of the United States—half of those in the House of Representatives and half in the Senate. It was among you that I learned my most important lessons. Among you, I acquired my most deeply held beliefs about government.[41]

While the legendary "Johnson Treatment" and the wholesale horse-trading of projects have been used to characterize Lyndon Johnson's work with Congress, he was as much a master of the small things that build congressional relations. Johnson insisted that he be notified any time a member of Congress was admitted to Bethesda Naval Hospital or the Walter Reed Army Medical Center so that he could send a note or flowers immediately.[42] Johnson knew the value of dancing with congressional wives at White House receptions, and the impact of having the president of the United States heap praise upon a spouse would carry. He became so adept at inscribing and signing photos that he could do so while carrying on a conversation. He was willing to spend hours signing photos and never complained about having to do so.[43] There was no such thing as a purely social event in the Johnson White House. Often the invitation lists passed along to the president had annotations that let Johnson know where members were on pending legislation or what a member might want to discuss with the president.

Johnson always tried to find time to see members of Congress, particularly senators and even Republican members or unsupportive Democrats. During trips out of D.C., Johnson always made sure that even Republicans were invited.[44] As a result, during the Johnson years, contact with the president became increasingly common and this created expectations that would lead to problems for the more distant Nixon.

A Fresh Mandate

Johnson's landslide victory in 1964 created a personal victory for the president but it did not necessarily indicate support for the Johnson agenda. In fact, a poll by Louis Harris suggested that there was strong opposition to an expansion of the New Deal.[45] After the Democratic landslide of 1964 set the stage for the Johnson legislative agenda, his administration worked aggressively to connect electoral victory to success in Congress. The president frequently reminded his staff that the election of 1964 had created a reserve of political capital that was to be spent freely rather than conserved.[46] Johnson told reporters, "We've got to do it now. The Presidential mandate runs out."[47] Johnson's comments to Harry McPherson demonstrate that he realized that his influence in Washington was a diminishing resource. Whereas Nixon would believe that he could wait for a better opportunity, Johnson told his staff that the time was now.

> You've got to give it all you can, that first year. Doesn't matter what kind of majority you come in with. You've got just one year when they treat you right, and before they start worrying about themselves. The third year, you lose votes; if this war goes on, I'll lose a lot of 'em. A lot of our people don't belong here, they're in Republican seats, and the Republicans will get them back. The fourth year's all politics. You can't put anything through when half the Congress is thinking about how to beat you. So you've got one year.[48]

To make the most of his political mandate the president scheduled his 1965 State of the Union Address during the evening, the first time since 1936 that a president thus used prime time. Thirty-one million Americans saw the president outline his legislative package, "The Great Society," and after the speech *Newsweek* proclaimed, "President Lyndon B. Johnson stood this week at a pinnacle of power that no American has reached before."[49] The speech succeeded in connecting his landslide election victory and his personal popularity to his legislative agenda.

Johnson's full court press paid off as he committed the full energy of the White House to the legislative process at a time when he held the most influence. While the election of 1964 created the potential for the victories of the Great Society, it was Johnson's commitment of that potential influence to his legislative agenda and his careful management of that electoral clout that insured the passage of a flood of administration legislation. Johnson deserves credit for making effective use of the opportunity. While legislative success may seem to naturally follow popularity in the polls, George Bush's inability or unwillingness to capitalize on his record approval ratings and Ronald Reagan's struggle to lead Congress during his second term suggest that the White House's commitment and skills play an important role.

Johnson had learned the value of assisting members of Congress at election time while still in the House of Representatives when he helped raise money for other congressional candidates in 1940.[50] His White House closely monitored congressional elections and watched for ways to avoid problems in the next election from the earliest days each session. Members of Congress were consulted about Republican activity in their districts and Vice President Humphrey was put in charge of looking after the seventy new Democrats elected in 1964. He made visits to their districts, invited constituents to Washington for conferences, and provided other forms of assistance.[51] The landslide victory in 1964 led many members to believe that Johnson would be an asset in their district and this became a strong incentive for some members to cooperate. One congressional assistant noted that suddenly a member of Congress was "all over me with good fellowship" and reached the conclusion that "he suddenly realizes he's up for re-election next year."[52] Elections are never far from the minds of lawmakers, a fact that was not lost on the Johnson White House. O'Brien insisted that the administration's lobbyists respect members of Congress and remember that they needed to be elected. Often the White House would begin lobbying by describing the benefits of legislation to a member's district. In a memo to Mike Manatos, one administration lobbyist reported that Senator Thomas McIntyre (Democrat-New Jersey) "is worried about rent supplements in this election year and wants a memorandum showing why he should support rent supplements politically." In the same memo Republican Senator J. Caleb Boggs (Republican-Delaware) is reported as wanting to support the bill but fearful of voter reaction, indicating his mind could be changed by a show of support from people in his state.[53] Members consider such assistance the most important help they could receive from the White House. One member of Congress discovered that a naval laboratory in his district was going to be closed and that the announcement of the closing would come about six weeks before the election. He desperately sought a delay in the announcement. "I could understand the [D]emocratic administration doing this to H. R. Gross or Wilbur Mills, but my God, I just couldn't survive."[54]

The election of 1966 was a major blow to the Johnson administration's legislative agenda as it shattered the image of Johnson as an electoral asset to his congressional allies. The Democrats lost forty-seven members in the House, almost all strong supporters of the Great Society. Further, the remaining Democrats could look to the 1966 elections as one measure of the cost of supporting the Johnson program, particularly in the area of civil rights.[55] Johnson, who had been a huge asset in the 1964 election, appeared to be a liability in 1966. While the Democrats retained their majority in Congress, the setbacks of the 1966 election created uncertainty as they looked to the next session of Congress. Johnson had been able to convince lawmakers that opposing him had its costs, but now members saw the electoral price of supporting the president.

The Full Court Press

Larry O'Brien, after service both as head of legislative liaison and commissioner of the National Basketball Association, recognized the Johnson approach as a full court press.[56] A full court press involves a team's aggressive and unrelenting pressure toward overcoming the defense and scoring a basket. According to Larry O'Brien, Johnson's full court press meant monitoring legislation at every step in the process and using every resource at the disposal of the White House.

> His efforts in the legislative program were intense. His involvement was as full as could be. He enlisted everybody possible. There were times in the White House when just about everybody on the staff was involved in one way or another in some legislative struggle. [They would] have assignments from him or from me to work with individual members.[57]

A productive strategy for the White House often begins by involving congressional leaders in the development of legislation. The Johnson administration followed the rule that said, "Bring them in on the takeoffs if you want them in on the landings."[58] Letting members shape legislation to avoid serious conflicts with constituent concerns or letting members portray themselves as more than simply following the White House's lead permitted members to support the president without damaging their own political standing.

BUILDING FRIENDSHIPS

Barefoot Sanders described the long-range goal of a successful liaison operation as maintaining a system of open communication and cultivating goodwill for the president and his administration.[59] One example of the institutionalization of the friendly relationship between the branches is the White House's system for dealing with congressional birthdays. The administration maintained a chronological listing of each member by birthday with the appropriate personalization for the card or letter that would be sent. The greeting reveals the level of favor between the member and the White House. For example, Congressmen Melvin Price and William Harsha Jr. shared the same birthday but not the same closeness to the White House. Cards and letters to Representative Price were to bear the greeting "Dear Mel," while Harsha was delegated to "Dear Congressman." The tone of relationships changed over time as the greeting next to Congressman Edwin Reinecks's name originally read "Dear Edwin" but was scratched out and replaced with "Dear Congressman."[60]

The Johnson White House tried to maintain friendly relations with Republicans as well as Democrats, again premised on the idea that you never knew when they might be in a position to support you. When southern Democrats defected on the Civil Rights Act of 1964, the Johnson administration found an ally in House Minority Leader Charles Halleck. Halleck had been a constant source of strong opposition to the Johnson administration but he and the White House always maintained a friendly personal relationship. The staff attributed the ability to work with Halleck as resulting from a friendly relationship that had been built by the White House staff.[61] On the Senate side, Minority Leader Everett Dirksen played a pivotal role in drafting and passing the Voting Rights Act.

One of the best examples of the Johnson administration's efforts simultaneously to lobby members of Congress and to build a friendly relationship was the series of congressional receptions put on by the White House. Several of the receptions were open to all members and their spouses while others included only Democrats or friends of the administration. Many congressional receptions included briefings by the president, the secretaries of state and defense, or the director of the bureau of the budget. This helped Johnson turn the reception into a show of respect for members of Congress by demonstrating that they were being taken seriously. Many members found these briefings useful since they did not have staff large enough to gather information on issues like foreign policy. In addition, stories of being briefed by the president in the White House could be used in constituency newsletters. White House staff were expected to attend these events and were briefed as to who they should talk to and what issues they should pursue. They were instructed to report back to O'Brien the next morning. To facilitate spotting assigned members, the Office of Congressional Relations maintained a "mug book" containing pictures of legislators.[62]

While members of Congress were at a policy briefing downstairs at the White House, upstairs their spouses were treated to their own briefing on the arts or a tour of the White House hosted by Lady Bird. The president and the first lady used their charm to build general goodwill, and members and spouses alike were flattered by the attention.[63] The White House made sure that members and their spouses could have their pictures taken with President and Mrs. Johnson. According to Jack Valenti, "Nothing pleases a Congressman more than pictures of his wife and him at the White House." Valenti considered the receptions in 1965 a "golden opportunity to reap the harvest" of the large freshman class and believed that the White House receptions would be "the high points of their lives—and we should make the most of it."[64]

In contrast to Jackie Kennedy, who maintained only a social interest in Congress, Lady Bird Johnson took an active interest in both the substance and progress of legislation.[65] Not only was she more interested in some of the issues, her years of living with Lyndon Johnson had brought her into frequent contact with legislators and gave her an understanding of congressional politics that almost equaled the president's.[66] Lady Bird was very popular on the Hill, especially with the senators with whom she had dealt extensively. The first lady and her assistant Liz Carpenter lobbied for the highway beautification bill. Generally, they spoke to members at White House social events, but at times they would call members by phone.[67]

DEPARTMENTAL LIAISON

Under Johnson the White House staff tried to make even more use of the departmental staffs and they effectively commandeered the efforts of the departments. Like everyone else in the executive branch, Johnson wanted the departments on his legislative team. The discussion in almost every cabinet meeting of the legislative status of the administration's program was a constant reminder to the departments of Johnson's commitment to his legislative program. According to Sanders, Johnson repeatedly drove home the importance of congressional liaison to his cabinet.

> In cabinet meetings, he would point to Bob Weaver or John Gardner or Bill Wirtz and say, 'Why haven't you passed that bill yet? What's wrong with you fellows?'—and the cabinet members, after being put on the spot once or twice, would redouble their legislative efforts.[68]

The president told his cabinet that each department's legislative liaison officers should be second in importance only to the cabinet secretaries themselves.[69] In order to upgrade each departmental liaison operation, quality people were needed in those offices. O'Brien explained the importance of placing a high quality liaison officer in each department and investing in their credibility.

> A government official must have status to make the proper impact on the Hill. He must have the ear of his chief, be able to speak for him, make decisions and not be just another guy with a legislation check list. It is to the best interest of his department or agency that he have this status.[70]

As part of their weekly reports to the White House, each department was expected to report any need for White House assistance and to provide information on congressional sentiment on departmental legislation.[71] Regular meetings were held that brought together the congressional relations operatives from the various departments and agencies, some departments bringing three or four people. Attendance was mandatory and these meetings might last two to three hours. These meetings provided an opportunity for departments to share notes and coordinate activities and gave the White House an opportunity to give departments a feel for their priorities and the overall legislative picture.

The White House maintained a list of "top echelon" personnel in each agency who had a personal relationship with members so they could be called in to gather "swing" votes. "When we get into a crisis, we bring 40 legislative officers into the act and all pull together."[72] The use of staff beyond the liaison staff for congressional lobbying picked up after the 1966 election as Johnson attempted to use additional manpower to offset losses in Congress and Larry O'Brien's departure.

GOING PUBLIC

Lyndon Johnson was not known for his oratorical ability and is considered to have been much better at working the cloakroom than the airwaves, but while he was an acknowledged master of the inside game of lobbying, he had an appreciation for the use of public opinion.

> When traditional methods fail, a President must be willing to bypass the Congress and take the issue to the people. By instinct and experience, I preferred to work within, knowing that good legislation is the product not of public rhetoric but of private negotiations and compromise. But sometimes a President has to put Congress' feet to the fire.[73]

Johnson described "This aura, this thing, this halo around the President, everybody wants to believe in the President and the Commander in Chief."[74] Larry O'Brien commented, "I don't think Lyndon Johnson ever was reluctant to envision where the camera locations were and he had a way of moving front and center. It came naturally to him."[75] Although Johnson's credibility problems contributed to the diminishing of this resource, his administration made some use of a public strategy. Barefoot Sanders considered public relations an important part of the liaison staff's strategy and later argued that Johnson used the president's ability to focus public attention on an issue more than other presidents did in the 1970s.[76]

Johnson's appreciation for public relations is evident in the transcript of his phone conversation with Ted Sorensen while he was still vice president. Johnson believed in the ability of the president to set out moral principals. Vice President Johnson urged Sorensen to put Kennedy on television to press for civil rights legislation.

> We got a little pop gun, and I want to pull out the cannon. The President is the cannon. You let him be on all the TV networks just speaking from his conscience, not at a rally in Harlem, but at a place in Mississippi or Texas or Louisiana and have the honor guard there with a few Negroes in it. Then let him reach over and point and say, "I have to order these boys into battle, in the foxholes carrying that flag. I don't ask them what their name is, whether it's Gomez or Smith, or what color they got, what religion. If I can order them into battle I've got to make it possible for them to eat and sleep in this

country." Then how does everybody—he goes home and asks his wife, "What's wrong with this?" and they go searching their conscience. Every preacher starts preaching about it. We ought to recognize this and put them busy.[77]

Once in the Oval Office, Johnson put this kind of appeal behind the Voting Rights Act. Johnson wanted a speech that used "every ounce of moral persuasion the Presidency held."[78] No president in nineteen years had appeared before a joint session of Congress for the purpose of proposing domestic legislation, but at nine in the evening of Monday, March 15, a southern president went before the Congress and the nation and called for civil rights legislation:

> What happened in Selma is part of a larger movement which reaches into every section and state of America. It is the effort of American Negroes to secure for themselves the full blessing of American life.
>
> Their cause must be our cause, too. Because it is not just Negroes, but really it is all of us who must overcome the crippling legacy of bigotry and injustice.
>
> And we shall overcome.[79]

The standing ovation was not quite unanimous but the reception was enthusiastic, giving the voting rights bill the strong send-off it needed. The reaction was impressive. Senator Edmund Muskie wrote, "It was more than a speech. It was an act of inspired leadership!"[80] Senator Thomas Dodd, after watching the president's address with a large group of constituents, wired the president, saying: "Never have I seen such a spontaneous, warm, emotional, and sincere response to any speech."[81] The president received telegrams from individuals ranging from Supreme Court Justice William O. Douglas to Mrs. Sidney Poitier.[82] Johnson had established voting rights as a great moral issue, making opposition difficult. Johnson likely understood that without a strong statement of the principles behind his legislation, other principals and stands might come to dominate the debate, as Ronald Reagan would two decades later. Through his speech to Congress Johnson made it more difficult for his opponents to raise the issue of state's rights as grounds for resisting the Johnson approach.

The Johnson administration used bill-signing ceremonies as public relations events and to reward friendly members. The administration tried to create unique events for each bill signing to enhance the drama and highlight the significance of a legislative victory. Johnson went to the Truman Library to sign the Medicare bill and to the Statue of Liberty to sign an immigration bill. Johnson returned to the one-room schoolhouse in Stonewall, Texas, where he began his education, to sign the Federal Aid to Education Bill in the presence of his first teacher. The Voting Rights Act was signed in the "President's Room" in the Capitol—the same room where, exactly 104 years earlier, Lincoln signed a bill that freed slaves forced to serve in the war by the Confederates—using the same desk that Johnson used as Majority Leader to work on the Civil Rights Act of 1957.[83] The administration was looking to make the most of their success:

> A touch of good drama might be added by having an automobile procession from the White House to the Capitol, carrying the President, the members of the Cabinet and various leaders of the voting rights fight—both white and Negro. For the greatest impact, advance arrangements should be made with the television networks to assure full and complete coverage, preferably live, at a convenient time segment. A signing at the Capitol—with live television coverage—would, in my judgment, have more impact, more dignity and be more nearly immune to criticism about the theatrics than signing out of Washington this soon after the trip to Independence.[84]

The president often used as many as sixty different pens to sign a bill and then distributed them to members of Congress as a token of the president's appreciation. While bill signings were generally ceremonial occasions for credit claiming and thanking members of Congress, Johnson used the momentum from one victory to build toward the next and was known to pull aside a member of Congress at a signing and ask for his vote on another piece of legislation.

The White House understood that the press's representation of the president's package was an important component of its strategy. Over time, O'Brien adopted the practice of sitting down with the president's press secretary so that more information on the progress of administration legislation could be worked into the press briefings. When the press put the administration on the defensive by reporting that little was happening when legislation was not being passed, O'Brien used one-on-one interviews and information passed to the press secretary to draw attention to the administration's efforts on bills still before lawmakers. Given Johnson's flair for dramatic bill signings and other events, this was less of a problem under Johnson than Kennedy, but the administration still needed a means of showing effort and interest while it was working behind the scenes.[85]

The administration wanted its message to come from Capitol Hill as well as the White House. In 1966 the administration began to orchestrate speeches (for insertion in the *Congressional Record*) and statements for use in members' constituent newsletters. Bob Hardesty was put in charge of developing and distributing these statements and then reporting back to the president on the number and nature of such speeches.[86] While Hardesty constructed some of these statements, most were to come from the departments and agencies with legislation pending. Hardesty constantly had to pressure the departments to provide the kind of material needed and then find friendly members to use the material. While many members were willing to support the administration, the White House realized that few would dedicate the staff time and resources to developing such statements and wanted to make it as easy as possible for members to express their support in a way that benefited the administration the most.[87] The White House watched the *Congressional Record* closely. Every morning Jack Jacobsen would go through it, looking for every reference to support or opposition to the administration. A report would be prepared for the president daily and the administration would try to get rebuttals to opposition statements into the *Record* by the next day.[88] Sanders reminded the staff that "Whenever any Congressman assigned to you makes a public statement in support of the President, be sure you call immediately and express our appreciation."[89]

In the battle to confirm Abe Fortas and Homer Thornberry, the administration anticipated a tough congressional fight and planned to shore up congressional support with public support. Sanders wrote to Johnson describing a plan to develop and push a public relations campaign to support their troubled nominees.

1. *Have one speech delivered by a Senator each day* before the recess, the Senator to issue a hard-hitting press release along with the speech.

2. *Utilize the Cabinet and Sub-Cabinet to stir up newspaper support in their home state.* They can be told now to do this. I believe the best impact will come if newspaper support and letters to the editors and letters to the Senators themselves start popping up all over the place about Labor Day and thereafter. . . .

6. *Is there anyway we can use the State Democratic organizations to stir up editorial support* and, where Republican Senators are in opposition, to have letters written to newspapers attacking those Senators for their opposition?[90] (emphasis in original)

The manipulation of public opinion was a strategy pursued through the departments as well. For example, when Secretary of Agriculture Orville Freeman found himself in a bitter struggle with members of Congress over the closing of agricultural research stations in some districts, he put together a public relations campaign that he outlined in a memo to the president:

> We are carrying forward an active campaign to reach the public. We've had a good bit of success in press, radio and T-V, but it has not gotten the public excited yet. . . . Briefly, I have personally been in contact with a dozen columnists and commentators and we have sent background materials to others I did not want to personally contact. Background stories and detailed information have been sent to the local newspapers in the vicinity of every station closed. Dr. Nyle Brad, Director of Science and Education, taped a series of radio interviews for use by radio stations in the areas where local criticism has been the most severe. Background material together with specific locality statements has been mailed to a thousand daily newspapers, radio, television stations, and farm magazine editors in the regions most affected. Four thousand copies of my testimony have been sent to newspapers, radio stations, trade publication, agricultural industry and commodity groups. We are now making a strong follow-up with columnists and commentators developing some new avenues as the result of yesterday's testimony. We hope to soon get a strong "fire" burning, hot enough to command Congressional attention and respect.[91]

While Johnson was willing to use a public approach to issues, he understood the risks of such an approach to Congress. He regarded the impact of a confrontational public approach to Congress as "mixed" and noted that, "It may serve to galvanize support in the Congress and the country, but it may also shorten tempers and polarize thoughts and emotions."[92]

D.C. HOME RULE

One example of the "full court press" as applied by the Johnson administration is the Johnson administration's push to gain "home rule" for the District of Columbia. After the 1964 election the administration began to lay the groundwork for passage of a D.C. home rule bill by trying to load the District of Columbia committee with likely home rule supporters. The liaison staff assembled a list of possible members for the committee, which they eventually pared down to eleven desirable possibilities. When Congress convened on January 2, all of the D.C. committee's five new Democratic members were from the administration's list. A third new committee member, George W. Grider of Tennessee, had been on their original list of eighteen but had not made the shorter list because, Charles Horsky concluded, "His reaction was one of doubt that a Negro city like the District was competent to govern itself. I am sure we can do better."[93] Congressman Grider did not come happily to the committee and informed Horsky that "he believes the President owes him something for his being on the House District Committee which he regards as doing a favor for the White House."[94]

Despite this careful planning, the bill languished in the committee. In response the administration attempted to dislodge the bill from committee through a "discharge petition." While the filing of a discharge petition was not rare, only eighteen had been successful since the rule was created in 1910.[95] Members were reluctant to put their willingness to undermine the D.C. committee's authority in writing and the administration's efforts to get more names on the petition was slowed by the problem of members wanting to remove their names. Johnson himself was needed to acquire the final signatures.

Katharine Graham and others from the *Washington Post* were recruited by the White House to lobby forty Republican members who opposed the bill.[96] While Johnson was administering the treatment to individual members over the phone lines, a public relations campaign was also underway. Johnson made repeated references to the failure of Congress to grant the citizens of the District the same control over their destiny that they had granted citizens of the Philippines and Puerto Rico.

This legislative battle demonstrates the full range of tactics used by the administration, and its defeat reflects the risks of such an aggressive strategy. The home rule issue provided members with a unique opportunity to demonstrate their independence from the president. Faced with the label of being a "rubber stamp" for Johnson, the home rule bill provided a visible issue to break with the administration. This issue was particularly ripe for opportunism since no member of Congress was elected by citizens of the District and few Americans outside of the District had strong feelings in favor of the District. Many people outside Washington did have strong feelings against the District, however. Since the city's population was 58 percent Black there was opposition to having the nation's capital run by a "minority." Republican opponents of home rule had reservations about extending power to a city that was predominantly Democratic.

A full court press has become the standard as presidents have had to scramble to find opportunities to influence legislation among dwindling political resources and increased political resistance. The defeat of D.C. home rule demonstrates that even committing the full resources of the White House is not enough to overcome a stubborn Congress.

Granting Favors: Who Gets What from the President

Lyndon Johnson did not invent dispensing presidential favors. However, he may have done it more effectively, enthusiastically, and openly than any president before or since. He had grown comfortable with the give-and-take bargaining among members of Congress during his service in the House and Senate, and once the resources of the executive branch came under his control he used them to build coalitions.

Trading votes for favors, while often not explicit, is understood between the White House and Congress. It is more accurate to examine the use of presidential favors in terms of "granting" rather than "trading" favors. The idea of trading favors implies a direct exchange of a vote for a favor. This was seldom the case with Lyndon Johnson, but providing favors did produce votes in an indirect manner. Presidents know when the White House is doing favors for legislators and expect compliance in return. Rarely will a member specifically ask for a favor in return for a vote. This is likely the product of pride and propriety. Often members of Congress simply turn the discussion from the pending vote to appointments or projects.

Johnson understood that granting a favor did not require an immediate return. He sought to build a general sense of indebtedness rather than engage in specific trades. House Minority Leader Charles Halleck recalls the president going down a long list of bills asking for his support, but generally receiving little. "But after it was over and I'd given these negative answers, 'Well,' he said, 'I'm going to appoint your friend Budge to Securities and Exchange Commission,' which indicates he didn't bear any grudge, or I never did think so."[97] The administration was anxious to reward its friends even when specific votes were not needed. When Congressman Robert "Fats" Everett (Democrat-Tennessee) had a problem with the behavior of a game warden, Henry Hall Wilson wrote to the Interior Department: "If you have a spare hour sometimes I will be glad to illustrate graphically the indispensability of Everett to this Administration in Congress." In a attached note Wilson commented, "I know this kind of thing ties your people in knots but it certainly helps to pass legislation."[98]

The administration realized that some of its friends in Congress were Republican and some of its most problematic members were Democrats. In 1968 they decided that additional flexibility was needed in the announcement of grant projects. A change in policy, approved by the president, sought to be more generous in awarding support to Republicans whenever possible.

> Bill Nichols supported the President only 43% of the time in the last session and I can see no good reason why he should be given lead time on an important Defense or agency announcement. . . . During the last session 13 Republican House members supported the administration more than 60% of the time. I believe it would be smart politically if we waived the rigid rule of not calling Republicans in this particular case. . . .
>
> I realize that in many cases this will have to be a question of judgment but I think that some flexibility in our policy is definitely required.[99]

The White House must often choose between rewarding old friends and making new ones. If favors are only granted to legislators who have supported the president in the past there will be little incentive for other members to join the president in the future. The White House must also remember that some members supported or opposed the president because of constituent pressure and that a vote cast against district opinion is much more of a sign of presidential support than a member facing no constituent pressure on an issue.

While alienating a member is always a risk, members themselves are reluctant to distance themselves too much from an administration of their own party. Most members will consider that there is always tomorrow and that they may find themselves in need of administration help at some time. O'Brien points out "that the White House remains awesome at all times, and there is always tomorrow. You don't want to be in a position where you can't pick up that phone."[100] Once members find themselves in opposition to the president, the White House staff has no reason to provide favors.

Photos with the president, messages of support from the president, or visits to the district by members of the cabinet or occasionally even the president were offered to members before they could ask for help.[101] Occasionally favors were done for Republicans. When Everett Dirksen sent Jack Valenti a list of small favors ranging from low-level appointments to the first lady's appearance at the dedication of a new courthouse, Johnson reviewed the items and told Valenti: "Please check carefully and help every way we *safely* can."[102] When a member of Congress requested that the president of the Lion's Club be allowed a meeting with the president, Johnson approved and would later use this to try to get this member's vote on the Farm Bill.[103]

The Johnson administration maintained a "favors file" that listed small favors done for members going back to the Kennedy administration. Each entry listed the day of the request (if a favor was requested), the date the favor was granted, a description of the favor, and the recipient of the favor. A sampling of entries (the sets of numbers and letters separated by dashes identifying the negative numbers used by the White House photographer) from Senator Dirksen's file (which totals four pages) reflects the kind of favors recorded in the file:[104]

5/13/65	Pen from H.J. Res. 447	
8/11/65	Photo from S. 1564, Voting Rights, 342-22A; 342-32A; 342-31A; & 339-2A	
8/31/65	6-6A signed: "To Mrs. Lily Carver, with my salute for ninety wonderful years and a great son-in-law, LBJ" and A-393 signed: "To Mrs. Lily Carver, Happy Birthday, LBJ"	Mrs. Lily Carver
2/12/63– 2/20/63	copy of "Profiles in Courage" signed "wbw-JFK"	For Senator's Leg. Assistant Mr. William A Stevens.

The White House had the Democratic National Committee report anything done on behalf of members of Congress. These ranged from transmitting messages to help with speeches to arranging a television taping with baseball star Stan Musial.[105] No favor was too small to be ignored. The White House maintained detailed records of members' visits to the White House for social affairs. Each member was listed along with marital status, party, state, seniority, committee assignment, and support scores. An additional column for comments permitted the staff to make notes like: "A *good* administration supporter on Rules," or "Strong supporter of the President in California." Even nonsupporters were examined for potential help in the future. Barber Conable, a Republican member of the Ways and Means Committee with a support score of 33 percent, was listed with the comment, "We are going to need all the help we can get on a tax bill."[106]

Barefoot Sanders, after being in charge of congressional relations for six months, pushed Johnson to permit the congressional liaison office to coordinate the president's appointments with members of Congress. Apparently, members had been meeting with the president and the OCR learned about it only after the fact.

> Why is this important? Because we are usually the people who are asking the Congressmen to help the Administration. But if we are not the people who do the favors—and a Presidential appointment is about the biggest favor that can be done for a Congressman—we are less effective when we ask for favors.[107]

O'Brien and Manatos had expressed similar concerns earlier in the administration. Manatos was embarrassed when Senate Majority Leader Mansfield asked him about details of a planned trip to Mexico City when Manatos knew nothing about the trip or the invitation from the White House to Mansfield. Manatos explained to Jack Valenti, who had issued the invitation, that "It would be helpful, Jack, if I can't dispense the goodies, to at least have a smell of the wrapper."[108] White House staffs have consistently attempted to control favors or at least to be consulted. Giving the Congressional Liaison Office some degree of control over presidential favors contributes to their ability to develop and maintain a working relationship with members of Congress. Furthermore, no one else in the White House has any need to gain favor with members of Congress independent of the legislative agenda of the administration. White House lobbyists need to be seen as something more than a simple conduit for information; they need to demonstrate clout within the White House and be capable of actively participating in the bargaining process.

Members of Congress believe that their ability to attract money to their district is an important part of their credibility with constituents, so every administration has tried to make sure that grant notification or other concerns that impact a congressional constituency are discussed with the liaison staff. The White House can attempt to provide some degree of cover or protection to congressional friends who failed to get action on an appointment or project. The Johnson administration would inform the member and tell them why they had lost and often provide a letter that confirmed that the member had been fighting for their district's interest.

The White House let members make the first announcement of federal grants and projects in their districts as one of the administration's chief means of helping members who had supported the administration.[109] The handling of grant announcements is done as much out of the fear of losing votes as in hopes of gaining support. Occasionally the Johnson administration's system broke down and members became angry. When Congressman Clarence Long of Maryland failed to receive notification on two Air Force contracts that affected his district, one for over twenty million dollars, he became irate at the White House. A member of the White House liaison staff made his anger with the Air Force clear in a memo to the Defense Department's liaison officer:

> It seems to me that whoever in the Air Force is responsible for these two inexcusable omissions is either grossly incompetent, unbelievably careless or both. The fact that I am on the receiving end of Congressman Long's wrath is quite unimportant but the fact that this kind of inefficiency reflects on the White House and the Administration is extremely important.
>
> There may be a good explanation for these two recent incidents and if there is I would appreciate your conveying it to me as soon as possible. If there is not, I would like to know the person or persons responsible in the Department of the Air Force so that steps could be taken to correct the situation.[110]

Sometimes the favors desired are legislative. Often legislators are hoping that the president will be supportive of their legislative agendas if they are sympathetic to the president's. One member was especially interested in seeing the administration get behind his Presidential Election Constitutional Amendment.[111] Not to dismiss completely the sincere policy preferences of members; but it is often the case that members are attempting to gain credibility with other members or constituents by securing the president's backing for their legislation. Access to the president represents power and prestige to voters and to other members of Congress.

Dispensing grants and patronage contributes to a member's credibility. Patronage indicates a member's influence in Washington and reflects on his or her ability to get things done for constituents. Tom Korologos, who worked for Nixon and Ford, pointed out that the White House can use its ability to influence the perception of members' importance as a tool of influence.

> You get a guy from the West who's causing you trouble, you have the Interior Department spread the word, quietly, that he can't get

things done in Washington. . . . You get a guy from Florida, let it be known that the Corps of Engineers can't work with him. Summertime, cut the allocation of tour passes for the White House. Keep him off Air Force One. Don't return his calls. Cut his wife from the First Lady's social list.[112]

The White House can be too effective at protecting members of Congress. The congressional relations staff realized that the proposed closure of seven Federal Aviation Administration offices would create serious problems for congressional friends but allowed publication of the listing on the grounds that, without an announcement of closures, protecting these offices would never become a favor. Wilson wrote to another member of the liaison staff, "I feel we can never get any appreciation from Congressmen by saving them from danger they never know exists, and it would be a far more effective operation if everybody was given the bad news and we rescued the good guys."[113]

One limit on the impact of granting favors to lawmakers is that Congress ultimately has control over many of these favors. Pork barrel projects like grants originate in legislation written by Congress, and while the administration ultimately may exercise some discretion, Larry O'Brien always understood that Congress controls the purse strings. "Anything the White House could do to accommodate Wilbur Mills was done. But as far as projects into Arkansas, Wilbur Mills didn't need the White House."[114]

Members quickly come to take for granted whatever they receive from the White House. Strom Thurmond was amazed to discover that many of the perks he received from a Democratic White House were cut off when he moved to the Republican party. He continued to request and expect the same level of appointments, White House invitations, and grant announcements. During the Johnson administration he was stunned to discover that he could no longer pick the postmaster of his home town. Claude Desautels recounts the response from the senator:

> So one day he calls me: "Kennedy gave me my postmaster. Johnson won't give it to me." Well, how do you say to a senator, "You've switched parties." So you try to be a little tactful, a diplomat and I said, "Senator, when Kennedy gave it to you you belonged to the majority party." I didn't want to use Democrat or Republican. I said, "You were a member of the majority party. But now, you're a member of the minority party. You made the decision, not us." And I

heard him yell to the big GOP guy down in South Carolina, Harry Dent—"Harry, what party did I belong to when Kennedy gave me that postmaster back in 1962?" I heard Harry say in the background, "Well, you were a Democrat. Then you switched later that year to Independent." "Oh, oh. Well, I guess you're right. I belong to the minority party."[115]

Members of Congress were already becoming quite demanding when it came to projects for their districts. Bill Moyers recounted to a liaison office his encounter with a member who wanted a new courthouse for his district.

Your good friend and mine, Carl Perkins, cornered me in a helicopter over Eastern Kentucky Friday. There being no escape but down, I chose the less fatal (although at the time I would not swear that it was) alternative of listening. . . .
    Next time, I will chose the other alternative.[116]

O'Brien found himself at odds with Majority Leader Mike Mansfield when the senator discovered that a VA hospital in his state was to be closed and without his consultation. O'Brien understated his predicament when he commented, "I must say, I was sitting with a very angered majority leader."[117] Not only had someone angered the White House's most powerful ally in the Senate, they had also undermined the workings of the congressional relations staff by not informing them. O'Brien found himself in a position in which the only two alternatives were that he had kept this information from Mansfield or that the White House was not briefing him of information relevant to Congress. Once a member publicly takes a position it becomes very difficult to back down. In this case, Mansfield remained committed to the hospital while President Johnson remained committed to the principal of cutting unneeded facilities, and by the time the issue came to the attention of the liaison staff it was out of their hands. Mansfied, who was a key ally of the administration, remained upset and confrontational on this issue and Johnson responded by planting editorials on the need for cost-cutting.[118] With both men effectively on the record in opposition before discussions began, there was no clean way out of the deadlock.

It is possible to work around members who have publicly stated their opposition. One example is when Les Arends had come out publicly against buying larger jetliners to serve as *Air Force One* and *Air Force Two*. Since he had publicly stated his opposition it was impossible to ask him to vote for the legislation. Instead the Johnson White House persuaded him to stay out of the battle. Aspin agreed to not participate in the debate and not try to persuade any member.[119]

The White House staff had no reservations about taking credit for favors it did not intend to dispense. In one case Wilson forwarded an appeal on behalf of a nominee to the Federal Communications Commission from a member who had been less than helpful. In forwarding the appeal Wilson commented that "I wouldn't pay it much attention, but you might just stick it in the file in the event she is appointed."[120] Wilson wanted to make sure that if this person were appointed the congressional relations staff would be notified so that it could at least claim credit with the member.

The White House staff had little interest in dispensing bad news. While they reserved the right to inform members of appointments and all except the smallest grants, the White House left bad news up to the departments. Henry Hall Wilson admitted, "As a general rule, we tried to bring only good news from the White House."[121]

Political legends in Washington often deal with presidents trading military bases or dams for votes. Lyndon Johnson allegedly told Senator Harry Byrd that "Bob McNamara says we have to close that Norfolk naval base of yours and I don't much want to."[122] Such trades make for much better storytelling than bargaining. Like handing out appointments, such trading once begun is hard to stop as it becomes the expected price of support. In addition, presidents have relatively few projects that can be manipulated in such a fashion.

The administration maintained its own set of detailed support scores for each member of Congress to help the president and the staff see the level of support that each member had provided. This proved to be useful information later when members sought favors from the administration.[123] For example, Sanders also sent a copy of members' support scores to the White House tour office with the suggestion that "you use these lists when Congressmen wish to exceed their tour quotas. Requests of Democrats with 90% and over support records should be honored whenever possible." Sanders went on to explain what level of generosity went with each level of support but admitted that "We may ask you from time to time to make exceptions for particularly helpful Republicans or for senior Democrats who are in the less than 50% category."[124]

One member of Congress suggested that Johnson's success had to do more with his appreciation of the value of these favors and his skill at dispensing them than with the volume of favors traded.

Johnson didn't have all that much to trade, but he knew how to trade somebody for something they really needed. A good speech or whatever it was Johnson would deliver for them, it wasn't always money or projects. By the time Johnson had come along we had stopped building dams anyway.

Johnson combined his understanding of legislators and the legislative process with the resources of the executive branch to create an effective bargaining strategy. While granting favors likely produced relatively few votes, Johnson made the most of these favors and the most of the votes they produced through careful bookkeeping and effective bargaining.

Conclusion

Johnson's success was a result of both the 1964 election and an aggressive legislative strategy. There is no doubt that the large Democratic majority created by the 1964 election facilitated Johnson's work with Congress, but Johnson had to convert the public's rejection of Barry Goldwater into legislative support of the Great Society. Further, the majority status of the Democratic party conceals powerful opposition to many of Johnson's programs as conservative southern Democrats continued to fight civil rights legislation. While the Johnson majority was larger than Kennedy's, it still held many divisions. Further, Johnson's civil rights agenda struck at the heart of the divisions in the party.

Lyndon Johnson's careful cultivation of the influence granted by the 1964 election contributed to the extent of his victories. Johnson came at Congress from every angle with his full court press. He took the high road and used the bully pulpit to define issues in a way that made opposition difficult. He also used the vast resources of the executive branch to provide himself with an array of favors to use to ply reluctant members. In the Oval Office, Johnson could be an intimidating presence, prodding and pleading his way to gaining the votes he needed.

Johnson's personal commitment to the legislative process goes beyond any president's in history, and while his obsession with the legislative process paid off in legislative victories, according to one member of Congress he neglected other aspects of the presidency.

I think one of the reasons that he wasn't a better president is that he never really understood the difference in being majority leader in the Senate and the president. On the one hand he had legislative responsibilities and on the other he had executive and administrative ones and I'm not sure he fully grasped the difference between those two.

The administration of Lyndon Johnson is both a high water mark and a turning point. Johnson's success has become the standard by which other presidents are judged, but his success helped spawn a congressional push for independence. Gerald Ford remarked years later, "Frankly, I got very disgusted with the performance of that Eighty-ninth Congress; it was a disgrace. They were not independent. They were tools of the White House."[125] The price the presidency would pay for Johnson's victories was high, as Congress responded to his aggressive use of executive branch power with a reassertion of congressional power.

5

THE NIXON
ADMINISTRATION

RICHARD NIXON RECOGNIZED TWO FACTS AS HE ENTERED office. First, he faced a Congress controlled by the opposition party. In 1968 the Republicans became the first party since 1848 to win the White House without winning control of at least one house of Congress. Despite Nixon's personal victory at the polls, Democrats outnumbered Republicans 245 to 189 in the House and 57 to 43 in the Senate. Second, he was not warmly regarded by the public. With just 43.4 percent of the vote in 1968, Nixon could not claim the same kind of mandate that Johnson had enjoyed after the 1964 election. According to one Nixon aide, "The president was a very smart guy. He knew he wasn't a very well-loved man and he knew that he had to have some help."

Underlying the partisan differences between Nixon and Congress was a growing institutional clash between the branches. Nixon inherited increasing congressional assertiveness. At the same time, Johnson had made the relationship between the president and Congress more intimate than any president before or possibly since. Even Republican members of Congress had grown accustomed to meeting with the president personally and receiving invitations to the White House for social functions. Ironically, while members of Congress had grown accustomed to perks and attention from the White House, they had also grown uncomfortable with the growing power of the White House. While Lyndon Johnson had tried to praise the 89th Congress by labeling them the "do plenty" Congress, some critics had embarrassed them by branding them a "rubber stamp." Lyndon Johnson's legislative successes in 1965 were not matched by Democratic success at the polls in 1966, leaving many congressional Democrats to pay for Johnson's legislative victories. The system of checks and balances as well as the electorate seemed to be suggesting that Congress should assert itself.

In response to these conditions the Nixon administration engaged in an intense public relations campaign that would make the president a more imposing figure and enable him to manufacture electoral fears in the minds of Congress. The emphasis on public relations is reflected in Nixon's selection of H. R. Haldeman, an advertising man, as his chief of staff. The only advisor in the Nixon inner circle with White House experience or with much experience with Congress was Bryce Harlow. Harlow was considered by many observers to be one of Washington's best political minds, but over time his contact with Nixon diminished, leaving the White House largely under the direction of people more familiar with public relations.

The Nixon public relations campaign never bore fruit and in the meantime may have hampered the ability of the White House to build coalitions by not fully developing other means of influencing Congress. The administration's reluctance to focus more of its resources on congressional relations limited its success with Congress as some opportunities to work with Congress were lost while the administration focused on public relations.

The Nixon Staff

Nixon selected Bryce N. Harlow to serve as the chief architect of his legislative strategy. Harlow became Nixon's first appointment after the 1968 election and Harlow set out to recreate the work he had done as Dwight Eisenhower's legislative assistant. Nixon wanted to return to a presidency more like Eisenhower's and he chose Harlow in part because he shared Nixon's belief that Johnson had "vulgarized" the presidency. Once in the White House they sought to revive the mystique of the Oval Office.[1] Harlow had spent the years since the Eisenhower administration as a lobbyist for Proctor and Gamble and as Eisenhower's representative in Washington. By 1968 Harlow had become known as one of Washington's most influential lobbyists and best political minds.

While Nixon's selection of Harlow brought a seasoned hand into the new administration, such was not typical of Nixon's top-level appointments. Nixon drew upon advertising and law firms from outside Washington for most of his top-level appointments, and key appointees like Haldeman and John Ehrlichman were unfamiliar to members of Congress. Evans and Novak suggested that "Not for decades had an incoming White House staff appeared so much a mystery to Congress or been populated with so many unknowns."[2] One veteran of the Johnson administration believed that many of Nixon's problems with Congress stemmed from the lack of experience, since Harlow was the only one with any real experience and he was spread too thin.[3]

Because Harlow was so highly regarded, members of Congress often assumed that any problems coming from the White House reflected the failings of Nixon. One article asserted that "Harlow's biggest problem is Mr. Nixon's lack of a firm hand at the controls, his extraordinary tendency to dither."[4] While many of these criticisms may have been true, when problems with Congress were attributed to the president rather than Harlow, Nixon was left without the traditional protection that advisors' service as a lighting rod can provide.[5]

Early on, the Nixon administration faced a wave of criticism in its dealings with Congress. Many Republicans were upset because they did not have their phone calls returned immediately.[6] Harlow attributed some of the criticism to unrealistic expectations on the part of Republicans in Congress: "After eight years out of the White House, each of the Republican Members of Congress wanted immediate service, to appoint this or that guy; to approach this or that project. When they couldn't get what they wanted, they complained about a lack of communication with the White House."[7] Presidents who inherit the White House from the other party find that members of their own party have unrealistic expectations about the treatment they will get. One of Nixon's House lobbyists complained that Johnson had made his job more difficult because Johnson made them feel at home in the White House, and once members realized they could not see Nixon as readily as they had Johnson they began to complain to the liaison staff.[8] Republicans had watched Lyndon Johnson and his White House heap attention and favors on Democrats, and even Republicans had enjoyed a few White House perks. Republicans likely overestimated how much attention Democrats had received from their president and expected such treatment once they won the White House. On top of this, Johnson had devoted an unprecedented amount of his energies to stroking Congress, and a similar effort from another president—especially Nixon—was unlikely.

Many of these congressional objections were the result of a conscious determination on the part of Nixon to return relations with Congress to a more healthy condition after what he considered the excesses in the Johnson and

Kennedy years. Evans and Novak argue that Kennedy and Johnson had transformed the congressional relations operation into a "service agency" for
members of Congress, and one member of Harlow's congressional relations
staff commented publicly, "We're going to wean the Congress off the White
House teat."[9] The weaning process proved to be a painful one as members
of Congress resented the withdrawal of favors.

The legislative staff did make efforts to build a friendly relationship.
From one to three on Wednesday afternoons Timmons and Harlow held "office hours" in Gerald Ford's Minority Leader's office and listened to members' concerns. Much of what they heard were complaints about members'
dealings with a cabinet department or not being invited to a state dinner and
were of little consequence to the legislative agenda. These sessions did provide an opportunity for Harlow to demonstrate his access. One Republican
member commented that "Sometimes, Harlow would get on the phone and
settle it right away. That would be very impressive."[10] By making members of
the House come through Ford these meetings enhanced Ford's credibility.
The liaison staff considered these meetings of some value in building up general goodwill, but of no use in furthering the president's legislative agenda.
Given the demands on the time of both Harlow and Timmons, they found it
hard to continue to invest that amount of time and the meetings were eventually dropped.

While the Nixon liaison staff retained the organization based on membership utilized by the Kennedy and Johnson White House, it resembled the
small Eisenhower staff in it size and approach. Some of the decline in liaison
staff resulted from Nixon's relative lack of interest in congressional relations
and maintaining congressional favor, but some of the motivation was a strategic concern for the proper use of departmental resources. They preferred to
leave as much as possible in the hands of the department liaison officials.

At several points in the administration, the Nixon White House attempted to reduce the size of the liaison staff and, in fact, the size of the liaison staff actually declined to six, after reaching a high of twelve earlier in
the administration. Nixon continually expressed a desire to reduce the size
of the White House staff overall and according to one aide believed that
"half the staff can do twice the work." Initially, the office was much smaller
than the Johnson staff, but as members of Congress continued to demand
the return of White House perks the congressional liaison staff began to
grow.

Initially, lobbying in the House of Representatives was headed by
Richard Cook. He was replaced in June 1973 by Max L. Friedersdorf, who re-

mained in charge for the rest of the administration. Lobbying on the Senate side was headed first by Eugene Cowen and later by Tom Korologos. The head of each operation was given the title of special assistant for legislative affairs and was assisted by a staff of two or three lobbyists who each held the title of deputy special assistant for legislative affairs. There was also an "internal" assistant given the title of deputy assistant for legislative affairs and assigned specifically to work with Harlow.

Harlow selected as his internal assistant William Timmons, a thirty-nine-year-old who had spent twelve years as an aide to Senators Alexander Wiley and William Brock. After Harlow's departure, the job of directing the congressional relations operation fell to Timmons, who lacked Harlow's reputation and had even less access to Nixon.[11] Stepping into Harlow's shoes presented a formidable challenge. Harlow had become a legendary figure to many in the administration and on the Hill. One aide commented that "No matter what happens, people lead a trail to Bryce Harlow's door. He probably has a greater memory of government than anybody else around today."[12] Timmons's credibility was further marred when Nixon took three months to name him as Harlow's successor. Johnson had committed a similar error after he named Larry O'Brien to be postmaster general. In both cases presidential reluctance to name a successor led members of Congress to keep turning to the original head of the department and cast a shadow over the eventual successor. Also, Nixon's reluctance to turn to an in-house successor like Timmons was interpreted as a lack of complete confidence in his liaison staff.

Timmons was often criticized for his distance from Congress. One Republican Senator complained in mid-1970 that "If he [Timmons] walked in here right now, I wouldn't know what he looked like."[13] Another member commented: "He doesn't get up to Capitol Hill much. Or he talks to the same people all the time—he is in constant touch with the leaders. To a degree he isolates himself."[14]

Some of the criticism of Timmons was the result of a general administration philosophy of avoiding overexposure on the Hill, especially for the person at the head of the legislative operation. Bryce Harlow had advised that whoever heads the operation save his contact with Congress for only the most important issues, leaving routine communication to the rest of the staff. Harlow felt that the assistant's presence should be used to indicate the importance of the issue. The intent was that when the head of the operation appeared on the Hill, members would know that the issue was a priority to the White House. Such distance was accepted coming from Harlow himself, because his credibility with Congress and journalists prevented people from reading the wrong message into Harlow's scarcity on the Hill. Harlow's many friends on the Hill and his well-known regard for Congress as an institution put his distance from Congress in a more favorable light. However, when Timmons took a similar approach many members construed it as a symptom of lack of respect for Congress. Timmons would serve as the primary lightning rod for congressional frustration with the White House from the time of Harlow's departure until later in the administration, when Haldeman and Ehrlichman became the target of choice. Many Republicans felt isolated from the White House but did not want to criticize the president directly, and Timmons became a more palatable target.

Interviews with members of Congress and others present a much more favorable view of Timmons. While readers of Washington's newspapers must have regarded Timmons as a failure, his continuation in office throughout Nixon's presidency and into the Ford administration suggests that he remained an effective White House lobbyist. When Timmons attempted to leave the White House at the beginning of the second term, Nixon urged him to stay. Further, after finally leaving the White House, Timmons and his assistant for the Senate Tom Korologos founded Timmons and Company, which quickly became one of Washington's most successful lobbying firms.

Under both Timmons and Harlow the staff operated in a quiet fashion. In part as a response to congressional rebellion to Johnson's very visible pressuring of Congress, the Nixon shop remained in the background, leaving more of the credit for legislation to members of Congress. The staff worried that upstaging members might revive congressional feelings of resentment or a perceived loss of independence that could damage relations in the long run and hurt congressional allies at election time.

Nixon's legislative aides were accused of framing issues into "a them-v.-us contest as they antagonize rather than persuade the lawmakers."[15] While the Nixon administration was often confrontational, attributing this to the liaison staff would be a mistake. As with many of the criticisms of the liaison staff, such complaints reflect conscious choices made by the president or others in the White House staff, contrary to the advice of the president's lobbyists.

LACK OF ACCESS

The congressional relations staff never developed a close working relationship with Nixon or his inner circle of advisors. While Bryce Harlow enjoyed access to the president, it was more restricted than the degree of access enjoyed by H. R. Haldeman, John Ehrlichman, and Henry Kissinger. Harlow never became as closely trusted by Nixon as others who had less experience in Washington. One of the reasons for the liaison staff's lack of time with the president was that Nixon's interest in foreign policy often came at the expense of domestic policy.

One member of the liaison staff commented that his relations with Haldeman and Ehrlichman were strained. "I was always bringing bad news. They never understood the congressional perspective and I was the one who had to tell them that something wouldn't fly." Another Nixon administration lobbyist reported often having his loyalty questioned when he represented the views of the Senate to Haldeman and Ehrlichman.[16] Evans and Novak reported tension between the "Downtown Staff" (those in the White House who set the legislative strategy: Haldeman, Ehrlichman, and Peter Flanigan) and the "Hill Staff" (Harlow, Timmons, and the rest of the liaison staff who had experience in Washington and worked with Congress daily).[17]

Over time Nixon increasingly came under the influence of the "Downtown Staff" and their allies who did not want to bargain with a Congress they distrusted and preferred to instead rely on public relations. By June 20, 1969, Haldeman noted in his diary that Harlow "feels (and rightly, I fear) that his working relationship with the P[resident] has badly deteriorated and is continuing downhill."[18] Harlow, frustrated by his poor working relationship with the president, eventually left the administration, leaving Nixon surrounded by advisors hostile to Congress. Nixon thus came to receive most of his political advice from Haldeman, Ehrlichman, Pat Buchanan, and Chuck Colson, all of whom had very little experience in Washington and a much more combative approach to Congress than Harlow or Timmons. In addition, members of Nixon's inner circle seldom sat in on the president's regular meetings with congressional leaders, perpetuating their insulation from congressional concerns. Over time, these voices likely shaped Nixon's view of the political world and set the administration on a more confrontational course with Congress. As this happened, the more conciliatory advice of those who worked with Congress on a daily basis was drowned out and many in the White House became distrustful of Congress to the point of being paranoid.[19]

The Office of Congressional Relations had the reputation of being on a "second-level rung" even while it was headed by Bryce Harlow, and the office seems to have received the same treatment regardless of who headed it.[20] Timmons had no regularly scheduled meetings with the president and was often kept waiting. Representative Barber B. Conable, Jr. (Republican-New York) said, "The result was that these [congressional relations] people became second-class citizens as far as the rest of the White House staff was concerned. Because they handled dirty goods and had dirty hands, they were so treated."[21] The dilemma of "boundary role persons" like legislative liaison staff has been discussed by Joseph Pika.[22] Pika described the congressional relations staff as a prototypical boundary-spanning unit because staff persons must serve both internal constituencies of the White House and the external constituency of Congress. Serving both constituencies places tension on staff members because they risk rejection by both sides. As one of Pika's sources explained, "We were trying to bridge the gap and were often neither fish nor fowl in the eyes of either."[23] One of the reasons why this tension was especially high in the Nixon administration is that the needs of the two constituencies served by the liaison office diverged so sharply. Many in the White House had little interest in the domestic policy process in Congress. By contrast, we will see in the chapter on Ronald Reagan the case of a White House that was oriented toward building the president's popularity through legislative success, thus bringing closer together the needs of the White House and Congress.

The credibility of those who worked with Congress every day was damaged by Nixon's repeated attempts to place some high-level administration official as the figurehead chief of legislative affairs. This process began when Bryce Harlow was promoted to the level of presidential counselor in late 1969. Harlow had been swamped with congressional phone calls and other details of the congressional office and had no time to dedicate to high-level strategy. Harlow was also needed for constructing broader political strategies and serving as a mentor to younger White House staff. Even though he moved up to get away from day-to day-duties, many of the demands followed him, and his promotion only encouraged members of Congress to seek him out rather than Timmons.

Harlow left the administration in December 1970 and the counselor role fell to Melvin Laird. Later, Nixon brought in Clark MacGregor to "fix" congressional relations, creating the impression that Timmons had broken it. One veteran of the Nixon White House believed that Timmons had been "shit on" by this move. MacGregor quickly declared that "The agonies of late 1969 and 1970 are a thing of the past."[24] Shortly after moving into the west wing of the White House MacGregor ordered red, white, and blue buttons that read "I Care About Congress" for White House staffers to wear. Although the *New York Times* reported that staff members began "dutifully" wearing these buttons,[25] veterans of Nixon's congressional relations staff assert that these buttons were almost never worn and quickly forgotten altogether.

In 1974, after Gerald Ford was confirmed, the new vice president was publicly given the role of "ambassador" to Congress. Kenneth BeLieu was put on the vice president's staff as a legislative consultant. He described Ford's role: "I don't think he'll be doing lobbying so much but will be kind of a conduit between the President and Congress."[26] Ford requested an office on the House side of the Capitol in addition to the office on the Senate side that the vice president traditionally used. One former White House aide warned against overestimating Ford's impact: "it would be a mistake for Jerry, the President and the Congress to think that just because of his experience on the Hill he is going to fix everything up."[27] Vice President Spiro Agnew had not played a similar role during his years as vice president. Early in the Nixon administration Agnew had walked out onto the floor of the Senate to lobby for votes. This was seen as a breach of protocol that led to considerable criticism of Agnew.[28] Agnew's energies, like those of most of the rest of the administration, were directed at public relations intended to protect Nixon's personal popularity.

The parade of higher-level supervisors for Timmons and his operation created the impression that they required supervision and could not be trusted to carry the president's message on their own. These high-level people were window dressing designed as a public relations ploy.[29] The press reported that these presidential counselors were placing tight restrictions on Timmons and his staff. While there is no evidence of this, press reports continued and it reinforced the idea that Timmons was not completely in charge. While he was described as taking over Timmons's job, MacGregor had little meaningful interaction with Congress or the congressional relations staff. One member of the staff remarked that the counselors after Harlow had "no controls that I can recall." Early on, MacGregor did have some meetings with members of Congress and did host some dinners to which legislators were invited, but such meetings were not part of the legislative strategy and likely would have occurred anyway given the friendships developed during MacGregor's ten years in Congress.

The White House used MacGregor and the other counselor appointments as a symbol of a change in attitude that never occurred. Clark MacGregor was brought into the White House because he needed a job and was owed a White House position as a payoff for being a "sacrificial lamb" and running against Hubert Humphrey. MacGregor was very supportive of Timmons and his team and in a meeting with reporters laid the blame for bad relations with Congress on Haldeman and Ehrlichman.[30]

The various counselors may have been brought in to bring some prestige into the congressional liaison office, but the transparent nature of this ploy was quickly seen by members of Congress. Further, in congressional relations, effectiveness and prestige in the long run have more to do with one's ability to speak for the president than a previous job or formal rank in the White House. Unfortunately, the president chose a parade of visible, high-level appointments made for the sake of public relations rather than granting meaningful Oval Office access to Timmons and his staff. This contributed to confusion about who spoke for the president, but it suggested that the liaison staff was not the definitive source.

Although the counselors had little to do with the specifics of congressional relations, they did play a role in the administration. Their primary focus, however, was development of policy rather than the implementation of strategy. Nixon's counselors were removed from the day-to-day line responsibilities and the barrage of phone calls that came with directing legislative affairs, to permit more time to think. MacGregor described his job as "related to the presentation, in the best possible form, of the President's legislative program, as opposed to 'back-scratching' or lobbying for votes as such."[31] In other words, MacGregor was brought in to supplement the public relations effort rather than work directly with Congress. Members of Congress likely saw this as a sign of disrespect, since the White House was showing little interest in dealing with them directly.

With the liaison staff continually passed over and counselors continually passing through, the only authoritative channels to the president for members of Congress were the relatively unfriendly Haldeman and Ehrlichman. Since members of Congress trusted neither of these men, their only hope was to speak to Nixon directly, but they were hampered by what they called "the Berlin Wall" of Haldeman and Ehrlichman.

The separation of long-term strategy and policy development from implementation does have advantages, especially in the face of the barrage of phone calls and meetings that the head of congressional relations faces. However, separating strategy development from implementation creates problems as well. One problem is that of credibility. These issues, discussed more broadly in the section below, affect the ability of the liaison officer to negotiate on behalf of the president and create uncertainty in Congress as to who speaks for the president. A second problem is that once the two functions are separated, those people engaged in long-range strategy do not come into daily contact with members of Congress and may lose sight of congressional concerns.[32]

THE CREDIBILITY OF WHITE HOUSE LIAISON

Members of the White House liaison staff need access to the Oval Office in order to serve as credible representatives of the president. Holding the trust of the president or being able to speak for the president enables a staff member to draw upon the prestige of the Oval Office. Access to the president also represents power within the White House. The importance of credibility is reflected in the views of a senior staffer in a leadership office: "There are two liaisons, there's the West Wing liaison and the East Wing liaison. The East Wing liaison we call 'mushroom people.' They are kept in the dark and fed manure. They are not part of the policy decision-making apparatus."

The ability to carry the words of the president to Congress permits a liaison staffer to act as the president's extension on the Hill. However, to be effective in negotiations they must be able to carry the president's word in a dynamic sense. It is not enough to be able to repeat what the president has said; staffers must be able to convey what the president thinks or will say and be able to provide definitive answers to lawmakers' questions and requests with the assurance that the president will follow the words of legislative assistants. The ability to speak for the president elevates the position to a high level, while failure of the president to place this trust in his congressional assistants can render the staff irrelevant. No one in Nixon's OCR held this kind of credibility, leaving members of Congress to seek out others for the definitive word of the president.

The problems of the Nixon administration were especially puzzling given Bryce Harlow's strong views on the importance of access. In speeches around town and in private conversations with other lobbyists, Harlow had made clear the importance of access to the president. Harlow argued that it is not enough to have access to the president—members of Congress must know that it exists.[33]

The access of the Nixon administration lobbyists was especially problematic because it contrasted so sharply with the clout held by Larry O'Brien under Kennedy and Johnson. While Nixon's legislative assistants were able to see him, their contact seems limited next to O'Brien's intimate interaction with the two presidents he served. O'Brien's greatest tool was his closeness to the presidents he served and they were always careful not to undermine him. This was not always the case under Nixon. Calls from members of Congress went to all offices all over the White House and members found that they could often easily circumvent Timmons by going directly to Haldeman or Ehrlichman. One Republican senator complained that Timmons did not hold the same kind of sway as O'Brien had: "The question really turns on how high a priority they place on liaison within the executive branch. With Larry O'Brien, you knew he had the authority and that you could get your views before the President. The new group has a much more narrowly based authority. If they are going to be effective, this must change."[34]

The imposition of presidential counselors in between Bill Timmons and his staff diminished their perceived access to the president. Members of Congress did not want to talk to the legislative relations staff, they instead wanted to talk with the president or with Harlow or other counselor-level appointees in charge of congressional relations.

> The trouble was that no one wanted to talk to the staff; they all wanted to talk to Harlow. Of course, they really wanted to talk to the President, but they would settle for Bryce. But no would settle for anything less than Bryce.[35]

With phone calls from Congress coming into the White House through numerous routes the liaison staff found it difficult to coordinate White House responses and remain informed themselves. Once members found that they could circumvent the legislative staff, the staff lost more of its credibility. Also, having members of Congress talking with numerous people in the White House made it much more likely that no consistent position was coming out of the administration.

Often presidential legislation is presented to members in terms of the president's needs. This is particularly true for members of the president's party, who will be told that "the president needs your support on this bill." This message, coming from someone who has infrequent contact with the president, carries little weight and will have little impact.

The access that lies at the heart of effective executive-branch lobbying encompasses access to all of the power structure in the executive branch. This goes beyond the president, to include the vice president and cabinet members as well as key White House advisors. Larry O'Brien had clout on the Hill because he had clout within the administration. Kennedy and Johnson gave O'Brien power to direct the efforts of cabinet members. Members of Congress realized that O'Brien was in a position to offer assurances from the president or virtually anyone in the administration. By limiting the credibility of his liaison staff, Nixon limited their effectiveness both with Congress and within the administration. This left the domestic policy goals of the president in the hands of individuals who were better acquainted with public relations than congressional norms.

Richard Nixon and Congress

According to Bryce Harlow, "Richard Nixon was the type of individual man who wanted to be President with the least possible interference from other actors in the political system."[36] Nixon did not enjoy the kind of personal politics that had absorbed Johnson and avoided dealing with members of Congress whenever possible. Nixon only attended meetings with members of Congress after considerable prodding, and his scheduled meetings with Republican leaders were held every other Tuesday in contrast to the weekly meetings hosted by Eisenhower, Kennedy, and Johnson.

Nixon warned the liaison staff in late 1969 that he did not wish to become intimately involved in dealing with members of Congress.

> With regard to our future Congressional relations, I want to emphasize a bit on what I told you earlier with regard to my future activities on issues like ABM and Haynsworth. In both of these cases, Presidential prestige was called upon far too often and I will not let it happen again. I think we are becoming too "common" with our letters and phone calls to members of the House and Senate, and I want you to watch these things closely to see that, with our new setup, I make such calls when they really matter, but not just routinely every time something happens on the House or Senate floor which we like. Above everything else, however, I want it clearly understood by the entire Congressional Staff that I cannot and will not intercede with individual Senators in order to enlist their vote for Administration programs. I will see some of them in a group only when the stakes are high and when we feel there is a reasonable chance we can succeed.[37]

Nixon could be persuaded to meet with members, but he did so as a duty. As one staff member said, "You had to drag him screaming into having a leadership meeting." This assistant reflected: "I don't know how he got elected. He didn't like being with people." Treasury Secretary John Connally called Nixon "A humorless man, and extremely private, almost antisocial."[38] One Republican member of the House who served with Nixon simply remarked, "Nixon wasn't Mr. Personality." Even those members who described their relations with Nixon as good qualify their praise. One Republican commented, "Nixon had a good relationship with members, if we could get to him."

When Nixon did talk with members of Congress he wanted to do so on his own terms because he felt it could diminish the mystique of the presidency. He made sure that "they come to the president, the president does not go to the Hill." Nixon expressed a willingness to schedule "congressional half-hours," time set aside for a number of short visits that would permit members of Congress to see the president in the Oval Office to make presentations and so on, so that they could claim they had seen the president.[39]

Even when Nixon agreed to participate, he wanted policy discussion excluded. "I think we should be pretty generous with regard to requests by Congressmen for photos with constituents and so forth. You could work this in these morning periods that you have available. What is important is that under no circumstances must we have anybody in if he's going to talk substance."[40] Nixon was generally less than pleased with these more superficial meetings. After one congressional half-hour Nixon remarked: "Boy, we had the damnedest collection today. Jesus Christ what a bunch of nuts."[41] Frequently, after informal meetings with members, Nixon would ask his staff, "Tell me what good that meeting did." Their response was often, "It was money in the bank—maybe you can draw it out next week."

Nixon did enjoy dealing with a few members (Senators Stennis, Mansfield, and Long) but generally, the liaison staff found Nixon to be shy and reluctant to deal with members. Gerald Ford found that he saw less of Nixon, whom he regarded as a personal friend as well as a political ally, than he had Johnson.[42] Nixon was persuaded to have a series of private breakfasts with Senate Majority Leader Mike Mansfield. Later Carl Albert was included. One staffer conceded that "I can't think of anything tangible we got out of those breakfasts—except that they might have opposed us more if the breakfasts would not have been held." Despise these lukewarm reviews the staff pushed Nixon to have more informal meetings with members in hopes of improving relations.

Within the White House, Nixon's reluctance to meet with members revealed to the staff a distance from Congress that may have confirmed their distrust and lack of respect. In an August 1970 meeting with the president, Senator Robert Dole of Kansas, who served as one of the administration's chief defenders in Congress, complained that he had not even met Ehrlichman.[43] When Gerald Ford met Ehrlichman, he was less than overwhelmed.

> We had a hot issue where he had to get the White House Domestic Council, which Ehrlichman headed, on the same wavelength with Republicans in Congress. So I got all the Senate and House Republican leadership and members involved to my office, and Ehrlichman came with two of his people. Everyone was trying to find an answer, but John Ehrlichman sat over in a corner in a big chair, obviously bored to death. He was silent, totally disdainful of the serious effort we were making to work out an accommodation. I'm not sure he didn't sleep; he had his hands over his eyes. I was disgusted.[44]

When Nixon could be persuaded to invite a member into his office to discuss policy, he was reluctant to press a member for a vote. While speaking to a group of Republican members whose vote was needed to pass an extension of a surcharge on the income tax, Nixon asked members to stick with the administration, but qualified his appeal: "You must vote in accord with your consciences. If you don't see your way clear to going along, I won't hold it against you."[45]

The liaison staff prepared detailed "talking notes" for the president for his meetings with lawmakers. These talking notes include background information on the members who would be present and specific points about the legislation that the president should raise. Some even provided specific wording to use. Even presidents like Johnson and Ford, who were familiar with members and the legislative process, made use of such notes to make sure that they were current on a member's situation and that no important details would be forgotten. Nixon used such talking notes and would faithfully follow staff suggestions with the exception of pressing for a commitment on a vote. Much to the consternation of his staff Nixon would consistently fail to "close the deal" and request a member's vote. One assistant considered this reluctance almost counterproductive. He would sit in these meetings and hear Nixon explain to a member that he understood if the member could not vote with him on a bill, and the liaison staffer would wonder "Why did I bring this guy here?" After seeing the president fail to press for a commitment, a member might feel that the president was not truly committed to the legislation; the failure of the president to apply pressure likely diminished the ability of his staff to make similar requests.

Contrary to some reports, Nixon did not object to his liaison staff pressing for votes.[46] Liaison staff rejected the suggestion that Nixon did not want them asking legislators for votes, but agreed that Nixon was personally uncomfortable doing so himself. One emphatically declared that "Nothing he ever said or implied told us we should not be up there." Looking back on his administration, Nixon told one staff member shortly before his death that "one of your strengths is that you were up there."[47]

While Nixon's refusal to press for votes would suggest to members that the issue was not important enough to merit some arm-twisting, Nixon was willing to punish those who failed to vote with him. In a memo to some of his top staff Nixon outlined his soft sell as well as his hardball response.

> 4. With regard to all those who opposed [the administration on the ABM and Haynsworth's nomination], I want one general rule followed without deviation. You are undoubtedly going to have instances where people like Jordan, Griffin, Schweiker, Percy et al. may contact members of the White House staff indicating their willingness to support us in the next nomination or on some other issue

which may be coming up. They will, of course, do this only when we are sure to win it. I want the answer in each case to be along these lines: "Thank you very much but the President wants you to feel free to vote your politics on this issue. He doesn't need you on this one." This will be quite effective and very hard for them to respond to.

· · ·

7. It goes without saying that those who are in this group should be given completely proper treatment so they cannot have anything obvious to complain about but none of them should get in to see me until I have gone through the list—one by one—of seeing all of those who supported us on these issues. I anticipate that this will take several months.[48]

The contrast between the president's soft sell and the discourteous hard sell from some of his staff undermined relations with Congress.[49] Members of Congress often felt that if they opposed the White House on any vote they would be regarded as enemies, regardless of their overall level of support for the president.[50]

While there was some legitimate interest in protecting the institution of the presidency, much of the administration's style in dealing with Congress is a reflection of Richard Nixon's personality. According to members of his staff, Nixon did not avoid asking members for their votes because of a deep philosophical objection; it was simply not in his nature to do so.

The Nixon administration publicly talked about restoring the "aura" of the presidency and restoring the credibility of the office. However, the Nixon administration's concern about the proper use of the Oval Office in lobbying seems inconsistent with their hardball politics. Nixon, like every other president studied, was certainly not above making deals. When Bryce Harlow advised Nixon that the Republican party was considering retiring a $250,000 campaign debt for Senator Saxbe without specifically linking this money to his vote on the pending ABM treaty, Nixon responded, "I disagree—Make the deal tougher with Saxbe—He doesn't understand anything else."[51]

For most of his presidency, Nixon received relatively little blame for the distance between the president and Congress. The press and Congress were generally content to blame either Bill Timmons or "the Berlin Wall" of Haldeman and Ehrlichman, but many of the problems came from the president himself and were merely reflected in the actions of others in the White House. Members of the White House staff were reluctant to ascribe these problems to Nixon himself in part out of loyalty but also because attributing blame to the president would suggest that relations were unlikely to improve. Haldeman and Ehrlichman took the blame silently and it was not until

Nixon's popularity began to plunge that staff were willing to blame the president.

Nixon's basic attitude toward Congress undoubtedly shaped the relationship between the White House and the Hill. Unfriendliness toward Congress all too often seemed acceptable in the Nixon White House. Nixon's dislike for Congress was clear to some members. According to Representative Barber B. Conable Jr. (R-NY), "Nixon didn't like politicians, and that included Congressmen."[52] Bryce Harlow said, "Nixon respected Congress as an institution but he was not often impressed by its individual members. He simply would not concede that a majority of congressmen were competent to deal with the rigors of managing the nation's affairs."[53] Once the Watergate tapes were released, members saw confirmation of a lack of respect from the White House.

Nixon's reluctance to trust even Republicans is revealed in a memo to Haldeman. The president planned to horde campaign funds that he thought would be wasted by congressional candidates.

> One of our most important projects for 1970 is to see that our major contributors funnel all their funds through us except for nominal contributions to the campaign committees. . . . What we need to do is to see that these funds are sent to the right people; but beyond that, we can also see that they are not wasted in overhead or siphoned off by some of the possible venal types on campaign committees. . . . If we can get funds channeled through our hands, we can also see that they are used more effectively than would be the case if the candidates receive them directly.[54]

Nixon returned to more conciliatory terms after the 1970 election, when Republican gains failed to materialize and the administration faced some criticism from congressional Republicans. With an eye toward the 1972 election Nixon seemed to soften his stand on nonsupporters:

> I think there is a tendency for us not to recognize that people like Brooke, Case, Schweiker, Saxbe, Cooper, Percy, even Javits et al., have their constituencies, or at least believe they are playing to their constituencies, but try to be with us when they can, and when they are against us do not try to make a virtue out of being against us, which of course was Goodell's major fault.
>
> I want you to emphasize with our staff that with all the Republicans that may be against us, I want even-handed treatment and once we have lost a battle in getting their votes, we forget that battle and

try to win the next one. This does not mean that we do not give some special attention to our friends, but it does mean that you don't read people out of the Party at this point when we're going to need every one of them with us in 1972.[55]

However, before the next election rolled around Nixon was again frustrated with Congress. "You have to remember that there are very, very few people with any backbone in the Senate or House anymore, and that they are really patsies for a group that comes in and puts it to them hard on an issue."[56]

Prior to the 1972 election, Bob Dole, as chair of the Republican National Committee, asked the Nixon campaign to share some of its resources. The Committee to Re-Elect the President had about $40 million whereas the national committee had only about $4 million.[57] The Nixon campaign argued that if Nixon won big enough he would help other Republicans on the ballot. Haldeman thought that the best way to gain clout with Congress was to run ahead of them while the liaison staff argued for giving money to congressional candidates and believed that the failure to put more money and effort into key races in 1972 may have cost the Republicans as many as thirty seats in the House.

An important difference between the Nixon approach to Congress and Eisenhower's approach is that Eisenhower maintained a friendly but distant relationship with Congress out of respect. While he occasionally privately expressed anger at the action of members, such outbursts were rare and did not implicate Congress broadly. Nixon, according to one legislative assistant, "crapped on" Congress often. Nixon's attitude and his willingness to express it to the rest of the White House staff served to poison congressional relations.

Given Nixon's reluctance to deal directly with members of Congress, the need for help from congressional leadership increased. Nixon and Harlow were both influenced by the Eisenhower approach to Congress and were comfortable leaving much of the administration's agenda in the hands of the Republican leadership. However, this did not mean that Nixon wanted to work closely with the Republican leadership. In fact he dealt with them as little as possible and seemed to have little regard for their abilities. Haldeman recorded in his diary that in a long conversation with some of his staff Nixon "got into quite a long thing on the lack of leadership in the Congress, particularly in the Senate, making the point that Gerry Ford really is the only leader we've got in either house."[58]

Presidents often express reservations about the party leaders with whom they serve. However, Nixon seemed to have little fondness for any of the congressional leaders or rank-and-file members. Eisenhower by contrast was often frustrated with some of his own party's leaders, but he enjoyed working with other high-ranking members like Everett Dirksen and enjoyed meeting in secret with Senate Majority Leader Lyndon Johnson and House Speaker Sam Rayburn. Nixon seems to have granted few exceptions to his dislike of Congress.

An entry from Haldeman's diary (March 6, 1973) reveals Nixon's frustration with Congress and his willingness to vent it directly to congressional leaders:

> E[hrlichman] reported earlier on the P[resident]'s leadership Meeting this morning. This was just with (Senator Hugh) Scott and (Gerald) Ford, and we knew that Scott intended to come in and complain about things on the Hill and suggest that the P[resident] have a series of meetings up there with the Republican senators. Scott started off doing exactly that, and said the mood was very bad, and whined on and on, for two or three minutes. The P[resident] just let him go, then stepped in and used a lot of apparently pretty strong profanity, and said that the senators are nothing but a bunch of asses. We never get anything from them, there's nothing that does any good, no matter what we do for them. We bring them down and give them cookies, and treat them nice socially in order to cover the things that we need to do, but we can't count on them for any vote and never have been able to.[59]

Whether Nixon's reluctance to see members resulted from personal discomfort with meeting with members or from a general lack of respect for Congress, members likely saw the distance between the White House and Congress as slight. After Johnson's relentless embracing of Congress, the Nixon White House's distance may have stung congressional egos. Members of Congress may have found themselves longing for invitations to the White House to have their arms twisted.

Public Relations

The Nixon public relations strategy was designed to help the administration's legislative efforts in two ways. First, these efforts would build up Nixon's popularity and make him a more formidable opponent for congressional battles. Second, Nixon believed that if he were personally popular, Republicans would gain control of Congress. Neither plan worked.

The Nixon administration's approach to public relations differs from that of other administrations in that it more narrowly focused on building up Nixon's personal popularity rather than building support for specific legislative proposals. While every White House has been anxious to build the popularity of its president, no other seems to have as consistently placed general popularity ahead of support for specific policies.

The Nixon approach to public opinion with its placement of legislative issues in the background can be seen in the administration's use of Lyn Nofziger. Although he was formally assigned to the congressional relations operation, Nofziger had little contact with the rest of the staff and did no lobbying. Nofziger did have some contact with members of Congress, but his efforts were directed at using members of Congress to counter attacks on the president and defend him personally rather than building coalitions for particular issues. His job was, in the words of one member of the staff, to get members to "cheer for the President when he does something right, to defend him when he's attacked by his enemies and to attack his enemies."[60] Members were often too busy to spend much time and effort in defense of the president and Nofziger found that the best way to get them to give speeches defending Nixon was to write them and send them over to the Hill. Every day Nofziger would write a half dozen or so one-minute speeches for House members and send them over to the Republican leadership so that they could be distributed to members on the Hill.

Nofziger was sometimes used to feed derogatory material to the media about Nixon's opponents.[61] Sometimes speeches would be sent to people beyond Congress. In April 1969, Nixon directed the staff to draw up a plan "to see that a number of Senators, Congressmen, Governors, etc. make appropriate statements on the first 100 days."[62] Later he told Haldeman that setting up a group "for the purpose not of cheering but solely of attacking and defending, is of the highest priority."[63] This function was transferred to the Republican National Committee when Bob Dole became chairman and Nofziger became director of communications. For the last two years of Nixon's first term the communications operation of the Republican National Committee remained an extension of the White House and was heavily involved in propagandizing the Nixon presidency.

In 1970 the White House recruited congressional allies for an unofficial "floor watch" system to respond to congressional critics. In the Senate they used a "man-to-man" defense that assigned allies to specific administration critics, specifically Senators Muskie, Kennedy, McGovern, Fullbright, and Proxmire. Each of these critics was assigned a principal defender and a backup. For example, Muskie's principal "defender" was Bob Dole, backed up by Henry Bellmon. On the House side the administration deployed a "zone" defense. Congressional allies were assigned to monitor specific days of the week. Each day of the week featured a defender—one of five Republican House members running for the Senate and "available to speak out on major issues which can give them favorable publicity exposure." For example, on Wednesdays Sam Devine was the principal defender who was backed up by Burt Talcott. Monday's designated Senate candidate was George Bush.[64]

Paralleling Nofziger's work with Congress, Chuck Colson was working with outside groups and organizations in a similar fashion. According to one member of the congressional relations staff, while the Colson operation was the best developed operation of its kind to date it did not serve Nixon's legislative goals as effectively as Anne Wexler's operation would serve Carter's a few years later. Colson ran an effective outreach program and developed a working relationship with many groups, but his office did not coordinate with the legislative affairs team very often and the interest group operation became another propaganda tool of the White House. Colson did coordinate the efforts of interest groups with the legislative team on a few major issues, but according to one of Nixon's legislative assistants, "I can't say they were always successful." The use of interest groups to assist with lobbying was most successful with the White House's efforts to gain approval of the Anti-Ballistic Missile Treaty. Interest groups were not effective at helping the administration with approval of the Super Sonic Transport or the nominations of Haynsworth or Carswell to the Supreme Court.

Despite the liaison staff's wishes, interest groups were never effectively brought under the control of the congressional liaison staff. They did work with Chuck Colson and others, but this never paid off with the kind of coordinated effort that would be found in later administrations. Some of the problems resulted from the administration's reluctance to take the interest group operations away from building support for the president personally.

NIXON'S WAIT-AND-SEE APPROACH

Nixon believed that in the long run the presidential popularity produced by public relations would lead to victory for administration legislation and Republican candidates. In contrast, Lyndon Johnson always attempted to press ahead as quickly as possible and believed that his chances of victory were constantly eroding. Nixon seemed to believe that the electorate would produce a transformation of Congress that would make future victories easier. Much of the difference between the two approaches is that between minority and majority presidents. Lyndon Johnson, given a landslide victory in

1964 and lopsided control of Congress, realized that the political climate couldn't get much better. Elected with just over 43 percent of the vote and facing both houses of Congress in Democratic hands, Nixon likely thought that things couldn't get much worse.

Nixon discounted the efficacy of bargaining and instead argued that good public relations would produce a popular president whom members of Congress would follow. According to Nixon a president could use his own popularity to shape electoral expectations by creating the fear of opposing a popular president: "His [the president's] popularity may go up and down, but if members of Congress see that he is determined to stay his course, they will hesitate to desert him when he is weak for fear that voters will hold them accountable when he is strong."[65] Nixon told his cabinet that they needed to make a "massive effort over a long period, and that Congress will change their minds because of public pressure if we keep it up."[66]

Haldeman described Nixon's posture in 1969 as "ready to take Congress on, and not cajole them into each vote. Let them vote us down and then stand on their record."[67] In August 1969, when a poll showed Nixon's popularity climbing to 60 percent, he had asked Haldeman and Ehrlichman to show the poll to congressional opponents "who may have thought that it will not be safe to give in to their deepest desires and kick us in the teeth.[68]

Shortly before the 1972 election the Nixon White House realized they would continue to face a large number of Democrats. Republican congressional victories never materialized and by January 1973, the White House realized that despite Nixon's landslide at the polls, little had actually changed in Washington.[69] Haldeman noted, "He [Nixon] now feels that we face a partisan situation right from the beginning of Congress, as evidenced by their approach on Vietnam, whereas we thought we would have a better relationship, at least at the start, because of the landslide election victory. Therefore, we've got to have a new attack organization directed at the top."[70] Democrats in Congress had learned that they could survive a Nixon landslide, reducing their fear of the White House further. James Cannon described the dilemma: "the voters had put in office a President that mistrusted the Congress, and a Congress that mistrusted the President."[71]

Nixon's wait-and-see approach held several drawbacks for congressional relations in the short run. At the very least, his lack of engagement signaled a lack of interest that discouraged congressional allies and emboldened potential congressional opponents. In the White House, Bryce Harlow had been disappointed that Nixon was unwilling to engage in an all-out battle for the ABM and the surtax battle in 1969.[72] Tom Korologos, Nixon's chief lobbyist in the Senate, noticed that Nixon never seemed interested in discussing domestic policy and would instead turn the discussion to foreign policy whenever possible.[73]

Congressional Republicans became frustrated with Nixon's own lack of effort despite his demands on them.[74] Notwithstanding his own reluctance to openly battle for legislation, Nixon often expressed the opinion that no one except himself was pushing legislation.[75] After a meeting with the congressional Republican leadership, Nixon complained to Haldeman.

> The P[resident] was really fed up with the attitude of the leaders. He told me to tell MacGregor that he's got to avoid letting these Leadership meetings becoming a crying towel. He's got to brief someone to step up and cheer a little bit. He made the point that if that had been a Democratic meeting, they would have cheered the P[resident]'s initiative and been babbling all over about it. He sighed and said it's such hard work for the P[resident] to have to buck them up all the time, which I can certainly understand.[76]

Nixon's attitudes provide some insights into both the administration's obsession with public opinion and the president's reluctance to meet with members of Congress. Since a Democratic Congress was unlikely to give Nixon what he wanted, he could only achieve his legislative goals by going through the people to change Congress. Since Nixon never worked with a Republican Congress it is hard to see how his approach might have changed, but it is clear that because of either his beliefs about the motivation of Congress or his personal shyness, Nixon avoided personal negotiations with members of Congress and instead waited for a more favorable Congress or public. As it turns out, Nixon would see little change in Congress and would watch his popularity decline.

DECLINE IN POPULARITY

Public support for Nixon never proved strong enough to give him the leverage with Congress that he sought. In fact, his approval generally declined over the course of his presidency. His victory in 1972 and inauguration for a second term created a brief reversal in this trend but this change was short-lived, and the erosion of support continued until the Watergate scandal caused his standing to plummet. Nixon's approval rating as reported by Gallup polls dropped from 67 percent in January 1973 to 23 percent at the time of his resignation in August 1974.[77]

This dramatic decline in popularity demonstrates the limits of the effect of public opinion on congressional support and influence. During his second term, Nixon staffers admit that it became easier to vote against the president as his approval dropped. One staff member commented that even though members of Congress will vote on the merits of legislation, low presidential approval often provides too great a temptation for members of Congress. When the president's popularity is low, "It's advantageous and even fun to kick him around." The Nixon staff also observed that Republican members were reluctant to attach themselves to administration legislation for fear of being linked to the Watergate scandal.[78]

As the president's approval dropped, the White House congressional relations staff publicly discounted the impact of Nixon's lack of popularity on their legislative package. Bryce Harlow pointed out that "Members don't vote on such things as farm problems, minimum wage, appropriation ceiling levels, national defense requirements and projects for their districts and state because of the President's expression on tapes."[79] Tom Korologos suggested that long-standing ideological and partisan divisions were being overlooked while many votes were being attributed to "impeachment politics." While he asserted that "On issues like school busing and military aid, they are going to vote their record, not on Watergate," one unnamed White House aide suggested that Korologos's explanation "sounds remarkably like whistling in the dark."[80]

While Nixon's legislative assistants were attempting to put the best face on a bad political situation, there is some truth in their explanations. Just as observers must be cautious not to overestimate the influence of a popular president, they must also be cautious not to assume that the entire legislative process changes because the president becomes less popular. Today, veterans of Nixon's administration admit that the drop in opinion made a difference, but they point out the limits to the impact of low public standing. One Nixon staffer commented that "Popularity matters except that things have to be done." As Charles Jones notes, "this nation has a government, not just a president."[81] Members of Congress are not going to vote against the president's position simply because the president is unpopular, especially on important issues. Unpopular presidents do not so completely taint legislative proposals as to make them unpalatable to members.[82] Ironically, Nixon's trouble in the polls offered a kind of freedom. Tom Korologos argued that since things couldn't get much worse, they were free to do what they wanted. He recalled the impact on his reception on the Hill:

> People used to laugh at me. A senator would come up to me and say about some bill they'd just passed, "You're not going to veto that

one, are you?" I'd say, "You don't think it could hurt our image do you?" When you're down to 25 per cent in the polls, there's not a lot you can worry about, is there? You don't stop and worry about what the Greeks or the Blacks are going to think. Actually, a lot of good government was going on in those days.[83]

The Nixon administration's experience suggests that the impact of popularity will vary across issues and according to the source of popularity. Constituent concerns dictate that most votes will be independent of a popular or unpopular president. However, members of Congress use votes of little or no interest to their districts to distance themselves from an unpopular president.

Nixon's lack of popularity in 1973 and 1974 resulted from concerns about his character, rather than from concerns about the policies of his administration. Therefore his decline in the polls served to implicate his character rather than his policies. This is not to say that a tarnished character is irrelevant, but that it creates a different dynamic in the process than more policy-oriented problems. Nixon's character-based popularity problems served to undermine his personal credibility and his general bargaining position with Congress. Watergate had little to do with most votes that members cast. A lack of popularity based upon public unhappiness over the political direction of his legislative program would produce general reluctance to support his program, rather than an increased likelihood of undermining him.

PRESTIGE

Nixon's belief that presidential popularity would translate into legislative success reflects one side of what Sam Kernell has termed "going public." Kernell describes going public as "a strategy whereby a president promotes *himself* and *his policies* in Washington by appealing to the American public for support"[84] (emphasis added). Nixon chose to promote himself rather than his policies.

The Nixon approach might be described as a general prestige effect. Researchers have attempted to correlate a president's public approval ratings with success in Congress with mixed results. For example, Jon Bond and Richard Fleisher suggest that as presidential prestige increases, support increases only among the president's partisans, and that partisan opponents actually responded negatively to increased presidential prestige.[85] In the more extensive analysis offered in their book, Bond and Fleisher's discussion of batting averages and individual and group support scores provides little evidence of a general effect.[86] They report low levels of correlation and statistically insignificant probit and regression coefficients. George Edwards, Mark Peterson and, most recently, Ken Collier and Terry Sullivan also failed to find any empirical linkage.[87]

Other researchers have used sophisticated models to uncover a small general prestige effect. Charles Ostrom and Dennis Simon use a structural equation to demonstrate what they call a dynamic or reciprocal linkage between presidential success in Congress and popular support. Their analyses suggest that declining popularity has a substantial and direct, though somewhat amorphous, effect on presidential successes. Ostrom and Simon estimate this effect at a three-point decline in roll-call victories for each ten-point decline in presidential popularity.[88] Douglas Rivers and Nancy Rose use a simultaneous equations model to suggest a slightly more complex, dynamic relationship.[89] Through it, a one-percent change in approval generates a one-point increase in legislative success. Most recently, Brace and Hinckley have uncovered a similar effect in which presidents gained 7.5 percent in victories for each 10 percentage points they get in the polls.[90]

If members of Congress are motivated by electoral concerns, the president's general level of approval will have a limited impact in most cases. As Rivers and Rose argue, the president's approval is not a good barometer of constituent interests.[91] Prestige may still play a broader role. George Edwards suggests that prestige may operate in the background and contribute to the effectiveness of other presidential resources. Also, as Charles Jones points out, there may be an asymmetry in the effect of presidential prestige, or limits on how much members are willing to oppose a popular president.[92] Supporting a popular president may do more to avoid opposition than to create support. Jones quotes one Republican member of the House who concluded that his ability to oppose a popular Reagan was limited: "Maybe I can get away with voting against him once, but with two, I'm dead meat."[93]

Bond and Fleisher point out that presidential prestige is unlikely to have a systematic effect, because most citizens lack the information to judge lawmakers on their continuing support of a president. Bond and Fleisher do note that while overall levels of support for a president are not likely to be important in congressional elections, on key issues support for the president could become a deciding factor in an election.[94] Voters likely see little importance in overall levels of congressional support and are more likely to judge members' willingness to work with the president based on a few issues that they regard as important, or issues on which members of Congress feel they share a common fate with the president.[95] Voters will only test congressional loyalties to the president on those issues they feel are worthwhile. However, the president's ability to turn specific legislation into important issues for voters creates an opportunity for presidential influence. Presidents also have the ability to make issues important to constituent definitions of "liberal" or "conservative" that may become important in voters' choices. We specifically examine the role of the president in shaping voters' views of issues in the chapter on Ronald Reagan.

Nixon and Departmental Relations

The Nixon administration relied heavily on departmental liaison offices, but in order to do so the staff needed to upgrade these offices. At the time they took office, there were only two people serving as legislative assistants in the departments at the assistant secretary level; the others were serving as "assistants to the secretaries." While the difference in titles is subtle, there are three important disadvantages to the assistant to the secretary position: lower pay, no Senate confirmation, and little clout within the department. The White House hoped that increasing salaries would attract higher-quality personnel.[96] Timmons also believed that by elevating the legislative affairs officer to the assistant secretary level it would give them more clout within the department and empower them to get other parts of the department to serve the legislative strategy and to cut through departmental red tape. Before the elevation of these offices, the liaison official for the departments often had little contact with the heads and instead worked under an assistant secretary.[97] Finally, by upgrading these positions and bringing in better people, Timmons hoped to transform these individuals into people with enough credibility to lobby Congress on issues beyond the immediate interests of their departments. As long as these individuals remained at lower ranks and wages, they would be capable of doing little more than pushing their departments' agendas.

Timmons also hoped to increase White House control over the appointment of these officials in order to control the quality of appointees and as a means of creating a team that would respond to the White House, rather than to departmental demands.

This process had begun in the Kennedy and Johnson administrations under Larry O'Brien, who had similar concerns about the effectiveness of these lobbyists. However, previous administrations had often relied upon cabinet secretaries to make these changes. As a result, changes were unevenly implemented and the officers remained more committed to their own interests than to the White House. In some cases, the organic legislation that had created the departments specified the title *assistant secretary,* making it difficult to add new positions. To overcome this problem, the Nixon White House turned to a pool of jobs available through the Office of Management and Budget. The use of the OMB pool also meant that the appointment could be made by the White House rather than the cabinet secretaries. After the 1972 election, Nixon gave Timmons control over the appointment of these officials. The upgrading of these positions and bringing their selection under the control of the White House worked perfectly, according to one member of Nixon's team.

The White House staff met regularly with departmental liaison officers on Saturdays to discuss strategy and to share information. Departments were also required to put together weekly reports that included the progress of various bills and the long-range outlook for legislative issues.

Departmental lobbyists had primary responsibility for their departments' bills but were also used to lobby members on bills outside their jurisdiction. This function was one of the primary motivations for the upgrading of their positions. Cabinet liaison officers were expected to develop very close working relationships with the committee chairs and members their departments did regular business with. The use of departmental lobbyists both as managers of departmental legislation and as auxiliary lobbyists on other administration legislation became more important as the size of the White House liaison staff decreased.

Conclusion

The Nixon approach to Congress was shaped by political weakness and by Nixon's view of Congress. Without a Republican majority or a strong electoral mandate the Nixon administration faced a struggle in Congress. One of Nixon's legislative assistants described the political and policy problems they faced early in the term as "immense."

In response, Nixon engaged in an aggressive public relations campaign that might be more typical of presidential leadership under individualized pluralism. This effort shunned traditional modes of bargaining in Washington. It was designed to build support for Nixon personally and seldom focused on getting citizens behind specific legislative proposals. Nixon gambled that this public relations effort would produce popularity for him and that this popularity could then be converted into legislative victories, because lawmakers would fear voter reprisals. Why Nixon expected that he would do better than the immensely popular Eisenhower, with whom he served eight years, is unclear. The Republicans had lost their majority two years into Eisenhower's presidency and by 1958 were barely able to win the one-third of congressional seats needed to sustain vetoes.

Nixon's personal distance from members of Congress took him out of the bargaining community that was essential to success under institutionalized pluralism, alienating congressional leaders who expected the president to work through them. As Nixon waited for the public to rally behind his cause, members of Congress from both parties became frustrated with his lack of commitment to legislation, and Nixon's unwillingness to invest in his congressional relations staff hampered their effort to build coalitions. The president's unwillingness to share more of his campaign money with congressional Republicans in the 1972 campaign reflects the extent to which some in the White House believed that what was good for Nixon was good for the Republican party. Thus, when the public relations effort failed to produce the groundswell of support for Nixon, the administration was left with few means of influencing Congress.

6

THE FORD
ADMINISTRATION

WHILE SCHOLARS HAVE DEBATED WHETHER AN ELECTION
can produce a mandate for a president, it was clear that Gerald Ford could
not claim one.[1] Ford's path to the presidency began when he was nominated
by Richard Nixon to replace Spiro Agnew and it was completed when Nixon
himself resigned. Ford had never been elected by a constituency larger than
the Fifth Congressional District of Michigan. He had been chosen as vice
president based on his reputation within the Congress, but outside of Congress Gerald Ford was far from a household name. The White House staff
noted that Eisenhower had been able to transcend partisan politics and institutional rivalries by drawing upon electoral strength, but that "President
Ford has not been tested at the polls and hence cannot rely on the mandate
argument which might allow him to present himself as being 'above politics.'"[2]

Congressional resentment of Nixon undermined the goodwill that Ford
brought with him from his service in the House, and pardoning Nixon only
reminded Congress of Ford's connection to his predecessor's problems. One
of the first legislative strategy papers produced by the Ford White House
began its conclusion on an ominous tone: "President Ford holds office at a
most unpropitious moment in history."[3] Outside the White House the sentiment was the same. One Republican member of the House concluded,

"Jerry was a marked president almost from the moment he became president."

The congressional revolt against executive power was in full swing. Congress was changing laws and building up its staff in order to bring down the "imperial presidency" that had developed under Johnson and Nixon. The election of 1974 brought in a large group of new members who embraced an open, decentralized legislative structure. The Ford administration could not rely on dealing only with a few party leaders and committee chairs. Rather, close attention had to be paid to virtually every member. Within Congress, power was dispersed by changes to the committee system, and party leaders began to lose their ability to deliver votes.

With no mandate and few partisans in Congress, Ford faced a resurgent Congress. What he did have was years of experience and friendship in Congress and the power to veto legislation. Thus the key elements of the Ford legislative approach were the use of friendly relations and, when that failed, a veto. He hoped to rebuild the relationship between the branches. Three days after becoming president, Ford told a joint session of Congress, "I do not want a honeymoon with you. I want a good marriage."[4] He got neither. The honeymoon ended abruptly when he pardoned Nixon, and the good marriage was precluded by continued tensions between the branches and a reassertion of congressional power. This left Ford reliant on the use of the presidential veto to try to restrain the agenda of a heavily Democratic Congress.

The Ford Staff

Ford selected John O. Marsh to oversee congressional relations and gave him the rank of counselor to the president. A four-term Democratic congressman, Marsh left the House of Representatives in 1971, but he returned to Washington in 1973 to serve in the Nixon administration as assistant secretary of defense for congressional relations. After serving on Ford's vice presidential staff, he was elevated to the position of counselor in the new Ford administration. Marsh played a role similar to the presidential counselors under Richard Nixon. He had formal authority over the legislative and public liaison operations in the White House, and Ford used him as a general troubleshooter and as a policy advisor on a wide array of policies including personnel, the economy, defense, and other major political concerns.[5]

Marsh's day-to-day contact with the liaison staff and Congress was limited, but he worked closely with the head of the staff on legislative strategy.[6]

While Marsh had jurisdiction over congressional relations, he generally left decisions in the hands of Bill Timmons and later, Max Friedersdorf.[7] The combination of Marsh's close working relationship with the president coupled with his willingness to place confidence in Timmons and Friedersdorf helped elevate the status of the liaison staff. The change was noticed, and in January 1975 Representative Barber Conable declared that the liaison staff would no longer be "at the bottom of the pecking order."[8]

Bill Timmons continued to run the legislative shop for Ford as he had for Nixon. Timmons stayed on with the new administration until the end of 1974, when he resigned and was replaced by Max Friedersdorf. Friedersdorf had served for ten years on the staff of Congressman Richard Roudebush before being named associate director of congressional relations with the Office of Economic Opportunity. He had joined the White House congressional relations staff in June 1973. Friedersdorf selected Vern Loen to be in charge of the House and Bill Kendall to be in charge of the Senate and bragged to a cabinet meeting that his staff had a combined total of ninety-two years of experience on the Hill.[9] The staff eventually grew to sixteen, including seven lobbyists and nine supporting staff people. Supplementing the White House team was the congressional liaison staff from the Office of Management and Budget. OMB's congressional relations person met with the White House team every morning, and Max Friedersdorf described OMB liaison as playing an important role and having equal status with White House liaison.[10]

One change in the use of the staff is that for the first time all of the White House's legislative assistants attended meetings with congressional leaders.[11] Previously attendance had generally been limited to the head of the liaison staff. According to one member of the liaison team, the inclusion of the entire team "contributed greatly to a team spirit and awareness of background and the President's thinking on important issues."[12]

According to one Nixon aide, "In many respects the congressional operations has improved. Max [Friedersdorf] has been given a lot more identity than Timmons. Ford put him up front and he has high status. It appears he has more access to the President than any congressional aide since Larry O'Brien in the Kennedy Administration. Whether he does or doesn't does not make any difference—as long as it looks like he does on the Hill."[13] Friedersdorf made sure that his assistants could demonstrate their access as well. "He always put us in the loop. I had a minimum of 10 Senators who worked directly through me. If they wanted a meeting or 5 minutes with the President they would have to deal with me.[14]

Gerald Ford and Congress: A Legislative Leader
in the White House

Gerald Ford brought a high level of legislative skill back into the Oval Office. While he may not be regarded in quite the same class with Lyndon Johnson, his years as Minority Leader in the House made him one of the most experienced congressional leaders to serve as president. Ford was described by one legislative assistant as a "House gym" type. Even after joining the executive branch he continued to make occasional use of the House gym and enjoyed meeting with members in other informal settings. One veteran of the Carter administration conceded Ford's connections: "Ford had been around Washington. He had a great Rolodex, knew everyone." The White House staff found that one challenge was keeping members of Congress from dropping in for Oval Office chats with the president.

Ford had regularly scheduled meetings with Republican leaders and a bipartisan group of leaders on alternating weeks.[15] In addition, Ford had frequent consultation on special concerns such as the war in Vietnam, and some weeks he ended up meeting with leaders almost daily.[16] This contrasted sharply with Nixon's avoidance of consulting with congressional leaders.[17]

Ford's legislative style was much less confrontational. His legislative assistants are divided on whether or not Gerald Ford played "hardball" with Congress, but this disagreement seems to have much more to do with the definition of "hardball" than with the president's legislative style. Even those who argued that Ford did play hardball believe that he did so differently than Nixon. Neither would threaten members to their faces, and each took firm stands in different ways. Ford's approach was described by one assistant as much more of a "curve ball" approach, in contrast to Nixon's "fastball." Ford would focus on outmaneuvering members of Congress, while Nixon preferred to overpower them. Evans and Novak concluded that "What was called 'hardball' in Nixon's day is still fitfully played in Mr. Ford's Oval Office, more closely reflecting the personality of Richard M. Nixon than Jerry Ford but lacking the ruthless Nixonian competency."[18]

Max Friedersdorf believed that relations with Congress were better under Ford than they had been under Nixon because members of Congress liked Ford better as a person.[19] Another liaison assistant summed up: "Jerry Ford was a people person and that paid off handsomely in congressional relations."[20] Representative John Anderson (Republican-Illinois) describes working with President Ford as more of a free-flowing conversation that built to a consensus, while Nixon was more prone to give congressional leaders "flip-chart talks" in which he simply presented what he wanted.[21]

Ford's ability to personally connect the two branches was limited by institutional barriers that would overwhelm the personal friendships he had developed over twenty-five years in Congress. One former White House official warned, "The fact is that once he becomes a part of the White House he can't straddle the Constitutional divide between the two branches. Things start out fine, but pretty soon they are at each other's throats. You can only be on one side at a time; that's the way the system works."[22]

Ford's attempt to build friendly relations with Congress was undermined by his need to do what he considered to be right. One congressional Republican believed that despite his skill, Ford's presidency was doomed from the start. "Jerry was probably as well prepared to be president as anyone. He never really had a chance to get off the ground. He pardoned Nixon and that cost him the presidency and challenged his effectiveness as president." Max Friedersdorf noted that Ford's decision to stick with the administration's decision to cut back on military bases hurt their legislative agenda, and he thought that if Ford had still been in Congress he would have lobbied to keep the bases open. Ford took seriously the need to serve national interests overall and stuck with the decision.[23]

Maintaining Favor

While journalists and other observers have focused on presidents trading favors for votes, John Manley has pointed out the importance of the White House being in favor with members of Congress. In his study of the Office of Congressional Relations under Kennedy and Johnson, Manley suggests that in reality the relationship between the White House and Congress does not focus on the exchange of specific favors; rather, favors are used to create a favorable atmosphere.

> Congressmen and presidents who enjoy each other's favor are more like long-term partners than temporary allies. As partners they may sometimes disagree. But, until the partnership is dissolved each knows that he can rely on the other for some if not all of his important political needs.[24]

Manley describes being in favor as distinct from simple bargaining and logrolling, in that being in favor is "the strategic background that allows repeated calls for assistance without embarrassment or worry that too much is being asked.[25] The key difference between "maintaining favor" and "trading favors" is that maintaining favor is a strategic activity designed to serve the administration's coalition-building effort in the long run, while trading favors is related to winning the support of members on particular votes. The White House provides services to members of Congress who have been supportive in the past or who they hope will be supportive in the future with little regard to any particular vote. The difference between gaining favor and trading favors is illustrated by the Ford White House's concerns about its relationship with Senator Howard Baker. As the liaison staff's comments reveal, their fear was not so much losing a vote as losing a senator who has contributed to a number of successes and whose loss could contribute to a number of future defeats.

> Frankly, Max [Friedersdorf], I don't know how much longer we can count on fellows like Senator Baker without doing SOMETHING for them in return. While they may continue to vote with us, they may, as Senator Pearson did after we rejected his nominee for FPC, become very uncooperative. In this regard I call your attention to the succession of failures we have had in the Commerce Committee with respect to Presidential nominations where Pearson is ranking Republican.[26]

Beyond the distinction between long- and short-range coalition-building, there is nothing that clearly distinguishes between gaining favor and trading favors, because often the favors traded for votes are quite small and the kindnesses extended in order to build friendships are large. Thomas S. Foley (D-Washington) would complain that Carter's White House "kind of misunderstood that small favors can translate into big switches."[27] Max Friedersdorf was known for his belief that if you take care of the little things, the big things take care of themselves. As one Ford lobbyist pointed out, while the favors might be small the votes requested may be of little import to the congressperson. "You could translate the little favors like White House tour tickets and trips with the president into votes on issues where Senators had no major interests to defend. Most members of Congress have a tremendous sense of appreciation and we just built on that especially on some of those 'yawn' votes which turned out to be more important from the perspective of the White House."[28] Often gaining favor involves making sure that the White House liaison staff claims credit for decisions that may have been made otherwise. When others in the White House started making calls to notify senators about the approval of nominees, Friedersdorf warned, "Remember, our guys have to ask the Senators for their votes."[29]

Part of the process of gaining and maintaining favor is the handling of congressional mail and phone calls. The White House maintained a small correspondence unit of two to four people who handled hundreds of phone calls and letters from members of Congress and their staffs. Each letter or call demanded a quick reply. One Ford White House staffer said, "Every piece of outgoing mail is a political bomb—and that's the routine correspondence." Small typographical errors like mentioning the wrong state or district number in a letter could easily turn into a political problem for the administration, and failure to respond quickly to a congressional concern about even the most seemingly minor issues can be interpreted as a lack of respect for a member or for Congress at large.

Manley was reluctant to generalize beyond the two administrations he examined, but it is clear every administration studied here made some effort to maintain favor with Congress, and Ford's pursuit of a "good marriage" rather than a honeymoon matches Manley's description of "long-term partners rather than temporary allies."[30] Dwight Eisenhower believed that congenial personal relations with members of Congress were not merely convenient, but in fact indispensable to effective leadership. Eisenhower thought that if members felt hostile toward the president, leadership would become impossible. He explained his approach saying, "If you're going to do anything, you've got to make Congressmen your personal friends; that's really what I tried to do."[31] Larry O'Brien referred to politics as "an intensely personal art"[32] and used cruises on the Potomac aboard the presidential yacht *Sequoia* to lay the foundation for trust among members of Congress and the White House staff. He hoped that "if the member enjoyed the trip, that was going to make it, hopefully, a little easier to talk to him about substance in a week or two."[33] Even Nixon reluctantly agreed to social meetings and other such activities with members in order to facilitate bargaining down the road.[34]

Maintaining favor with Congress appears across administrations and in the periods of individualized and institutionalized pluralism for a number of reasons. First, the process of gaining favor facilitates coalition-building by permitting the president or congressperson to build up a reserve of goodwill rather than requiring a specific tit-for-tat exchange on every vote. Members of Congress need not have a list of patronage or other favors ready when approached by the White House staff, and the president need not have a reservoir of favors ready as each important vote approaches. Since projects, state dinners, and other such favors seldom coincide with key congressional votes, the White House can simply dispense these favors as they become available, building up a pool of goodwill with both sides making some kind of cumulative judgment rather than relying on a basic tit-for-tat or basing their response on their last exchange. As one Carter liaison staffer described it, "It's sort of like we're in the Green Stamps business. But we have to give out a lot of stamps before members will trade them in."[35] If the White House wants to trade appointments or projects for specific votes, trust between the White House and the legislator facilitates bargaining by insuring that both would fulfill their ends of the bargain. Because politics operates without written contracts, trading partners depend on trust to prevent bargaining from breaking down entirely. In this regard, gaining favor has persisted after the decline of institutionalized pluralism because it facilitates bargaining regardless of whether the president is offering institutional or electoral resources.

Second, gaining favor is widely used by the White House because it remains one of the norms within Congress. While broad political forces may drive much of the behavior in Congress, members expect some degree of civility from each other. Congress is an organization guided by rules and norms that are both institutional and personal. Tip O'Neill commented that, "Congress is a very human institution. People like to be asked, and they like to hear 'thanks.'"[36] As this civility or *comity* within Congress continues to decline,[37] lawmakers may expect this less and less from the presidency in general. However, those who are part of the president's coalition will likely continue to expect friendly treatment from their political allies.

Finally, gaining favor is relatively inexpensive. When Jimmy Carter sold the presidential yacht *Sequoia* in order to save money, many believed that it cost him much more in goodwill, and it was considered by some veterans of the White House a missed opportunity to create friendly relations with Congress.[38] Next to the expense of many of the water projects he ended up having to return to the budget, the occasional trips on a presidential yacht or White House reception were inexpensive. Other rewards handed out to members, whether appointments or dinner invitations, will be offered to someone in any event and pose no additional costs.

Gaining favor became an important feature of the Ford administration's style in particular for several reasons. First, it played to the president's strengths by building upon relationships developed during Ford's twenty-five years in Congress. With Gerald Ford in the Oval Office the White House liaison staff did not have to build favor, only to maintain the favor that already existed. Second, following on the heels of many real or imagined slights from the Nixon administration, congressional egos were bruised and could easily have continued to be a serious barrier to cooperation. When stories of "snubs" or slights from the Ford White House reached the press, the congressional liaison staff responded quickly because, according to one staff memo, as a result of "the wounds and bruises lingering from the Nixon days, the pardon furor, and the economic message (surtax) just prior to the [1974] election, plus general vacillation by the Ford Administration in the closing days of the 93rd Congress, there is a lot of fence mending to be done with House GOP Members to establish better Congressional Relations."[39] The White House instructed cabinet departments to establish good working relationships with members of Congress, especially new ones, and stressed this frequently during cabinet meetings.[40] The large freshman class of 1974 was a primary target of the administration's efforts to build friendly relations. These new members represented potential votes regardless of their party because of their loose ties with congressional leaders. At the same time, the White House had to honor the seniority system and talk first with more senior members. Jack Marsh urged cabinet secretaries to approach new members of related committees, but only after making sure to "pre-notice ranking members before contacting the new members. It is a mistake that the White House has consistently made and which had offended many people."[41] Congress was shifting away from the system of institutionalized pluralism, with its seniority system and heavy emphasis on working through congressional leaders, to individualized pluralism that rewarded the independence of members.

The Ford White House needed to maintain favor with a large number of members because the fading loyalty to party within Congress necessitated that the administration rely upon a strategy of constructing "floating" coalitions—building a new coalition on each issue. The liaison staff found that after the 1974 election they would generally fail to get the support of about twenty of the 144 House Republicans and eight to ten of the thirty-seven Senate Republicans, requiring them to seek out Democrats even to sustain a presidential veto. The task was much greater to pass their own legislation. The administration knew that they could often pick up some Democratic votes, particularly southern Democrats, but that the coalition between southern Democrats and Republicans was beginning to fall apart and that the White House had to be prepared to seek out potential allies throughout the ranks of the Democratic party. As a response to the waning party loyalty that marked the decline of institutionalized pluralism, Ford, first as Minority Leader, then as president, developed a strategy of "floating coalitions" that reached out in whatever direction necessary to bring in the votes to win.[42] The White House emphasized that members of Congress would not be penalized for not going along with the administration on individual votes.[43] Because the coalition that the Ford administration relied upon for success in Congress changed with every vote, the administration was always anxious to cultivate friendly relations with any member. One Ford aide described the importance and functioning of gaining favor under Ford:

> The bottom line, in legislative bargaining, is that you have to create a positive environment. That holds whether you are initiating programs or sustaining vetoes. . . . It was the bicentennial and we had many requests for Rose garden appearances with the President. We made ourselves available at all times. We brought congressmen up to the White House for briefings in the Roosevelt Room of the White House and they just loved it. There is always a need to keep communications flowing and Gerald Ford did his utmost to make sure that individual Congressmen felt that the White House was not out of touch.[44]

The "congressional half-hours" reluctantly scheduled by Nixon became "congressional hours" under Ford, who understood their value. While the subject matter of these meetings was minor, they provided members an opportunity to demonstrate to constituents their access to the president or to have their photo taken with Ford for a newsletter. These sessions were declared a success at the end of 1975 by the White House staff: "Most of these sessions were of minor significance, but very important to the Members involved. They contributed to the President's desire to be readily accessible to Members of Congress."[45]

By building friendships the White House made it more difficult for members to vote against the president. While a friendship between the president and Congress facilitates support it does not guarantee it. One Republican member of Congress said, "I would hate to vote against him [Ford] on something he wanted badly, but I did, plenty of times."

The rewards of maintaining favor are generally subtle. By taking pressure off of each individual vote, maintaining favor helps stabilize the relationship among members of Congress and the president. No one vote should dramatically alter the workings of the relationship between a legislator and the White House, giving each the flexibility that they need to survive the next election. The administration could seek a short-term benefit by pressing for a vote from a member that will cost them the next election, but the loss of a congressional friend could represent many votes lost in the future. Some votes in support of the White House may come at a very high price for members and expecting their support on every presidential initiative is implausible and eventually counterproductive. Ford, according to Max Friedersdorf, was always sensitive to the electoral concerns of Congress:

Ford's philosophy was not to ask a man to do something that might damage his chances of coming back. Don't hurt yourself, was his constant advice, both as minority leader and as president. . . . I would try to show the moderates, on each issue, how they could vote with the administration without hurting themselves.[46]

Both the White House and members of Congress try to make sure that the other is fully aware of the level of goodwill between them. Members frequently remind the president or White House staff of their level of support and are anxious to explain any failure to support in an effort to maintain favor. The White House maintains its own set of support scores to record how often each member has supported the president on key votes. One member of the Carter liaison team recalled, "I remember sitting in the president's study and we'd say you need to go out and do a fund-raiser for Congressman So-and-so and he would literally open his drawer and pull out this scorecard and say, 'Why should I, he's never been with me?'" At the same time the White House keeps a record of the favors done for members of Congress so that staffers can remind members at a key moment that the White House has extended kindness in the past. The White House tries to demonstrate that remaining in favor is rewarded. One congressional relations aide asked President Johnson to see "how we can give more assistance and recognition to those who support us most of the time—in other words, how to get it across to the members that their support or opposition to your program makes a difference on how we handle their problems and requests for favors."[47]

The White House can benefit from building a long-term relationship simply by making members feel like they are part of the president's team. With the White House representing the focus of power and prestige in the government, by becoming part of that team members can feel some share of its glory and increase their image of importance among constituents and within Congress. For example, when members of Congress complained that the press was getting copies of President Ford's addresses to Congress before his allies in Congress, the liaison staff made sure that the press no longer received this favor before the president's friends in Congress.[48] Shortly before Ford announced his selection of Nelson Rockefeller as vice president, Republican Senator Hugh Scott of Pennsylvania called the White House repeatedly to ask that he be told at least a few minutes in advance of the announcement so that he could say: "yes, I knew about it."[49] The White House is conscious of status within Congress. The Johnson White House liked to call members while other members or important constituents were present because members like to be "interrupted" by the White House; they want to feel that they are part of the White House team.[50]

The Ford White House created a strategy for consulting with members of Congress as part of their program to build cordial relations. Early consultation with members helps the White House build a relationship through inclusion of members and avoid political trouble by sounding out members' stands on developing legislation. Charlie Leppert warned the rest of the staff: "My experience on the Hill and association with Members of Congress establishes the lack of consultation as the primary reason for confrontation between the Administration and Congress."[51] This is based on the principal that if you wanted members with you for the landing you should have them with you on the take-off. As one legislative assistant described, "One of Ford's goals was clear communication. Ford wanted it to be an absolute rule that nobody in the leadership of the Congress would read about an important political event in the paper before we told them about it."[52]

The impact of gaining favor in terms of converting members may be small, but the impact of losing votes must also be considered. While gaining favor does not seem to be a major component of legislative victories, the absence of favor can become a serious barrier to coalition-building. As the Carter administration would find out, when relations with Congress are strained, building coalitions, even among partisans, can be difficult. Gaining favor is often a defensive action, with the White House being more concerned about the risks of falling out of favor with a member than the benefits of being in their good stead. Members of Congress eventually came to take these favors somewhat for granted, leaving the White House in fear of disappointing potential supporters. When Tom Korologos passed along the demand of Senator John Stennis of Mississippi for immediate action on a favor, he noted that the demand was "nothing personal—strictly business! He calls me *every* day including Sundays and Holidays."[53]

The friendly alliance between a member and the Ford White House was threatened and the reputation of a senator and the liaison staff was compromised when the White House considered changing its mind on appointing Senator Curtis's wife to a health board. Tom Korologos described himself as "hysterical" over the matter and outlined why the administration should go ahead with the nomination.

The Senator is embarrassed before his colleagues—many of whom cleared her; he is embarrassed to his constituents where they announced it; to his new wife, who thinks he can't deliver on a commitment; and he feels (coupled with our inability to get his group in) that Ford is against Curtis because Curtis was so strong for Nixon and Ford wants to cut off all such ties.

He [Curtis] will be Ranking Republican on Finance where ALL

of the big domestic, financial, tax and trade legislation goes; he is senior on Budget Committee; he is senior on Agriculture Committee;
he is senior on Space Committee and next year he plans to run for
Cotton's leader seat as Chairman of the GOP Conference.

This is so patently absurd a situation and one which will prove
detrimental not only to my effectiveness but could harm the President as well.[54] (emphasis in the original)

The issues that might cause congressional irritation range widely in importance. As much as executive-congressional relations during this period
were driven by broad constitutional struggles over the principal of checks
and balances and separation of powers, they could also result from concerns
much more personal than policy. The White House liaison office battled
those policy advisors in the White House who felt that there were too many
days and months designated in honor of various interests, for example, when
Senator Howard Baker wanted to have October declared Country Music
Month. They had a similar struggle for a disaster declaration for the mushroom industry on behalf of Republican Senator Hugh Scott.[55] When Bob
Dole became irritated over a patronage issue a member of the liaison staff
warned Friedersdorf of the possible consequences.

Just spoke to Bob Dole on the S. 1849 override attempt. He's "boil-
ing" mad about "Rummy [Donald Rumsfeld] screwing me on Kent
Frizzell for Secretary of the Interior. I'm sick and tired of those guys
doing it to me and, as a direct results, you may not get my vote to sustain the President's veto."

He asked that his exact words be conveyed to the powers that be
in the White House.[56]

Despite occasional problems the result of the Ford White House's liaison
efforts was a reduction in tension between the branches. Max Friedersdorf
asserted, "The main difference [between the Nixon and Ford administra-
tions] is the atmosphere and the cordiality that exists between the President
and Congress."[57] The Ford administration succeeded in reducing the tension between the branches despite the wounds of Watergate.

One testament to the value of gaining favor is that the two modern presidents who knew Congress the best made it an integral part of their legislative strategy. Both Johnson and Ford understood that legislative victories are
built a little at a time, often months in advance.

The Postimperial President and the Postreform Congress

The power wielded by Johnson and Nixon had come to be widely known as the "imperial presidency."[58] Members of Congress had grown weary of Johnson's heavy-handed legislative style and Nixon's attempts at budget impoundment. The eventual disclosure of the Nixon administration's abuses of power, including wiretapping, the political use of the IRS, and (eventually) Watergate, gave rise to specific fears of a presidency that might become too powerful for Congress to effectively check. One Nixon aide suggested that the reseparation of powers was inevitable. The presidency, he reasoned, had become too powerful, and some kind of change was inevitable: "Congress was just going to slap them [the executive branch] down. Something had to give." A legislative strategy memo from the early days of the Ford administration noted, "The bulk of the media and the academy have called for a diminution of the power and status of the Presidency."[59]

Arthur Schlesinger Jr., in *The Imperial Presidency*, suggested two possible responses to the excesses of the Johnson and Nixon administrations: "Congress could tie the Presidency down by a thousand small legal strings, but, like Gulliver and the Lilliputians, the President could always break loose. The effective means of controlling the Presidency lay less in law than in politics."[60] A veteran lobbyist commented, "When Nixon defied the government, he weakened the presidency. Then the Congress moved in on him. Hard to believe what they wrought."[61] Congress used laws like the Budget and Impoundment Act and the War Powers Resolution to attempt to restrict the president and at the same time empowered itself to more effectively do political battle with the president. By creating a Congressional Budget Office and expanding personal staff, Congress was better arming itself for the struggle with the White House. Beyond that, individual members increased their independence from congressional leadership and their party, and although the dispersion of power in Congress was not designed to diminish the role of the president, it certainly created additional headaches in the White House.

Part of the new challenge to presidential power on the Hill was a shifting of spending authority. Bill Kendall of the liaison staff noted that "Many people don't seem to remember that we were operating under a completely new budget process that was designed to control presidential discretion."[62] One of the ways Congress reclaimed authority was by gaining control over federal spending so that it could not be used as leverage against them. One member of Congress who served during this period admits that one of the reasons for some of the changes to the budget process was to prevent presidents from being able to use federal spending to extract votes from members.

> We earmark things. Under the old system prior to 1974 presidents could just not spend it [money appropriated by Congress]. So if I put a couple of million dollars in for a dam and the president didn't want the dam built, he just didn't do it. But under the Budget Reform Act of '74 whatever is in the legislation is mandated and has to be done. Presidents no longer have discretion on that. They can send up a rescission but unless we approve it, nothing changes.

The creation of the Congressional Budget Office (CBO) provided Congress with another means of resisting the White House. Members of Congress had previously been forced to rely heavily upon economic forecasts and spending projections and budget information from the executive branch. Previous presidents had enjoyed a virtual monopoly on detailed economic projections, giving them much greater latitude in shaping the policy debate. The Congressional Budget Office became a tool for challenging executive proposals because it provided an alternative to the executive branch's generally optimistic estimation of the cost of programs favored by the president. Johnson had always managed to present favorable cost estimates for his programs. With the CBO prepared to examine and question the cost of every program, the executive branch could no longer use favorable cost and revenue estimates to pave the way for expensive programs. Now, the budget estimates attached to a program need not arise from the same organization and assumptions that originated the idea.

The Budget and Impoundment Act of 1974 that created the CBO also attempted to reduce presidential use of impoundment by requiring that the president report any delay in the implementation of the budget. Reporting requirements were also included in other legislation. The Case Act required the secretary of state to submit the text of any executive agreements within sixty days, while the War Powers Resolution required that the president immediately report any use of military forces in a situation in which they could be put at risk. The National Emergencies Act mandated notification of Congress in advance of the use of presidential emergency powers.

Congress expanded its staff resources to keep up with the increased monitoring of executive branch behavior and to avoid reliance on the executive branch for information. Joe Califano, who had served in the Johnson White House, noted that "Congressmen are so busy and understaffed that a strong president can virtually set their complete agenda."[63] In 1972 Senator Walter Mondale remarked at a conference,

> I have found that whenever I am on the side of the Administration, I am surfeited with computer print-outs and data that comes within seconds, whenever I need it to prove how right I am. But if I am opposed to the Administration, computer print-outs always come late, prove the opposite point or always are on some other topic. So I think one of the rules is that there is utterly no reason why Congress does not develop its own computer capability, its own technicians, its own pool of information.[64]

The expansion of congressional staff resources went beyond the CBO. In 1975 Congress created the House and Senate Intelligence Oversight Committees to help monitor the Central Intelligence Agency and similar agencies in the executive branch. Congressional staff increased dramatically in the years following the 1974 election.[65] By 1976, one member of the Ford White House liaison staff was complaining that the White House was now at a relative disadvantage to congressional offices.

> Congress is very liberal in voting itself staffs. Their staff have expanded tremendously in the past few years, particularly in the last two years. But they are very niggardly with the White House. For example, our secretaries had to use old fashioned typewriters that they hadn't used on the Hill in ten years. Yet we had them in inventory, we had to use up those typewriters and run them into the ground. We couldn't dispose of them through GSA [General Services Administration]. Every congressional office had telecopiers, a device by which you can transmit the written word over the telephone. We didn't have those. We could have save ourselves a lot of time if we could have transmitted things from the Hill back to our office that way.[66]

Congress also strengthened other policy analysis tools. The Legislative Reference Service of the Library of Congress was reorganized and expanded into the Congressional Research Service. The General Accounting Office was given more authority and the Office of Technology Assessment was created. These offices were provided with independent sources of expertise so that lawmakers had less need to turn to the executive branch for answers to its questions.

While many of the resources the Congress developed were used to hold off presidential intrusion into its authority, many were also aimed at winning election. Nonetheless, the results were the same. One Nixon lobbyist argued that Congress was using the franking privilege and other public funds to develop public relations in their districts that would help make them more independent of their party and the White House.[67] Congressional offices were no longer content to simply answer mail, and the amount of mail generated by Congress grew. Many offices began to compile lists of constituents who had written letters in the past on an issue, and they sent out letters after key votes on which they wanted to claim credit. Constituents who had written letters on the budget would receive letters from their representative announcing that "Knowing your interest in a balanced budget, I thought you would like to know that today I voted for Gramm-Rudman."[68] Sophisticated uses of constituent mail enabled each lawmaker to claim credit within their own district and with the voters most interested in the issue.

As the cost of campaigning climbed, members spent more and more of their time chasing money. This often involved talking with interest groups whose agendas were in conflict with the White House. In the past, party leaders had been able to provide political "cover" of sorts for members of Congress who had cast votes unpopular with constituents or interest groups. However, as the public became less partisan, members could no longer hope that unpopular votes would be politically neutralized by the assurance that it had been done in their role as a "good" Democrat or Republican. Interest groups no longer saw following party leaders as being sufficient cause for a vote against their position. Interest groups understood that as members became more independent of the party financially they would become more independent on policy as well. With party diminished, interest groups could hope to put their priorities ahead of those of a member's party or president. A decentralized system made members more directly accountable to constituent and contributor demands.

Congressional efforts paid off as reelection rates climbed. Morris Fiorina suggests that the electoral strength of congressional incumbents has made members less responsive to national forces like the president and party leaders.[69] Whether this increased level of security was caused by Congress's own actions or broader electoral forces, the increased security emboldened members. In 1977 Hubert Humphrey described how the members of Congress regarded their ability to survive presidents. "I'll tell you something I hear people say now that you never heard before: 'I've seen them come and go, and I'm still here.' They're talking about presidents, you know. I've run through seven of them myself."[70]

Not all of the reforms that hampered presidential coalition-building were aimed at the presidency. The dispersion of power in Congress, while part of a broader change, made winning votes more difficult for the White House. The dispersion of power in Congress began in earnest during the Nixon administration and proved to be a major liability for the White House. A key component in the decentralization of power was the weakening of the seniority system and the rise of subcommittee autonomy. Subcommittee membership and the opportunity to chair important subcommittees became more open to junior members, and the autonomy of subcommittees grew.[71]

Gary Hymel, a veteran lobbyist, considered the "subcommittee bill of rights" one of the most significant changes because "All of a sudden, we had 157 subcommittee chairmen with power, space and jobs, instead of a closed shop of 19 committees where all the action took place—and where all the lobbyists concentrated because that's where the job got done."[72] Not only did subcommittee chairmanship give legislators power within Congress, the influence they gained over parts of the policy process created a base for fundraising among interest groups under their jurisdiction. Subcommittee chairs had less need of fund-raising help from the president or congressional leaders because many political action committees were lining up to try to buy access to these new sources of power.

The decline of congressional leadership would seem to offer an opportunity for the president to step into the vacuum left by their departure. However, the decline of congressional leadership did not leave Congress in want of leadership; it reflected a growing move toward independence. The new members who entered Congress with the 1974 elections were anxious to rebel against the existing system, especially the presidency. Power in Congress was factionalized at the same time that distrust in the presidency was institutionalized. One White House veteran noted that the change in Congress had made it much harder on the president.

> The destruction of the seniority system in Congress has made it tougher for the president. When Bryce Harlow was running things both in the Eisenhower administration but also early in the Nixon administration before the leadership had begun to melt down, you could get done what you wanted to get done by getting the agreement of the party leaders.

The independence of congressional Republicans in particular became a significant problem for the Ford White House. According to Max Friedersdorf, "The tendency of the moderates to oppose the administration was partly just to show independence from the White House—to prove they were not rubber stamps."[73] The eagerness of the Watergate class of 1974 in Congress to demonstrate their independence was reflected in a spat between Freshman House Member Larry Pressler, a Republican from South Dakota, and Vern Loen, a White House lobbyist who was also from South Dakota. After defecting from Republican ranks on a natural gas bill and contributing to a loss on a close vote, Pressler wrote a letter to Ford complaining about Loen's tactics. According to Pressler, Loen complained that the congressman had let the administration down and warned that "If you want any further favors from the White House—call the AFL-CIO." In another conversation, while Loen was somewhat apologetic about his tone he continued to point out that "we've done more for you than any other freshman Congressman."[74] While Loen publicly denied issuing a threat, the intent of his warning is clear. Pressler's complaints, however, reflect a level of sensitivity and resistance to pressure that Johnson and Nixon had not encountered from freshman members. Previous administrations had used similar levels of pressure, but in the post-Watergate climate such pressure was not readily accepted. In late 1975 Max Friedersdorf sent a memo warning his liaison staff to avoid using visible hand signals to members entering the chamber before a vote.

> There have been complaints about the White House lobbyists outside the chamber flashing signals on votes occurring on the Floor.
>
> This is annoying to our friends who may be voting with us, but appear to be in our pocket if we yell or signal them on votes as they enter the Chamber.[75]

The White House found that it could use the independence of members, particularly the Watergate class, to its advantage. Although it made it harder for the White House to keep Republicans in line behind the president, it also made it easier to attract the vote of Democrats. As one member of the liaison staff reported to Friedersdorf, "By cultivating key members of the 75 Democratic freshmen, we succeeded in keeping that voting block fragmented to a large extent."[76]

As a member of Congress Ford had watched Lyndon Johnson build coalitions, first as majority leader, then as president, but had Ford as president tried to operate in the same fashion he would have failed. The old strategies were no longer appropriate for the new Congress. Early in the administration William Timmons warned the president that traditional strategies were now much less productive. "Few results will come of our meeting because Congress is not one whole, but rather 535 parts."[77] One Ford aide told an interviewer, "I remember hearing Carl Albert say that he was with the President but that he wasn't Sam Rayburn. He told the President that he would have to go down to the grassroots to get votes. The era was past when you could make a deal by calling in just the leaders and the senior committee people."[78] One of Nixon's lobbyists observed in 1977 that the Congress was more fragmented and complex than it had been during his service just a few years earlier.[79] Years after serving in the White House Larry O'Brien was amazed to discover how much things had changed:

> I was lobbying on behalf of the National Basketball Association on a bill that had something to do with tax on sports tickets, in the Ways and Means Committee, and I had Wilbur Mills's successor asking me if I could provide him with a head count of his committee so he could determine where his committee stood. Well, that really stunned me, because [in] my years with the Ways and Means Committee and Wilbur Mills, that wasn't the way it [was done]. You might work a head count on his behalf but, believe me, he would never say he didn't know what was going on. He never allowed that to happen.[80]

Dispersion of power throughout Congress posed two related problems for anyone attempting to influence the legislative process: complexity and reliability. First, there is an increasing number of individual members that need to be approached. More individual members need to be approached in part because there are fewer indirect, centralized channels like congressional leadership to utilize. Without centralized power in Congress, it is very difficult to find any one source who can "deliver" votes. You could no longer find a Lyndon Johnson or Richard Russell who, if persuaded, could bring along other votes. Persuading such power centers was difficult, but they at least simplified the process of coalition-building. One Ford White House strategy memorandum noted, "Congressional leadership is presently so fragmented that there are no real leaders to co-opt."[81]

Under the old system there were relatively few serious obstacles. A bill that did not enjoy the support of key congressional leaders or committee chairs was almost certainly doomed. Wilbur Mills or other powerful committee chairs would likely succeed in stopping any legislation they strongly opposed. Under this arrangement the system may not be friendly, but it is simple. If Judge Smith says that no civil rights bill is coming through the Rules Committee, then there is little point is asking other members of the committee. At the same time strong committee chairs provided a stabilizing influence on legislative debate. One senator pointed out that without strong committee chairs you can no longer bring a bill to the floor without fear of being buried by amendments. As Paul Light has pointed out, the legislative "road map" has become increasingly tangled for the president attempting to maneuver legislation through the process and "[t]hough there are few single obstacles to passage of the President's program, there are many more potential dead ends and delays."[82]

Not only was the new order in Congress more complicated, it also created more unreliable bargaining partners. A veteran of the Ford White House felt that it was much easier for the White House to deal with a limited number of established leaders within Congress. "With power dispersed you've got 535 monsters out there and you've got to deal with every one— many of whom are liars and cheats." Beyond simply reducing the number of bargaining partners, the White House found that the old leadership system in the Congress had produced a stable and reliable set of leaders that the president could deal with. Years of service in Congress and the climb through the leadership system provided a testing ground that sorted out the reliable from the unreliable. The old system also produced a more reliable environment for bargaining. Because the old system elevated a few people to leadership positions through a process of experience and selection by the party caucuses, before an individual rose to the level of being in a position to bargain seriously with the White House, they had been tested. Unreliable bargaining partners would fail to move up in the party hierarchy, while more reliable bargaining partners were promoted. Thus, the seniority system created a process in which natural selection of leadership could take place.

In 1973 Congress began opening up its committee meetings, bringing the White House more scrutiny and competition during the development of policy. This precluded some of the cozy markup sessions that executive branch lobbyists had used to work out deals on legislation. Often, White House or departmental staff were invited into these markup sessions, and while they were usually careful not to intrude into congressional prerogatives, they were able to play an important role in these sessions. Questions from members would allow the administration's representative to provide information, suggest alternatives, and bring the president's views into the room before interest groups had a chance to intervene.

The congressional reforms of the 1970s represent a major turning point in presidential power.[83] John Marsh concluded, "When Ford came into the presidency the executive power was very much under attack."[84] According to one Republican member of the House, "The president had gained in power and authority and that has destroyed some of the balance." Another Republican member of the House noted the same resurgence of congressional authority.

> I think the president's role has been reduced. For example, we did the budget act in '74 that took away the ability to impound funds which greatly reduced the president's impact on spending issues. Then we passed the War Powers Act which was the result of excesses under Johnson and to some extent Nixon which again debilitated the president's authority. So there's been overall a gradual erosion of presidential impact on policy versus that of Congress. Congress has become more and more jealous of its powers.

A White House briefing paper from the Ford White House noted the new limits on presidential power.

> The passage of certain laws in the 93rd Congress weakened his [the president's] leadership of the bureaucracy and legislation in the 94th Congress threatens to continue this trend. Examples of legislation which weakens the Presidency are the Impoundment Act, the War Powers Resolution, the extension of the confirmation requirement to lower ranked officials, and such proposals as that of requiring the agencies to submit budget and legislative recommendations directly to Congress at the same time they are sending them to the OMB. The President must be aggressive in protecting his prerogatives and powers.[85]

While some observers believed that the struggle between the branches was largely partisan, the continuation of tensions into the Carter administration would reveal the institutional roots of the conflict. In 1977 the congressional relations staff warned Carter of the institutional problems facing the White House.

> Many of the tensions have a Congressional ancestry rather than a Presidential one. The growing institutional independence of Congress, the "democratization" of the House and the reduced power of committee chairmen, the evaporation of party loyalty, and the growing political independence of individual Members have all contributed to the current situation. Many seeds of difficulty were sown long before your campaign for President was announced, let alone the advent of your Administration itself.[86]

The Ford administration tried to work upon the rapidly shifting land-scape of Congress. They became the first administration to work under the new challenges presented by the independence of individualized pluralism and the assertiveness of the Congress. Once Congress had begun to reassert its authority and members began to enjoy their independence there was lit-tle Ford could do. One senator noted that there was little interest in return-ing to a more centralized system and that "you can't get the genie back in the bottle."

Vetoes

Gerald Ford entered the presidency as the nice guy who was going to open the doors of the Oval Office and repair relations with Congress. His smiling friendly face in contrast to the dark jowls of Nixon was supposed to signal a change in the tone of the relationship. However, in his first address to Congress, after telling the assembled members that he wanted a good marriage rather than a honeymoon, he went on to say, "Tonight is no time to threaten you with vetoes. But I do have that last recourse and am a veteran of many a veto fight in this very chamber."[87] Soon thereafter Ford adopted an aggressive veto strategy that demonstrated the limits of the friendship. Ford began using the veto power of the presidency within three days of tak-ing office and by the next year Majority Leader O'Neill would refer to Ford as "the world champion on how to sustain a veto."[88] Reviewing the 1975 leg-islative year the White House staff saw the veto strategy as a success.

> There is little doubt that the leading achievement of the Office of Legislative Affairs in the First Session of the 94th Congress was to es-tablish the credibility of the Presidential vetoes in the so-called "veto proof" Congress where Republicans are outnumbered two to one in both Houses.
>
> In rapid succession we managed to sustain vetoes in the House of the Farm, Strip Mining, Jobs, and Housing Bills, among others. At year's end the House again sustained the President's veto of the Tax Bill and was forced to come up with a tax cut extension which gave lip service, at least, to the concept of a spending ceiling.
>
> For this year it was necessary for the President to veto only 17 bills, out of 1,436 measures passed. Of these vetoes, three were over-ridden (Nurse Training, Education Appropriations, and the School Lunch Bill), each of them a "motherhood" issue. Had we not made credibility in the veto threat areas in the session, the majority party would have rolled over us with all kinds of undesirable legislation.

Many, many measures were cleaned up and made acceptable for fear
of a veto.[89]

The president's power to veto legislation has often been discussed as a
constitutional power, but the effectiveness of the veto threat is predicated on
the political skills of the White House in sustaining vetoes.[90] The administration helped itself by creating an "early warning signal" that was designed to
influence the process at the subcommittee level in order to avoid a need for
a veto on some issues and to avoid a veto that could not be sustained. In early
1975 one member of the liaison staff pointed out to Friedersdorf:

> From the standpoint of setbacks, the President was forced to make a
> turnabout on the Common Situs Picketing Bill and veto it. Probably
> the most important improvement that could be made in our opera-
> tion would be to keep open the President's options in dealing with
> key legislation. The entire staff should guard against getting him too
> far out front too early on major issues for one never knows what
> shifts in public and congressional sentiment will occur along the
> way.[91]

By pushing the departments to be more hands-on with departmental legislation and keeping members informed on possible administration objections to legislation, the White House managed to facilitate changes to legislation that made it more palatable to the president.[92] Ford told his cabinet,
"In many cases our veto strategy will not be to block the enactment of legislation, but to cause the Congress to make legislation more acceptable either
because of threat of veto, or because it has been successfully vetoed. If we can
establish a beachhead early on, using the veto to demonstrate strength, we
may not have to use it as frequently in the future."[93]

Conclusion

Gerald Ford and Lyndon Johnson entered Congress with similar levels
of legislative expertise. Ford, like Johnson, entered the White House after
having served as a congressional leader, with only a brief stint in the vice
presidency separating the Oval Office from Capitol Hill. However, while the
two men were similar, their political situations were very different. Johnson
won a landslide reelection victory and enjoyed a lopsided majority, while the
unelected Ford had to work with the smallest partisan coalition behind a
president since Eisenhower's last two years in office. Distrust over presidential handling of the war in Vietnam had weakened the ties between the pres-

ident and Congress, and Watergate shattered whatever foundation of trust remained. Ford had to attempt to govern on the rapidly shifting landscape as the norms of institutionalized pluralism that he had operated under in Congress were giving way to the extreme individualism that was beginning to dominate Washington politics.

According to one Ford lobbyist, "We came in facing a tremendous task in just repairing relations with the Hill."[94] While Ford's previous close relationship with many members of Congress was an asset to rebuilding trust, his status as an unelected successor to the presidency left him without enough credibility to rebuild the relationship during his short time in office.

Ford's earliest decisions in the White House served to alienate members of both parties and encouraged them to distance themselves politically from the White House. When Ford pardoned Nixon and considered pardoning the rest of the Watergate conspirators, Senator Bob Packwood phoned Tom Korologos to tell him that sentiment was already against a pardon and that pardoning the rest would make things even worse. Packwood went so far as to suggest that Ford was becoming a greater political burden than Nixon would have been if he were still president.[95] In October 1974 William Timmons conceded to the president that "the administration so far is a handicap to most GOP Members."[96]

Gerald Ford worked to create a friendly atmosphere of trust between the branches. However, weighty forces were at work, driving a wedge between him and his old congressional colleagues. As one veteran of his liaison staff said, "Ford was immensely popular in the House and his personality leaned toward making friends, but once you cross the barriers between the two branches things change." Ford's problem might be best summarized by a conversation between Ford and Speaker Tip O'Neill that occurred when Ford called the Speaker to invite him to his swearing-in as president on August 9, 1974. After discussing arrangements, Ford and O'Neill exchanged vows to work together. Then after a brief silence O'Neill remarked to Ford, "Christ, Jerry, isn't this a wonderful country? Here we can talk like this and you and I can be friends, and eighteen months from now I'll be going around the country kicking your ass in." They both laughed as Ford replied, "That's a hell of a way to speak to the next President of the United States."[97] While Ford had hoped for a good marriage and O'Neill had pledged cooperation, partisan and institutional pressures were too intense to permit harmony between the branches.

7

THE CARTER
ADMINISTRATION

LIKE GERALD FORD, JIMMY CARTER NEVER HAD MUCH OF
a "honeymoon" with Congress. A *National Journal* headline from just one
week after the election asked, "Carter's Honeymoon on the Hill—How Long
Can It Last?"[1] The tension between Carter and the Ninety-fifth Congress revealed that the struggle between recent presidents and Congress went beyond partisanship. Carter's mandate as he perceived it conflicted directly
with the goals of some individual lawmakers. Carter's campaign against
Washington politics and pork-barrel spending had clearly implicated Congress and contributed to the atmosphere of mutual suspicion that would
continue throughout his presidency. While the idea of cutting out pork-barrel projects and reducing the size of government overall proved popular during the election, specific cuts would face stiff resistance within Congress, particularly from the congressional Democrats who could have formed the base
of the president's support. Carter's policies were conceived with a national
perspective but had to be voted on by members representing individual districts and allied with specific interests. While some observers expected Carter
to be able to work with the Democrats in Congress to pass his agenda, most
incumbent Democrats had little appetite for fundamental changes to the political system in which they were thriving. Parties were weakened and party

leaders lacked the ability to deliver votes for the president, and Carter's agenda did little to help the situation.

Carter's high-principled approach to Congress, described by Charles Jones as the "trusteeship presidency," presents a precarious foundation for congressional relations.[2] Carter stepped into the Oval Office at a time when congressional distrust of the executive was at a high point. Congress had not only rearmed itself after its conflicts with Johnson and Nixon, it had internally dispersed power, making any coalition-building difficult. One Carter liaison staffer believed that most members of Congress had no experience with working with the White House and no desire to change. "The Democrats in Congress had been in an attack mode. In their eyes Nixon and the executive branch could do no right and it's difficult to teach an old dog new tricks."

The Carter administration was thus fated to a difficult four years with Congress. While the presence of a Democratic Congress and Democratic president held out the promise of cooperation, the two had very different orientations that were predicated on the fundamental need to win reelection. For the next four years each side would remain stubbornly on track; and, although blame may be placed on either side, the political costs proved to be much higher for Jimmy Carter.

In response to the failure of his party to provide a stable foundation for a winning coalition, the Carter White House turned to the public for support for his agenda. Carter's attempts to go to the public found limited success and generated resentment in Congress. The White House found a grassroots strategy engineered by Anne Wexler and the Office of Public Liaison more successful at shaping the electoral expectations of members of Congress. With Carter failing to demonstrate an ability to transform the public at large into a political ally, the White House set out to build constituent support among a narrower segment of constituents.

The Carter Staff

The first step in assembling the liaison staff began in June 1976 when Carter sent Frank Moore to Washington to establish contact with congressional leaders and to coordinate joint appearances with congressional campaigns. Moore had served as Carter's liaison to the Georgia legislature and municipal governments during Carter's service as governor. After working on the transition, Moore would be named as the head of White House congressional relations.

In May 1977, William C. Cable was brought in to head the House lobby-

ing team to replace Rick Merrill who had been blamed by some congressional leaders for problems with Congress. Cable had been serving as staff director of the House Committee on Administration and had previously served
on the staff of the House Committee on Education and Labor. The House liaison team was rounded out by James C. Free, Valerie F. Pinson, Robert W.
Maher, and Terrence D. Straub. Free had worked in the Tennessee legislature, but the rest had held positions on the Hill. Valerie Pinson had the distinction of serving as the first Black and the first woman in the White House
congressional relations office. With almost thirty years of experience in
Washington, including service on the staff of Senator Thomas Dodd and in
the Johnson White House, she was the most experienced member of the liaison staff. Despite being a landmark appointee on two counts, she encountered no problems in working with Congress, perhaps because Speaker
O'Neill made sure she felt welcome.

Lobbying on the Senate side was headed by Dan C. Tate. Tate had served
on the staff of Senator Herman Talmadge of Georgia. Bob Beckel worked
primarily with the Senate but was responsible for foreign policy, national security, defense, and intelligence issues as they arose in either house. Robert
Thompson joined the staff from the Senate Democratic Committee. He
served as Moore's deputy. His responsibilities were primarily inside the
White House and he did little lobbying. Thompson was responsible for making sure that the office ran smoothly and that the congressional concerns
were incorporated into decision making in the White House. Eventually the
White House congressional relations office would have a full-time perma-
nent staff of twenty-six (including the eight lobbyists and clerical staff) with
an additional seven long-term detainees and consultants on loan from other
departments.[3]

It is tempting to portray the Carter administration's problems with Congress as resulting from Frank Moore's lack of congressional experience, but
there is clearly much more to the problems the administration would experience. A veteran of the Nixon liaison staff believed that the administration
committed some errors early on but conceded that this was in part the result
of an arrogance found in most new administrations. He pointed out that
Kennedy, Larry O'Brien, and his staff entered the White House with similar
levels of ignorance and arrogance, but the price in the 1960s was much lower
than it would be for Carter in the 1970s. Bryce Harlow suggested, "This is
chronic. You can go back to early 1961, with John F. Kennedy in the White
House, a fresh, shining new President, with a beautiful wife. Presidential
aides were throwing each other into the swimming pool and Camelot was in
full bloom. Yet, on Capitol Hill, they were kicking the hell out of Larry

O'Brien."[4] For all his Washington experience and connections, George Bush's White House also ran afoul of congressional personalities, but less was made of his early problems than Carter's.[5] Frank Moore, like Bill Timmons before him, spent his years heading congressional liaison to a chorus of public criticism. However, like Timmons before him, Moore endured, remaining in the White House all four years of the administration. The longevity of these two liaison chiefs reveals the importance of closeness to the president. Members of Congress can tolerate the occasional slight from the White House liaison staff, but they have no use for a head of congressional liaison who is not close to the president. Moore's access to the president was never in question and the White House often went out of its way to demonstrate this. Moore had a standing 8:15 appointment with the president every morning and it was not unusual for him to see Carter four or five times a day.[6] Moore was a personal friend of Carter and the two families were very close. One of Moore's assistant's complained, "One of the things that Frank Moore never gets any credit for is the fact that he was really part of the family team—he was close to the president. That helped enormously in us getting what we needed done by the president."

Much was made of the liaison staff's move from the White House to the Old Executive Office Building. Many critics suggested that it revealed the low status that the staff enjoyed. However, Frank Moore and his assistant remained in the West Wing of the White House, which houses the Oval Office. The rest of the liaison staff had been housed in the East Wing of the White House but moved because Carter increased the size of the staff. One member of the staff pointed out that in terms of proximity to the Oval Office the Old Executive Office Building was just as close and that their new offices were much more spacious than their cramped quarters in the East Wing.

It is difficult to gauge how much of the Carter staff's poor reputation was deserved. Years later one congressional Democrat described Frank Moore as a lovely man who faced too much criticism. He reflected that while Moore may not have been aggressive enough, he had quality people working for him. A Republican leader, not known for his kindness toward Democratic presidents, described the Carter liaison staff as "a pretty good operation." Frank Moore even received some public support from the unlikely source of Orrin Hatch (R-Utah). "His poor image is unjustified. . . . He does an excellent job, tells the truth, shoots square with me."[7] Eventually most of the criticism of the liaison staff ceased. Tip O'Neill forgave Moore for early problems but remained unsure about the rest of the White House. "I'm not mad at Frank [Moore]. Out of all that damned crowd down there, he's the only one who's ever been very friendly to me."[8]

LEGENDARY MISTAKES

A series of blunders by Moore received more attention than the overall effort to win friends. One of the most widely discussed mistakes was Moore's failure to attend a scheduled meeting with the Democratic chair of the House Ways and Means Committee. Moore was also criticized for being generally unresponsive and failing to return phone calls. Six months after Carter took office, a veteran of the Nixon White House liaison staff was surprised to learn from Tip O'Neill that the Speaker still had not had a private meeting with the president. One reporter noted that "To an outsider, such improprieties may seem like social misdemeanors, but to most Members of Congress, they are political felonies."[9] A little over one month after the inauguration one article quoted a Capitol Hill veteran as saying, "At the rate it's going now he's not going to last. He's going to be the first sacrificial lamb." One House aide said in November 1977, "Carter's people had good intentions, but they're ignorant. People now say the hell with them."[10] Other sources considered the attacks on Moore an "overplayed story."[11] It is interesting to note that at the same time that Moore was being blasted in the press, Carter was receiving a number of letters from members supporting Moore.[12]

When Frank Moore arrived in Washington after the election he was put in a transition office in the Health, Education, and Welfare building and given one secretary. During the campaign and the transition Moore was the only known contact for lawmakers wishing to communicate with the administration. He dealt with members of Congress, both those currently in office as well as those who had just been elected, who flooded his office with policy and personnel suggestions. When Moore showed up in his transition office after the election, six hundred messages were sitting on his desk waiting for him. It was impossible to respond to all of these as well as those that would continue to pour in. One member of Moore's staff tried to find humor in Moore's reputation. "I kid poor Frank that his middle name is Frank-Who Never Returns His Phone Calls-Moore." Another of Moore's assistants expressed resentment about how quickly people in Washington labeled Moore.

> Mary Russell who was a *Washington Post* reporter wrote a story during the transition that Frank Moore didn't return Congressmen's phone calls. That was part of his epitaph in this town from that day on. It was in the clip file of every reporter when they called up Frank Moore and Congress. The first thing they read chronologically was this Mary Russell story that Frank Moore didn't return the phone

calls of important members of Congress. In fact he didn't return their phone calls and I would submit that he probably never could have.

The mistakes of the Carter administration's relations with Congress became legendary. One member of the Reagan liaison staff commented, "Moore did a couple of dumb things and this town can seize on one or two things and draw conclusions. People on the Hill take offense easily." However, like most legends, the tales of Carter administration bungles were as much myth as reality. One of Carter's legislative assistants described the problem.

> Once you get a reputation, especially in this town, it just sticks with you like glue. My favorite example to underscore this is the story of Norm Mineta being invited to a dinner for the Japanese Prime Minister that was told and retold until it became the legend that Mineta was invited to attend the state dinner for the Italian Prime Minister because the White House thought that he was Italian rather than Japanese-American. That was reported in the *Wall Street Journal,* and other places to prove that even after two and a half years that we were still incompetent and it became the accepted wisdom. The problem was that it wasn't true. The true story was, and I know because I was a principal figure in the story, that when Norm ran for city council and mayor in San Jose, we used to joke with him that the only reason he got elected in San Jose was that people thought we was Italian rather than Japanese American. So we wouldn't put his picture on the billboard, for fear that voters would find out. Even Norm would joke about it.
>
> The story began when the Japanese Prime Minister came for a state dinner. I noticed that Mineta had not been invited. We had a meeting to reconcile that and someone asked how they should explain the late invitation and I said to tell him that we thought he was Italian. Everybody laughed. But the story got told and retold until it was the point that it was no longer a joke and it was Mineta being invited to the Italian Prime Minister's state dinner. That's a long way of making the point that once a story sets in this town it is impossible to knock down no matter what the facts are.[13]

While the slights against Congress were often overstated, the White House understood that it had a problem by July 1977. The liaison staff warned Carter, "*Regardless of the relative accuracy or fairness of these complaints, it is the perception with which we must deal and the perception on the Hill is not good"*[14] (emphasis in the original). On another occasion Moore reminded the president, "We have often said that, as far as the Hill is concerned, perception is more important than reality."[15]

The White House took steps in mid-1977 to improve relations with Congress. Beyond expanding the liaison staff in order to keep up with the demand from Congress, meetings with members of Congress were scheduled for both the president and senior White House staff. Vice President Mondale was put in charge of a task force to prioritize the administration's legislative agenda and the Congressional Liaison Office began to work with the rest of the administration to increase congressional input into patronage appointments.[16]

Another problem was that Congress viewed the administration overall as disorganized and indecisive. One Carter veteran confessed: "We made some real mistakes, there's no doubt about that. We pulled the plug on the $50 [tax] rebate without letting Ed Muskie, the chair of the Budget Committee, know in advance." This switch, among several others, was cited by Frank Moore when he reported to the president in April 1978 that "They [Congress] believe that we send conflicting signals; that cabinet officers run their own fiefdoms; that you do not have any experienced Washington-based political operative close by; and, most importantly, that we are frozen by indecision on many fronts—the most common being personnel." Moore believed that this undermined the administration's efforts overall because members were doubtful of the administration's commitment to positions and its ability to effectively follow through. "In summary, we have a Senate that is drifting and somewhat confused. In such an environment, a small minority of Senators, adamant in their opposition, can take advantage of Senate rules to prevent action on any issue they choose. This has happened repeatedly."[17]

It is hard to pinpoint why Congress was so unforgiving of Carter's early errors. While some of the tension had to do with growing congressional independence and lingering problems from the Johnson and Nixon administrations, part of the explanation is that Carter and Moore were unknown to members of Congress. Without a foundation of trust, members of Congress were more likely to interpret what the White House said or did in an unflattering light. Some of the reaction from Congress resulted from Carter's tone in the 1976 campaign. One member of the liaison staff suggested that it went beyond a simple dislike for an outsider president.

> Washington is a mean city and it's a bigoted city and there was a bigotry against southerners. I can say this because I'm not a southerner, but there was a northeastern elitist view. It's a very definite part of

reality in this city. This administration is fighting with it. Those same people resented people from Georgia with southern accents and made fun of them and their accents—called them hillbillies. On the flip side of that, we reacted to that and had a bit of a chip on our shoulder.

Organizing the Liaison Staff: "Substance Versus Shoe Leather"

The Carter administration had mixed results from some of its changes in the way the White House organized its work with Congress. The staff's attempt at making assignments along policy lines rather than assigning lobbyists to members was a short-lived experiment that failed. Simultaneously, the Carter administration's more extensive use of the vice president and the creation of task forces to manage legislative issues paid off handsomely.

As the White House Office grew larger and more specialized, a gap developed between those who created policy and those who pushed it through Congress. The White House staffs of Franklin Roosevelt, Harry Truman, and Dwight Eisenhower had flexible job assignments that often involved staff members in both development and advocacy of policy. For example, in the Eisenhower White House, Bryce N. Harlow, who would eventually head the congressional liaison staff, spent much of his first two years in the White House writing speeches for the president and working on civil rights issues. While their jobs were primarily those of general legislative liaison agents, the Eisenhower congressional relations staff had policy backgrounds and became involved in speech writing as well as lobbying on the issues they had expertise with.

Over time, however, specialization of function became the norm and the two functions moved to different parts of the White House. Meetings were used to coordinate policy development and advocacy but tension between these units often arose. The people who develop policy tend to be very protective of their ideas and are generally more reluctant to accept compromise than administration lobbyists. Policy staff can afford to be more ideological and principled, while congressional liaison people must be pragmatic. One member of the Nixon and Ford liaison staff commented, "It's easy for the Domestic Council or OMB to recommend a veto, it's up to me to get the votes. I looked at it from the practical standpoint. That's what I was supposed to do."[18]

As anti-Washington presidents like Carter have become more common, this conflict has become more intense and a significant part of running the White House. White House congressional relations staff members are often selected because of their years of experience on and around the Hill, but when distrust in government brings people into the White House, this experience presents a liability in dealing with others on the White House staff who see their own role as undoing what has been done before.

The Carter White House initially shunned the geographic division of labor employed by previous legislative shops that had lobbyists assigned to work with particular members based on region. They chose instead to organize along issue lines. For example, initially on the House side Jim C. Free was responsible for lobbying on issues related to the Departments of Agriculture, Transportation, Interior, and the proposed Energy Department; Valeric Pinson was responsible for matters in the jurisdiction of the Justice, Health Education and Welfare, Housing and Urban Development, and Labor Departments; and Rick Merrill was responsible for those issues relating to the State, Treasury, Defense, and Commerce Departments. Their reasoning was that it was better to have lobbyists that were more familiar with the issues they were talking about than the congressperson to whom they were talking. This organization reflects Jimmy Carter's belief in depoliticizing government and advancing legislation based on logical arguments rather than back-slapping and trading favors.

While the Carter White House was the first to attempt to organize along issue lines, this distinction reflected a continuing concern about the organization of the White House liaison staffs. The question was framed by one source as "substance versus shoe leather." Some administrations have advocated spending more time with the White House policy experts, developing a stronger background in policy (substance), while others have believed that time was better spent walking the halls of the Capitol becoming acquainted with Congress and its members (shoe leather). As one veteran of several administrations pointed out, "Congress is an expertise all its own." As power was diffused throughout Congress and as congressional committees and staffs proliferated, the effort required to maintain an expertise on Congress and its centers of power has grown further.

Each approach has its advantages and liabilities. On one hand, the people with the closest contact with Congress will best be able to judge what Congress is willing to accept in legislation. Policy people may have a clearer view of the most efficient form for a policy to take, but their research and policy expertise amount to little if the policy cannot gain congressional support. Bryce Harlow would often say, "you can't come running in here and give us a lead weight and tell us to float it across a pond."[19]

One member of the Carter staff admitted that, in the end, the issue-based organization was not a good idea. "Too many members simply fall through the cracks. You might be assigned an issue, and that issue might never come up during the entire two years of a congressional session. Also, with the issue-based system, you don't get around to talking to many members until it's too late."[20] At the same time, it is very difficult for administration lobbyists to effectively advocate legislation that they do not fully understand. In the give-and-take of the legislative process, administration lobbyists need to be familiar enough with the legislation to know which sections of a bill are essential to achieving the administration's policy goals and which can be sacrificed. As legislation becomes more and more complicated, it has become even more difficult for White House lobbyists to stay informed on the content of legislation. Members of Congress have also had trouble keeping up with the implications of increasingly complex legislation, intensifying their need to ask lobbyists questions about sections of bills and their significance.

Liaison officers realize that if they attempt to push the details of legislation that they do not fully understand, they may damage their credibility. Several White House staffers reported that while it helps to have enough expertise with a subject matter to deal with it comfortably, it is not absolutely necessary, because you always have access to people who are specialists in the subject. Frequently, when lobbying for legislation that involves technical issues beyond their grasp, liaison officers will bring along policy experts or "technicians" to help them with specific language or provisions of a bill.[21]

When William Cable was put in charge of lobbying the House for Carter, he insisted that responsibilities be divided geographically. Cable divided assignments by giving each staffer a small cluster of states rather than the broad regional distinctions that some previous administrations used. Each House lobbyist was assigned about ninety members and told to become familiar with them and make occasional visits independent of seeking specific votes. One liaison staffer reported that when he suddenly began to drop in for these visits, "Some members would be happy to see you, others would look at you like you were from Mars."

An issue-based organization was retained on the Senate side, but this was possible because the smaller number of members enabled liaison staff to establish a credible working relationship with members while retaining their issue expertise. Such an organization has been used on the Senate side by other administrations, especially on matters of foreign affairs. In the case of the Carter administration, Bob Beckel was responsible for national security issues and coordinated the administration's effort to gain ratification of the Panama Canal Treaties.

The triumph of the member-oriented "shoe leather" approach provides some insight into what members of Congress expect from the White House.

Congress is an institution that operates on the basis of personal relationships. In addition, both the executive and legislative branches are full of policy experts, and the credibility of the White House liaison staff has more to do with their access to the president and understanding of the electoral needs of Congress than their grasp of the details of proposed policies.

THE VICE PRESIDENT AS LOBBYIST

The person in the Carter White House most knowledgeable on the legislative process was Vice President Walter Mondale. A legislative role for the vice president seems natural given the formal position of presiding officer of the Senate and, since many vice presidents have been drawn from the ranks of Congress, their potential to assist seems obvious. As the vice presidency grew from a position of awaiting presidential demise to something closer to a full partner in White House affairs, the potential for the use of the vice president in legislative matters grew as well.[22] John Nance Garner, while serving as Roosevelt's vice president from 1933 to 1940, attended FDR's meetings with congressional leaders and assisted the president with his program on the Hill. He reported to Roosevelt in 1934, "as I have said to you before, I think my greatest contribution can be while the Congress is in session in keeping contact with the Senate and House. I have had some experience and, I might add, what seems to be luck in that particular. As your messenger, I will try to hypnotize, mesmerize and otherwise get our friends to approach matters in a helpful way."[23] As vice president, Nixon had been brought into all legislative leadership meetings as well as all Cabinet meetings. He was also very active working on Capitol Hill, holding meetings and working on behalf of the president's programs. Hubert Humphrey had been an active lobbyist for the Johnson administration, although his role was often overshadowed by the president's personal involvement.

The increasing importance of the office put the vice president in a position of serving as a credible voice for the White House. At the same time, the importance of the office also increased other demands on vice presidents. So, just as vice presidents had developed more potential for working with Congress, they found they had less time.

Mondale worked closely with Frank Moore's liaison staff on general legislative strategy as well as lobbying members on specific votes.[24] Mondale used his weekly lunch meetings with Carter to advise him on legislative matters. Bill Smith, from the vice president's staff, sat in on meetings with the congressional liaison staff. The staff also used Mondale's Senate office as a staging ground for their lobbying in the Senate and the vice presidential

mansion for entertaining members of Congress. Equally important, Mondale
had many friendships on the Hill. After Carter struggled through 1977, Mondale advised the White House on reducing the size of its legislative agenda
to prevent overwhelming Congress. One of the ideas produced by the vice
president's review of Carter's legislative priorities was that if legislation were
a presidential priority it would be managed by a legislative task force run out
of the White House that would be assigned to manage it. Each task force was
chaired by a senior White House official and provided a written work plan to
Hamilton Jordan and Frank Moore that outlined congressional, public outreach, and press strategies.[25]

One of Mondale's most significant contributions was that he provided a
high-level advocate of the congressional perspective and helped the congressional relations office educate the rest of the White House staff on congressional needs. Mondale's clout also helped insure that the White House
would stay focused on its legislative strategy and stay within its limits.

Educating the White House

One of the most important functions of the congressional relations staff
is educating the rest of the White House on the needs and functioning of
Congress. This role ranges from providing specific pieces of political intelligence about the timing and support for pending legislation to creating a
broad understanding of the norms of the legislative process. Bryce Harlow
offered seminars for White House staff during his service in the Nixon White
House, but the education is more often an ongoing process of socialization,
accomplished through day-to-day interactions with other staff members. The
role of educating the White House is one way in which the liaison office goes
beyond what we traditionally think of as lobbying.[26]

The congressional relations office in the White House and other executive departments must play a dual role and serve as a conduit for information
both to and from Congress. While carrying presidential wishes to Congress
is the most obvious function of the liaison operation, the information they
bring back is also important. This information can be used to educate others
in the executive branch on the norms and political realities of the legislative
process. One Carter liaison staffer stated, "We would go in and meet with
Eizenstat or Jordan and explain you can't do that or if you let this member
introduce the bill then you're going to piss off this chairman of a key committee. That's the role of congressional liaison to be both the president's advocate on the Hill, and the Hill's advocate inside the White House."

Members of Congress consider the liaison staff an important channel to the president. One senior member of the Appropriations Committee believed that this function was especially important for the work of his committee. "Especially in the appropriations process, we need access to the president so we can call him and tell him, 'Look, Mr. President what you're asking us can't be done. We need to be able to work together more closely.' Someone is needed in the executive branch to remind appointed staffers and career bureaucrats of the electoral concerns of members of Congress."

Joseph Pika has pointed out that organizations like the White House Office of Congressional Relations are "boundary role persons" who must serve constituencies both within the White House and in Congress.[27] Often the most important "lobbying" that can be done by the legislative relations team is to convince White House staff to be more cordial toward Congress. A veteran of the Nixon and Ford White House described educating the White House as a big portion of the congressional staff's responsibilities, particularly for the head of the staff. According to him, "Clearly, 50 percent of the time is spent working on internal things." Harlow and the rest of the liaison staff attempted to temper Nixon White House hostility toward Congress but with little success. The lack of familiarity in the Nixon administration contributed to an "us vs. them" feeling that was referred to as "paranoid" by one of Nixon's legislative assistants.[28] In a similar fashion, the Carter liaison staff worked to keep Hamilton Jordan and Jody Powell from exacerbating tensions with Congress. One member of Carter's liaison staff described diffusing tension as crucial to correcting the White House's problems with Congress: "[I]mportant to that was an education of the rest of the White House staff to the importance of Congress and how you treated it. You couldn't leave it exclusively to the congressional liaison to handle it. We could do a lot of good work and one person at a party or [social] function could blow it. A vote or a carefully cultivated friendship could be undermined, just in terms of attitude."[29]

This educating of the White House staff is by no means unique to the Carter and Nixon administrations. The Reagan administration would include many experienced political operators but their experience was from outside Washington. During the Ford administration, sources in the White House seriously undermined the liaison staff's efforts on the Education Appropriations Bill by telling the *Washington Post* that the White House was not really putting up a fight to sustain the president's veto. Max Friedersdorf complained to Jack Marsh that such stories left congressional supporters who had taken positions on issues resentful of the administration. "When we appear to back off on these vetoes, whether we can win or not, it destroys our credibility and makes it more difficult to obtain support for other vetoes. I am particularly disturbed about persons outside the White House Congressional Relations Staff making 'source' statements that cut our legs off."[30]

The ability of the liaison staff to provide a steady stream of fresh information was particularly important as the norms of Congress shifted and Washington moved from institutionalized pluralism to individualized pluralism. With the decentralization of power and the rise of the individualized style of politics, the locus of control and means of influence were continually shifting.

What is unique about the Carter administration is that the education of the staff extended to tutoring the head of congressional liaison, the person who usually takes the lead in teaching the White House about Congress. As one Carter liaison staff member described it, "This was a whole new era for Frank. Frank had to learn a lot. So we were kind of teaching Frank along the way." During the early days of the Nixon administration Bryce Harlow's credibility provided a degree of protection and his experience provided guidance as the rest of the staff learned their way around Capitol Hill. Frank Moore could not provide that kind of credibility with Congress and the administration's reputation suffered a decline that could never fully be reversed.

Presidents like Carter who come to office by running against Washington are faced with a dilemma of either leaving congressional relations in the hands of people with little or no experience with Congress or in the hands of people that newcomers to Washington on the staff may believe helped create the current problems. Drawing staff people from Congress led some in Carter's circle to question where the liaison offices' loyalties really lay. Outsider presidents like Carter are distrusted in Congress, making the job of congressional liaison staffers, the professional allies of Congress, difficult at best, since by nature their job is to give aid and comfort to the enemy.

This often has led some in the White House to distrust those members of the legislative staff who possess any experience on the Hill. This tension inhibits the education of the White House staff when it may be needed most. The task of educating the White House staff was especially important in the case of many of the people that Carter brought from Georgia, but also was more difficult because of their anti-establishment perspective. One Washington veteran on the Carter liaison staff reported: "The Carter people that came into the White House were entirely new to the game. Carter himself was completely new to the process, in fact he ran on that. So they came in with that whole perspective. It was difficult to relate to them how important it is to be political and work with the process."

The role of educating the White House staff involves much more than providing particular bits of political intelligence. Interpreting these bits of information and placing them in the proper context is equally important. Educating the White House requires transmitting information and making sure that it is taken seriously by the president and the senior White House staff. It is not enough to tell those who write policy in the White House of the position of members of Congress, but to also make clear the full importance of certain members and the need to accommodate their views. This is one reason why the congressional relations staff needs credibility within the White House as well as on Capitol Hill. Sometimes the rest of the White House will defer to legislative affairs on what should be done, but the problem, as described by one White House lobbyist, is that "everyone in Washington is an expert on Congress."

The liaison staff provides the mechanism for feeding the White House the information on congressional thinking that is necessary in crafting a successful legislative strategy. Once this communication link is weakened, the White House begins making strategic decisions with little or faulty information. As Nixon had less exposure to the information provided by the congressional relations operation (or direct contact with individual lawmakers) and more exposure to the new summaries of Pat Buchanan or the political intelligence of Chuck Colson, his view of the world was changed. Ultimately the counterattacking strategy of the Nixon White House may have helped the public standing of the president but cost him votes in Congress. According to one liaison staffer, attacking the Democrats only hurt the administration on legislative battles and the congressional relations staff had to try to rein in counterproductive efforts. "We were in a battle with the public relations people a lot. Part of the White House wanted to continually do battle with Congress on public relations."

By contrast, Carter's closeness to Frank Moore and his congressional relations staff helped prevent Carter's relations with Congress from deteriorating over the course of his administration. Some legislators noted that Carter became more friendly toward Congress after his early problems. Some of this can be credited to the ability of Frank Moore and the congressional relations staff to make Congress's voice heard in the Oval Office. Given Carter's closeness to Hamilton Jordan, a leading contributor to friction with Congress, only someone as close to Carter as Moore could consistently make his voice heard.

One member of the Carter liaison staff talked about the difficulty of getting through to the "Georgians."

It's difficult to teach members of the White House staff—who don't know much about Washington and don't have much appreciation about congressional politics—that President Carter was not crowned king. There wasn't a coronation on January 20, it was instead an inauguration. Many people on the White House staff then believed that the world revolved around 1600 Pennsylvania Avenue. They were rudely awakened. And, while our initial efforts to, if you will, "teach" the White House staff, some of whom were fairly high ranking, that Congress had to be taken into account in virtually all aspects of policy and personnel were met with skepticism initially, and then after several of their policies got bludgeoned on Capitol Hill, many members of the White House staff realized that hey, there is another force here in Washington and that force is known as Congress. Of course, they also began to realize that there is a force known as the lobbying community, and the bureaucracy, and the press. This was not certainly unique to the Carter White House staff. It's true with most White House staffs. People are not born to be White House assistants. In order to be a White House assistant you have to have particular knowledge or expertise in an area. You can rarely get that knowledge without going through the school of hard knocks.

Educating the White House staff is generally accomplished by insuring congressional relations staff representation in important meetings. Occasionally, the liaison staff will circulate memoranda to impress upon others the concerns of Congress. The Carter administration made sure that the congressional relations staff was included in the decision process. Before a policy paper went to Carter for a decision it would go to Frank Moore so that the congressional relations staff had input on every policy. A member of the staff explained their role. "We would say, 'This policy is fine but before we proceed any further we've got to talk to Senator Russell Long and the Chair of Ways and Means.' We'd list out who he should talk to, who he should call. Literally, on every single policy we would include a congressional assessment, along with others, [Office of Management and] Budget, [Office of] Political [Affairs]. Sometimes our point of view would prevail."

The president is the legislative shop's most important student. While many presidents, like Ford and Johnson, were as experienced with Congress as anyone who served on their staffs, other presidents have needed a broad education on Congress. Ford and Johnson needed specific political intelligence like the positions of members and the status of legislation, while presidents like Carter, Reagan, and Clinton were entirely new to the legislative process as practiced in Washington. Even with an experienced legislative hand in the Oval Office, Bill Timmons was concerned about keeping President Ford current on legislative matters.

> As a suggestion, you may want to include the President's Assistant for Legislative Affairs in briefings for the President before any press conferences.
> While the WH press corps seldom asks questions on legislation, there is always the possibility the President could be embarrassed by failing to properly respond to tough questions on measures he should know about.[31]

Over time, the liaison staff helped ease relations between Congress and Carter. According to one member of the liaison staff, "It was tough to get Carter to relate to the Congress. I guess after a while, he realized how important it was that he do some of the things we had suggested he do. One thing I will say about Carter is he would listen to staff."

Jimmy Carter and Congress

The tension between President Carter and Congress had begun as candidate Carter defeated candidates with congressional backgrounds in the 1976 primaries by using anti-Washington rhetoric. Many in Washington believed that an outsider like Carter could not win the nomination, but as Carter gained momentum some Democrats from inside the Beltway, led by Senator Paul Simon of Illinois, tried to organize to prevent Carter from winning the nomination.

Carter's attacks on Washington were vaguely threatening during the campaign, but once Washington realized Carter intended to follow up on his promises, tensions began to rise. Congress became alarmed when they realized that Carter's assault on the way they had been doing business was more than campaign rhetoric. One Carter aide commented: "Carter's campaign was that he was going to do something very different than Washington had been used to. . . . Water projects was a great example at the beginning of the administration. He said he was going to do that and I don't think anybody in this town believed him." When asked if Carter's campaign undermined his work with Congress, another legislative assistant replied, "I think it probably did, but my goodness the man has to get elected before he can do anything with Congress." Another Carter assistant saw a definite impact.

Yes, it [resentment of Carter] was real, it was very real, it was palpable, you could feel it in the process, there was some real tension between the Hill and the White House. Some of it was style, some of it was substance, but it was there. I think that most of it was based on expectations unfulfilled. Unreasonable expectations on both sides. Carter's expectation was that if you could show people that two plus two equals four they had to agree that it was four and that we would proceed from there on the basis of an understanding. But as you know in politics it isn't as simple as a straight line to get from point A to point B. It took the president a while to learn how to work well in this town. I think that ultimately he did, but it sure wasn't easy in the beginning.

The combination of Carter's personal and political styles compounded to alienate lawmakers. Carter felt that his mandate enabled him to make broad policy decisions without extensive consultation with Congress and he felt that the development of good policy rested more on determining what was right or wrong than on bargaining. Members of Congress were irritated by the president's moralistic tone. To oppose a president who regarded his alternative as right was to be cast as being immoral or incorrect. The problem according to Charles Jones was that "A common cause monarch is bound to make members uncomfortable."[32]

Early in the administration, members of Congress were not consulted in a meaningful way. This had two effects. First, members of Congress did not have an opportunity to develop a working or personal relationship with the president through such meetings. Carter did not enjoy spending time socializing with members as much as Lyndon Johnson or Gerald Ford had relished passing time with old colleagues; so, members had to rely more on learning about Carter by working with him. Early on they got few chances to get to know the president. If members of Congress had been provided with more or better opportunities to meet with the president it might have been possible to overcome the lack of trust between them. Conversely, had a sense of trust existed already, perhaps Carter would not have experienced the same reaction from members. Charles Jones points out that "Since Congress is an institution that depends heavily on personal communication and trust, a more impersonal style causes perplexity, even suspicion."[33] Second, by the time legislators were brought into the White House, Carter had already made his judgment and was moving ahead. This left members who had reservations to either reluctantly fall in line behind Carter or to oppose him, driving the two sides further apart.

Some reports indicated that Carter was reluctant to ask members of Congress directly for their vote.[34] One member of his staff disagreed.

> Carter was not uncomfortable asking for votes. In fact, he enjoyed calling members who had publicly announced against him. He was uncomfortable in doing business in the "help me and I'll help you" kind of way, horse-trading if you will.
>
> I can remember Jim Wright and Carl Perkins telling me that they couldn't make Carter understand how important this was and how much it would do to help further his agenda if he could just find a way to go along and help us out and get over these little rough spots. And these little rough spots were "my dam" or "my road" or my highway or bridge. Members perceived Carter having a hard time doing that kind of business. I think there's validity to that.
>
> However, I can show you examples of where he made deals like that. I think he was very pragmatic. I remember on an energy vote we needed a vote from a member and we got his vote by trading for some California water project. There was a negotiation that wasn't with the president, but it was authorized by the president who said "go take care of it—we need this vote."

Carter was comfortable asking for votes and even seemed to relish doing so when he could do so on the merits as he saw them. But the president remained uncomfortable with the give-and-take of political bargaining. As one of his assistants described it, "He would have liked to have thought that, given a fair chance, he could have convinced everyone that his position was right for substantive policy reasons."

While Carter would later be faulted for being too bogged down in administrative details and failing to delegate enough, his knowledge of legislative issues impressed many members and made him an effective lobbyist when pressing the merits of a case. One congressional Democrat reported:

> You could go to the White House when Carter was president and you had committee chairmen and others from the legislative branch who had a great deal of expertise in a given subject area because they had been on committees that dealt with that issue. . . . They would ask questions of President Carter and he had the answers—chapters and verse—in detail.

Another member of the liaison staff remembers the impression Carter made with his grasp of details.

Early in the administration in the spring of 1977 he had the California delegation in. I was sitting next to one member whose district was involved in a controversy over the use of certain kinds of nets in tuna fishing that were harmful to dolphins. So this member gets up to talk about how big of an issue this is in his district and how many jobs are involved and he wants to make sure that his district didn't suffer under new regulations. So then he asks the president for his view. Those of us who had put together the president's briefing paper for the meeting missed the issue completely and hadn't put anything about this issue in the briefing. We're sitting there thinking "Oh shit, did we miss that one completely." Carter not only answered the question, he did so in detail. He knew about every different kind of tuna, every different kind of net. And this member said to me, "I'll be damned, he knows more about the subject than I do and it's my district."

Carter's work ethic was also an asset to his lobbying. His legislative assistants note that he always completed the lists of phone calls. "You never sent a list to be called into Carter or Mondale that did not come back with all the calls made. . . . Carter would sit methodically and make the calls." Also, the administration's files are filled with photocopies of hundreds of handwritten letters from Carter to members of Congress, some of them several pages long.[35]

Carter's approach to Congress and politics in general contributed to both his successes and failures. Many failures resulted from Carter's unwillingness to compromise, and his insistence on pressing ahead on unpopular issues, lawmakers believed, created unnecessary electoral risks. Even after the administration cut back on the flow of legislation after the first year, criticism of the Carter agenda continued. Frank Moore reported to the president that "Many Senators are grousing about the number of tough legislative issues they feel we are forcing them to act on this year. Several resent our sending the arms package, Greek-Turkish initiatives, and the Labor Law Reform hard on the heels of the Panama Treaties votes. Some will use their pro-treaty votes as excuses to vote against us on other tough issues."[36]

Much of the friction between Carter and Congress resulted from his refusal to back off some issues. Carter resisted compromise on his agenda and specific pieces of legislation. He continued to press for policies based on whether he saw them as right or wrong, often seemingly oblivious of the risk that lawmakers saw in taking these positions. Historian Burton Kaufman wonders why Carter continued to push for a ten-cent-per-gallon surcharge on imported oil. "Why the president insisted on challenging Congress on such an unpopular measure when relations with Capitol Hill were already so strained and his administration was in such deep water politically remains something of a mystery." Kaufman answers his own question when he notes that Carter believed the tax was necessary.[37] This was simply Carter's view of politics. One legislative assistant notes that Carter's problems came from his belief that he could depoliticize the process. "My criticism to this day of Jimmy Carter is that he was wrong, but so were the voters. They did in fact say that's what they wanted and he believed it and tried to give it to them, but the fact is you can't depoliticize government."

Another legislative liaison staffer saw two sides to Carter's stubbornness. "I think that Carter was willing to take on a lot of stuff that other presidents would not take on. Some of it, like the Department of Education, I wish had not happened but some of it, like the Panama Canal treaty, I'm glad he did." Carter's unwillingness to avoid a fight because of the likelihood of losing contributed to a number of legislative defeats that only served to increase tension with Congress, undermining other legislative initiatives.

Carter's approach is reflected in his handling of water projects. Carter considered many of the water projects prime examples of pork-barrel projects and announced soon after taking office that they would be reviewed and, if found to be wasteful, canceled. Carter pursued these projects regardless of the party or power of the members who represented the districts involved. As one liaison staffer admitted, "We took on water projects when we should have been selective, but we went after some projects that were near and dear to members' hearts." Carter saw the issue in terms of the monetary costs of various projects, while the liaison staff saw the costs in terms of goodwill lost and future votes undermined. Still, as one aide described it, "The worst way to persuade Carter to do anything was to go in and make the political case for it. He just wouldn't hear it. He'd say, 'you do your job and I'll handle the problem,' or 'The politics will take care of themselves.' Maybe it should."

Jimmy Carter was not apolitical. However, he often seemed unaware of the political realities of life in the legislative branch. The president saw electoral reward in pursuing the legislative agenda that he thought would best serve the nation as a whole. Members of Congress, on the other hand, saw a need to serve their districts or organized interests that were powerful in their district. Carter certainly failed to fully recognize the electoral demands of congressional districts, but at the same time members of Congress failed to recognize the political realities that confronted the president. While party seemed to unite the president with congressional Democrats, there were significant differences in the needs of the two as they looked toward reelection.

The Decline of the President as Party Leader

Carter was the first president to operate in a system that Sam Kernell has labeled "individualized pluralism." Individualized pluralism is a system of "independent members who have few group or institutional loyalties and who are generally less interested in sacrificing short-run, private career goals for the longer-term benefits of bargaining."[38] Such an environment creates challenges to presidential leadership in Congress in two ways. First, members have no connection to political institutions like party from which the president can draw strength. With rewards through collective organizations being available, the president cannot rely on those organizations as channels of influence. Members realize that they cannot rely on political parties to win elections for them and have developed independent sources of resources.

Joe Califano, who served in the Johnson and Carter administrations, wrote that "the political party is at best of marginal relevance to the performance of the duties of the White House."[39] This became increasingly clear during the Carter administration as the Democratic majority in both houses openly resisted much of what the White House wanted. Carter arrived in office hoping to change the way that Washington had been working. During the election, he and his forces wrested control of the party from a more Washington-oriented group and the president's goals were not always enthusiastically embraced by Democrats in Congress, in part because his national goals (austerity) clashed with member's local needs (district spending). Eight years of divided government had prevented the president's leadership of the party from being put to a thorough test as the system of institutionalized pluralism fell apart. However, when Carter took office, the limits of party leadership quickly became apparent.

The new president faced new leaders in his own party. Not only were these new leaders headstrong, they seemingly represented the least harmonious match for a president like Jimmy Carter. The House selected Thomas P. (Tip) O'Neill of Massachusetts as their new Speaker. O'Neill was known for the premise that "all politics is local." Senate Democrats elected Robert C. Byrd of Virginia, an acknowledged master of pork-barrel politics, as their new leader. Carter's assertion of a national mandate and his disdain for pork-barrel projects put him at odds with the leadership of his own party.

Speaking at a dinner in his honor less than a month after the inauguration, House Speaker O'Neill sent a strong message to the new administration about congressional independence. He suggested that Congress wanted to cooperate with Carter but pointed out that during the last eight years Congress had developed an independence and "gained back the powers to make us equal."[40] He warned that members of Congress were ready to challenge the White House and their own congressional leadership. O'Neill went so far as to assert that members of Congress would "just as soon take on a Mr. Carter as they took on a Mr. Nixon or the war [in Vietnam]."[41] Given that Congress had taken Nixon to the brink of impeachment, such a warning to a fellow Democrat seems especially strong. Even if O'Neill was overstating the sentiment of members, this comment coming from a congressional leader of the president's own party reflects a desire to demonstrate a very high level of independence. When members of the Carter White House made similar statements they were accused of being hostile and needlessly irritating Congress, but with Congress asserting itself few seemed shocked by the Speaker's warning.

Despite the differences between the Carter White House and the Democratic leadership, O'Neill and Byrd worked closely with the White House. Carter liaison staffers generally praise both men, although one suggested that Speaker O'Neill was easier to deal with.

> O'Neill was willing to rise above his premise that all politics was local and work with Carter on national issues. Byrd was a very difficult guy to deal with. He perceived himself to not only be a great national statesman, but a great world statesman. When you had to sit in there with him between his cigar and playing his violin with his long lectures about the history of the presidency, that was tough to deal with.

Although many of Carter's failures can be attributed to the White House's failure to understand Congress, some problems were created because congressional leaders failed to understand or recognize the political forces that had brought Carter into office. It seems unfair to criticize Carter for failing to understand the political realities of Congress without at least considering congressional leaders' failure to understand the nature of Carter's election. In 1992, one senior Republican senator laid much of the blame for the soured relationship between Carter and congressional Democrats at the feet of the Senate leadership. "I think Carter tried hard, I think he learned the hard way like Clinton if he's elected. A lot of these guys around here, it's not the right attitude, but they think, I'm going to be here for twenty-four years, that guy is going to be around for four or eight years at the most. So I'm not going to change my philosophy to satisfy some guy that is just passing through town." Just as many members of Congress could claim that they would remain well beyond Carter's service, Carter can today claim that the frustration with Washington that swept him into office has remained well beyond the service of most of those same members. The success of presidential candidates running as outsiders suggests that Carter's high-toned rhetoric had some lasting resonance with voters.

Some of Carter's problems keeping Democratic members in line behind his proposals resulted from growing congressional independence. Congress had just come off a string of victories in reestablishing congressional power. They had helped drive Richard Nixon from the presidency with the threat of impeachment, helped force an end to the war in Vietnam, and rewritten the budget laws to restrict the president's ability to impound funds. The last few years had been heady ones for Congress and they were in no mood to give up what they had gained.

Almost two-thirds of the 95th Congress had been elected in 1968 or later. These members were trained in a period of divided government and distrust of the president. In his memoirs Carter noted that few Democrats had served with a president of their own party and described their attitude as "one of competition rather than cooperation with the White House."[42] David Broder noted that, "In the years of conflict with Republican presidents, congressional Democrats developed a sense of their own power, and they have largely lost the habit of deference to the White House."[43]

Members of Congress were happy to assert their independence from the executive because there seemed to be little electoral advantage to working with the president. Democrats enjoyed a solid grip on both houses of Congress. After the 1976 election Senate Democrats held a 61-38 margin (with one Independent) and in the House the Democrats enjoyed a comfortable 292-143 advantage. However, the Democratic majority in Congress was not considered Carter's majority. Jimmy Carter had not brought the Democrats into majority status; it was a status they had enjoyed since the Eisenhower administration. Democrats had gained a large majority in Congress in 1974, well before the first appearance of Jimmy Carter in the national polls. Carter ran ahead of very few congressional incumbents, and one House aide remarked, "Congress doesn't owe Jimmy Carter anything."[44] Representative Elliot Levitas (Democrat-Georgia) claimed, "I didn't run on his coattails; he ran on mine."[45]

Carter did attempt to help congressional Democrats both in 1976 and 1978. In 1978 the White House lined up over three hundred appearances for the president, first lady, vice president, senior White House staff, and cabinet secretaries to help congressional candidates, and in the final weeks of the campaign the White House dispatched most of the congressional liaison staff out into the field to implement a national get-out-the-vote program.[46] Still, Carter received little for his efforts. One Democratic senator asked, "Is he [Carter] going to help you raise money? Good, that's about all he can do for you."[47]

Several trends provided congressional Democrats with ample evidence that there was little to fear from a failure to follow their president. Divided government was becoming the norm in Washington, and while the Carter years provide an exception, it may have been apparent to members of Congress that voters saw little connection between the White House and Congress when they cast their votes. In addition, congressional incumbents had become entrenched in Congress by high reelection rates.

There was also a large expectations gap. In several ways, Congress was disappointed in what they were getting from the White House. One veteran of the Nixon and Ford liaison staff commented, "Ford got along better with the Democrats in Congress than Carter so far has done [in 1977]. This was partly because the Democrats did not expect too many favors from a Republican administration and were always pleased with what they got. But from Carter, the Democrats expect a lot, and because there are so many more Democrats than there are Republicans, there just isn't enough to go around."[48]

Some members of Congress regarded Carter as less qualified than themselves and, according to one Carter aide, did little to conceal that feeling. "I can remember several instances in the White House where senators particularly made it fairly clear that they felt they had every much a right to be in that office, even though they hadn't been elected to it, as the president did. It wasn't superiority or disdain, but a feeling that some of these guys had been around and deserved it." These feelings carried down to congressional staff who had toiled in congressional offices during the Nixon and Ford administrations and fully expected to be drawn into the next Democratic administration. When Carter brought in people from outside Washington it triggered resentment of congressional staffers who felt they were entitled to graduate to an executive branch position.

The decline of the president as the leader of their party in Congress was as much the result of the decline of the party as a decline in the presidency. Parties were losing their clout in elections. Carter as a candidate benefited from this trend, but as president he suffered. Political parties no longer had the cohesion that they once had. It had been the case in the many districts that all someone needed to get elected was the nomination of their party, if they could provide the funds and people necessary to mount a credible campaign. Increasingly, candidates were able to raise their own funds and put together their own campaign organizations. According to one congressional veteran, "They [members] learn very early in the game that the party cannot elect them. So they don't necessarily feel an obligation to take a position just because it's the party's position."

One member of the Carter liaison staff was disappointed to discover that even those members who were usually politically close to the president and may have owed some debt to Carter failed to support him on key votes. "When we lost hospital cost containment, which was on a bipartisan vote, the two guys who stick out in my mind visibly costing us the vote are Marty Russo on the Energy and Commerce Committee and Dick Gephardt on Ways and Means. They were both big Carter supporters on almost any scale. I mean, Carter went and campaigned for Russo in 1974 while he was at DNC. He picked this young suburban Democrat out and helped him. They had a relationship. Gephardt was elected in 1976. Those were the defectors who cost us the vote." One House Democratic official commented, "It's every dog for himself up here these days. They won't do anything that's not in their own interest and I know of very few members who consider Carter an asset in their campaigns."[49] Congressman Cederberg (R-Michigan), who had been in Congress twenty-five years, told one administration official that "everyone in Congress is elected a Democrat or Republican but when they get to Washington, they are all Independents."[50]

Party loyalty was often overwhelmed by a general liberal-conservative distinction or by district concerns. One White House assistant described Carter as being amazed when he looked over congressional support scores because many of the members that he knew best or had campaigned for did not support him as much as northeastern liberals. The Chrysler Loan program brought together Republicans and Democrats from districts that manufactured automobiles. One liaison staff member noted that they worked closely with Dan Quayle on the Chrysler loan guarantee. Energy legislation often united Republicans and Democrats from the same region, as the Northeast squared off against the energy-producing states.

Despite these limitations on cooperation, there are commonalities between the White House and Congress. In contrast to Bond and Fleisher's emphasis on party as shared ideology, George Edwards emphasizes party membership creating a psychological bond between the White House and members of their party. This loyalty can be translated into votes when necessary.[51] Carter did what he could to use party to his advantage. In a meeting with Senator Russell Long, Carter attempted to get Long not to pass a tax cut that Carter considered bad politics and bad economics just before the 1980 election.

> In the next few days you can irreparably damage the re-election chances of both myself and, I venture to say, several other Democrats. If you pursue your present course, I have no choice economically and politically but to fight you. The Republicans will simply sit back and gloat.
>
> You have some formidable weapons in your arsenal. You have a unanimous Committee behind you. You have virtually every Republican in the Senate on your side. You have 24 nervous Democrats who are up for reelection considering whether they should hedge their bets. You can win. But even if you do not, you will not be harmed. You have already won your campaign. I have not and I have an uphill fight. If the most powerful Democrat in Congress defies me on this fundamental economic issue, only Governor Reagan will benefit. I may win, but the price will be too costly.
>
> I need your help. I must ask you to consider the consequences if you do not.[52]

As reforms dispersed power more evenly throughout Congress, the White House found it more difficult to find the kind of powerful congressional ally that can carry a major piece of legislation through the process. Richard Neustadt has noted that "As recently as Johnson's time a bargain with a standing committee chairman was a deal; now it often only is a hope."[53] Frank Moore explained the dilemma to President Carter. "In a way, it is unfair to look to Senator Byrd for leadership on every major policy issue. Nevertheless, since the death of Senator Hubert Humphrey, few other senior Senators are willing to get heavily involved on any major issue."[54]

The Office of Public Liaison and Interest Groups: Special Publics

The Carter administration used interest groups differently than previous administrations that had worked through a small collection of influential interest group lobbyists.[55] The Carter administration's methods sought to bring in a much larger number of people and to bring grassroots pressure to bear on Congress through interest groups. This transformation of interest group lobbying began during the Nixon administration, but their potential for influencing the legislative process was not developed until Anne Wexler took over the Office of Public Liaison in the Carter White House.

Carter faced an interesting dilemma. After the congressional reassertion of power, the president lacked many of the tools that had given the White House power to work inside the Washington system. In some sense, Congress had created a public approach to presidential influence by taking away the president's institutional resources. Carter chose to go public based on his experiences in Georgia, but what he would have discovered anyway was that Congress had hindered other approaches by diminishing presidential power within the system. At the same time, congressional resentment limited the effectiveness of using "outside" forces to move Congress. O'Neill warned Carter publicly that going over the head of Congress to the people would be a mistake. "It upsets me when they say, 'We'll bring it to the people.' That's the biggest mistake that Mr. Carter could ever make."[56]

Another reason why Carter did not make more use of direct appeals to the general public for support is that these were not considered successful in gaining legislative support. Even Carter's staff admits that he lacked Reagan's television communication skills, but as an outsider president he needed some means to draw upon support from outside the Beltway. "Carter needed Wexler's assistance in a way, because he did not have the kind of stylistic communication skills that Reagan did. He needed that kind of Wexler grassroots organizing effort to get his agenda through." Carter needed some means of going to the public without stirring congressional anger.

Although Ronald Reagan would often gain influence by going to the public at large to plead his case, presidents need not turn to the entire citizenry to apply pressure to Congress. The general public may not support the president's legislation or, while supportive, may remain too disinterested to be motivated enough to become a factor. In this case the White House may attempt to selectively mobilize the public or turn to what might be called "special publics."[57] A special publics strategy attempts to manipulate an especially influential segment of a legislator's constituency or a group within the district that is naturally interested in an issue on the presidential agenda.

In May 1978 Anne Wexler took over as head of the Office of Public Liaison, and although much of the Carter administration's legislative operation was often considered ineffective, Wexler's operation was much admired.[58]

Although the Office of Public Liaison continued to work with Washington-based lobbying groups, they became known for their "outreach programs" that built grassroots support by bringing constituents into the White House. These outreach programs were designed to activate potential allies, convert opponents to the administration's point of view, or neutralize those who could not be converted.

Public Liaison's effort to build support through outreach programs began early in the process as the legislation was taking shape. One member of the public liaison staff discussed how the White House made use of input from groups.

> Our attitude about a lot of this policy development was—especially on the big issues—that there was no way people were going to be with us on the landing if they weren't with us on the takeoff. And we tried very hard to bring them in early on. We didn't always agree with them, we didn't always do what they wanted, but we certainly listened. And Stuart [Eizenstat] and his people [the Domestic Policy Staff] were always great about that. . . . If there were major concerns about the constituent groups they were heard early and certainly taken into consideration.

A similar effort was made to build support for Carter's 1979 and 1980 budgets. In the fall, about the time that the Congress went home, the White House would bring in program assistant directors from the Office of Management and Budget and have them meet with constituent groups to talk about budget priorities. This created an exchange of ideas with mayors and governors, and a cluster of public interest groups in which the administration could tell these groups what their priorities were and get feedback from the groups. According to one veteran of the OPL staff, "They would lay out their priorities and we would lay ours out. People had a sense of where we were going to be able to be helpful and where we were not. But most of these people went away with an understanding of the areas in which we could not be helpful so that their expectations were not overblown, which helped us immensely with problem avoidance in the sense that when numbers came out nobody was really surprised. It lowered the temperature dramatically."

A special publics approach creates less congressional animosity because it presents less of a public confrontation between the president and Congress. The Carter White House further diffused tension by contacting members of Congress and asking them who from their district should be invited to these events. One member of the OPL staff described how invitation lists were constructed:

> We did a tremendous number of outreach briefings on hospital cost containment and we did them essentially by calling members of

Congress and saying the president would like to meet with some of your constituents on hospital cost containment. Would you give us a list of people you would like to have invited? We explained that what we were looking for was a combination of people who were supportive but even more people who were neutral or leaning against. We were looking obviously for community leaders. What we got was that, as well as a sprinkling of friends of members who wanted to go meet the president. It was very good for members because they were able to call up their constituents and say, "I got you an invitation to the White House."

By involving members in the invitation process, the White House began the process by doing a favor for a member of Congress. Letting members provide these lists enabled members to demonstrate access to the White House and reward supporters. As one staffer mused, "I mean, if a member of Congress also wanted to invite his largest constituent, we didn't ask who they were." Perhaps equally important, including Congress from the beginning avoided the resentment that could be produced by going to a member's constituents behind his back. Members of Congress also benefited from this strategy because it provided an opportunity to diffuse potential problems in the districts if the member voted with the president. Lawmakers are willing to help a president of their own party if the electoral risks are low. By having key contributors or constituents brought into the White House, members of Congress could gain political cover if the White House succeeded in converting or at least neutralizing opposition in the district. Rather than having to go back to the district and explain an unpopular vote to constituents, members could hope that constituents would learn firsthand why a bill was needed and diffuse the opposition of others.

The Carter administration would bring in these people from "out of town" (their phrase for constituents) for White House briefings by the president, senior White House staff, and cabinet members. After the meeting they would often have a reception in the State Dining Room. Sometimes members of the liaison staff would be brought in to talk to these groups about issues and strategies and why their help was needed.

Wexler described the purpose of their outreach programs: "Our job is to create lobbyists."[59] However, one member of the staff was anxious to point out that the White House was careful to not violate the law. "We never asked them to lobby, because that was against the law, but we basically brought them and saw to it that they were thoroughly educated on an issue. Often the follow-up to their meetings came with some outside organization with whom we worked who would ask them to lobby. Many came to the White House and then, on their own, just went to the Hill. Many came to the White House and went directly to the Chamber of Commerce or some other organization that had helped organize the whole thing."

The congressional relations and public liaison staffs worked together rather loosely. Each built support for the president's policies among their respective clientele with a general knowledge of the other's activities. Both Congressional Relations and Public Liaison were always represented on the task forces coordinating work on important issues, and it was not unusual for these task forces to be headed by Wexler, Moore, or one of their assistants. As one staffer commented, "We [Public Liaison] were a part of every White House task force. We had a very close relationship with the congressional liaison office and the policy shop run by Stuart Eizenstat. On international policy we worked closely with the NSC and with the State Department." However, there were some instances where Wexler's office worked with Moore's staff more closely to target specific members by geographic area or by issue interest (farmers, etc.). As the final vote grew near, the two staffs would sit down together to establish a list of members to be targeted.

The Carter public liaison operation as run by Wexler was distinguished from the Nixon operation run by Charles Colson by its exclusive focus on policy.[60] One Carter public liaison staffer contrasted their work with that of the Nixon White House's efforts to build up support for the president personally: "All of our work was building support for issues. The public liaison office was not involved in personal public relations for the president at all. To the degree that the two are synonymous we certainly were, but the public liaison office of the Carter White House was organized around building support for the president's priority issues."

The special publics approach is also less risky because it may alert those groups most likely to support the president without necessarily stirring opposition as well. The White House often used an outreach program to "activate" individuals who shared their views. While this was usually done by the staff or by the president speaking to large groups in the White House, occasionally the president himself talked one-on-one with important individuals. One example of this can be found in a memo from Hamilton Jordan to the president recommending a number of phone calls to business leaders whose support on a natural gas vote could prove pivotal. In the margin of the briefing paper Carter noted the response he received from each. Next to the background information on William A. Klopman, chairman of Burlington,

Carter scrawled "*100% support.* Will call Hollings—need other names"[61] (emphasis in the original).

The White House also succeeded in these events in converting many opponents into supporters. One member of the staff reported that "In many, many cases people would come in, especially on the international issues but also on energy or urban policy issues, people came with a preconceived notion and changed their mind. And they'd go out to the press and say afterwards, 'I talked to the president. I've decided I'm going to support him.'" While individuals would often deny that they had been awed by an invitation to the White House or by a pitch from the president, many found themselves supporting the president after these sessions.[62]

One member of the congressional liaison staff argued that Wexler was very good at building support on issues and translating that into support on other things. "You would take manufacturers who wanted an investment tax credit and then get them involved in something like employing Vietnam veterans by bringing them in for the goody of being part of the coalition to get a tax break and then saying, 'By the way would you be willing to talk to your senator about this targeted job tax credit?' . . . You bring them in on what they're interested in and then you broaden it to help with the things you're having a hard time selling."

Perhaps as important as attempting to convert opponents is the ability to neutralize potential opposition before it has a chance to build. Some constituents who could not be persuaded to support the administration's policy could be dissuaded from openly opposing a member of Congress who voted with the president. This helped limit public opposition to the policy and eased the fears of election-minded members. One member of the congressional relations staff suggested, "It's very important to neutralize potential opponents. It's almost as important to neutralize potential opponents as it is to energize potential supporters."

The administration's outreach meetings also provided a conduit into local news outlets. The local press was invited to these programs, leading to positive stories in congressmen's hometown newspapers. Local media, like the citizens they were accompanying, could be impressed by the White House and often went out on the front lawn to do an interview.

Every member of the Carter liaison staff interviewed offered praise for Public Liaison's organization and impact. One member of the congressional relations staff considered OPL's efforts a major contribution to important legislative victories.

I think the Wexler model, the constituent outreach stuff, was ahead of its time. She deserves a lot of credit for having broken that ground and recognizing, before it really became in vogue, that you absolutely had to have public interest pressure around the president's agenda or you get overwhelmed from the other side. . . . had it not been for her effort I don't think that the Panama Canal treaty would have passed. I know for a fact that the sale of the AWACs and F-16s to the Saudis and Egyptians would not have worked. That was a very valuable tool for us.

Another member of the staff summarized the importance of the administration's outreach program: "The public liaison office can serve an absolutely vital role in the president's initiatives simply because the congressional relations office talks to the senators and the congressmen, but the public liaison office talks to their campaign supporters and their constituents. And nothing is as eloquent to the ears of a politician as the voices of his constituents."

The Office of Public Liaison was successful because it built support for presidential legislation in a way that did not interfere with the electoral security of members of Congress. Carter's general approach was to advocate the policy he considered best and leave members of Congress to make the case to constituents; by going to constituents first, the outreach program began by lowering the risk to members of Congress. This "special publics" approach to legislative influence reflected the highly individualized politics that was becoming common in Washington.

Conclusion

Many observers believed that Carter's election signaled at least a temporary pause in the struggle between the branches. However, Carter's troubles with Congress demonstrated that many of the barriers to cooperation between the White House and Congress were institutional, rather than simply partisan. Contributing to Carter's problems with Congress was his anti-establishment campaign. As one of his aides reported, "You don't spend a year and a half running against Washington, then come to Washington, and not have to pay for some of that rhetoric."[63] Members of Congress may have wondered what kind of reelection assistance a president who seemed hostile to Congress would offer them.

This tension created a hostile environment that contributed to the heavy price the administration paid for early mistakes. As Max Friedersdorf, who would head the Office of Legislative Affairs for Ronald Reagan, reflected, "The Hill is a very unforgiving place. If you make one mistake, they remember it forever; if you do something right, you never hear about it."[64]

One of the most often cited criticisms of the Carter White House was that it did not understand the political realities of Washington.[65] Carter and much of his White House staff did not seem to fully understand or appreciate Congress. Such has been the conventional wisdom for years. However, it is not fair to lay the blame for miscommunication on one side. It may be fair to fault Carter for not understanding the reality of Congress, but it is also fair to criticize members of Congress for failing to come to terms with the reality of Carter's mandate and the citizen concerns behind it. Charles Jones concludes that, "A review of how the Ninety-fifth Congress came to Jimmy Carter suggests that Congress did not altogether understand itself or the new president.[66] Political scientists, the media, and citizens in general expect presidents to heal the rift between the two branches while members of Congress are encouraged at the polls to remain independent. Congress was becoming more and more unmanageable, both for the president and party leaders. One White House aide complained, "There's no consensus on the Hill, just roving bands of marauders."[67] While the growing independence of members of Congress was undeniable, the political reality was that citizens expected the White House to forge a working coalition.

Carter's unwillingness to compromise deepened the divide between his administration and Congress, but his resistance to bargaining may have been overstated. Carter was often willing to negotiate, but he was much less willing to trade political favors for votes. However, by the time of the Carter presidency, presidential bargaining resources were declining as Congress continued to reassert itself so that Carter gave up little when he shunned bargaining within Washington. The rise of individualized pluralism left little within the Washington bargaining community that the White House could use to effectively prod reluctant members, so the president had to look beyond Washington for a source of influence. Carter lacked the communications skills to transform public opinion and move constituents, and so the Office of Public Liaison worked to construct coalitions at the grassroots level. This approach proved to be the administration's most effective tool of legislative influence because it connected an outsider president with his natural base of support outside Washington, while not unnecessarily irritating an increasingly difficult Congress.

THE REAGAN
ADMINISTRATION

BY 1980 MANY OBSERVERS WORRIED THAT THE PRESIDENCY
was too feeble to sway Congress.[1] Lyndon Johnson and Richard Nixon had
begun their presidencies on optimistic notes, but each left under a cloud,
while Gerald Ford and Jimmy Carter had been battered throughout their
presidencies. Ex-president Gerald Ford described the presidency as "imperiled" rather than "imperial," and outgoing vice president Walter Mondale described the American presidency as "the fire hydrant of the nation."[2]

Ronald Reagan campaigned against Washington with the same fervor as
Jimmy Carter and seemed headed for a similar showdown with Congress.
Reagan faced a Democratic House that had been more than willing to confront a Democratic president and was led by senior members who had
helped create many of the programs that Reagan wanted to take apart. However, by the time the president-elect arrived in Washington, he had assembled an experienced legislative liaison staff and took a conciliatory tone in
his meetings with congressional leaders. While attacking Democrats in public, privately Reagan was, in the words of one member of his transition team,
"kissing their ass like you wouldn't believe." The president-elect consulted
with key Republican leaders on important appointments and courted Democratic Speaker Tip O'Neill with private meetings and an invitation to the
president's intimate seventieth birthday party.[3]

Reagan's role in bringing a Republican majority to the Senate fostered a sense of optimism among congressional Republicans, convinced many in Congress that Reagan held sway with the electorate, and gave the administration some control over the timing of legislation. Also, with the Senate Republicans under the leadership of a loyal Howard Baker, the administration could focus its efforts on the House of Representatives.

Reagan enhanced his electoral clout by his successful appeals for public support and won several impressive victories in his first term through his ability to create electoral insecurity on Capitol Hill. However, after the 1982 and 1984 elections, more members of Congress became confident that they could survive an election after opposing Reagan on legislation. As Reagan lost his ability to reshape the public agenda and the electoral expectations of members of Congress, his clout within Washington declined and the administration found itself unable to sustain its early level of success.

The White House Staff

While Reagan won office on an anti-Washington platform, his legislative victories were engineered by Washington insiders. William Timmons and Tom Korologos, who had spent the years since their service in the Nixon and Ford liaison offices setting up one of Washington's most influential lobbying firms, were given leading roles in the Reagan transition team. Max Friedersdorf was selected to head Reagan's congressional liaison staff, and although he was the most experienced member of the staff, every staffer had some Hill experience.[4] Friedersdorf had begun his Washington career as an assistant to Representative Richard L. Roudebush (Republican-Indiana) and later served on both the Nixon and Ford White House liaison staffs. After the Ford administration he served on the staff of the Senate Republican Policy Committee before President Carter appointed him to the Federal Election Commission.

Friedersdorf enjoyed easy access to the president and, through the Legislative Strategy Group, played a leading role in shaping the efforts of the White House. Friedersdorf had the authority to speak for the president. "That's why I meet with him [Reagan] everyday. If I have questions about his position on a piece of legislation or an amendment, I ask the president where he stands, and then I can convey that to my staff and the Hill."[5] Friedersdorf stayed in close touch with the president and Congress, spending more time on the Hill than his predecessors. "I think the worst trap you can fall in is to be chained to the White House. If you don't get to the Hill, you lose that touch."[6] His efforts paid off; as Representative Conable declared, "He knows everybody up here. There's a personal relationship that makes a difference."[7] Friedersdorf believed that "If you take care of the small things, the big things will take care of themselves."[8] One veteran of lobbying described Friedersdorf's strength:

> He knows the Hill, what makes them tick and he knows what kinds of cigars Tip O'Neill smokes. That's what's important. The big things, like welfare reform, the MX missile, SALT, take care of themselves. What's really important is knowing what door to send the car to when you're picking up a senator.[9]

Max Friedersdorf selected Powell A. Moore to head liaison with the Senate. Moore had served on the staff of Senator Richard B. Russell (Democrat-Georgia) before working in White House liaison for Nixon and Ford. At the end of 1981 he was replaced by Pamela J. Turner who headed up Senate liaison for the remainder of the Reagan administration. Turner was a veteran of Senator John Tower's (Republican-Texas) staff and had worked on the staff of Senator Edward J. Gurney (Republican-Florida).

Kenneth Duberstein headed liaison on the House side and would replace Friedersdorf as head of congressional liaison when he left the White House at the end of 1981 to become U.S. consul general to Bermuda. Duberstein had served on the staff of Senator Jacob Javits (Republican-New York) before becoming director of congressional relations first in the General Services Administration (1972–1975) and then in the Labor Department (1976–1977). He would later serve as deputy chief of staff and eventually as Reagan's final chief of staff.[10]

M. B. Ogelsby would replace Duberstein, first as head of House lobbying and then, in December 1983, as head of the entire liaison operation. Ogelsby had served on the staff of Representative Edward Madigan (Republican-Illinois) and on the House Energy and Commerce Committee. In the eyes of some, Ogelsby lacked the extensive experience and connections of Friedersdorf, and Duberstein and was assigned some of the blame for the administration's legislative troubles.[11] While Ogelsby's credentials were not as impressive as Friedersdorf's, the administration's problems were the product of Republican losses in the 1982 election and the increasing partisanship leading up to the 1984 election. During Ogelsby's service as head of congressional relations, Max Friedersdorf was brought back into the White House to help map out a legislative strategy for Reagan's second term. This created "a

crowd at the helm" of the White House liaison staff and some observers felt
that Reagan seriously undermined Ogelsby with this move.[12]

Friedersdorf ended his second shift in the White House in 1985 and
Ogelsby left in March 1986 to be succeeded by William A. Ball, who left in
early 1988 to become secretary of the navy. Ball had begun his Washington
career in the navy's Congressional Relations Office before going to work for
Senator Herman Talmadge (Democrat-Georgia) and then Senator John
Tower (Republican-Texas). Ball was replaced by Alan Kranowitz, who headed
the staff for the remainder of the administration. Kranowitz had served on
the staffs of Senators Dodd and John Tower and then as chief of staff for
Congressman Tom Leoffler. He had also worked in congressional relations
in HUD under Richard Nixon and in the Ford White House.

While Ronald Reagan's public appeals and his work with individual
members were the administration's most visible tools, his congressional relations staff was as effective and hardworking as any to date. While they toiled
in relative obscurity next to Reagan's very public visibility, their contributions
were significant and they were highly regarded on the Hill.

The congressional relations team averaged ten to twelve lobbyists over
the eight years of the Reagan administration, with a support staff of about fifteen.[13] Reagan's staff had issue specializations, although all were called in to
work on big issues. House lobbyists were assigned to work with members who
served on the committees that fell under their issue specialization, while Senate liaison staffers were expected to be able to work with any member of the
Senate.

The Reagan administration moved congressional liaison back into the
White House. During the Carter administration the liaison staff had been
housed in the Old Executive Office Building (EOB) next door to the White
House. While Frank Moore's connection to Jimmy Carter was never ques-
tioned, the Reagan liaison shop made much of its move back into the White
House. Tom Korologos noted, "The EOB is not the White House. In this
town images mean a lot. The Hill saw congressional liaison go back in the
White House. They saw the pros go in. To that extent we tried to do what
Carter didn't."[14]

The Reagan White House learned from the early mistakes of the Carter
administration, but Friedersdorf sympathized with Frank Moore's problems
during the Carter years. "They got off to a bad start. Frank was chastised for
four years for not returning one telephone call."[15] The Reagan liaison staff
set out in the first months of the administration to visit every member of
Congress and let them know that the White House wanted to help.[16] Duber-

stein characterized the liaison office as "a service organization" and said, "Our first, second and third priorities has to be 435 members of the house and 100 members of the Senate."[17] Friedersdorf planned to have "someone practically live in the majority and minority leaders' offices."[18] The congressional leadership and their staffs welcomed this attention and a close working relationship developed.

The Reagan White House was careful not to overload the congressional agenda as Carter had. Even before the inauguration Friedersdorf indicated that the administration would focus on economics and attach a lower priority to the administration's more controversial positions on busing and abortion.[19] The White House understood that in the long run it would be hard to steer clear of social issues unless they could control the congressional agenda. This made the GOP majority in the Senate especially important. One member of the staff told Stephen Wayne, "It will be harder to control the agenda as time goes on. Issues will converge at the wrong time. A lot [of our success] has to do with our ability to control our own destiny. We have been lucky so far."[20]

THE LEGISLATIVE STRATEGY GROUP

While the administration did enjoy some good luck, its willingness to fully commit the White House's energies to the president's legislative agenda became the key component of its success. Because of the importance of winning in Congress to the success of the administration, legislative strategy became a primary focus of the Reagan White House. According to one member of the liaison staff, the Reagan administration became organized around winning legislative victory.

> Everything was tied to the legislative process for Reagan, to legislative victories, to establishing him as being a victor on the Hill. The president got polling once a month and looked at it, but that was worthless. That was to get a feel for where the American people were. It was to raise some issues before Congress during the coming months. It was not to boost Reagan's popularity.

At the suggestion of his assistant Richard Darman, Chief of Staff James Baker assembled Reagan's top policy, public relations, and congressional liaison staff into the Legislative Strategy Group (LSG). The LSG included the highest-ranking individuals in the Reagan White House, and the "Troika" was represented with Baker generally in charge of the meeting.[21] Michael Deaver also attended, and Ed Meese was invited but often stayed with Reagan throughout the day and missed the meetings. The regular membership of the group during the first term included Deaver, Darman, Friedersdorf, Duberstein, Communications Director David Gergen, and Budget Director David Stockman. They were sometimes joined by presidential pollster Dick Wirthlin and cabinet secretaries with major initiatives coming before Congress. According to Larry Speakes, the Legislative Strategy Group became "the engine that ran the White House."[22]

The Legislative Strategy Group coordinated the development and implementation of the administration's strategy for gaining approval of its legislative agenda. The group, according to one member, "took congressional liaison and moved it up to legislative strategy. It wasn't just the care and feeding of the Congress. It was also how to strategically accomplish the president's goals." While the Carter administration had taken the step of using ad hoc task forces to coordinate work on major issues, the Reagan White House provided effective coordination of the entire legislative program through the Legislative Strategy Group.[23]

The LSG provided a forum for directing a growing array of White House resources toward common legislative goals. The Reagan White House had in-house polling as well as a Planning and Evaluation Office that was used to track trends in public opinion. An Office of Political Affairs was created to work with Republican constituencies, while the Office of Public Liaison continued outreach programs as it had under Carter. The Reagan White House also used the Office of Intergovernmental Affairs to gather support from state and local government and the Office of Communications to generate favorable press relations. These offices, combined with congressional liaison, were coordinated to create a broad-based approach to winning in Congress. According to one member of the LSG, "We had the press office and the communications office singing off the same hymnal. Because we knew the president had decided what he wanted to get accomplished. The LSG ran it for him." While other administrations had developed similar resources, it was the Reagan administration that most successfully brought them together into a cohesive strategy.

According to one member, the LSG was able to succeed because the membership carried weight with the president. "The people you had around the table in the Legislative Strategy Group were the people who could decide what to recommend to the president and have a pretty good chance that they would be the people to implement that recommendation. That gave us an awful lot of sway over things that happened." The Legislative Strategy Group was able to make decisions rapidly and to bring the full array of White House resources to bear quickly. Another member of the LSG recalled one of their finer moments:

> The meeting I recall was the INF [intermediate-range nuclear force] treaty. The difficult factor was that the president was due to be in Moscow to sign the treaty and it was extremely important that we have the treaty ratified by the Senate before the president set down in Moscow. We made it by the skin of our teeth and not without a lot of planning and effort. Senator Byrd in one of his more partisan moments as majority leader decided that he favored ratifying the treaty, but after it had been debated thoroughly on the floor of the Senate, and if it happened after the president was in Moscow who was he to care. In an LSG meeting, Howard Baker had the brilliant inspiration to invite Senator Byrd and Senator Dole on the plane to go to Moscow and be there for the signing. Suddenly all the barriers that had been there dissipated.

Just as in the Nixon and Carter administrations, tension existed between the congressional relations staff and some of the more ideological elements of the White House staff. One of the founding members of the LSG noted the importance of the group's role in resolving conflicts within the White House.

> I got some advice during transition in 1980 from somebody I knew well in the Carter administration in legislative affairs. He said to me my biggest battles would be—not be on Capitol Hill—but within the gates of the White House and the halls of the administration because fundamentally people in the executive branch don't understand the Congress and you come to personify the Congress.

Early in the Reagan administration Meese and Deaver often pressed the conservative agenda with little regard for the realities of Congress. Congressional suggestions for nominations to federal courts often came in conflict with a litmus test on abortion advocated by some in the White House. Over time, these ideologues left and were replaced by more pragmatic staff people. Still, the liaison staff had to remain on guard to prevent flare-ups. One member of the liaison staff, who was included in the LSG, spoke of educating the White House staff on the need to balance ideology and pragmatism.

In the early eighties (through about '85) we had some very hard-line, very conservative members of the White House staff and you had some pragmatists who were interested in getting the Reagan program passed. There were others on the staff who were more than willing to take a loss and stand on principal. Consequently [there was] a constant need for education. They were at loggerheads all the time. We were trying to persuade some of the rest of the staff that conservative principals were nice, and no one was suggesting that you discard them, but if you wanted the president's programs to pass you had to make some pragmatic efforts to get Congress to support them.

The clout of the LSG helped control some of these conflicts between the Hill staff and the conservatives in the White House. Many of the "Californians" considered Congress "a more annoying version of the institution they had faced in Sacramento"[24] and this division could have created problems like those found in the Nixon and Carter White Houses. By making the legislative goals of the administration central to the functioning of the White House, the Reagan administration avoided the problem of congressional liaison staff becoming "boundary role persons," as described by Joseph Pika.[25] This also helped manage to keep the ideological battles within the White House from taking a toll on congressional relations. Conservatives like Pat Buchanan sought to press for a more confrontational approach to Congress and were frequently at odds with those who had to work with Democrats and moderate Republicans in the Congress. According to Larry Speakes, "In dealing with Congress, Pat lived to veto. He was always looking to pick a major fight with Congress, although every poll we did showed that the American people wanted the President to get along with Congress, not be confrontational."[26] According to one member of the LSG from the liaison staff, one of their functions was to avoid having someone in the White House make congressional relations more difficult.

Some of the speech writers spend a lot of time putting in paragraphs that bashed the beejeepers out of the Congress, and the legislative affairs operation would narrowly excise those paragraphs because we were the ones who had to work with the Congress and get them to be cooperative, which was pretty hard to do if they were being slammed in presidential speeches. There was a constant education process.

While part of the success of the Legislative Strategy Group was its ability to reduce conflict within the White House, much of the contribution of the LSG was the commitment of the White House to long-range planning of the legislative agenda and strategy. According to one member, "We did react, but we tried to raise the questions that would let us develop not only priorities and strategies to know in advance where the forks in the road were, to know in advance where our numbers would be." By bringing together those who could control the administration's policy agenda with those who would promote these policies, the White House was able to avoid some unnecessary confrontations and defeats in Congress. The Reagan administration chose to focus on gaining control over the budget and passing tax cuts because it felt that it had strong public support on those issues and stood a good likelihood of victory in Congress. David Gergen admitted, "We recognized early on when we went for a simple agenda, we were staking the Reagan presidency on one issue. If it failed, we didn't have a big fallback. If it succeeded in terms of legislation, that would give us a second burst."[27]

Through the Legislative Strategy Group, the Reagan administration remained more focused on winning legislative victory than any administration since Johnson's, and the commitment of the White House to congressional matters and the long-term planning that the LSG permitted provided the foundation for much of Reagan's early success.

CHIEF OF STAFF

The variety of individuals who served as Reagan's chief of staff demonstrates the significance of that office in dealing with Congress. Ronald Reagan would draw his numerous chiefs of staff from the campaign (Jim Baker), the corporate world (Donald Regan), Congress (former Senate Majority Leader Howard Baker) and Legislative Affairs (Ken Duberstein). According to one member of the liaison staff, "The operation was very much dependent on the chief of staff. There were very different experiences based on who was the chief of staff."

Chief of Staff Jim Baker's role in congressional relations contributed to Reagan's early victories in Congress. His friendly relationship with Senate Majority Leader Howard Baker provided a strong foundation for smooth congressional relations. The two Bakers shared a moderate approach to policy and a pragmatic approach to politics. This contributed to the Majority Leader's willingness to let the White House lead on many issues. One of Howard Baker's aides described the chief of staff's role: "He spent his whole

day on the phone holding people's hands. He knew that if you beat someone, you might need him again. He knew the most important time to stroke
some senator was right after you'd beaten him. Baker would roll [over] Jesse
Helms on a cloture vote, and then he'd sit Helms down in the cloakroom
and have a talk with him afterwards."[28] Members developed a level of trust
with Baker through frequent contact. Referring to a series of meetings on
bailing out the Social Security system that were held in Jim Baker's home,
one participant observed, "We had been there off and on for the budget
talks, parties and such. No one had to tell us where the bathrooms were."[29]

The chief of staff does not have to play a leading role in legislative affairs,
but it is of great benefit to the White House liaison staff to have a chief of
staff who recognizes the needs of Congress. Carter's chief of staff, Hamilton
Jordan, had a rocky relationship with Congress, and Speaker O'Neill frequently referred to him as "Hannibal Jerkin." If the chief of staff can keep
the rest of the White House from interfering with congressional relations,
the lobbying staff can focus its efforts on pressing ahead with the president's
agenda, rather than mending fences between the White House and lawmakers. Otherwise, more staff time has to be devoted to convincing those in the
White House of the need of compromising on policy and taking into account
congressional concerns.

When Jim Baker and Secretary of Treasury Donald Regan traded jobs in
Reagan's second term, the congressional liaison office lost a valuable asset
and inherited a problem. As chief of staff, Regan was willing to commit fewer
of the administration's resources to legislative affairs. Regan's caustic style
did little to help relations with Congress, which were already suffering from
early signs of Reagan's lame duck status. Regan and his staff revived some of
the tensions between the White House and Congress that the administration
had diffused during the first term. Representative Newt Gingrich complained that Regan lacked respect for Congress.

> Our message does not get through at the Reagan White House, as
> also was the case with Carter and Nixon and other Presidents, be-
> cause Congress is seen there as a peculiar body with mere politicians
> who are grubby and demeaning and do not understand very much.[30]

Max Friedersdorf described Regan's first visit with congressional leaders,
whom he proceeded to lecture: "It was just embarrassing. Regan had little respect for politicians as a class. What he respected was wealth."[31]

Further compounding the Regan problem was a perceived dilution of talent in the Legislative Strategy Group. With Baker, Meese, and Deaver gone the group lost clout in the administration and the new members lacked the old group's experience on the Hill. One Regan assistant conceded, "You do have some different players who aren't as comfortable in the legislative process. From my perspective, a Stockman and a McFarlane were just unbelievable assets, both internally as well as on the Hill."[32] The LSG became less adept at long-range planning and eventually ceased functioning under Regan and was supplanted by an informal system that included fewer people. The White House became engaged in short-term planning and damage control. Indecision coming out of the administration contributed to a weakening of its position and to growing irritation in members of Congress who were unable to get commitments from the administration on policy.[33] The LSG was reinstated when Howard Baker took over as chief of staff and this, in the eyes of several on the liaison staff, contributed to a stronger performance in Congress.

Reagan and the Public: Merchandising

Ronald Reagan, like Jimmy Carter before him, came to Washington expecting little support from the political forces inside Washington and planning to turn to the people for support.

> In Sacramento, the most important lesson I learned was the value of making an end run around the legislature by going directly to the people; on television or radio, I'd lay out the problems we faced and ask their help to persuade the legislators to vote as they wanted, not in the way special-interest groups did. As president, I intended to do the same thing. It had worked in Sacramento and I thought it would work in Washington."[34]

Carter had been criticized for believing that he could go over the heads of Congress in the same way he circumvented the Georgia legislature,[35] and Reagan likely would have faced the same criticism except that he quickly proved his critics wrong. One Democratic member of Congress conceded Reagan's effectiveness.

> If you want to put down a president who got his way with Congress, Reagan came as near to doing that as any president since Lyndon Johnson. He came to office in 1981 and got his major economic pro-

gram through a Democratic-controlled Congress by working with a coalition of Republicans and so-called Boll Weevil Democrats. And interestingly enough Ronald Reagan did it the same way that Roosevelt had. . . . They both had engaging personalities, they projected an air of sincerity, and they were able to go over the head of Congress and successfully appeal to the American people. I don't know who coined the name the "Great Communicator," but it was an accurate one. He read his lines beautifully.

He was extraordinarily effective with Congress not because he was liked, admired, and respected by a lot of individual members of Congress but because he had the ability to communicate with the American people and he was advocating a program that at that time a working majority in Congress really favored.

Presidential attempts to sell his programs to the people and mobilize them behind his legislation might be labeled merchandising.[36] The Reagan administration treated public appeals as an integral part of its legislative strategy, but the Reagan approach to public relations was, in the words of one veteran of both administrations, "completely different" from the Nixon approach. Nixon had hoped to use the approval of the American public to increase his influence in Congress. The Reagan White House believed that winning in Congress was the key to gaining public approval and that building public support for the president's agenda was the most productive strategy. Merchandising emphasizes promoting the product more than the salesperson.

The Reagan approach linked public appeals to specific legislative battles. Many of Reagan's addresses were carefully timed to generate support as the crucial vote approached and the president specifically asked citizens to pressure Congress on behalf of his proposals.[37] As Reagan described the battle for his tax cuts when he ran into opposition, "That meant I had to dip into FDR's bag of tricks and take my case to the people."[38] Actually, what Reagan offered was a more aggressive version of Roosevelt's addresses to the people. Reagan mobilized voters behind particular issues. In contrast, the only case where Franklin Roosevelt urged voters to pressure members of Congress was with his court-packing plan.[39]

The merchandising approach is more specific than the public prestige approach described in the chapter on Nixon, both in the scope and the timing of the appeal. Whereas Nixon attempted to create a general pool of public support to draw on at some later date, Reagan attempted to create a specific public response that could be used to pressure Congress on a pending vote before it could dissipate. One member of the Reagan liaison staff noted that the White House was prepared to go beyond the simple popularity of Reagan and let him build support for issues. "We relied on his popularity to a large degree, but clearly when you have the 'Great Communicator,' you let him communicate greatly." The link between general public support for the president and support for presidential initiatives is ambiguous, whereas public support for specific presidential legislation is clearer and harder for lawmakers to ignore.

As discussed in the chapter on Richard Nixon, Samuel Kernell has described going public as "a strategy whereby a president promotes *himself* and *his policies* in Washington by appealing to the American public for support"[40] (emphasis added). The Nixon administration chose to emphasize promoting the president's popularity directly, hoping that popularity or prestige would translate into congressional support for Nixon's policies. Reagan, by contrast, used his frequent appeals to the public as a tool to winning on legislation that the administration believed would in turn translate into public support for the president.

This distinction is important on several counts. First, it represents a theoretically distinct form of influence. A general prestige effect involves a relationship between citizens and the president, while a policy-specific appeal relies more on a dynamic between citizens and issues. Samuel Kernell has suggested that going public undermines the legitimacy of others in the system as the president attempts to usurp the representative role of members of Congress.[41] The degree to which this is true varies with the form of going public. If the president uses his general prestige to intimidate other representatives of the people then he is supplanting their representative role. If, on the other hand, the president advocates his policies in a manner that activates public interest in an issue and that makes it difficult for lawmakers to oppose his ideas that have been made popular with the public, the White House is not short-circuiting Congress's representative role.

Second, this issue-based public opinion strategy may help explain why presidential popularity has not consistently produced any statistically significant links to success in Congress. While presidential popularity or prestige is a constant force that operates continuously in the background,[42] specific appeals for support on policies are sporadic, even for enthusiastic practitioners like Reagan. While there may be a general prestige effect, the skilled use of public persuasion can be a powerful tool in selected legislative cases and, further, can serve as a deterrent to future political resistance.

While the Reagan administration focused its efforts on specific legislative victories, it was not unconcerned about the president's general level of approval and never lost sight of the broader goal of building an image of Ronald Reagan as a successful president. One veteran of the Reagan White House emphasized the importance of passing legislation on public approval.[43]

> In the modern presidency, to be viewed as successful you need to be viewed as effective on Capitol Hill. If you are perceived as King of the Hill, you will be perceived as a strong president who can pretty much get his way. That is certainly something we decided early on and then again coming into the last two years of the Reagan administration. If the president were perceived as coming out ahead on Capitol Hill, then he'd be viewed as an effective president. Therefore, we gave a priority to having good congressional relations which is important in your ability to get things done.

Another member of the liaison team noted that the feedback between presidential success and presidential popularity plays a role in member's response to a popular president.

> When the president is unpopular and when the programs that he proposes are unpopular, one presumes that he is unpopular because his programs have not been popular with the American people or he has failed to communicate with the American people and then it just drags that proposal down.

Reagan focused the nation's attention on his legislative victories on economic policy, while his defeats on infant formula, wilderness areas, aid to El Salvador, and social security were downplayed.[44] Veterans of the Carter administration were amazed by Reagan's ability to claim victory.

> Reagan was a master at taking credit on an issue on which he won only 15 percent of what he proposed and lost on the other 85 percent. He was a master at making that a 15 percent victory, as opposed to an 85 percent defeat. You contrast that with Jimmy Carter who seemed to have just the opposite ability. If we won on 85 percent and lost on 15 percent, and somehow the focus was on the 15 percent we lost.

Unlike other administrations, the Reagan team considered public appeal an integral part of its legislative strategy. According to one member of the liaison staff and the Legislative Strategy Group, "The LSG gave ideas to Reagan about what topics should be in the weekly address based on what was coming up in Congress in the next week and what had happened last week that would be leading into next week. It's all a part of the agenda setting that the LSG controlled." Because the LSG understood Reagan's ability to communicate and was able to keep the White House focused on long-range planning, they often made public appeals an integral part of the legislative strategy throughout the process rather than using such appeals only when other techniques had failed.

To some degree Reagan capitalized on the congressional reforms that had hampered congressional leaders and created the context of individualized pluralism. The reforms that spread power throughout Congress made members only beholden to their districts. Therefore anyone who could move constituents the way Reagan did could influence members with little interference from party leaders.[45] Reagan stepped into a void left by the decline of Washington institutions. He communicated effectively with the public on issues before other congressional and interest groups developed this strategy.

Kernell has argued that "going public fails to extend benefits for compliance, but freely imposes costs for noncompliance."[46] However, as one member of the liaison staff pointed out, Reagan was able to offer members a political cover by making issues popular.

> There were many members who came into the office to be pitched by the president and said, "Look, Mr. President, I really want to vote for what you've talked to me about, but I'm not hearing anything from back home about it." For Ronald Reagan that meant he had a job to do convincing that congressperson's constituents to be in favor of what he wanted. So we'd go to work with Public Liaison, etc., doing that. I think that's an important part of building support for your program, giving the congressman or the senator cover.

David R. Gergen, who at the time was staff director for Reagan, also noted the desire to provide some protection for congressional supporters:

> It's our sense that there are a fair number of Democrats who would like to vote with the President on this program. They feel in some in-

stances that they may be in hot water back home from some of their constituency groups. We want to let them know that the water may be warm, but it's not going to be scalding.[47]

Reagan's ability to appeal to the public was dramatic in the eyes of many. Jeffrey Tulis warned that the Reagan presidency had completed a transformation of the presidency that was now empowered by rhetoric. The presidency, which had grown to imperial proportions under Johnson and Nixon and then shrunk during Ford and Carter, had returned to dangerous proportions.

> Among the consequences of Reagan's election to the presidency was the rewriting of textbooks on American government. It was no longer possible to maintain that interest groups, subgovernments, the checks and balances system, iron triangles, and a demoralized public would frustrate the efforts of any president to accomplish substantial policy objectives, to maintain popularity, and to avoid blame for activities beyond his control.[48]

Walter Mondale, writing after his service in both branches of government, described the importance of going to the public as key to leading Congress.

> When the going gets tough, a president must be prepared to take his case directly to the American people and make full use of the persuasive powers of his office. In fact, a president's responsibility for public education may be the most important responsibility he has and, when properly conducted, the most significant power he possesses.[49]

Still, the impact of going public is often overrated. Congressional Democrats were anxious to point out that Reagan spoke to the nation on Latin American policy several times but lost in Congress. One congressional leader described Reagan's success in Congress by saying, "He had a window when he was great, beyond that. . . ." Reagan took his message to the public in part because it made use of his skills as an actor. However, as Kernell has noted, the reason for the rise of going public has more to do with the changes in Washington. It can be argued that the rise of going public is a reflection of presidential weakness rather than strength. With the decline of parties and the dispersion of power previously discussed, going public became an attempt to replace resources lost. As Kernell described the presidency's needs, "As Washington comes to depend on looser, more individualistic political relations, presidents searching for strategies that work will increasingly go public."[50]

As much as going public may have empowered the Reagan presidency at times, some in the administration believed that reliance on the technique ultimately limited their legislative success. One veteran of several Republican administrations believed that the administration became too reliant on Reagan alone: "Everybody thought that all they had to do is get Reagan to say something." This came at the expense of bringing in other voices to "resonate" the president's ideas throughout Congress and the country. One aide remarked,

> I always thought that the Reagan administration did not do as well nearly as it should have done. They relied almost entirely on Ronald Reagan, "The Great Communicator," and they thought they could put him on television and the public would respond and they could bring in congressmen and they would do pretty much what he asked them to do. Sometimes it worked, but sometimes it didn't.

Reagan's use of the airwaves also made Congress somewhat defensive. One Republican member saw the threat from Reagan as minimal and even counterproductive at times.

> He often would take to the airwaves and say I'm coming to you because Congress won't do this. I suppose maybe he did imply somewhat a threat against members of Congress. . . . If anything most of us of had just kind of set our feet and said he can't get away with this. Congress has equal power among the three branches.

Even before Reagan developed presidential appeals to the public to a high art, forces were at work that would counter this presidential tool. Speaker Tip O'Neill had provided the first warnings that Congress would grow to resent presidential appeals to the public when he warned that if Carter attempted to turn to the public for support in a legislative battle it would be "the biggest mistake that Mr. Carter could ever make."[51] Jimmy Carter was in the Oval Office when C-SPAN began televising from the floor of the House. While Representative Al Gore was the first member to have a speech from the floor of the House televised, the Republican minority learned that they could use C-SPAN to get their message out as well. Reagan faced a televised House, and beginning in June 1986, a televised Senate as well. The increasing access of members to television made it more difficult for the president to dominate media coverage. One senior Republican member of the House felt that the introduction of television into Congress had compromised the president's control of the agenda.

> There is no question it has diminished to some extent the role of the president because any member can command a certain amount of national attention on the tube and the bully pulpit doesn't quite have the same impact it did when the president had more or less command of the air waves. Roosevelt with his fireside speeches was able to move the country and they [citizens] didn't even know what Congress did. You see that day is gone, because, sure the president has access to the tube, but so does everybody else.

Bargaining with Congress also became more difficult because lawmakers were now much more closely watched by their constituents. According to one representative, "If there is a controversial thing on C-SPAN—and even more so on CNN—well my phone starts to ring and I'm immediately sensitized to that issue. Whereas if you just had the print media it might be weeks before the thing would catch up. Television has had an enormous impact." A veteran of the Carter White House echoed this concern.

> You're going to be challenged because there's going to be someone watching the 3 A.M. repeat of the hearing on C-SPAN who's going to write you a letter. I think C-SPAN, CNN, and public television have changed the nature of the political debate dramatically. They have created a multiplication of pressure on members of Congress. Good, bad or indifferent, it's there.

The intense coverage given to the White House and Capitol Hill has reduced the flexibility that both sides need to bargain. In making members of Congress more sensitive to their districts, television has limited the ability of members to bargain within the Washington community. Barefoot Sanders suggested that more intense media coverage has made it more difficult for the president and Congress to communicate privately and that it is tempting for them to communicate through these public channels. "That practice clearly imperils the maintenance of the close relations which are basic to effective executive-congressional relations."[52] Kernell makes a similar point in his discussion of the transformation of Washington from a system of "institutionalized pluralism" to "individualized pluralism." Kernell points out that this transformation has made bargaining more difficult because, having stated their position publicly, it is more difficult to accept a compromise.[53]

One veteran of the Carter liaison staff and a Washington lobbying firm argued that bargaining in Washington had changed, because thirty years earlier members were more afraid of the president than of their constituents since the president could watch them more closely.

> You didn't have to be a representative. You could actually make a decision based on what the common good was and not represent the sort of NIMBY [Not In My Back Yard] syndrome that you do now. Unless you're out there being more protective toward your local constituents you're going to get challenged. . . .
>
> And imagine what it was like thirty years earlier when there was no transmission of that information on any kind of a real-time or generic basis. Congressmen and senators could go into their district and say one thing and come back to Washington and say another and no one would ever notice. It wasn't until C-SPAN and CNN came along when you get where what you said outside out of Washington ever mattered in Washington. I can remember guys in the mid-eighties being decimated because they had to say the same thing in both places. . . .
>
> That's only going to continue. You can't go home and tell the good ol' boys on the courthouse steps that you're against civil rights and not have it reflected in the *Washington Post* the next morning, whereas twenty years ago you could.

While the openness of government is generally considered desirable, one member of Congress worried that there is only the appearance of accountability. "Cosmetically, constituents are able to monitor the activities of their representatives more with the advent of C-SPAN. They see the surface. And maybe that's bad." Constituents may believe that by watching floor speeches and voting they are able to judge the behavior of their members, but because floor activity can often be used to create a facade, there is little meaningful accountability.

In addition, television has contributed to the dispersion of power in

Congress, with every member having access to C-SPAN's cameras. According to Hedrick Smith, "Television has given relatively junior members of Congress a platform to become policy entrepreneurs, and the highest ranking leaders on Capitol Hill are sometimes forced to chase after junior back benchers, to find the head of the political parade."[54] Also, television has, according to at least one veteran of Congress, changed the character of the members. "Members' access to television has changed how they respond to television quite a bit. Once television is involved it becomes show business. If I were king we'd eliminate it."

The presidency has become responsive to the same forces. A veteran of the Carter White House suggested that presidents had become increasingly aware of public opinion trends, so much so that attempting to follow public opinion has become a distraction: "The presidency has changed too because the president has become much more responsive to his constituency on a real-time basis—much more so than I think we had the ability or desire to know."

Electoral Clout

Republican control of the Senate after the 1980 election seemed to indicate Reagan had the ability to influence congressional elections. Members of Congress brought in on Reagan's coattails felt gratitude, while other members saw the potential impact that Reagan could have. The Reagan administration reminded members of this often. One member of the liaison office described the importance of Reagan's ability to demonstrate influence at election time.

> You also have to remember that the vast majority of congressmen elected in 1980 and 1984 ran behind Reagan's numbers in their districts. So a member would say, "My god! Reagan got 62 percent in my district—I only got 54 percent." So the president would be seen as more popular. That was part of the juggernaut that was Ronald Reagan.

Another member of the staff described members' concerns about the next election in a similar fashion.

> Up on the Hill they have got to worry about what is going to be the effect of their decisions to support the president or not to support

the president. They are going to look at the bottom line as being the next election. In a situation where it is not going to cost you votes in the next go-around, then there is no reason to pay a lot of heed to what the president wants from a straight political standpoint. . . . I just can't imagine somebody saying that there is not a connection.

One Senate Republican described Reagan's clout as coming from fear. "Part of power is fear. [Senator] Byrd gets what he wants because we don't want to cross him, but no one really fears [Senate Majority Leader] Mitchell. No one fears Bill Clinton. No one feared George Bush. But members were worried about Reagan. Part of the success of Ronald Reagan in his first term was a level of public support that implied a threat to members." A member of the liaison staff came to the same conclusion.

To be an effective president you must be both revered and feared, and Reagan was both. A lot of members didn't want him to come into his district and campaign against them or speak on behalf of an issue they might oppose. Because they knew that the "Great Communicator" had a chance to turn people around.

One reason that observers have not given much credibility to Reagan's electoral clout is the high reelection rates of members of Congress, who seem invulnerable to defeat. During Reagan's eight years in office reelection rates for members of the Democrat-controlled House rose as high as 97 percent, suggesting that members had little to fear from Reagan. However, the electoral security of members of Congress may be much more fragile than it would appear, or at least it is perceived by members as more fragile. As one senior congressional staff member described it, Congress did worry about Reagan's clout.

Congress is a very human institution, complete with all the insecurities that humans have. This helped Ronald Reagan create the fear that he could have you defeated at the polls. Members just aren't that sure that they can win next time.

If nothing else, members of Congress understand that presidents have the ability to turn out voters to a rally or, more importantly, fill the room at fund-raising events. While many members are generally secure in their district, the president holds the kind of visibility that can raise big enough issues to undermine a congressional campaign. While members of Congress are generally able to dominate news in their district, a visit from the president can easily overwhelm them. Presidents have the ability to single-handedly transform an unknown candidate into a serious challenger in a congressional race. Reagan had the potential go into a district to raise an issue and win over citizens to his side.[55] A visit from Reagan might lead voters to ask the representatives unwanted questions about their failure to support a tax cut after hearing the president define the issue in the light most favorable to his perspective.

The president's clout in elections is generally more potential than real. However, any chance of defeat may look large next to nervous members. Often when the White House approaches legislators for their support they must ask them to choose between the president's wishes and those of constituents, but Reagan's ability to bring these two together made congressional decision making much easier. Lawmakers found during Reagan's first year that the president and his policies were popular and that voting against either was risky, and when Reagan's popularity and that of his policies worked in tandem they became almost irresistible.

There was more to Reagan's electoral clout than simply fear of defeat at the polls. Norman Ornstein suggested that Republican control of the Senate was the most important element in the success of Reagan's policies: "A minority party that moves into the majority after a long period wandering in the desert exhibits early and striking party cohesion."[56] Had the Republicans not gained control of the Senate, Reagan's victory could have been narrowly interpreted as a personal rejection of Carter rather than a Republican mandate, further limiting Reagan's claim to a policy mandate.

Reclaiming the White House always brings perks to members of the president's party as everything from grant announcements to invitations to state dinners become more common. After feeling locked into a minority party status in Congress for almost thirty years, the 1980 election provided Republican members of Congress with an opportunity to serve in the majority party and to play a more meaningful role in governing. The 1980 election and early Republican victories in Congress held out the promise of policy success to Republicans who had experienced few real opportunities to lead in the policy process. Suddenly, Republicans were chairing committees and organizing the congressional agenda. House Republicans, while not in a majority, saw their ranks swelling and could see the fruits of majority status in the Senate. Republicans were playing a central role in the coalition-building process. No longer were Republican votes sought only to replace those of defecting Democrats. Republicans formed the core of coalitions and were key in building winning coalitions. Conservatives found a role other than as naysayers. They could draft bills or amendments that had an opportunity of passing.

Talk of a Republican realignment was everywhere, and Republicans could dream of putting together the kind of electoral majority that had kept the Democrats in power for years. The transformation of the Republican party was apparent to Max Friedersdorf, who observed in 1981:

> The freshman and sophomore classes make up almost half of our 192 members. They are extremely aggressive to make their mark. They want to win and they are fully aware that they have power in unity. They have an influence on the more senior Republicans who have developed a minority complex over the years. They sense that they're getting close to having a majority in the House. This makes for an esprit that I've never seen before.[57]

This sudden activation of the Republican party in Congress reflected well on Reagan, and the expectations of future gains mobilized and unified Republicans in Congress. Republicans now found themselves more fully engaged in the legislative process and were anxious to do everything they could to insure that their good fortune continued. Reagan represented a rebirth of the Republican party in Washington. According to one member of the liaison staff:

> I think it was tremendously important that we could show the House Republicans that if they stuck together that we could get the Boll Weevils and they could win. For so many years they had a minority mentality and we helped them get a governing mentality. In the Senate, it was "we can get done what Ronald Reagan needs to get done if we stick together, because we have the votes." Therefore there was more deference to the president's agenda.

Republicans could see majority status on the horizon. Representative Richard B. Cheney (Republican-Wyoming) believed that Republicans had developed a national sense of party because of "the burning desire, especially by younger Members, to become the majority."[58] Still, some Republicans considered staking these hopes on the Reagan agenda, which was, in the words of Senate Majority Leader Howard Baker, a "riverboat gamble."[59]

Jimmy Carter had been unable to offer these things to a party that had held a lock on Congress for over twenty years, but the wave of Republican optimism gave the Reagan administration a strong start. However, as George Edwards points out, governing places stress on the connection between the president and party.[60] Just as Carter before him, Reagan found that the details of many of his broad policy goals were seen as problematic by members of Congress interested in winning reelection. As Reagan pushed for budget cuts, Republican members of Congress found their president cutting into programs that were often popular in their district. Once the Reagan coalition in Congress moved beyond the popular tax cuts, working together became more difficult. As their role in government increased, Republicans found that the electoral stakes of their decisions increased. They could no longer argue for budget cuts in principal; they had to make specific cuts, all of which risked the support of some constituents.

Thus, the conflict between the national constituency of the presidency and the local concerns of members reappeared. Members sought exemptions for local projects or interests, much to the dismay of the White House. Describing one meeting with Republican leaders, David Stockman complained, "At a White House strategy meeting, Minority Whip Trent Lott summed up the mood: 'Everybody else is getting theirs, it's time we got ours.'"[61]

Reagan's second term was a major disappointment despite his stronger electoral showing. The second term problems began the day after his landslide victory in 1984 when Bob Michel complained that the Reagan campaign had been consumed with making its electoral victory as large as possible rather than helping to elect Republicans to Congress. Michel noted that Reagan had won 59 percent of the vote, but the Republicans had only gained fourteen seats in the House. This not only left congressional Republicans uncertain about their connection to the political success of the White House, it also emboldened Democrats. Congressional Democrats now had evidence that they could survive a campaign in which Reagan was actively engaged. 192 House Democrats had won election in congressional districts that Reagan carried and lawmakers on both sides of the aisle found less to fear from the White House. Something similar had occurred in the 1972 election, when congressional Republicans saw their presidential candidate run away with the election while they made only minor gains in the House and actually lost a seat in the Senate. In both cases Republicans lost some of their loyalty and Democrats lost some of their fear. One member of the liaison staff felt that the nature of the campaign and Reagan's lame duck status undermined the impact of the 1984 election.

> In 1980 he took in the Senate and in the House he had 191 Republicans and he was elected on a mandate for a specific change. In

1984, it was "Morning in America," there were not the specifics, it was "continue what we have developed over the last four years." It was also the fact that everyone knew that Ronald Reagan wouldn't be on the ballot again in four years.

Grassroots Lobbying—Special Publics

Reagan, who engaged in the most publicly oriented style of leadership, also made use of grassroots pressure. The Reagan public relations style included both broad appeals to the public and specific efforts to work members' districts. According to one member of the liaison staff:

> Part of the function of the Office of Public Liaison and the political operation as well was to make sure that the folks back home knew what their member was doing and I suspect they did a very good job of notifying locals of who was where on a given issue. I don't think we would have been doing our jobs if all aspects of the White House would not have been working on this.

Computerized lists permitted the White House to target direct mail to key supporters within a district. The administration also used the Republican National Committee, Republican Congressional Campaign Committee, National Conservative Political Action Committee, the Moral Majority, Fund for a Conservative Majority, the U.S. Chamber of Commerce, National Association of Manufacturers, Business Roundtable, American Medical Association, and other groups to bring indirect pressure to bear on behalf of the president's tax cuts. The Reagan administration compared lists of contributors to the Reagan campaign. The administration found it was able to win some votes by having common donors put pressure on the legislator, but without mentioning the White House.[62]

In what has been described as a nice cop–tough cop routine, members of Congress would be invited to a friendly meeting with Reagan and then return to the office to find a blizzard of constituent response beginning to build. Representative Butler Derrick described his experience in this way:

> I've been here since 1974, and I've never seen an operation as well orchestrated as the way the Reagan administration has handled this budget battle. The president invited me down to the White House one morning with five other congressmen. It was very pleasant con-

versation. There wasn't any pushing. He was giving his views—kind of good-guy conversation. . . . They have apparently gone back through my contributor files and pulled prominent conservatives that have contributed to my campaign over the years and also probably have supported the national Republican ticket. They have gotten in touch with them. It's been very effective in the business community . . . probably sixty or seventy percent of the large-business community people in my district have contacted me. And of course, I have had many small businessmen contact me. I don't recall that I've ever been lobbied quite as hard from my district.[63]

The White House's grassroots appeals on behalf of tax and budget cuts were complimented by those of an outside group, the Coalition for a New Beginning. The coalition was a privately funded effort organized by Charles Z. Wick and William A. Wilson, two members of Reagan's informal "kitchen cabinet." The coalition was involved in funding and implementing a nationwide "education" campaign that featured the distribution of materials and appearances by prominent citizens.[64]

The Reagan White House realized that it could not win votes in Congress simply by putting the president on television, and staffers incorporated Reagan's ability to communicate with the public into a broader legislative strategy. One liaison official described how the kind of outreach program first developed during the Carter administration was integrated into a broader public relations approach.

Before the President goes on television we would first bring in our allies. Reagan would meet with them in private—several hundred at a time and give them an advance view of what he is going to do so that they can alert their allies to be prepared to go.[65]

Reagan and Congress: The Gipper "Treatment"

Reagan, according to one Senate leader, had a "star quality" to him. According to one member of the liaison staff Reagan used his "Irish charm" and star quality to good effect.

One member of the House called me into his office one day and said, "you'd better not have the president call me because here's what I'm going to tell him. And I don't want to say these things and he's not going to want to hear them." So, the president didn't call him, he invited him into the office for a one-on-one meeting in the Oval Office. The congressman walked in, and there's just some aura about the Oval Office, the guy melted and not a single adverse comment came out of his mouth and he went back to the Hill happy as a skylark.

Speaker O'Neill conceded that the president had an impact.

The members adored it when he called, even when they had no intention of changing their vote. The men and women in Congress love nothing better than to hear from the head guy, so they can go back to their districts and say, "I was talking to the president the other day." The constituents love it too, because they want to believe that the representative is important enough to be in touch with the chief.[66]

One member of Reagan's liaison team went so far as to claim, "There were some folks who dreaded getting a phone call from the president because they were well aware that he could charm them off their feet."

Members of Congress interviewed by the author consistently denied being overwhelmed by Reagan and the aura of the Oval Office. One congressional Republican denied that Reagan or any president impressed him. "I was a holdout on the tax bill in 1981. I got the Oval Office treatment. I decided to go along with him out of party loyalty and there were some good things in it. But awed? I see these guys, they're pretty damn ordinary. Very, very ordinary."

Reagan, who disliked conflict, sometimes resisted pressing for members' votes in one-on-one meetings in the Oval Office. David Stockman noted, "He [Reagan] could resolve conflicts of great principle sometimes, but those between people almost never."[67] One staff member found that he needed to have a follow-up meeting with members after their visits with the president to make sure that they had been pressed for a commitment.

I guess if I had any frustration from time to time it was that he would not ask the hard question at the end: "Will you vote with me?" So could he be tough? Sure. Would he be tough in those one-on-ones? No. And I finally learned that what you needed to do was after the president had charmed a member of Congress that someone else had to be the bad cop and ask, "What are you going to do? Are you going to be there?"

At the same time this staffer noted that Reagan would press members for their vote when using the phone. "In person it was one thing, on the phone it was another."

In sharp contrast to Carter, who relied on businesslike reasoning to persuade legislators, Reagan offered warmth. According to one member of the liaison staff, Reagan's personal warmth may have been especially influential with members because they realized that this same warmth was often felt by constituents.

> I think when members of Congress go home and speak to their constituents and pick up this well of affection for the man in the Oval Office, they catch on real quick that this guy has communicated emotionally to the folks back home and there's no question that they are going to help him when they can.

While much of the Reagan administration's public and legislative strategy was carefully crafted by the Legislative Strategy Group, the administration gained an unexpected boost when the assassination attempt helped energize a presidential agenda. Polls within the administration had shown Reagan's popularity beginning to slip, but the sympathy that resulted from the shooting and the admiration for Reagan's personal response gave the president a much-needed surge in the polls. Richard Darman admitted the importance of this incident to Hedrick Smith.

> That [assassination attempt] was crucially important. I think we would have been way out of the normal presidential honeymoon at the time of the crucial votes on the budget and tax cuts if there hadn't been a "second life." The shooting and Reagan's recovery was not only a second life for Reagan but a second life for Reagan's honeymoon. Sheer chance—and extraordinarily important. In fact, I think we would have had to compromise on the tax bill without it.[68]

David Stockman noted a similar sentiment in his account of the Reagan administration. "There were two miraculous recoveries in April—the President's and his tax cut's—and the former had everything to do with the latter."[69] A member of the congressional relations staff described how Reagan's character was revealed and how the administration used the public's response and the subsequent passage of Gramm-Latta to build Reagan's reputation.

> One of the things that people need to look more at in terms of the success of the Reagan administration is the failed assassination attempt. Remember, everything was very problematic in the first year of the Reagan administration. Things were not going that well. There were fights everywhere. The outlook for the various budget proposals was very poor. And then he got shot. And Reagan responded in a fashion that absolutely enchanted the American people who respond to him very warmly after that event. What that did was to extend the honeymoon for the presidency for a great amount of time and as a result you had Gramm-Latta pass. And, what enactment of Gramm-Latta did was signal to these congressmen in Washington that things had changed.

After the assassination attempt Reagan appeared before a joint session of Congress on April 28, 1981, to deliver what could be described as an inaugural address for his politically reborn presidency. One White House aide said, "He gave that joint address to Congress and we were off." This address gave Reagan the opportunity to place his personal popularity before members of Congress and to connect that to his legislation. The personal standing of Reagan shifted the political debate from the rising doubts about the validity of OMB's budget estimates and the validity of supply-side economics to Reagan himself. By the time of the assassination attempt, the Reagan administration's economic projections and spending cuts had come under close scrutiny. With the public having little or no understanding of the technical issues underlying the debate, its confidence in Reagan became a deciding factor.

While his ability to go to the public and the assassination attempt provided Reagan with clout in Congress, over time members of Congress saw a lack of connection between the public and private sides of Reagan. According to one Republican member of the House, Reagan's ability to generate confidence was both impressive and problematic.

> Reagan seemed to have a knack for generating confidence, not only in the Congress but in the people. People to this day say that if we just had Reagan in there we wouldn't have all this big spending. In

reality he was the master big spender. The deficit went from a trillion and a half to about four trillion in his administration. But he
would talk about the veto pen and balancing the budget. He was a
con artist in many respects. In a very nice way. Then he lucked out
and the economy got strong by the time he ran for a second term.

Using stories and passion, Reagan attempted to win over members in a
manner that could be as emotionally draining as receiving the Johnson treatment could be physically draining. One Republican recalled sitting in the
cloakroom while another member took a call from Reagan just before a crucial vote. Listening to one end of the phone conversation he heard his col-
league saying "Yes sir . . . Yes, sir" as the president talked with him and then
finally, with tears welling up in his eyes, "No sir." After hanging up the member confided to his colleagues: "I just felt like I told my grandfather I couldn't
go to the ball game with him."

There were limits on Reagan's use of the emotional appeal. Shortly after
recounting the story of the teary-eyed congressman having to say no to Reagan, the member concluded, "His heart was in the right place, he just didn't
know what was going on." Over time, members of Congress began to consider Reagan less effective in their meetings with him, and the warm image
of the Gipper was replaced by that of a stiff president reading from notes he
did not completely understand. Congressional leaders were often frustrated
when Reagan avoided a serious discussion of issues by repeating anecdotes
about "welfare queens."[70] One senior Democrat complained, "He'd read his
index card and make his remarks, then he'd want to swap some Irish jokes
with you." A senior Republican congressional staffer noted that "Reagan
didn't know these guys, he needed cue cards to know who they were." One
senior Republican leader commented that "I'm never sure if he knew what I
was doing as chairman of the —— committee. He didn't look at the jurisdiction of committees: somebody gave him a little card and said, 'Call up
Senator —— and read this to him.'" At the same time this Republican conceded that this was in part a strength of Reagan's approach. The president
was not intimidated by not knowing the names of members or exactly what
they were doing. Reagan was willing to dive into situations and exercise the
clout of the office. Had Reagan been intimidated by the situation, he would
have been detracting from the aura of the office and any uncertainty would
have diminished the power of his message. "I think Reagan appreciated that
we never really let him know what we were doing. He didn't want to know all
of it. Even in Congress."

Reagan's inability or unwillingness to engage members in a discussion of the mechanics of legislation seems to have given members reasons to dismiss his arguments. While Reagan was generally considered likable, his lack of understanding of the intricacies of policies may have kept him from being less than a full member of the club. One senior Democratic member felt that even Clinton, who lacked Washington experience, had the policy expertise to be taken seriously in discussions with members.

> Reagan was a little distant. He just didn't know how to visit with members and talk about legislation. He didn't really understand legislation that much, the issues at stake, what was involved in making it work. He knew where he wanted to go. Understanding details wasn't his strong suit. He wanted to go in there with his 3 by 5 cards instead of living and breathing an issue [as compared to LBJ or Clinton].

Another Democratic member of Congress who had been clearly impressed by Reagan's ability to lead public opinion was less impressed with Reagan's meeting with members.

> It was really a stark contrast to hear some of his public speeches and his flawless performances and to visit him in the White House with small groups of congressmen. His presentations for them were the same as his presentation for the public. He went through his 4 by 6 cards and read them and when he got through he had his cabinet officers and others there and when someone would ask a question he would point and say well you take that one. . . . It was very clear that when he got through reading his 4 by 6 cards that was just about the extent of his knowledge. And that was a very stark contrast to Jimmy Carter.

Reagan's ability to influence members of Congress had more to do with his ability to charm voters, but the president got much less of what he asked for after the 1984 election. Against the objections of his legislative staff Reagan went to the Capitol in April 1987 to lobby members to uphold his veto of a highway bill. One Senate Republican recalled Reagan's inability to defeat the constituent interests of members.

> I remember Ronald Reagan coming up here and pleading with us to veto the highway bill. And he begged us, but he didn't get a single vote out of our caucus. And we only needed one vote. He said "I'm

begging," but he couldn't budge these guys, because they each had their own highway goodies in their states—they wouldn't listen to Ronald Reagan. There are some things you can't move, and again, I don't know how we change that. It's always been that way.

One member of the administration noted, "Reagan throughout his political career never found it in his heart to play consistent hardball with his political enemies. Fortunately, some around him, including his wife, didn't have that problem."[71] While the Reagan White House lacked Nixon's hardnosed approach to politics, they were, according to one member of the liaison team, willing to trade for votes.

On the MX missile, one Democratic member of Congress from a landlocked state in the Southwest was on the Armed Services committee. In order to get his vote in subcommittee, somehow or another, he got a water project, in order to get his vote in the full committee he got another water project, so it went on the floor and in conference committee. And that landlocked district is now a port!

One difference between the Nixon and Reagan administrations is that the Nixon White House would reward members of Congress for their support while under Reagan staffers would do things for members in hopes of future support. One source close to both administrations pointed out, "In the Reagan administration they ran all kinds of people and groups through the White House to meet with the president. There would be Democrats and liberals and afterwards they would go out and kick the shit out of the president. In the Nixon administration we never allowed that to happen. In the Nixon administration we went to them, if they did something for us then we saw what we could do for them."

Reagan's steady course proved to be an asset. As one legislative assistant pointed out, while Bill Clinton had undermined his bargaining position by changing his mind on the BTU tax, Reagan's more consistent approach strengthened his position on Capitol Hill.

The most important thing, and I say this with all due respect to George Bush and to a degree Bill Clinton, Reagan stood for things. It was always clear what his [Reagan's] line in the sand was and what he stood for. And that makes it very easy for an Office of Legislative Affairs because no one is afraid that the rug is going to be pulled out from under them. If they support the president, they know he is

there. If they oppose the president, he's against them and they know
he isn't budging.

One of the problems with Mr. Clinton is that no one is entirely
sure where he really stands and they are scared to death of being
"BTU"ed all the time.

Ironically, Fred Greenstein was leading a revision of scholarly opinion of
Dwight Eisenhower's activism at a time when America had a president who
was even less engaged in the specifics of policy.[72] As Greenstein pointed out
in subsequent research, Reagan succeeded in effectively advocating broad
policy goals with little interest in the details of the policy, in contrast to Eisenhower, who took more direct control over policy.[73] Eisenhower was portrayed
as inactive because he appeared to often leave decision making in the hands
of others. Reagan delegated everything except going public, but by taking
the most visible form of leadership, he was viewed as more active than Eisenhower.

Conclusion

The Reagan presidency provides a prime example of the president's
ability to reshape the electoral expectations of members of Congress. The
administration surprised those who had argued that the presidency was in
decline by convincing members of Congress, at least temporarily, that he
could reach into their district and make their next election more difficult. A
Reagan White House staffer described their influence over a senator on a
key vote in terms of electoral survival: "We stood him in front of an open
grave."[74] Members feared crossing a popular president and feared Reagan's
ability to define issues in a way that would put them at risk in the next election. However, congressional fears of Reagan were short-lived, and by the
end of the administration Congress had gotten over much of its fear of the
presidency. *Congressional Quarterly* commented, "an undertow of constitutional power continues to flow away from the White House toward Congress,
while the presidential luster of the Reagan years has only increased the public's expectations for the chief executive and his ability to take command of
the federal government."[75] One writer went so far as to conclude that
"Ronald Reagan's Hill history has been so extreme a riches-to-rags story that
many feel the relationship has nowhere to go but up [for the next presi-
dent]."[76] In his farewell address Reagan noted that "we have not restored the
constitutional balance, at least not fully—and I believe it must be restored."[77]

Although Reagan's legislative style is distinct because of his effective use of television, his administration succeeded in Congress because the White House made effective use of other resources as well. Reagan's relationship with Congress went much deeper than his smile. The president's television and radio appearances were just one component of a carefully constructed and implemented plan created by the Legislative Strategy Group and carried out by the men and women of the Congressional Relations Office. Because the president's public appeals just before a crucial vote seemed to bring in final votes needed, Reagan's command of the airwaves was given much of the credit for his victories. However, before Reagan used his public appeals to bring in those final reluctant members, they had been softened up by one-on-one lobbying from departmental and White House liaison as well as from the president, cabinet members, senior White House staff, and congressional leaders. Such lobbying was often backed by pressure applied through inter-est group constituents. By the time that Reagan made one of his famous tele-vised appeals to the public a solid foundation had been laid, leaving the pres-ident to finish the job and receive the credit. Although Reagan's communications skills deserve credit for winning many votes, they built upon the work that had come before.

9

THE BUSH
ADMINISTRATION

WHILE BUSH OFFERED THE ELECTORATE THE PROMISE TO stay the course and continue the Reagan revolution, his approach to Congress would differ significantly from Reagan's. Bush was the first president since Gerald Ford to have close friends in Congress and to possess an understanding of how Washington works. He was comfortable working within the system and was not comfortable campaigning against Congress or going over the heads of Congress as Reagan had. He had campaigned using what one journalist described as "only moderate Congress-bashing."[1] According to one senior Republican, "Bush knows the system and knows the players and has been around here for a long time," and one reporter described the new president as having a "golden Rolodex of Hill contacts"[2]

In contrast to Carter and Reagan, who had made no significant mention of Congress in their inaugural addresses, Bush spoke of a need to work with Congress and used it as an opportunity to reach out.

> To my friends—and yes, I do mean friends—in the loyal opposition—and yes, I mean loyal: I put out my hand. I am putting out my hand to you Mr. Majority Leader. For this is the thing: This is an age of the offered hand. We can't turn back clocks, and I don't want to. But when our fathers were young, Mr. Speaker, our differences ended at the water's edge. And we don't wish to turn back time, but when our mothers were young, Mr. Majority Leader, the Congress and the executive were capable of working together to produce a budget on which this nation could live. Let us negotiate soon and

hard. But in the end, let us produce. The American people await action. They didn't send us here to bicker. They ask us to rise above
the merely partisan. "In crucial things, unity"—and this, my friends
is crucial.[3]

Bush even appeared reluctant to assert a mandate. The day after his election to office, when asked to describe his mandate Bush shied away from the
term: "Well, I don't know whether I want to use the word mandate. . . . I
would say the people have spoken, the verdict was clear, and therefore I will
take what I think the prime issues of the campaign was and work construc-
tively with Congress to attain the will of the people."[4]

While Bush offered his hand, he inherited a restless Congress, frustrated
by eight years of Reagan and emboldened by the Iran-Contra scandal. Frustrated by absence from the White House, congressional Democrats became,
according to one Republican lobbyist, "feistier and feistier while out of the
presidency longer and longer."

Ultimately, congressional relations would suffer because George Bush
would attempt to lead the Congress he had left decades earlier. Bush's numerous friendships with lawmakers and his experience within Washington
made him better suited for leading Congress under a system of institutionalized pluralism. In 1990 Bush seemed to acknowledge that he had not yet
fully taken the reins of the modern presidency: "I think sometimes that I as
a person—as the president—perhaps underestimate the bully pulpit aspect
of the presidency. Or perhaps the fact that the presidency has a very special
and thus specific role in exhorting or encouraging people to do whatever."[5]

The Bush Staff

Perhaps because Bush had served in Congress, he selected a staff with respectable congressional experience but lacking a "white-haired" Washington
insider who could play a strong role both on the Hill and inside the White
House. Bush selected Frederick D. McClure to be his first head of congressional liaison. While McClure was relatively young (thirty-four), he had considerable Washington experience. He had served as an intern in the Ford
White House and on Senator John Tower's (Republican-Texas) staff. More
importantly, McClure served in the Reagan White House as a liaison with the
Senate before taking a position as a lobbyist for Texas Air Corporation in November 1986. While little attention was paid to his race, McClure became the
first African-American to head White House Office of Congressional Relations. McClure knew the Senate well and was highly regarded for his ability

to work with people, but some in the administration doubted his ability to formulate strategies.[6]

Initially, McClure was given a smaller liaison staff than the Reagan administration had used. While the Reagan administration had used nine lobbyists supported by a staff of twenty-seven, the Bush White House began with seven lobbyists and a staff of twenty.[7] One explanation offered was that Bush would be "his own best advocate with Congress."[8] However, by the end of the administration, the number of lobbyists rose to nine.

The Bush White House followed the traditional division of labor by dividing the legislators they worked by chambers. Within each chamber the staff divided their work by committee, although the staffers were expected to be generalists who could talk with any member. Dividing members by committee allowed them to specialize somewhat on the issues that came before that committee while still working with particular members on a regular basis. For example, on the Senate side, the head lobbyist, with the title of special assistant to the president for legislative affairs, was in charge of national security issues. Lobbyists with the title special assistant to the president divided up the rest of the issues with one responsible for budget, tax, and appropriations, one focusing on health, labor, education, and other social issues, while a third dealt almost exclusively with confirmations for presidential appointees.

McClure selected E. Boyd Hollingsworth, Jr., to head relations with the Senate. Hollingsworth had worked on the Judiciary Committee staff and as the top floor assistant to Senate Assistant Leader Allan K. Simpson of Wyoming. After Hollingsworth's departure, James W. Dyer, who had worked in congressional relations under Reagan, returned to the White House to head the Senate liaison operation for Bush.

The House liaison was initially headed up by Nicholas E. Calio, who was regarded by some as a "star."[9] Calio had begun his Washington career as litigation counsel for the Washington Legal Foundation. He served as senior vice president of the National Association of Wholesale Distributors just prior to coming into the White House. Calio left the White House in 1991 and was replaced by Gary Andres, who headed House liaison for the rest of the Bush administration. Calio returned to the White House in February 1992 to take over after McClure left the administration to take a job with a Dallas investing firm.[10]

McClure kept a low profile. In fact, one Reagan aide worried that McClure and his staff were too nice, especially as assistants to George Bush. "I wish he [McClure] were a little meaner, I don't know how he is as an arm-twister. . . . This is a kinder, gentler White House, I understand that. But somebody has to be a nut-buster, if it's not going to be George Bush."[11]

The Bush Congressional Relations Office was greeted by early criticism that sounded remarkably like the concerns expressed about Carter's White House. Republicans complained about unreturned telephone calls, failure to be consulted on appointments, lack of timely notice about grants, and presidential or cabinet visits to their district.[12] Representative Gerald B. H. Solomon (Republican-New York) voted to override Bush's veto of a minimum wage bill allegedly because of his frustration with not being able to arrange a meeting with Environmental Protection Agency officials. Representative Guy V. Molinari (Republican-New York) warned that the White House must "build up a reservoir of goodwill so that when critical votes come up, the White House congressional liaison people can call up [members] with a feeling that there's a reasonably good chance of getting their votes."[13]

While the Bush White House committed some mistakes early on, these complaints reflect deeper problems with the administration. Many in Congress were becoming frustrated by Bush's lack of strong stands on issues and some Republicans felt neglected by Bush's attention to congressional Democrats. Many Republicans in Congress wanted Bush to continue Reagan's confrontational approach with congressional Democrats.

The biggest hindrance facing members of the liaison staff was that they did not carry enough weight within the White House to play a leading role in forming strategy. This lack of clout within the White House also limited their influence on the Hill. The liaison staffers were viewed more as functionaries who carried messages than as heavyweight advisors involved in making strategy. One member of the liaison staff conceded that McClure's relationship with Chief of Staff John Sununu had not been good. As a result, members believed that McClure was out of the loop and turned to cabinet members or others to get their messages through to the president.[14] One Senate Republican complained that Sununu neglected congressional Republicans and the congressional relations staff.

> Part of the problem that President Bush had is that he has never been that close to the head of that office [Legislative Affairs], Mc-Clure and Calio. I regard them highly and I have a strong friendship with them, but they have never been perceived around town and on the Hill as having a close relationship with President Bush or as having the strength within the White House to be able to make a difference. Either the House or the Senate leader or the rank-and-file Republicans just haven't felt that if you want to get something done or if you want to get a message to the president that you call the head of Legislative Affairs. They will call the chief of staff.

Sununu attempted to retain too much authority and failed to invest sub-ordinates like McClure with the kind of stature they need.[15] Sununu was also widely criticized for his poor personal relations with Congress. One senior White House aide suggested that Sununu had "an enormously low opinion of members of Congress and the press," while another Bush advisor noted that rather than listening quietly to congressional notions, Sununu would say, "That's stupid."[16] The chief of staff went so far as to cancel a congress-man's use of the presidential box at the Kennedy Center.[17] One member of the liaison staff saw two sides to Sununu's style.

> Sununu was very good with some members and at times he was good with all members, but frankly at times his contacts with members could be counterproductive because he would evidence in some cases a lack of respect. There were times when he made Republicans on both sides of the Hill angry for a variety of reasons. By the same token, he could get in there during a negotiation and be tremen-dously effective and productive.

Another member of Bush's liaison staff defended Sununu because he was often forced to be both the president's representative on the Hill and, in Haldeman's famous description, the president's "son of a bitch." Discussing his relationship with members, Sununu conceded that his style had consc-quences. "Hey, every time you're dealing in a community in which any time anybody has to be the person that says no or deliver bad news, there's always going to be criticism, and I'm resigned to that."[18]

The Bush White House initially did not continue Reagan's use of the Legislative Strategy Group. Instead, legislative strategy was often determined by John Sununu, Richard Darman, and Dan Quayle.[19] Sununu did meet with senior staff to do some long-range planning, but this planning lacked the focus on winning legislative battles that had made Reagan's Legislative Strat-egy Group a success. When Nick Calio took over the operation in February 1992 he played a stronger role in strategic planning, as Samuel K. Skinner, who had been named chief of staff in December 1991, revived the Legislative Strategy Group. A new Legislative Strategy Group began to meet at five o'clock each afternoon and included Skinner and Calio as well as Budget Di-rector Richard G. Darman, Bush campaign chairman Robert M. Teeter, Deputy Chief of Staff W. Henson Moore, and Clayton K. Yeutter, who had just become Bush's new counselor for domestic policy.[20] This larger group in-cluded more people and a broader range of talent.[21]

By failing to include McClure fully in legislative strategy development, the administration diminished the quality of the strategy as well as McClure's effectiveness on the Hill. Without strong input from the legislative affairs people, the strategy was less likely to be in tune with the congressional mood. McClure's lack of clout in the White House diminished his clout on the Hill. One administration official asserted, "He [McClure] needs to create the perception by setting strategy that he's a player at that level. Otherwise, Members of Congress will go over his head."[22] Because Fred McClure was not seen as carrying enough weight in the White House to offer definitive answers, members of Congress began calling others in the White House. The impact of too many voices speaking on behalf of the president was, according to one veteran of the administration, problematic.

> You can't have two or three people talking to these guys because even the difference of inflection in the voice can result in a different message being received. "Hey, Frank, let me tell you something, the president cares about this," or, "Hey Jerry, let me tell you something, the president cares about this, understand? He really cares about this." So, Frank gets one message and Jerry gets another. You have got to have people that are operating off of the same page. The chief of staff can talk to members of Congress but he should do it when the Legislative Affairs guy says, look, you need to talk to this guy, it is time for you to make a call to this guy. The good chiefs of staff will listen to that.

In the end, the problems of the Bush liaison staffers originated with their position within the administration rather than with their own efforts. While the staff, like all others, committed some early blunders, their efforts were generally praised. One member of Congress expressed a high regard for the Bush staff: "He doesn't have to call someone to get the vote he wants, they can get the votes." However, the White House lacked the kind of commitment to winning legislative battles that had contributed to Reagan's success. One White House aide claimed that "Long-term planning goes on individually rather than collectively."[23] This suggests that while some individuals in the White House were thinking in the long term, there was less interest in the kind of coordination that helped the Reagan White House make effective use of its resources.

One specialized function of the liaison staff in charge of the Senate is handling nominations. Some administrations have had individuals assigned specifically to handle nominations. Each administration must handle 2,500 to 2,700 appointees, and while most are routine, some require some kind of management from within the departments or from the White House. Successful confirmation by the Senate is expected, and as one staffer pointed out, "The importance of nominations really doesn't come through until you lose one."

The battle to confirm John Tower as secretary of defense was considered by some to be Fred McClure's "first big test."[24] No one on the liaison staff had any experience working with a controversial nomination, and Tower's rejection by the Senate was the first time in U.S. history that a president's initial cabinet selection had been rejected. The *National Journal* concluded, "The Tower affair left ill-feelings at both ends of Pennsylvania Avenue and—perhaps worse—questions in some Washingtonians' minds about the White House's political talent."[25] Bush waited until the nomination seemed doomed before approving a pitched partisan battle that seemed certain to maximize the damage he would suffer from a loss. Senate Republican Leader Bob Dole questioned the motives of Senator Sam Nunn and other opponents, denouncing Democratic intentions and helping to put an end to whatever was left of the president's political honeymoon. One reporter concluded:

> The loss in the first major test Bush has faced also has raised questions about his ability to wage the tough battles on other issues that are sure to follow. Republican theoretician Kevin Phillips said Bush already reminds him of President Jimmy Carter, who never fully recovered from a rocky beginning in which he was forced to withdraw the nomination of Ted Sorensen as CIA director.[26]

Handling nominations requires that the liaison staffers work with Congress and the nominee themselves. Most nominees have never been through this process, and according to one liaison aide, "It's like nothing you've ever done before." The liaison staff has to "tutor" each nominee before approaching Congress. The challenge for the liaison staff is that, in the words of one staffer, "Everyone's nomination is the most important thing in the world to them, but you're handling hundreds of them."

George Bush and Congress

Like Gerald Ford before him, Bush attempted to open up the White House and treat members like friends and peers. Departing from the more regal presence of Reagan, Bush invited members of Congress into the family quarters of the White House and gave them a tour that included the private bathroom he shared with his wife. During one tour, Bush grabbed a Polaroid camera and took snapshots of members and their wives sitting on the Victorian bed in the Lincoln bedroom.[27] Bush's willingness to invite members into areas of the White House that he had not been invited to during his service as vice president and his eagerness to share his excitement about the White House helped to build a friendly atmosphere and reduce some of the distance between the president and Congress.

Many members of Congress had become frustrated with Reagan's lack of familiarity with the legislative process and details of policy and Bush's ascendance to the Oval Office represented the arrival not only of a president who had many personal friends on Capitol Hill, but of someone who understood Washington and enjoyed working closely with Congress. Early on, one story reported that lawmakers "gush about Bush's hands on style" and that Democratic Senator Don Nickles of Oklahoma said, "It is a tremendous asset to have a President who does not read from note cards and is well aware of what is going on and has a good feel for politics."[28] Senator John B. Breaux (Democrat-Louisiana) noted, "He knows the players. When Bush walks down the inaugural steps and waves to members of Congress, he knows who he's waving to."[29] In a call between the election and the inauguration, Representative William H. Gray (chair of the House Democratic Caucus) asked whether to address Bush as *Mr. Vice President* or *Mr. President-Elect,* and Bush suggested, "Just call me George." Gray later praised Bush for being "one of the guys."[30]

In the eyes of many lawmakers, Bush's friendly approach paid off. Representative Charles Pashayan (Republican-California) admitted, "It's harder for someone who has some personal affinity with George Bush to deny him when he makes a request."[31] One House Democrat conceded that "If he [Bush] hadn't had his personality and established his good relationship with Congress he wouldn't have gotten as much as he did." A senior Republican member also confirmed the importance of Bush's personal popularity.

> George Bush was a friendly fellow. Everybody liked George Bush personally. And really that goes a long way. It's remarkable how much difference that makes. You would think that with elected representatives in the House and the Senate that it doesn't make much difference what they personally think of a president. . . . A likable guy can still influence a lot of people. George Bush did, he called and talked to members personally. He had a very engaging personality. He was likable. That gave him, I think, more influence than he otherwise would have had.

Bush was anxious to work with Congress. One Republican leader commented, "He'll make dozens of calls. I tell him we need five [calls] on a certain bill, and he will make five; if we need ten, he'll make ten." As one member of the White House admitted, the problem was not to persuade Bush to schmooze on Capitol Hill, but it was hard to make him stop.[32] One member of the liaison staff noted that while the administration made some use of "hidden-hand" leadership, Bush was more than willing to work with members of Congress.

> There was an awful lot of hidden-hand work and certainly the president played a part in it. But he was also very visible in meeting with people. If you look at the fast-track vote in 1991, I can't tell you the number of phone calls that the president made, the number of meetings we had in the cabinet room with fifteen or so members, or the number of meetings in the Oval Office with five members, two members, one member. The lead up to the Persian Gulf vote was the same way.

However, one criticism was that Bush was too nice when it came to Congress. The administration's reluctance to go public on issues originated with George Bush. According to one aide, "He'd get upset at [the notion] of going over the heads of his friends."[33] During his first days in office Bush delighted many members by providing some political coverage when he endorsed the 50-percent congressional pay raise.[34] Bush also put aside the contentious issue of military aid to the Nicaraguan rebels, or Contras, an issue that had produced tension between the Reagan White House and Congress. Members of both parties also knew that Bush was reluctant to play hardball politics and would be forgiving in defeat, but many were stunned in 1989, when Paul Weyrich, an influential Washington conservative, disclosed that Bush had sent him a friendly note after Weyrich helped scuttle Bush's nomination of John Tower as secretary of defense by testifying about Tower's drinking habits.[35]

While the members of Congress interviewed for this book all spoke highly of Bush as a person, all expressed some reservations about him as an effective politician. While Bush's grasp of issues was strong, his passion was weak. One Democratic member of the House who generally spoke kindly of Bush had reservations about the president's commitment to policy.

> I think very clearly one of his problems was that he really didn't have any kind of program to push in Congress. I sort of agree with what was said in the campaign, that he was very poor at the vision thing. He really didn't have one. I think presidents come to office with a clear idea of what they want to do and what they want to accomplish

and I don't think he did. He had been vice president for eight years and the vice president didn't have any responsibilities, policy or otherwise. I think George Bush wanted to be president and enjoyed being president. But I don't think he had a personal view or commitment of where he wanted to take the country; that's one of the reasons his administration didn't accomplish more than it did.

Jack Germond and Jules Witcover noted in March 1989, "The absence of an agenda is becoming painfully clear now, as the new Administration struggles to get off the mark."[36] A veteran of the Reagan White House complained that the Bush administration had no direction and no focus. "I think they're pissing away their honeymoon and getting nothing in return for it. Their agenda isn't pushing anything."[37] Another veteran of Republican administrations used similar terms to describe Bush's failure to capitalize on his post–Gulf War popularity. One high-ranking Republican Senate aide complained, "There has been nothing significant the administration has offered and fought for."[38] One reporter summed up the feeling of many about Bush: "Reinforcing Bush's ideological mildness is his passion for prudence."[39]

Bush's lack of presence on issues eventually translated into a lack of clout on the Hill. Senator John Kerry argued, "There is no intensity to his [Bush's] presence on the Hill at all."[40] One Senate Republican pointed out that Bush, in contrast to Reagan, was seldom a concern to members. "Bush never commanded fear, in part because we never knew where his plumb line was, we never knew where he stood."

This image of Bush is consistent with Bush's failure to capitalize on his high approval ratings following the Gulf War. Many Republicans felt that Bush simply did not have a domestic policy agenda to pursue. Also, Bush had consistently failed to connect his popularity to possible sanctions against members. In 1989 one Democratic House staffer commented, "Unlike Reagan, there isn't any cost to crossing him."[41]

The idea that Bush lacked a domestic agenda was reinforced by the lack of a strong Democratic agenda. In 1989 the Democrats were hamstrung by embarrassments like the congressional pay raise and the resignation of Speaker Jim Wright. As one Democratic insider described it, "We could not have a congressional message when we had a Speaker who could not be seen in public."[42] With no agenda coming from Capitol Hill, Bush's lack of policy initiative was more evident. While much of the blame has been laid at the feet of George Bush, his lack of clout on the Hill reflects the larger decline of presidential authority described in this book. Jack Germond and Jules Witcover noted in 1989 that Bush was less likely to be able to intimidate Congress because of a general decline in influence that they traced back to the Reagan administration.

> The days when Members of Congress, in either party, could be intimidated by the political popularity of the President probably ended during Reagan's first term and certainly when the Democrats managed to recapture the Senate in the 1986 election. If Reagan couldn't save his fellow Republicans, the notion that Bush might do so is fanciful.[43]

A member of Bush's liaison staff echoed that sentiment. "That's a tough road to hoe. People generally do vote on local issues. It takes a lot for a president to go and directly threaten people in their district." Many in Congress and the White House believed that if the great communicator could not go out and stir up voters, Bush certainly could not.

The Veto Threat

George Bush set no records for the number of vetoes; he vetoed forty-six bills over four years. By comparison, Gerald Ford vetoed forty-eight bills and use his pocket veto eighteen times in just over two years in the White House. Ronald Reagan had developed a reputation on the Hill for threatening vetoes but failing to follow through on his threats. Reagan would sometimes talk at length about using his "veto pen," but members of Congress paid less attention to his very visible threats and considered them more for public consumption because he often failed to follow up on his threats.[44] In the end, Reagan only vetoed seventy-eight bills over eight years.

The number of bills actually vetoed by the president only tells part of the story. Bush's advisors convinced the president that the veto power of the presidency could be turned into a positive tool for negotiating with Congress.[45] Through this strategy the administration would make good use of veto threats to motivate changes in legislation or to discourage Congress from passing objectionable legislation. The Office of Management and Budget reported that by mid-1990 the Bush administration had issued 120 veto threats.[46] Representative Robert Roe (Democrat-New Jersey) complained, "Every time we go to the bathroom around here somebody says: 'Check on the White House. They are going to veto.'"[47]

One congressional leader reflected that Bush was much more effective at being a barrier than an advocate. Interviewed just before the end of Bush's string of sustained vetoes, this Democrat felt that the president's ability to stand in the way of legislation was generally underestimated, and he contended that citizens believed that just because Democrats held a majority they could do whatever they wished. This member felt that they would need two-thirds to get anything significant done. Kevin Moley, deputy secretary of the Department of Health and Human Services, noted some of the fallout from the president's aggressive use of the veto. "We don't have a lot of allies on the Hill. We are the victim of our own success in veto overrides. We are the grid in gridlock."[48]

In order to facilitate their veto strategy, the Bush administration began to look for ways to clearly signal its intentions early. As the legislation approaches floor consideration, the OMB will put out a "Statement of Administration Policy" (SAP). Even though cabinet secretaries' letters on legislation (discussed in the next section) required approval by the OMB and White House, SAPs were considered much more credible. SAPs resemble press releases and serve as the official signaling device for presidential vetoes. These "veto threats" were placed into several categories. The most serious warning is a senior advisor's threat, which states that if a bill were presented to the president, "his senior advisers would recommend that he veto it."[49] Such a warning indicates that unless outlined changes are made a veto is certain. A slightly less certain threat warns that if the bill is presented to the president the secretary of the relevant agency will recommend a veto. However, the president's position is never directly stated, leaving some room to back away from a veto. SAPs change as the bill changes, if these changes cause a shift in the administration's position. For example, the administration often puts out a separate SAP on legislation after it has gone through conference committee.

The battle to sustain a presidential veto involves drawing upon friendships and loyalty to the president. According to one Ford assistant, the use of a veto shifts the focus of the debate.

> Once a bill is vetoed, the issue behind it disappears and it becomes us against them. The battle become institutional and partisan. The president must win this institutional battle if his threats of future vetoes are to remain credible. The president's party in Congress is called upon to support "their" president in order to protect the party. The struggle to sustain the president's veto is a test of the strength of the party and the strength of the presidency.

The personal nature of veto overrides was emphasized frequently both by Bush aides and members of Congress who served during the Bush administration.

Because of this, sustaining vetoes is where Bush's approach to Congress paid off. Bush's thank-you notes and his frequent visits to the House gym paid off when the appeal became personal. Members of both parties admitted that their fondness for George Bush made it very difficult to vote to override his vetoes. Certainly, few legislators were willing to risk reelection to support the president out of personal fondness, but Democrats seem to have lost their interest in embarrassing a president of another party and Republicans were more willing to put aside their concerns about distancing themselves from the White House.

Bush succeeded in blocking objectionable legislation through a combination of vetoes and veto threats. Bush's streak of sustained vetoes became an object of pride in the administration.[50] Someone in the White House even had buttons printed in honor of the streak. Others in the administration, however, worried that the White House became more concerned with protecting the veto streak than with the policies themselves, and they felt that the streak eventually became detrimental because the White House was reluctant to risk an override. While the White House may have at times been overly concerned about having a veto overridden, the strategy seems to have been a success if measured by nothing other than the frustration of congressional Democrats.

The Institutionalized Hidden Hand

The Bush administration often pursued a quiet, behind-the-scenes approach to leading Congress. The White House made extensive use of hidden-hand techniques, but according to one member of the liaison staff, the president generally was not involved in hidden hand leadership.

> Most of the hidden-hand work comes from the staff. We quite regularly activated various networks to contact members and say, "vote with the president." Politically important people back home, financially important people back home, constituent groups that had a major presence in the district, that was done at the staff level. The president would directly call people occasionally, but you never wasted the president. It had to be an important issue and the calls had to count.

The hidden-hand approach was institutionalized during the Kennedy administration. The Kennedy staff prepared a "backgrounder" on each member of the House. This file would contain biographical information such as religious affiliation, hobbies, social activities, organizational affiliations, and what schools members of the family attended. It also contained sources of campaign support and other information that might lead the White House staff to key constituents that the staff could use to influence the member.[51] For example, when a liberal congressman from Chicago publicly proclaimed his desire to block any civil rights legislation that did not accomplish all he thought was needed, Kennedy's liaison staff contacted Mayor Daley, whose Democratic machine controlled the nominating process in Chicago. The member soon announced that he would not be seeking re-election.[52]

While the Johnson White House probably had fewer qualms about openly wielding power than any other administration, it too used the back channels of hidden-hand leadership, and evidence of hidden-hand leadership can be found in every administration studied here. The institutionalization of this style represents how subsequent White Houses built upon the style of leadership generally ascribed to Eisenhower.[53] And, while Eisenhower's use of a hidden-hand approach deserves noting, it should be viewed in the larger context. Hidden-hand leadership did not suddenly reappear during the Bush administration, nor was it the first administration to institutionalize the hidden-hand approach. Such an approach had existed for years, but had often been overlooked because other, more visible presidential power was being wielded at the same time. In addition, the hidden-hand technique was used by the Bush White House because it complemented the president's personal approach to Congress and his resistance to public confrontations with his friends in Congress.

Departmental Liaison and the Intrabranch Lobby

The Bush administration made somewhat limited use of its cabinet resources. Through weekly reports compiled by the legislative staffs of the departments, the White House kept apprised of departmental activities. There was some consideration of having regular meetings of departmental staff with the White House liaison staff, but these were never followed up and meetings between the two were sporadic. The paths of the two offices did cross as they did their work on the Hill, but the departments were left to pursue their own strategies.

At the same time, the Bush administration faced a struggle to control the departments. According to one White House staffer, one of the most important jobs of the congressional liaison office is to make sure that the various executive departments are "reading from the same sheet." While this will be a problem for every administration, the difficulty in this case was due in part to Bush's lack of a clear agenda.

Bush's problems with the cabinet were similar to Carter's. Carter had attempted to recreate cabinet government by giving cabinet secretaries more autonomy, while Bush's cabinet created autonomy in order to advance its legislative goals. One consequence was that the administration's legislative program lacked coherence and the departments pursued their own goals regardless of whether or not they conflicted with the president's stated goals.[54] Carter's legislative chief warned the president that the number of messages coming from the administration contributed to his image problem and his problems with Congress: "If there is one reason for the criticism we receive from the Hill about being in 'disarray' it is because Cabinet and sub-Cabinet officers are frequently going off on their own on decisions contrary to previously enunciated policy or simply making new policy which must then either be contradicted or 'eaten.'"[55]

How closely the Bush White House worked with the departments was largely left to the departments. One assistant secretary for legislative affairs commented that he had to lobby the White House as much as Congress and that the process was an "outside-in" approach that often left the departments pushing the White House rather than leadership coming from the White House. Some use was made of the cabinet secretaries as lobbyists on issues beyond the scope of their departments, but lesser officials in the departments were seldom put to use in this way. Some liaison officials from both the White House and the departments felt that this left a significant resource untapped.

Departmental liaison did work closely with the members of committees with related jurisdiction. While departmental lobbyists usually do not get to know large segments of Congress very well, they do develop close working relationships with a subset of members. Tapping into these relationships could provide the administration with a few crucial votes in a tight battle. The White House kept lists of lawmakers indexed by any source in the administration that had worked closely with them. Cabinet lobbyists were assigned particular members to talk to as key votes approached.

One advantage of engaging the departments' lobbyists more is that such activity elevates their status. While many lobbyists have little interest beyond their own departments, they welcome an opportunity to become part of the White House team and work on presidential legislation. As long as the departments are treated as a thing apart from the White House, they are more likely to behave in a similar fashion. Inviting them into White House meetings and drawing them into White House efforts builds a sense of teamwork and importance. Many White House assistants have considered regular meetings with departmental staff of little value beyond morale-building, but still considered this sufficient justification to hold these meetings.

It is difficult to generalize about the legislative liaison operation of the different cabinet departments, because while they operate under the general control of the White House, their organization and style vary from department to department. Some of the differences in activities reflect differences in the policy areas they cover. Departments with programmatic agendas deal with more case work and grants. This provides the department with a channel for some influence but it usually requires some staffing to handle these issues. One staff member from the Treasury Department highlighted the difference:

> We do not run programs. Which is different than other departments, Agriculture, for instance, which runs programs—we don't. We do policy. We don't give out grants. We either enforce laws, like Customs, or IRS, or BATF, or set policy. We don't hand down a lot of money or make plans.

Departments also vary in their importance. High prestige departments like Defense or Treasury are better received because they handle "death and taxes" issues. Some of this is undoubtedly related to the high influence departments receive with high quality (or influence) secretaries, but the prestige of the department itself plays a significant role.

The cabinet departments had congressional liaison operations that in many ways resembled the organization found in the White House. This is in large part due to the fact that cabinet secretaries and the president face very similar kinds of problems. Both are involved in many diverse and time-consuming functions. The diversity of the functions means that cabinet secretaries must now be responsible for mastering such political skills as administering a large organization, developing and implementing detailed policies, handling public opinion, and maintaining friendly relations with Congress. Given the job description of a cabinet secretary today, it is unlikely that a secretary will have highly developed legislative skills. Even in those cases where legislative skills are present, the ability to dedicate large amounts of time to congressional liaison is not. Cabinet secretaries, like the president, face many demands that preclude giving Congress the kind of attention it demands. For these reasons, cabinet departments have developed offices that specialize in lobbying members of Congress. These offices provide both manpower and expertise so that the secretaries' energies can be devoted to other pressing demands.

These operations are headed by political appointees, usually assistant secretaries or deputy assistant secretaries. While the rank of the officer is not in itself important, their access to the secretary is essential to the success of the operation. Assistant secretaries are presumed to have direct access to the heads of their departments, while deputy assistant secretaries and similar ranks are more likely to directly report to an assistant secretary or someone else in the department. Jack Marsh, who had served as assistant secretary of congressional relations for the Defense Department under Nixon, told Ford's cabinet, "The secretary should identify with the legislative affairs people and should be seen with them on the Hill. Congressional members should know that the legislative affairs people in the various agencies have access to their Secretary."[56]

Departmental and agency lobbyists are most often drawn from congressional staff, particularly those of committees with related jurisdiction. Cabinet secretaries drawn from Congress often bring key staff members into their departments with them, and often into the role of legislative liaison. These officers are provided with assistants, usually assigned to deal specifically with either the House or the Senate and given staffs to handle routine matters. These operations often combine lobbying with case work so that all communication with Congress is coordinated. This connects those who ask for members' votes with those who provide information, grant notification, and other favors. Some departments have experimented with combining congressional relations with intergovernmental relations, bringing communication with Congress together with communication with other entities within the federal system. Since many of the grants and other services provided by the departments flow throughout local governments, such a combination makes some sense. Mayors and governors can be altered to congressional actions of interest to them so they can be turned into lobbyists. However, there is some potential benefit in connecting the legislative affairs unit with virtually every other section of a department, and some involved have worried that combining legislative affairs with intergovernmental relations brings together too wide a range of functions.

The distinction between those involved in case work and the lobbyist is not always clear. One assistant secretary commented: "With the weekly contact that a congressional relations person is going to have on case work, you are going to have the chance or opportunity to talk about other kinds of policy besides case work. You are going to have a chance to say, hey, this bill is going to come up soon and we would like you to keep this in mind."

Working with Congress often involves a great deal of "staff-on-staff" contact as departmental liaison agents work frequently with congressional staff, especially those of the committees. Because so much of the department's efforts are directed at legislation early in the process, their ability to work with staff on the shaping of legislation is key.

THE INTRABRANCH LOBBY—DIVIDED LOYALTY WITHIN THE EXECUTIVE BRANCH

Every administration has had trouble relying on departments to provide the kind of absolute loyalty that it desires. Some in the Eisenhower White House believed that trouble keeping the congressional relations offices of the departments in line with the president's wishes resulted from New Deal holdovers. Eisenhower's White House staff worried that assistant secretaries were "crawling into the pocket" of Senate Majority Leader Lyndon Johnson. Harlow saw this as inherent in the way the relationship worked, since the help of a powerful Senate leader is always valuable to an assistant secretary.[57]

This problem became more serious during the Bush administration because the lack of a strong agenda coming out of the White House left the departments unsure about the president's priorities and restless to advance their own. The White House often must struggle to keep the departments in line. Each department would like to see its priorities at the top of the president's agenda and often becomes restless when its legislation receives less that a wholehearted effort from the White House. While some cabinet secretaries will sit quietly and wait for their favorite policy initiative to work its way onto the president's agenda, other secretaries see the president's four-year term ticking away and will begin to push their legislation ahead. This problem became acute during the Bush administration as several department heads became impatient waiting for Bush to embrace some of their policies. This was especially the case with Secretary of Housing and Urban Development Jack Kemp. As a visible member of the Republican party and a presidential candidate in 1988, Kemp had a keen interest in housing policy and possessed the visibility to press those ideas without the help of the president. As a former member of Congress, Kemp was familiar with the legislative process and was anxious to bring his ideas before Congress.

I label this the *intrabranch* lobby because often the job of the secretary and his or her Congressional Liaison Office begins with lobbying the White House to advance legislative priorities. The departments must also lobby the Office of Management and Budget to get their agendas approved, and the White House must lobby the departments to keep them in line with the president's program.

There are also struggles within the departments, and in some departments the struggle within can be difficult to manage. One lobbyist from the Defense Department pointed out that each of the military services had a lobbying staff larger than his in the Pentagon. He also noted that the service branches also had their own offices located on Capitol Hill and many "toys" at their disposal:

> They can take congressional staff or members on trips. "Do you want to go see an aircraft carrier?" "Do you want to go underneath the water in a submarine?" "How would you like to go out to Fort Airwood at night and watch the army do tank battle maneuvers?". . .
>
> When the members of Congress travel abroad on these congressional delegations, they are escorted by military officers and enlisted people who work in the congressional liaison operation of the various services. There's nothing like travel abroad with somebody to get to know them personally.

While these advantages can be used to the benefit of the Defense Department's liaison office, it does represent an independent source of political favors and, combined with many lawmakers' attachments to various service branches, can make the control of the service branches difficult.

One of the most crucial supporters of any piece of legislation coming out a cabinet department is the president. Beyond a superficial claim of support, departments seek out a commitment for a meaningful effort on the part of the president and the White House. Members of Congress are much more interested in bills that are of interest to the president. This is especially evident at the committee stage, where the decision for members of Congress is not so much whether or not they favor an issue, but which bills have a chance of reaching the floor and thus merit their attention. Departmental liaison people know that if they can demonstrate the White House's interest in their department's legislation it is much more likely to receive the attention of members of Congress. One assistant secretary commented that he had to spend as much time lobbying the Bush White House as Congress. Many members of Congress are waiting to hear the president's position on an issue before going too far in any direction on a bill. Members often want to withhold public judgment because they do not wish to disagree with the White House on an issue. At other times, members of Congress will avoid taking a position on a controversial issue unless they are sure that the White House will provide them political cover by also supporting the legislation. Many members fear that they will take a tough stand on a controversial issue only to find later that the president has backed off the issue, leaving the member with what one source described as some "unpleasant surprises." Members of Congress have learned the "myth of the unitary executive" and do not believe that just because the department takes a position that the

White House will agree. Therefore, they want to hear from the president. This occurs, however, early enough in the process that the White House has not yet engaged on an issue. Some sources feel that the White House is losing an opportunity to influence policy because it is not at the table.

At the same time, the departments are usually very committed to their own issues while the White House must maintain a much broader perspective and save its efforts for legislation seen as key. Some departments are very protective of their legislation and are reluctant to hand bill management over to the White House for fear that they would quickly compromise on some key element or let the bill die of neglect. The White House must make sure that the departments are willing to accept the compromises needed to get legislation passed, and the department lobbyists make sure that the White House does not sacrifice policy goals in order to claim success.

While the departments, the product of presidential appointments, can be thought of as extensions of the president's electoral concerns, they are not usually as concerned with simply obtaining victories and claiming credit. The departments see presidents as much too anxious to compromise principals in order to avoid defeat. At other times, departments are much more willing to sacrifice some principals in order to gain a much desired program. Veterans of the Reagan and Bush White Houses complained that Democratic members of Congress were successful in turning administration proposals into "Democratic Christmas trees." This left presidential legislation serving the reelection needs of opponents and made it difficult to explain why the president opposed administration legislation.

Caught between these two forces is the Office of Management and Budget. The OMB has its own set of priorities. Particularly in the budget restraints of the nineteen seventies, eighties, and nineties, the OMB has been handed the task of reining in departmental spending ambition. Cabinet secretaries, while generally committed to budget austerity, often see more opportunities for budget cuts in other departments. The OMB becomes a "choke point" for the spending wishes of the departments, a role that often puts them at odds with the departments. They survive this in large part because they are "inside the gates" and much closer to the president than the departments. Such conflicts, when serious enough, are resolved between the cabinet secretary and the director of OMB.

Cabinet Secretaries as Lobbyists

Cabinet secretaries represent important constituencies and hold the potential to be powerful allies in legislative battles. Fenno argued that they do little to help the president's program in part because opportunities to do so are rare.[58] They do help the president by creating a friendly atmosphere and taking on some of the burden of maintaining the relationship between the branches.

Cabinet secretaries are inherently limited in their effectiveness as lobbyists for several reasons. As Fenno points out, cabinet members find themselves in the dilemma of having to be both presidential advisor and departmental head. While the role of presidential advisor dictates loyalty and service to the president, the role of department head involves presidential direction and legislative control. Fenno concludes, "Where his ultimate responsibility is concerned, he cannot serve two masters."[59]

In choosing cabinet secretaries, presidents often must implicitly decide whether to serve public or congressional constituencies. While the two are not mutually exclusive, cabinet nominees who satisfy electoral constituencies may not have the ability to deal effectively with members of Congress. Cabinet secretaries with large public followings may hold some influence with Congress due to their popularity, but legislative skills are required to turn this support into influence in Congress.

One way to examine what constituencies presidents intend to serve through the selection of cabinet secretaries is to look at recruitment patterns. Pendleton Herring suggested that presidents have not made full use of their cabinet secretaries to work with Congress because few secretaries were drawn directly from the House or Senate.[60] It is plausible to assume that presidents seeking to create alliances to the Congress will draw their nominees from there. Those presidents seeking to serve other constituencies will be less likely to select members of Congress.

Cabinet secretaries can be seen as trying to balance between their own policy goals as well as those of their president and the Congress. Clearly, the goals of the president must direct much of their action. The president, after all, carries the electoral mandate of the executive branch. Given cabinet secretaries' appointment and removal by the president, the chief executive's goals must be considered. However, the concerns of Congress must be considered as well. Finally, cabinet secretaries may hold their own sets of policy goals, independent of the president that appointed them or the Congress that confirmed and funded them. The goals may have been brought into the government or be the product of "capture" as the secretary begins to be drawn into departmental concerns. In either case, the cabinet secretaries and their departments may wish to serve goals that have little to do with Congress or the president.

Although Fenno is correct in seeing limits on the impact of secretarial lobbying, the cumulative impact of their efforts is significant. Clearly, no individual cabinet member will prove pivotal in the passage of administration legislation, but no one president or congressional leader will have this impact either. The relationships developed in frequent dealings with Congress provide some advantage. Through their work with members of Congress, secretaries may develop relationships that facilitate lobbying on departmental or other issues. Frequent contact with Congress can also provide secretaries with information that is useful to the administration. Secretaries may also develop sources of information and friendships on the hill that provide the foundation for influence.

Some administrations have gone so far as to institutionalize such channels of communication. For example, the Carter administration maintained a list of congressional friends of cabinet secretaries so that when a member's support was needed an administration official who held their trust could be located quickly. The Kennedy and Johnson administrations brought in lesser cabinet officials and made extensive use of departmental liaison on issues beyond their departments' jurisdiction. On some occasions they became too involved and too many individuals were running around pressing members for votes. One member, who had been involved in developing the administration's strategy on a bill, found himself being questioned about his position on the bill. When the member asked why he was being called, the liaison officer replied, "Because, your name was on my list."[61] The Johnson White House staff limited departmental liaison to working during the committee process because of the confusion generated by the many voices lobbying for the legislation and because often the White House found the department's headcounts unreliable.[62]

While the payoffs to such a system may be very small, the cost is equally small as well. The White House simply sends out a questionnaire asking secretaries to list members with whom they share a special relationship and the liaison staff compiles and maintains these lists for use at key points. Such use of cabinet officers is selective, to prevent overuse of a personal connection. The Bush administration was reluctant to use such connections, much to the dismay of some liaison personnel.

The White House needs cabinet secretaries that are both credible political figures and team players. The stronger the secretary is politically, the more weight he carries with Congress. Cabinet secretaries drawn from Congress can use their expertise and connections to create a legislative strategy for passage of their own bills and occasionally lobby on behalf of other administration legislation. At the same time, cabinet members who know Congress (or think they know Congress) may not be willing to defer to the White

House liaison office and may initiate their own strategy. Such was the case with Secretary of Housing and Urban Development Jack Kemp during the Bush administration. Kemp's congressional experience and national recognition provided the administration with a powerful advocate of Housing Department policy but, as a veteran of Congress, Kemp was not always willing to defer to the Bush Legislative Affairs team, and at times the tension between HUD and the White House seemed higher than that with the Democratic Congress.

EARLY ACTION

Officially, the executive branch is precluded by law from lobbying.[63] Therefore, cabinet officers are quite anxious to define their tasks in terms of "providing information" rather than "lobbying," and while their emphasis on providing information is in part a rhetorical attempt to avoid the admission of a crime, providing information is an important part of their job. Because these departmental liaison staffs are involved with the congressional committees that know the topic the best, they are most likely to face questions on the details of legislation. Undoubtedly, there are times when the departments go beyond providing information and begin pressing their agendas, but there are several functions of their organizations that simply provide information. The form that this information takes varies with the stage in the process.

Generally, the work of the departments' legislative affairs offices is done prior to legislation reaching the floor. Once the legislation reaches the floor, the White House takes over, although the departments play a supporting role, assisting with vote counting and managing amendments to be presented on the floor. Occasionally, on very important legislation, the White House will begin its effort earlier, usually with full committee consideration. However, managing legislation throughout the entire process is demanding and can only be reserved for the most important bills. Through the early stages of legislation the departments handle bills with the White House remaining advised through weekly memos on the progress of their agenda and their activities.

The role of departmental liaison often begins with providing political intelligence that may be used in the drafting of legislation within the departments and then working with members during the committee process. Given the kind of sweeping changes that committees may make during markup sessions, departments must watch the legislation closely and keep in mind what both the secretary and White House want out of the legislation. During markup sessions on major administration legislation, the departments stay in close contact with the White House and cabinet secretaries.

Early in the legislative process, when bills are before committees or subcommittees, departments provide letters from the secretary that outline the department's stand on pending legislation. While major pieces of legislation may be handled differently, in general the department uses this letter to inform members of Congress what the concerns of the department are and, when needed, to suggest possible changes in the legislation to make the bill more acceptable. These letters can be short notes briefly stating general support or opposition to a bill, or long letters providing detailed analysis and suggestions. Often this will involve a detailed, title-by-title analysis of the bill with suggested amendments. This is designed to help the committee avoid conflicts with the administration. This puts OMB in the role of referee between departmental interests and as a keeper of the White House perspective. Because these letters, while signed by the department's head, are cleared through OMB and the White House, they add credibility to its contents.

The departments begin working on legislation as it develops in the committee system. Administration lobbyists consider the markup process an ideal opportunity to resolve disagreements in bills because once legislation reaches the floor the issue often becomes very public, with too much position-taking and credit-claiming going on to produce healthy legislation. The White House inherits the bill after it has cleared the full committee and the terms of the bill are less fluid because of the difficulty of floor amendments and because members have already begun taking positions. Especially given the lack of centralization in Congress today, it is very difficult for the White House to engage in give-and-take once a bill reaches the floor. Such bargaining on the content of legislation could have been done throughout a strong party leadership structure, but when interests are fragmented, offering changes in legislation in return for support is unwieldy at best. Bob Bonatati, assistant to the director for congressional relations for OMB for Ford, noted the opportunity provided by working with committees early in the process.

> As most of us know, the place to effectively impact the legislative process is the committee consideration stage where one is dealing with fewer rules and few players. At this stage of the process it is much easier to rewrite, initiate, delay, or kill legislative proposals. One is usually dealing primarily with the committee staff members

and relatively few Members of Congress. The longer one waits to interact with the legislative process the more difficult it becomes to effectively exert influence.[64]

Further, once legislation reaches the floor, the process is much more closely watched. The media and members of Congress who do not serve on the committee with jurisdiction do not have time to follow all of the legislation flowing through the committee system. However, once a bill reaches the floor, much more attention is given and bargaining and changes to the content of the bill are easily observed. Changes in the content of legislation become more visible during the floor consideration, which the White House oversees, and such signs of bargaining may signal weakness and encourage others to seek concessions. Further, as the process is more closely monitored, the electoral costs of bargaining may become prohibitive as concerned interests or the public in general apply pressure to avoid compromise.

Departments find their work with committees easier because they are usually working with a smaller group of members that they deal with frequently. Since each department maintains close contact with a few committees with which they share jurisdiction, they generally enjoy a smooth working relationship with committee members and their staffs. Their frequent interaction permits a long-term relationship to develop naturally. The department may alter what it proposes in anticipation of the response of powerful members of committees with jurisdiction.

The administration may use the committee process to develop congressional supporters who can help influence other members. Departmental lobbyists seem especially proud of the number of members of Congress who will cosponsor their legislation. Other members of Congress will turn to committee members as cues (guides) to their own votes, and having committee members actively supporting departmental legislation provides the department with valuable lobbying help.

Sometimes involvement at the committee level is effective because the composition of the committee provides the best opportunity to stop the legislation. The Nixon administration, facing a Democratic Congress, believed that often the best chance of stopping legislation was at the committee level, especially in those committees chaired by relatively sympathetic southern Democrats. The White House understood that once legislation reached the floor Democratic leaders would be in a position to foil the administration. Compounding this problem, congressional Democrats realized that a defeat on the floor was a public defeat for Nixon.

The Office of Management and Budget

The Office of Management and Budget, while an important part of the overall liaison operation of the executive branch, is unique in several regards. The Bureau of the Budget (BOB) as originally created under the Budget and Accounting Act of 1921 was part of the Treasury Department but was directly responsible to the president. The BOB's original functions centered on assisting the president with the preparation of a budget and reviewing agency proposals for legislation for budgetary considerations. When the Executive Office of the President was created under Roosevelt, the BOB was moved into a position closer to the president and became more involved and more important in the policy process. Roosevelt considered it wasteful to have agencies working at cross purposes on substantive issues and expanded the use of central clearance to include substantive as well as budgetary concerns. The BOB became a logical repository of this function, given their central clearance responsibility on financial matters, and the use of the presidential advisors to provide central clearance on substance was taxing the small staff.

As the Bureau of the Budget and later the Office of Management and Budget (OMB) began to grow in power, it became natural to include it in the legislative lobbying process. The Nixon administration, in particular, wanted to centralize decision making and used the OMB toward that end.[65] They were invited into the leadership meetings with the president because of their responsibility for seeing that the president's budget guidelines were followed.[66] The OMB's role in legislative relations began to grow as the budget became an increasingly important issue in politics. During the Ford administration the OMB's congressional relations person met with the White House team every morning. According to Max Friedersdorf, who headed the Office of Congressional Relations for most of the Ford administration, the OMB person played an important role and had equal status with White House liaison.[67] Reagan gave his OMB directors cabinet rank, and the position has come to be regarded as one of the president's most important appointments.

The Office of Management and Budget became more central to the policy process through its role in central clearance and through its own lobbying. While central clearance has become the most important function, the role of the OMB in lobbying Congress is not insignificant.

The growth in OMB's importance has empowered its lobbyists, who have come to be regarded as more important than those of the departments. The

OMB lobbyists are important players in the legislative process because they may influence policy development and lobbying. Their level of prestige is high on the Hill and they enjoy ready access to the White House. They are "inside the gates" and get answers, whereas assistant secretaries are not always able to get their phone calls returned. OMB lobbyists have the "face time" in the White House to become known by the key players there. Kenneth C. O. Hagerty, who served as deputy assistant for congressional relations under both Nixon and Ford, described his job:

> As Deputy I share responsibility for OMB's overall Congressional relations effort which involves: explaining and promoting the President's Budget and the policies contained within it, fostering passage of Administration legislation, especially bills which cut across the entire government or establish new entities; abetting the defeat of legislation contrary to Administration policy; providing information and staff assistance to the White House Congressional Relations office; promoting and defending the appropriations and other institutional needs of OMB as an agency; and speaking to groups on Administration policies and the role of OMB. I developed and produce the weekly schedule of Administration positions on bills slated for floor action.[68]

The politics of balancing the budget and the increased importance of the budget director made the OMB's lobbyist increasingly important. Because of their role in the budget process, their proximity to the White House, and their jurisdiction over issues that go beyond the boundaries of a single department, these lobbyists, by the time of the Bush presidency, had become second in importance only to the men and women who worked directly for the president.

Conclusion

By the end of the administration, both Republicans and Democrats had become frustrated with George Bush. The president's interest in foreign policy was not shared by the public or by lawmakers. Further, Bush lacked a connection to the public, leaving both Democrats and Republicans largely unconcerned about his impact on the next election. Republicans felt a lack of leadership, and one writer derided the president's use of the bully pulpit as the "silly pulpit." George Will concluded that "Congress likes Bush, but does not respect him because it doesn't have to, which is why they like him."[69]

Conservative Republicans in particular were frustrated with the 1992 campaign. According to one veteran of the Bush White House, conservatives "washed their hands of the last four years and set out to be whole again—pure again, reclaim their virginity." Another veteran of the Bush White House saw that Bush's loss of public confidence seriously undermined his ability to work with Congress:

> With the Bush presidency, the last six months were very bad because our side was worried about being too closely affiliated with the president. It is not, "Hey, the main man is in trouble, let's rally around the president." Are you kidding? It is "every man for himself!" That never happened with Reagan, even through Iran-Contra that didn't happen because everybody stood behind him. Because of the basic popularity that the man enjoyed with the American people. The problem with Bush is that he lost that, he lost the trust of the American people. His last year, when he was kind of flip about what was going on around the country, if he had come out and acted like he cared about getting reelected a lot earlier, maybe people would have thought, "Hey, this guy is worried about us."

George Bush often walked away from the public appeals that were one of the few remaining tools of the presidency. Burt Solomon suggested that "President Bush didn't merely disdain attempts to appeal past Congress for public support: he hindered them."[70] This created the irony that Bush's many friendships became a problem for his legislative agenda. As veterans of his White House explained, the president did not like the idea of going over the heads of his friends in Congress.

However, Bush's friendships paid off in his battles to sustain vetoes of legislation, and the administration's system of veto warnings increased the effectiveness of the veto as a bargaining tool. The Bush administration often succeeded by making its objections known very early in the legislative process, while legislation was just taking form in committees and subcommittees. Had these threats come later in the process, too much energy would have been invested by members of Congress and their staffs and too many members would have taken public positions to make bargaining effective.

Beyond the innovative use of veto threats, George Bush seemed to be trying to exercise leadership in the old system of institutionalized pluralism. Most of the complaints lodged against Bush and his White House were relatively minor, but the sum of his efforts did not impress lawmakers. Bush relied on his friendships and the goodwill built through years of service and the writing of countless thank-you notes. He refused to go over the heads of his friends in Congress, but his friendship was not enough to secure their votes. Lacking a strong domestic agenda or the Republican majority to pass it, the president focused on foreign policy. What the Bush years demonstrate is that presidential politics as usual is not enough to produce influence in Congress. Without the public appeal of Reagan or an aggressive attempt to stimulate support at the grassroots, Congress will politely go its own way.

10

THE CLINTON
ADMINISTRATION

BILL CLINTON'S ARRIVAL IN WASHINGTON SEEMED TO hold out the promise of the end of gridlock. Clinton brought an activist's agenda to a Congress controlled by fellow Democrats, and the new president seemed to possess the kind of rhetorical skills that could provide enough public leadership to prod the process along. However, Clinton had won the White House with less than 43 percent of the popular vote (roughly the share that Richard Nixon had in 1968). The three-way race cut into Clinton's share of the vote and he ran behind the winning House candidate in all but five districts,[1] insuring that he could make no claims that he had brought members into Congress. The Democrats' loss of a few seats convinced members of both parties that Clinton would have little impact on reelection. Clinton's mandate would be challenged even before all his votes were counted, when Senate Republican Leader Bob Dole appeared on television on election night to point out that a majority of voters had chosen someone other than Clinton.[2] Dole went so far as to claim to represent the voters who had voted for Bush or Perot. Despite the dubious nature of Dole's claim to a mandate, he helped diminish or at least distract from Clinton's victory.

The Democratic majority in Congress produced in the election of 1992 was neither large nor cooperative. Jimmy Carter had begun his term with 14 percent more House Democrats and 11 percent more Senate Democrats.[3] This meant that the Democrats lacked the sixty votes they would need to end Republican filibusters. Clinton inherited the unenviable task of trying to bring together a Democratic coalition that had operated largely as an opposition force. After twelve years of being locked out of the executive branch, congressional Democrats had settled into a disruptive strategy. Many congressional Democrats had built their careers around being rebellious rather than cooperative, and they felt better served by a course of independence from the White House rather than a partnership. Representative George Miller (Democrat-California) noted, "Divided government gave everyone a place to hide, we no longer have the luxury of criticizing," while one Democratic senator concluded, "A lot of senators don't know how to act with a Democrat in the White House." Cooperation requires adjustment, especially for those who have sought notoriety.[4]

The presence of unified government and an activist president created high expectations. Unfortunately, these expectations did not work to Clinton's advantage. The Clinton administration gained passage of the Family Medical Leave Act, the "Motor Voter" bill, and national service, as well as the components of his economic passage. The administration also won congressional approval of the North American Free Trade Agreement and the General Agreement on Tariffs and Trade. However, these successes were considered disappointing because more was expected. Without domestic policy victories and buffeted by allegations of various forms of personal wrongdoing, Clinton became a liability to the party in 1994, and the loss of a Democratic majority further undermined Clinton's influence.

The Clinton Staff

While Clinton's lack of influence in Congress was largely the result of broad political forces, the Clinton administration contributed to its problems. Some observers in Washington expressed doubts about the Clinton liaison staff, and Clinton was criticized for using the congressional relations staff as a device for bringing diversity to the White House and repaying campaign workers. The legislative affairs team was certainly the most diverse ever assembled and one campaign worker was included in the team, but the remainder of the Clinton team had Hill experience.

The office was initially headed by Howard G. Paster, a "short, personable man, with a Brooklyn accent and an appealing scrappiness."[5] Paster had begun his Washington career as an administrative assistant to Representative Lester Wolff (Democrat-New York) and later served as legislative assistant to

Senator Birch Bayh (Democrat-Indiana) for six years. Paster had spent twelve years at Timmons and Company, a high-powered lobbying firm, working with veterans of the Nixon, Ford, and Carter White Houses, and most recently he had been the head of the Washington offices of Hill and Knowlton. Paster was the most experienced member of the liaison staff, while he was not a White House veteran, the Democrats having had few recent administrations to draw talent from.

The Clinton staff followed the organization that had become standard. Directly below Paster were three people with the rank of deputy assistant to the president. Two were housed in the East Wing of the White House, with Steve Ricchetti heading Senate lobbying and Lorraine Miller in charge of the House. Ricchetti had served as executive director of the Democratic Senatorial Campaign Committee during the 1992 campaign. Susan Brophy served with Paster in the West Wing as an "internal" assistant to Paster, dealing with matters internal to the White House and making decisions when Paster was busy. Brophy, who had been in charge of congressional relations during the transition, had served as chief of staff for former Senator Tim Wirth (Democrat-Colorado) before joining the Clinton campaign. The staff included seven people holding the rank of special assistant to the president, with three working with the House, three with the Senate, and one working as an administrative aide to Paster. There were also eight assistants providing staff support. Two additional people were assigned to the legislative correspondence unit.

Paster left the administration at the end of the first year, citing "burnout" and a desire to spend more time with his family. Reporters attributed Paster's departure to clashes with Chief of Staff Mack McLarty or to Paster's abrupt style.[6] Paster had been criticized for not returning phone calls and was described by some as confrontational and unsympathetic to congressional concerns,[7] but some sources saw Paster's problems more as the product of the workings of the Clinton White House. One veteran of the Carter administration attributed Paster's departure to the chaotic organization of the Clinton White House and to people cutting deals behind his back: "This is the sort of thing that drives Howard crazy, there is the politics of campaigning and there is the politics of governing, and the two are not the same necessarily. Not every battle is between good and evil. Not every legislative fight has to have a villain. Some do, but not all of them." While Paster denied that he departed for these reasons, the style of the administration did make his job more difficult. Bob Woodward concluded that Paster's job was made impossible by a White House that was "too often like a soccer league of 10-year-olds. No one stuck to his part of the field during the game."[8] Paster enjoyed access to Clinton, but so did many others. One of Paster's friends explained why the flexible assignments that produced the open exchange of ideas that Clinton liked did not produce an effective legislative operation.

> There seems to be a much larger number of people who have carte blanche to muck around in things that were a little more orderly or a little more functionally organized in the past. There wasn't a George Stephanopoulos in many administrations, at least I don't think there was, who kind of was without portfolio, just sort of out there doing congressional relations, and doing public affairs and doing this and doing that. This interferes with the head of the office's ability to function because, if Dick Gephardt can pick up the phone and get what he needs from these people, he doesn't have to go work with Pat [Griffin—head of Congressional Relations at that time]; it's harder then for Pat to be sent back to deal with Gephardt and get something out of him because he hasn't been the one delivering the goodies.

Ironically, the only other senior member of the Clinton White House with significant experience with Congress was George Stephanopoulos, who had been Majority Leader Dick Gephardt's chief legislative assistant before joining the Clinton campaign. With Stephanopoulos as a competing source of congressional strategy and as a natural conduit to the Hill, the Office of Legislative Affairs' biggest ally could also be a competitor.

Paster was replaced by Patrick J. Griffin who was president of the Washington consulting firm of Griffin, Johnson, and Associates. Griffin had previously served as Secretary to the Senate Democratic Conference, as well as floor assistant to Senator Robert Byrd (Democrat-West Virginia) when he was Minority Leader. Griffin departed the administration in February 1996 claiming that "two years in this job is like a career in most others"[9] and was replaced by John Hilley. Hilley had served as chief of staff for Senate Majority Leader Mitchell and, after Mitchell's retirement, on the staff of Tom Daschle when he served as Senate Minority Leader.

The Clinton administration limited itself by the failure to bring the congressional relations operation closer to the president, and word circulated throughout Washington that Clinton's congressional operation had been relegated to B-level status. Regardless of whether or not this rumor was true, once it became the conventional wisdom, it set in motion congressional responses that would undermine the Office of Legislative Affairs. Because Paster and Griffin were not clearly part of Clinton's innermost circle of advisors, the liaison staff lacked the ability to educate and direct the rest of the White House and keep them focused on a legislative strategy. When problems in the White House began to appear, one White House veteran suggested, "I'm sure Howard [Paster] tried to stop it. He must have died a thousand deaths. But Howard couldn't stop them, because he's not an FOB [Friend of Bill]. I don't envy Howard for his job at all." The kinds of divisions predicted by Joseph Pika[10] and observed in previous administrations appeared within the Clinton administration. Howard Paster and his congressional liaison staff were seen by some in the White House as being too concerned with congressional needs.[11] At the same time, sources on the Hill criticized Paster as being insensitive to congressional concerns, and comparisons were made to Carter's liaison chief, Frank Moore. The suggestion that Frank Moore, the Washington novice, and Howard Paster, the experienced Washington operator, were similar reveals as much about congressional complaining as about Paster, who had his defenders. Representative John Dingell (Democrat-Michigan) suggested, "The President's problems are in the Senate, which has the same rules as the San Francisco Zoo. There's no way Paster can be blamed for that."[12]

The Clinton liaison staff was also criticized for not spending enough time with members of Congress, especially those outside the leadership.[13] Several lawmakers commented that they had seen little of the liaison staff, and veterans of past administrations noted the White House's lack of a presence on the Hill. Without a close day-to-day interaction with Congress, the liaison staff was unable to provide the kind of political intelligence needed to construct an effective strategy.[14] The White House stumbled into some losing battles when they underestimated the size or intensity of opposition to nominees or policy initiatives. After the administration's economic stimulus bill was stalled by Senate opposition, one House Democratic aide commented, "It bothers me that the White House was surprised by the Senate situation. That's an indication that they have been developing a strategy without good information."[15]

Despite their newness in Washington, Clinton White House staffers were not shy about playing hardball. After Senator Richard C. Shelby (Democrat-Alabama) embarrassed Vice President Al Gore in front of cameras with a lecture about the shortcomings of the administration's proposal, the White House sent their own message by moving some government spending out of Alabama.[16] Some critics of the administration claimed that the White House's retaliation against Shelby only stiffened his resistance, but one member of the liaison staff believed that they were not going to get Shelby's help anyway and that "It proved we were willing to get tough." Tom Korologos, who had played hardball with Congress during his service in the Nixon White House, found humor and similarities in the Clinton approach. "I give these guys six month before they have a team of plumbers. Pretty soon they'll be at the Watergate. Seriously, they're playing hardball and I admire them."[17]

The Clinton administration suffered from the arrogance typical of new administrations. They failed to sit down with veterans of the Carter administration on a regular basis and listen to what they had learned from Carter's problems with Congress. One veteran of the Carter White House noted, "They could have learned a lot from us. We made all those mistakes, they didn't have to make them again." He went on to worry that the Clinton staff had too much confidence in the political skills of their president.

> Early on I was talking to someone from the Clinton administration who said that their trouble is that Clinton is always smarter than anyone else in the room. And I thought, oh man, are we headed for trouble! There are a lot of smart people in the room, and there are a lot of smart people in this town, and some of them get paid big money to stop what the president wants to do. And they've stopped other presidents.

Clinton and Congress

Bill Clinton was willing to spend time with Congress and avoid the criticisms that Carter had faced. Clinton began with a visit to Congress during the campaign and he made several visits to Capitol Hill in the months before his inauguration.[18] Clinton enjoyed the give-and-take of the process and was always available to work with members. During the battle for his economic plan, Howard Paster returned from the Oval Office where Clinton had been calling members and remarked, "He likes this. He thinks this is fun."[19]

While congressional Republicans would justify their complete lack of support for most of the Clinton legislative package by claiming that they had been left out of the process, the president did make several trips to Capitol Hill to see Republican lawmakers that were described as "unheard of," but within a few months they were complaining that they had been ignored.[20]

Clinton was eventually overexposed in the bargaining process on his stimulus package and his first budget. The president began making calls to members while these bills were still in committee and Clinton personally engaged in bargaining for votes. This was seen by some White House veterans as overusing the president. As a veteran of the Reagan administration said, "The president had to learn not to get into the process himself." Treasury

Secretary Lloyd Bentsen worried that Clinton had made it too tempting for members to hold out in the hopes of gaining benefits for their district.[21] One Democratic congressional aide complained, "Whoever heard of a President calling a junior member of a committee on an amendment?"[22] This type of involvement connected Clinton directly to the bestowing of favors to members of Congress. One veteran of the Reagan and Bush administrations noted the risk of such close presidential involvement in favors.

> They started dealing openly. The president had to learn to not get into the fray himself. That was a huge mistake. When you have the president calling members of committees before votes. Jeez!! You don't do that. You're just throwing away presidential resources. The president calling up members and making deals—you let the president get involved in that, you want him away from that so he can say later on, so that he can deny that. You've got to have that as a backstop.

Clinton and Public Relations

Clinton did not have the luxury of high approval ratings as he began his presidency. Clinton's approval ratings were in the mid–50 percent range in the early months of his administration, but they declined as the divisiveness of the 1992 election coupled with the anger over Clinton's early efforts on behalf of gays in the military took him into his earliest congressional battles with as weak public support as enjoyed by any president during their first one hundred days.

The president's support early in their administration may be especially important as lawmakers take stock of a new president. This is especially the case with a president from outside Washington because many members of Congress are taking their first measure of the person and his political skills. During this period legislators begin to form their expectations of the president and his impact on the electorate. Elizabeth Drew described the process during the Clinton administration.

> The Congress takes its measure of every new President—the members watching and sniffing the air and feeling the pulse of their constituents. It is constantly judging how strong a President is and how popular he is, as they make their calculations of how important it is to support him and the consequences of doing so. These judgments can change over time, but first impressions are very important.[23]

The president's ups and down in the polls made excellent fodder for journalists and pundits. With opinion polls on presidential approval becoming more frequent, every variation in the president's performance could be speculated upon on a near-daily basis. Clinton's ups and downs with the public and Congress reinforced each other and created what Fred Greenstein termed a "roller-coaster presidency."[24] These ups and downs may have undermined what public support the president enjoyed. With the president's approval constantly moving, observers were certain to wonder about the depth and meaning of Clinton's support, and this may have distracted from the aura of the office. Having seen the president's repeated rise and fall in the polls, lawmakers could feel that if they were confronted by a popular Clinton, all they needed to do was wait for the next downturn in the polls.

Clinton's lack of popularity translated into problems in Congress because lawmakers increasingly considered him an electoral liability and doubted his value as a fund-raiser. Whereas even unpopular presidents had often been involved in congressional fund-raising in past midterm elections, congressional Democrats turned increasingly to other celebrities to bring citizens to fund-raisers. Representative Dave McCurdy (Democrat-Oklahoma) passed on having Clinton appear at a fund-raiser saying, "I had a fund-raiser in Washington and I had Garth Brooks."[25] Clinton was not the first president to be passed over by lawmakers putting together fund-raisers, and as interest groups and congressional opponents became better organized around the congressional election, the president's relative attractiveness as a source of electoral support declined.

The Clinton staff wanted to use the public to move Congress and some were frustrated with the amount of time that Clinton spent talking with members of Congress rather than with the public at large. One staffer argued that Clinton should play to his strength by talking to the public who would in turn pressure Congress. "It's a bank shot. What you say to the American people bounces back to the Congress."[26] The administration suffered because, according to one alumni of the Carter staff, their public relations approach was inconsistent.

> You need to decide that you've got enough muscle to use the grass-roots—that you're going to muscle Congress and get what you need or you are going to go the American people and stir them up and be willing to take on Congress and be willing go into members' backyards and do it. But trying to have it both ways won't work. An example is this feud with [Senator Bob] Kerrey of Nebraska and Clinton. You can't on the one hand be giving a wonderful speech about

giving all Americans health care and the same time having the Democratic National Committee spots attacking Kerrey in his home state.
It's inconsistent and not smart politics.

Clinton also suffered from problems coordinating public opinion with
his legislative agenda. Clinton's first health care address succeeded in shifting public support behind his cause, but because the legislation would be
bogged down in committee for months, opponents had time to construct
doubts in the minds of citizens. The ability to draw out a fight had proved an
advantage to congressional opponents before. Senator Tom Connally noted
that Roosevelt's popularity made resisting his court packing plan difficult in
the short run, but that by delaying, some of the president's advantage could
be reduced.

> As for our strategy in the Judiciary Committee fight, we knew we had
> the advantage in a long drawn-out fight. Since Roosevelt was so pop-
> ular throughout the country, we assumed that the first reaction of
> the nation would be to favor his bill. Our job was to prolong the
> committee hearings until we could sell our case to the country and
> the Senate.[27]

The president has the power to initially define an issue in the public
mind, but this initial advantage may fade with time. Opponents of President
Clinton's "stimulus" package found that by delaying, they were able to take
away the president's agenda-setting power and redefine the package as "pork
barrel" spending. Clinton failed to define the terms of the debate on his economic package in 1993. Republicans and their allies on talk shows succeeded
in labeling the Clinton plan as "tax and spend" liberalism. While the increased taxes in the Clinton plan were directed at the wealthiest Americans,
a CNN–*Time* magazine poll showed that 67 percent of the public believed
that the middle class would pay the new taxes, while only 27 percent thought
that the wealthy would be paying the new taxes.[28] The loss of control over the
debate represented the White House losing control of one of the few advantages that the presidency had enjoyed under individualized pluralism. Clinton's critics were especially adept at using the airwaves. Entire radio and television programs were built upon criticizing the president. During the health
care debate virtually every member of Congress got some chance to publicly
criticize the president's plan and the health insurance industry launched several very effective ads. While some of the blame for the failure to define
these issues to the president's advantage resulted from the White House's

failure to remain focused on one issue or to stay "on message," the barrage of criticism reflected an unprecedented level of public relations coming from the opposition. Clinton's communications skills were well developed and the administration engaged in extensive public relations efforts like town hall meetings, suggesting that the explanation for the problem lies as much with the effectiveness of the opposition as with the ineffectiveness of the White House.

Presidential efforts to lead the public were also becoming increasingly difficult because of growing media cynicism over its role in the process. Steven Waldman suggested that journalists often resisted covering Clinton's efforts to promote his national service plan to avoid being manipulated by the White House and to protect their image as skeptics.

> Cynicism, after all, not liberalism, is the dominant ideology of the Washington press corps. Reporters have always treasured their image as hard-boiled skeptics spitting tobacco juice on the powers that be. They truly believe that the politicians will trumpet the good news, so it is up to the journalist to find the bad. By that logic, anything the president pushes, the press should duly ignore. Clinton wanted us to know about national service—ergo, no story.[29]

The administration did clearly succeed in one use of public relations, ironically by using Vice President Al Gore. As Democratic lawmakers faced the supporters of Ross Perot and organized labor, both of whom were adamantly against the approval of the North American Free Trade Agreement (NAFTA), the White House began to look for ways to diffuse opposition and reduce the electoral risks of casting a vote with the administration. As one White House official said, "Most members wanted cover. They wanted to get labor off their backs. They wanted to get Perot off their backs. They wanted to make it politically possible to support it."[30] The vice president debated Ross Perot on national television, letting Perot discredit himself in the process. A *Time* magazine–CNN poll taken after the debate showed that only 18 percent of those surveyed said Perot won the debate, compared to 47 percent naming Gore.[31] The joint appearance did not increase the White House's clout so much as it reduced Perot's perceived threat to lawmakers. In this case, the White House won the battle of electoral expectations by removing a threat to lawmakers, rather than posing their own. Sidney Blumenthal wrote, "A house landed on the Wicked Witch, and the Munchkins nervously came out of hiding: more than thirty representatives endorsed NAFTA the following week."[32] The administration followed up on their public relations victory with some attention to individual lawmakers' districts. U.S. Trade Representative Mickey Kantor was sent out to reassure business people in the districts of Democratic supporters of the treaty's value.

Clinton used a wide variety of venues to advance his ideas, particularly in support of his health care reform proposals. In pressing his case for action, Clinton used his State of the Union address, an additional address to Congress just on health care, as well as town hall meetings and campaign-style rallies. Hillary Rodham Clinton spoke to numerous groups on behalf of the plan, and many cabinet members were involved in promoting the plan in public as well. Appealing directly to voters on behalf of health care reform, Clinton talked explicitly of electoral expectations. At a rally featuring a member of the House and both of the states' senators, Clinton called on their constituents "to persuade your members of Congress, without regard to party, that they can do this and be re-elected."[33]

Occasionally, Clinton's ability to promote or merchandise his proposals created some shifting of electoral expectations on the Hill. Clinton's first State of the Union address made some lawmakers take note of the president's ability to use his communications skills. *Newsweek* magazine described the president's ability to suddenly transform his standing before Congress by taking his ideas to the public:

> It was a virtuoso performance, and not a moment too soon: his presidency was in jeopardy, especially in the corridors of power. "There is no fear here," a Senate staffer has said a week earlier. There may be some now: Clinton showed that he can make them seem timid, foolish, craven. He can go around them, to the American people, and make a case that sells.[34]

Clinton's 1996 State of the Union address succeeded in successfully defining his position in a way that put congressional Republicans at a disadvantage. The president's improved standing helped discourage the opposition of Republicans and led some congressional Democrats to consider Clinton an electoral asset.[35] Ironically, Clinton became most effective at defining issues after seeing much of his legislative package fail to pass and witnessing the loss of a Democratic majority in Congress.

Clinton and the Republican "Revolution": A Return to Divided Government

The election of 1994 surprised most observers as the Republicans gained control over the House and the Senate. Clinton was blamed by many observers for the demise of the Democratic majority, although the number of people assigned blame or taking credit for the 1994 election involves most of the political universe.[36] Clinton became the first president to lose his majority in both houses since Eisenhower lost his Republican majority in the 1954 election, although Reagan had lost his Senate majority after the 1986 election. Clinton's "loss" of Congress was treated differently, in part, because Clinton lacked Eisenhower's public approval. Because most Americans liked "Ike" few Democrats in Congress were willing to openly confront Eisenhower, while Clinton's lack of popularity made him a likely scapegoat.

The challenge Clinton faced went beyond the numbers of the Republicans alone. With Senate Majority Leader Bob Dole, new House Speaker Newt Gingrich, and several other members of Congress campaigning for president or considering a run for the presidency, Clinton faced congressional Republicans who had little incentive to work with the White House on any issue that might reflect well on Clinton. The presidential contenders and the large (seventy-three members), aggressive freshman Republican class were both strident in their positions and visible in the national media.

Even while political scientists have doubted the validity of a president's claim to a mandate, congressional Republicans had no problem claiming that they held a clear mandate from the people. Senate Majority Leader Bob Dole laid out the Republican position in terms that laid claim to a mandate that precluded compromising with the White House.

> But he [Clinton] should know that we will never compromise away the mandate the American people gave us last November. This will not be an autumn of compromise. This fall we will win our fight for revolutionary change vote by vote, bill by bill.[37]

From the White House, the new Republican majority was neither friendly nor predictable. Beyond their general contempt for Clinton and the Democrats in Congress, the new Republicans represented a different set of electoral concerns from their more senior colleagues. The Republican freshmen were not content to quietly follow congressional leadership, and they became an independent power in Congress. One writer compared the hardline Republican's chants of "Shut It Down!" during the budget battle to the chants of antiwar protesters during the war in Vietnam.[38] Their rhetoric suggested that they saw no need to compromise. Putting aside concerns of separation of powers and bicameralism, House Republican Whip Tom DeLay (Texas) asserted, "We are going to fund only those programs we want to fund. We're in charge. We don't have to negotiate with the Senate. We don't have to negotiate with the Democrats."[39] This bravado was not supported by their numbers in either House. The Republican majority in the House of Representatives was the slimmest since the Democratic majority coming out of the 1956 campaign that reelected Dwight Eisenhower, and their seven-seat advantage in the Senate was far from historic and not large enough to preclude Democratic filibusters or other disruptions. The Republicans' lack of electoral strength was compensated for by their willingness to use every possible source of political leverage.

Senator Jesse Helms (Republican-North Carolina) used his chairmanship of the Senate Foreign Relations Committee to try to shut down the State Department, much as House Republicans tried to shut down the government. Helms held up the nominations of over four hundred State Department promotions as well as approval of over a dozen treaties in an attempt to force the reorganization of some agencies that dealt with arms control and foreign aid. At one point, about 15 percent of American embassies were left without new ambassadors.[40]

The new Republican majority and their leader, Newt Gingrich, stole much of the president's spotlight. While past Speakers like Tip O'Neill had made use of media coverage to challenge the president's monopoly of the public agenda, none had been as aggressive as Gingrich was. Gingrich held frequent press conferences during the early portions of the 104th Congress, and while the constant exposure led him into controversy, he succeeded in shifting much of the media focus in Washington from the White House to the Speaker's office. As part of Gingrich's attempt to win a majority in the House, he and his supporters in Congress had assembled a platform labeled the "Contract with America." Because many observers gave the Contract with America partial credit for the Republican victory in 1994, and because Gingrich and the Republicans made frequent references to the contract and held several staged events, this program became the focus of Congress and the nation for much of 1994. By spring 1995 Clinton was arguing that he was still relevant.

Gingrich made sure that his efforts translated into electoral influence. As the 1996 election approached, Gingrich became heavily involved in fundraising for congressional Republicans. During one break in the budget deadlock, Gingrich departed on a ten-day, thirty-stop fund-raising tour for incumbent Republicans. And, much as past presidents had done before, the Speaker carefully chose whom he would provide assistance to, leaving out some members who had opposed him on key votes.

For the first time since congressional leaders like Lyndon Johnson channeled money from wealthy donors to needy candidates, the leadership of

Congress represented a fund-raising force that rivaled the presidency. And, for the first time ever, the Speaker of the House enjoyed a level of visibility and agenda-setting that rivaled the president's.

The most visible example of the degree to which the new Republican majority was willing to use whatever tools were at its disposal was the budget battle of 1995 and 1996. While still the minority, the Republicans in the Senate had been willing to utilize a record number of filibusters to slow down or kill Clinton's legislative proposals, and with the power of the majority Republicans were able to find new challenges to presidential power.

The Republican leadership had to find a way around the president that relied upon commitment rather than strength because the Republican majority could not override a presidential veto of their budget. However, because Republicans saw the shutting down of the government that resulted when funds ran out as consistent with their goal of reducing the size of government, they felt that they had an advantage that would force Clinton to accept their version of the budget. Many Republicans were willing to fight for a balanced budget regardless of the political costs. One Republican freshman claimed, "Maybe not all 73 of us, but 50 to 55 of us don't care if we get reelected or not if we fold on the balanced budget."[41] On two occasions, Congress refused to pass a continuing resolution that would have kept the government funded while the White House and Congress negotiated, and parts of the government were shut down on two separate occasions, on the first occasion for six days and the second time for twenty-one days.[42]

Congressional Republicans also refused to raise the debt ceiling, a move that threatened to force the government into defaulting on its loans for the first time in history. The Treasury Department sidestepped the problem by postponing interest payments to some federal pension funds and tapping into others for loans to avoid a default for several months until public opinion turned against the Republicans, leading them to rethink their approach and agree to raise the debt ceiling.

While fault for the government shutdown and the inability to reach an agreement were tossed around by both sides as well as by numerous Washington pundits, it is clear that the Republicans in Congress were willing to take conflict with the executive branch to a higher level than previous Congresses. House Republican freshmen in particular were more than happy to shut the government down indefinitely until the White House conceded to their demands. Democrats in Congress had been willing to force a brief shutdown during the Bush administration, but their willingness to use this leverage fell far short of the assertive Congress that Clinton faced.

Republican attempts were successful in that the Clinton administration did eventually agree to a seven-year plan to balance the budget, but the Republicans failed to get the president to agree to their versions of some programs and finally gave up and left the issue in the hands of the voters in the 1996 election. One House Republican freshman conceded, "We just underestimated Clinton." While conceding that mistakes were made, this Republican went on to describe their experiences as something like being battle tested: "We just had to go out and get shot up a little so that we could come back better prepared for the next battle."

Ironically, this challenge to Clinton's leadership improved his public standing and helped his reputation within Washington. When faced with the strident challenge from Republicans, Clinton became strident. Because many of Clinton's reputation problems on Capitol Hill resulted from his vacillation on issues like the energy tax, the presidential resolve brought on by the congressional challenge created a new image for Clinton. Public opinion polls showed citizens blaming congressional Republicans more than Clinton for the shutdown. Speaker Gingrich assisted the president's cause by conceding at a press conference that one of the reasons for the budget impasse was that he had felt slighted when, after a long flight to Israel for the funeral of Prime Minister Yitzhak Rabin, he was not allowed to exit *Air Force One* from the same front door that Clinton used. In the end, Republican tactics and Clinton's response created a context that worked to the electoral advantage of the president. As Congress watched Clinton's approval rise and disapproval of Speaker Gingrich and the Republican Congress increase, lawmakers began to feel that allying with Clinton would produce benefits at the next election.

The Challenge of Interest Groups Under Individualized Pluralism

Threats of government default and shutdown, and growing media resistance to cooperate with presidential attempts to promote their policies or "merchandise," reflect only some of the ways in which the political landscape has grown increasingly resistant to presidential leadership. Clinton faced a more difficult political landscape than had existed even during the Carter administration. One Carter aide argued that for all the trouble they experienced with Congress, it was easier under Carter than under Clinton.

It was a lot easier for us to do it in '76–81. There was so much more party loyalty, there were fewer people to deal with, the major committee chairmen, the senior system was much more in place at that point. . . . Even after the '74 Watergate baby class, that great explosion of new talent and interesting people. They began to overturn the seniority system but you also have to remember that they were the last of the old-school politicians. They got there by upsetting Republicans in districts that hadn't elected a Republican in a while but most of them came with the blessing of the party leadership back in their districts. I look at these guys now and see what they had to go through to pick up a few votes here and there. For a Democratic president after twelve years, and they had to go through that? It was unbelievable. It really has changed a lot and therefore I'm glad I'm not there.

The growing ability of interest groups to play a role in the public debate over legislation represents the degree to which tools of presidential influence have been emulated by interest groups. In the environment of individualized pluralism, interest groups have succeeded by making opposition to their agenda electorally risky through advertising and other forms of going public.

The Clinton administration faced a well-organized and well-financed coalition of interest groups on many key issues. Insurance companies (among others) opposed health care reform, and the National Rifle Association opposed several components of the president's legislative agenda.[43] One Democratic member of Congress pointed out that the health care battle represented a sophisticated challenge to Clinton's leadership of public opinion.

This [the health care battle] is not classic interest group politics. It's interest groups that have gone public and have learned to excite public apprehensions and public opposition. And that's what's really hurting politically. It's not that some insurance lobbyist comes in here and twists my arm. Who cares about that? But when the insurance association runs these ads that get everyone spooked—that has political impact.

The Clinton administration found itself facing interest groups that were often trained and led by veterans of previous White Houses. White House staffers have followed up a few years of service to the president with a career in the private sector since the White House congressional liaison office was created. In the field of congressional relations, the overwhelming majority of these people go into lobbying for the private sector, either to individual businesses, trade associations, or increasingly they join firms that specialize in lobbying for a variety of clients. Especially after the 1994 election, the Clinton White House faced a talented band of veterans of Republican administrations who were working closely with the administration's congressional opponents. These ex–White House lobbyists worked with congressional Republicans on vote counting operations, putting together talking points for members, running briefings for congressional aides, and even helping to draft the House rules behind the passage of many bills. House Speaker Newt Gingrich recruited Nicholas Calio, who headed Bush's congressional relations office, to head the Congressional Institute, Inc., which put together annual retreats for House Republicans.[44] Gingrich also consulted frequently with Kenneth Duberstein, who had served in the Bush administration, and with other veterans of past Republican administrations.

When interest groups draw their lobbyists out of the White House one of the resources they are co-opting is credibility. One of the most serious challenges faced by lobbyists today is gaining access to members of Congress. The growing number of lobbyists in Washington makes it harder for any single lobbyist to gain access to a member of Congress. Members of Congress are besieged by lobbyists, and old friends and familiar faces are the most likely to gain the member's ear. While interest groups can attempt to buy a little of this credibility from well-connected lobbying firms, a new White House staff must struggle to develop such a reputation over time. A new administration can hope to attract a veteran White House lobbyist, but this inevitably requires that they take a large cut in pay to return to public service. After Howard Paster left the White House, his new salary with Hill and Knowlton was estimated to be around $1,000,000. He had been earning around $130,000 in the White House (near the top of the White House pay scale—his staff averaged $67,000).[45] While Paster's million-dollar salary is impressive, it is not unheard of in top firms. One veteran of the White House pointed out that top White House or congressional staff people can easily increase their salary two or three times by moving to even the "mid-range" positions as lobbyists. He would have not been able to take a position in the Clinton White House because he had two children in private colleges and could not afford the pay cut.

The disparity of financial resources extends beyond salary. One veteran of both the Carter administration and a downtown lobbying firm concluded, "We're better at grassroots lobbying because, frankly, we're better funded." The White House does command the political resources of the executive branch, but because the law limits the use of federal money for grassroots lobbying, the executive branch's political resources are modest in comparison to the interest group community. One magazine estimated that interest groups spent almost $800 million on grassroots lobbying during the 103rd Congress.[46] Referring to the lead characters in an advertising blitz financed by interest groups opposed to the Clinton health care plan, one analyst suggested, "Even Lyndon B. Johnson couldn't have brought Harry and Louise around."[47]

Clinton even faced congressional challenges in foreign policy. There was a massive interest group campaign against the ratification of the North American Free Trade Agreement and the General Agreement on Tariffs and Trade. One Carter aide noted that the president's ability to enjoy unchallenged leadership on foreign policy had evaporated. "I don't think you could pass the Panama Canal treaty today. . . . There was not nearly as organized an effort against the Canal Treaty as against NAFTA."

Interest groups also began to organize their efforts earlier in the process. Anticipating the impact of Clinton's proposal of direct lending from universities to students, numerous banking interests involved in the current student loan system began to organize. After the election a lobbyist for the Consumer Bankers Association gave questions to congressional staff that could be used to question Clinton's appointees during their Senate confirmation. In January 1993, a number of financial institutions banded together under the label "Coalition for Student Loan Reform" to block Clinton's proposal to change the system. This forced the White House to mobilize interest group efforts and engage the president in personal lobbying of members just to get the bill out of the House Education and Labor Committee.[48]

Clinton faced the best trained, organized, and funded collection of interests to date. While some of this opposition resulted from the nature of health care reform and other issues, Clinton's experience with interest groups is an extension of the kind of opposition that often challenged other recent presidents.

Conclusion

Many in Washington seemed to claim that the White House didn't win more legislative battles because the White House was inept. Despite the proclamations of various Washington pundits, the Clinton administration has had its successes. Jon Bond and Richard Fleisher found that Clinton had a very high level of success at winning controversial votes, and *Congressional Quarterly* found that Clinton's success rate was over 85 percent for his first two years in office.[49] The administration was ridiculed for pointing out that its success rate was comparable to the allegedly passive Eisenhower, and other observers suggested that Lyndon Johnson's success in the 89th Congress was a much more legitimate yardstick. Students of the presidency would be better served by noting that either standard requires that we look back almost thirty years for an example of success. A standard of success that is seldom met needs revision.

The return of a Republican majority in Congress sharply altered Clinton's success and his success rate in Congress dropped to 36 percent, well below the previous record low set by George Bush in 1992.[50] Clinton's failures, like his successes, lay with electoral concerns. Many congressional Republicans resisted any legislation that might boost Clinton's plans for reelection.

Clinton, like other presidents studied here, made mistakes in dealing with Congress. However, focusing on these mistakes overlooks both the barriers to presidential leadership in the constitutional framework and a political context that rewards independence. Clinton's problems getting congressional cooperation had more to do with his marginal victory in the 1992 election and the difficulty of fostering cooperation in an increasingly individualized system. As James McGregor Burns noted early in Clinton's presidency, "[W]hatever human mistakes he [Clinton] has made, the president is mainly a victim of our constitutional system of deadlock combined with a media that heats up every trivial gaffe into a momentous event."[51] The political system has become too practiced at resisting presidential leadership, and Clinton's lack of influence results not from his misapplication of the old tools of influence, but from his inability to find innovative tools of leadership that have not yet been emulated by other political institutions.

11

CONCLUSION

A striking feature of our recent past has been the
transformation into routine practice of the actions we once
treated as exceptional. A President may retain liberty, in
Woodrow Wilson's phrase, "to be as big a man as he can." But
nowadays he cannot be as small as he might like.

Richard Neustadt, *Presidential Power*

PRESIDENTIAL LEADERSHIP OF CONGRESS IS HARD AND
getting harder. Successful cases like Franklin Roosevelt and Lyndon Johnson
represent exceptions, when unusually large electoral majorities and the perception of a clear mandate overwhelmed the separation of powers and created the appearance of presidential dominance of the legislative branch.
However, even Roosevelt and Johnson experienced setbacks. One senior
member of the House noted both the decline in presidential power and the
limit on even great presidents like Franklin Roosevelt.

> There has been overall a gradual erosion of presidential impact on
> policy versus that of Congress. Congress has become more and more
> jealous of its powers. And of course we haven't had a Franklin D.
> Roosevelt—but he couldn't get the court packed in his heyday.

Many journalists continue to use the standard of Franklin Roosevelt's
first one hundred days, despite the fact that the length of one hundred days
was set because Congress convened March 9, 1933, and went home for the
year on June 15.[1] Thus, Roosevelt's first hundred days made up the entirety
of his first session with Congress. The standard of the first one hundred days

measures presidents at a time in which they have the least experience. It is ironic that Americans are more patient with the counter help on their first day working at a fast food restaurant with a limited menu than they are with the president of the United States trying to master the workings of a separated system and the role of leader of the free world. This is especially odd given the public's fondness for choosing outsider presidents who inherently have little knowledge of Washington politics.

Americans continue to expect a level of legislative leadership from their president unsupported by the system of the separation of powers created by the founders and made even more unlikely by the independent-minded lawmakers that voters send to Washington.[2] Presidents are blamed by voters for failing to lead Congress while members of Congress are often rewarded for *not* following the president. One member of the House reminded me of the challenges inherent in moving Congress:

> This is not an easily manageable place. It wouldn't be any more so for Republicans than for Democrats. Members are highly individualistic, often getting elected by going home and proclaiming how independent they are. The parties are in decline in the electorate and in local party organizations. What incentives do you have to make the institution work? Or to be a team player? Your incentives are very weak for that.

Vice President Al Gore was reminded of the support for congressional independence when he drew applause from a crowd at a fund-raiser for a Democratic incumbent when he told them, "I can tell you from personal experience and with some regret that David [Mann] does not vote the way we want him to every time a vote comes up, but the American people want a member of Congress to exercise independent judgment."[3]

Analysts often approach presidential leadership of Congress attempting to explain why presidents have failed to move Congress. However, expectations based upon a consideration of the realities of the U.S. political system would acknowledge that the chief executive attempts to exercise influence in the legislative branch *despite* constitutional barriers. Recent history certainly provides ample examples. Presidents Eisenhower, Kennedy, Nixon, Ford, Carter, Bush, and Clinton have all struggled to lead Congress throughout their presidencies. Ronald Reagan enjoyed significant successes his first year, but struggled with a reluctant Congress throughout the remainder of his service. Lyndon Johnson enjoyed phenomenal success in 1965, but even his legislative skills could not guarantee success once the war in Vietnam became a distraction and his party lost its lopsided majority in Congress. As one senior member of the House remarked, "Congress has lost its fear of the president—if it ever had it." Lack of presidential success is inherent in the system and the idea of a president aggressively attempting to lead Congress is relatively new. Hubert Humphrey described the change shortly before his death.

> Up until the time of Woodrow Wilson, with the exception of Teddy Roosevelt, we had congressional government. Congress was the predominating influence. Now Congress had reasserted itself again. I can't overemphasize the importance of this. Congress is no longer afraid of the executive—particularly when you look at things like the budget.[4]

Writing for the *New York Times* in 1952, William S. White noted, "it is more or less in the American way for there to be trouble with Congress for any except the most supine executive. Those famous 'checks and balances' are quite real."[5] Bringing together the White House and Congress is harder than is often portrayed, especially when the two branches are in the hands of the same party. As Ken Duberstein, who headed congressional relations for Reagan and served as his chief of staff, has pointed out, even when the White House and Congress are in the hands of the same party, as it was during the first two years of the Clinton administration, there is still much that divides them. "Yet in spite of both ends of Pennsylvania Avenue being controlled by the same political party, we still will have two competing governments—one on the Hill, one at the White House; one focused on the national interest, one focused on 435 separate districts of 50 states."[6]

The View from Between the Branches

The workings of the White House congressional liaison office illuminate much about the exercise of influence between the two great branches of government. The positioning of the White House liaison operation between the two branches reflects the problems inherent in presidential leadership.

> In the perennial war between the executive and legislative branches, few warriors are as unsung as those who toil in the no man's land in between.

Such is the lot of the White House congressional relations staff, the presidential envoys whose job it is to forge a truce between two forces that in recent years have behaved as natural enemies.[7]

Both the Congress- and the presidency-centered approaches described in chapter 1 will not fully advance our understanding because the relationship between the president and Congress is not the product of either branch, it is the product of both. While it would seem that the White House Office of Legislative Affairs would be an extension of the president, it must take the role of a "boundary" organization and reflect the concerns of its congressional constituency as well as the organization in which it is placed.[8] A member of the Reagan administration's congressional relations office described the dilemma created by the constituent pressures of the two branches. "The fellows up on the Hill are up there to make demands on behalf of their constituents' interests and people in the White House are there to serve the interests of the country through their service to the president." Max Friedersdorf described how the electoral concerns of members are brought into the White House by the liaison office's work with Congress. "Congressmen are subjected to the whims, fancies and demands of 555,000 people and those translate into demands on us, which we try to satisfy."[9] One veteran of the Bush and Reagan liaison staff commented on how little impact the change of presidents had on how the staff did business.

> I don't think there are tremendously substantive changes in the way we have done business around here. We are very much creatures of the Congress. They very much dictate our lives. When they want to start, we start, when they want to finish, we finish. Everything else we do works around that schedule. So, there has not been a major restructuring of the way that the Congress does business and I don't think there has been a major overhaul in the way that we approach the Congress.

A veteran of several White Houses described "the struggle between serving the White House and Congress as a significant problem that continues to this day between parts of the White House and the congressional staff" as a key problem for the staff and suggested that, ironically, the staff must serve the Congress in order to serve the president.

> A person is probably not doing his job if he tilts too far one way or another. If he represents only the White House he will not be too ef-

fective and if he represents only the Congress he will not keep his
job very long. . . . If communication only goes one way the relationship will fall apart.

The White House liaison staff members must be effective advocates for
both branches because cooperation between the branches is unlikely in the
absence of understanding. By understanding Congress the president's lobbyists can work effectively with lawmakers, and by being well placed in the
White House they can bring an understanding of Congress into White
House decision making. As one Carter staffer commented, "That's the role
of Congressional Liaison—to be both the president's advocate on the Hill,
and the Hill's advocate inside the White House." Powell Moore, who headed
Senate relations for Reagan, expressed the same requirement. "We see our
roles as people who are advocates for the President on Capitol Hill and advocates for the Senate inside the White House. If we don't deliver in the
White House [with respect to congressional requests], then we're not going
to deliver for the President on the Hill."[10] Members of Congress see a similar function. Representative Nancy Johnson (Republican-Connecticut)
noted her desire to see influence flow both ways. "They try to influence me,
but I try to influence them just as much."[11]

Being the advocate for two branches puts the Office of Legislative Affairs
in an uncomfortable position. One member of the Carter staff recounted a
warning he passed along to one of his successors:

Let me share with you some advice I gave Ken Duberstein when he
was named President Reagan's chief House lobbyist. I said, "Ken,
you will come to believe that when you go outside the wrought iron
fence that surrounds the White House and the Old Executive Office
Building, when you're headed to the Hill that you're going home.
When you come back inside the wrought iron fence you'll find that's
where you have most of your problems."

The White House Office of Legislative Affairs is important to the White
House for the same reason that it is a valuable source for an academic study
of White House relations with Congress: it provides information about both
branches to create an understanding between them. Often this information
is used to shape White House strategy, while at other times it is used to shape
policy to determine what proposals can hope to survive the legislative
process.

The role of White House liaison is to keep the connection between the

White House and Capitol Hill as open as possible so that each understands the other. One of the most common words in the vocabulary of the White House Liaison Office is *trust*. Veterans of the staff spoke frequently of the importance of holding the trust of both their clientele on the Hill and their colleagues in the White House. Without the confidence of lawmakers, the president's lobbyists will not be able to accurately judge congressional moods or bargain on behalf of the president. Without the confidence of the president, these lobbyists will not be able to represent congressional concerns to the White House.

The Future of the Legislative Presidency

Presidential influence over Congress and the many forms that it takes is largely the product of a president's ability to shape how members of Congress view the White House's ability to influence and shape their reelection. As Walter Mondale put it,

> If the president has the American people on his side, Congress will take notice—because, like a hanging, the prospect of defeat in an election concentrates the mind.[12]

The changing political context has shifted how the president attempts to gain influence over congressional elections as elections have changed. The most important shift has been the "deinstitutionalization" of Washington, the decline of parties, and the rise of congressional free agency as legislators have become increasingly detached from their parties and more independent. Norman Ornstein has decried the "failure of followership" in Congress and in the country and its effect on the ability of anyone to lead in the legislative process. "The individualization of American politics has created a Congress of 535 entrepreneurs, elected and financed individually, in an institution that has bent over backward to give individual leeway and resources to act as they wish."[13] Ken Duberstein noted a similar set of problems. "The system is biased toward inaction. There is little leadership or followership on the Hill. Members of Congress do not feel beholden to any president, let alone one who trailed them in their district."[14]

Richard Neustadt observed that presidents derive their power from the dependence of others but depend on others to carry out their wishes. "The needs of others for a President's initiatives creates dependence on him. Their dependence becomes his advantage."[15] But the dependence of others is limited. Several members of Congress admitted that the legislative process overall may benefit strong centralized leadership, but the reelection prospects of individual members may best be served by decentralization. Congress as an institution may benefit from the energy and direction that the executive can bring to the policy process, but individual members of Congress need independence from the executive so that they can serve local constituent needs. As one Clinton White House staffer commented, "Nowadays, the most successful Senate candidates are elected by going against the grain, picturing themselves as standing up for their state or region against the evil knights of Washington."[16]

Power has not simply shifted from the president to Congress; rather, power has become more scattered. As Paul Light points out, "the price of policy has increased dramatically, with little growth in the President's ability to absorb the 'inflation.'"[17] Members of Congress are urged to go their own way by a host of interest groups who can provide the campaign finances to compete with the limited ability of parties to help candidates or who may run television ads to turn up the heat on a member who wants to buck their interests in favor of party unity. As the Clinton agenda began to bog down on Capitol Hill, Larry O'Brien III (a lobbyist and the son of Kennedy and Johnson's congressional chief) noted, "All the potholes this thing has hit are reflective of how difficult this is. What you're seeing is the contours of the modern legislative process. It's very reactive, very much organized interest group-oriented and sensitized."[18]

Contributing to the dispersion of power in Washington is the ambiguity in the message sent by voters at election time. Republican presidents intent on balancing the budget have been elected along with Democratic Congresses committed to protecting and expanding social programs. Paul Taylor of the *Washington Post* argued, "At a time of dizzying social change and nagging economic anxiety, Americans are of two minds about the role of their government. They want its protections but not its intrusions; its benefits but not its costs. Each Election Day, they bundle up these cross-pressures into a confusing package of instructions and mail if off to Washington."[19] With no clear message coming from the electorate, the disparate voices of interest groups are able to play a larger role in guiding lawmakers to their next election.

The future of presidential influence, while generally the product of broad political forces, depends to some degree on the ability of individual presidencies to respond to changes in the politics of the nation. The presidency was considered under siege until Ronald Reagan's communication skills helped reestablish the leadership of the office. While his work was not completely successful, it reflects the potential of the presidency to learn and adapt. Ken Duberstein has argued that Lyndon Johnson would not succeed in the 1990s if he used the techniques he had in the 1960s. "He would be blind-sided constantly by people he would have paid no attention to 20 years ago because then they were not factors in the congressional power equation."[20]

This struggle for congressional independence from the executive has set into motion what Senator Daniel Patrick Moynihan has called "the iron law of emulation."[21] Every presidential innovation has been met by congressional emulation of the new technique. After presidents like Lyndon Johnson used the dispensing of spending in districts to bargain with lawmakers, Congress responded through the "earmarking" of spending in legislation that precluded presidential discretion of the use of funds. Similarly, Congress matched the growing expertise of the executive branch by beefing up its information and expertise with the creation of the Congressional Budget Office and the Office of Technology Assessment, and through the enhancement of committee and personal staff and other congressional service organizations. Lawmakers equipped their offices with long-distance phone lines, built their own congressional television studios, invited in the cameras of C-SPAN, and funded numerous offices back in their districts, all in order to increase their communication with constituents to limit the president's ability to "go over their heads."

Today, the presidency faces an unreceptive political environment and is challenged by a talented collection of congressional leaders and interest groups. House Speaker Newt Gingrich represents just one player who is willing to take control of some of the communication tools that have previously been left largely in the hands of the president. He and others in Congress have seen the potential of the White House's domination of the public discussion and emulated some of the president's techniques. Every member of Congress, numerous interest groups, and a host of pundits and talk show hosts have gained access to some segment of the public. Each enjoys greater freedom to play a negative role than does the president, who must maintain some degree of civility with all of the nation. These competing voices enjoy the freedom to turn up the volume and test the credibility of their message selectively, while the demands of presidential leadership provide little opportunity to lay low and wait for an opportune moment.

The challenge facing Bill Clinton and future presidents will be to find the means of influence against which congressional opponents have not yet inoculated themselves, to find some innovative use of presidential resources that can create a window of opportunity for leadership until Congress emulates those techniques in an attempt to restore the balance. While leadership of Congress has once again become a struggle, it is a struggle built into the system by James Madison and others who might review the balancing of the electoral ambition of the two branches at the heart of presidential relations with Congress today with some satisfaction. Although the president and his assistants in the Office of Legislative Affairs have not been completely successful in their attempt to, in the words of one veteran of several administrations, "uncheck the checks and imbalance the balances,"[22] they have succeeded in helping the branches work together more effectively.

APPENDIX A
Interview Information

Personal interviews were conducted with many of the actors involved in the congressional liaison process. These interviews were conducted between August 1992 and January 1996. Most of these interviews were conducted in person and on a not-for-attribution basis in order to facilitate an open discussion. Fifty-seven people were interviewed, some on several occasions, totaling seventy-five interviews. Interviews ranged from twenty minutes to over two hours.

The individuals interviewed do not represent a random sample. They were sought out because of the positions they held, or because they were recommended by other subjects as being especially valuable sources. In particular, members of Congress who were senior and had worked with several presidents were sought out. This gave me an opportunity to talk with members of Congress who had worked firsthand with presidents from Kennedy to Clinton. In addition, members of the congressional leadership and their staffs were targeted because of their more frequent contact with the White House. Four of the seventeen members of Congress interviewed currently held key positions in the party leadership. All except two of the remaining members except one held or had held positions as chair or ranking minority member on a committee.

The positions held by those interviewed are detailed below. Subjects are identified by the most senior position they had held at the time of the interview. All of the subjects categorized as White House staff were from the White House Office of Legislative Affairs, with the exception of three people from the Office of Management and Budget who were involved in congressional relations, including the director.

TABLE 1.

Position	Number of Subjects	Number of Interviews
White House Staff	26	43
Member of Congress	17	19
Congressional Leadership Staff	7	7
Departmental Liaison	6	7
Totals	56	76

APPENDIX B

Partisan Breakdown of Congress

TABLE 2.

Years	Congress	President	HOUSE		SENATE	
			Democrats	Republicans	Democrats	Republicans
1953–54	83rd	Eisenhower	211	**221**	47	**48**
1955–56	84th		232	**203**	48	**47**
1957–58	85th		233	**200**	49	**47**
1959–60	86th	283	**153**	64	**34**	
1961–62	87th	Kennedy	**263**	174	**65**	35
1963–64	88th		**258**	177	**67**	33
1965–66	89th	Johnson	**295**	140	**68**	32
1967–68	90th		**246**	187	**64**	36
1969–70	91st	Nixon	245	**189**	57	**43**
1971–72	92nd		254	**180**	54	**44**
1973–74	93rd		239	**192**	56	**42**
1975–76	94th	Ford	291	**144**	60	**37**
1977–78	95th	Carter	**292**	143	**61**	38
1979–80	96th		**276**	157	**58**	41
1981–82	97th	Reagan	243	**192**	46	**53**
1983–84	98th		269	**165**	46	**54**
1985–86	99th		252	**182**	47	**53**
1987–88	100th		259	**176**	55	**45**
1989–90	101rst	Bush	260	**175**	55	**45**
1991–92	102nd		267	**167**	56	**44**
1993–94	103rd	Clinton	**259**	175	**57**	43
1995–96	104th		**204**	230	47	**53**

Note: Shaded cells indicated majority party status.

Entries in **bold** represent the number of members of the same party as the president.

NOTES

PREFACE

1. Arthur M. Schlesinger, Jr., *The Imperial Presidency* (Boston: Houghton Mifflin Company, 1973), 381

1. INTRODUCTION

1. Pendleton Herring, *Presidential Leadership: The Political Relations of Congress and the Chief Executive* (New York: Rinehart and Company, 1940), 110.

2. Richard E. Neustadt, *Presidential Power and the Modern President: The Politics of Leadership from Roosevelt to Reagan* (New York: Free Press, 1990), 29.

3. Bryce N. Harlow, "Text of Harlow Keynote Address at Nashville Symposium, October 21, 1973," *Center House Bulletin of the Center for the Study of the Presidency* (Winter 1974): 7.

4. Ibid.

5. Richard M. Nixon, "Needed: Clarity of Purpose," *Time* magazine, November 10, 1980, 35.

6. Neustadt, *Presidential Power and the Modern President*, 185.

7. Throughout the text, *departments* is used to describe both cabinet departments as well as the various executive agencies.

8. During some earlier administrations this office was known as the Office of Congressional Relations, and prior to that the White House lobbying team had no official title. The title *Office of Legislative Affairs* is used throughout for simplicity.

9. Stephen J. Wayne, *The Legislative Presidency* (New York: Harper and Row, 1978).

10. Abraham Holtzman, *Legislative Liaison: Executive Leadership in Congress* (Skokie, Ill.: Rand McNally and Company, 1970); Nigel Bowles, *The White House and Capitol Hill: The Politics of Persuasion* (Oxford: Clarendon Press, 1987); and Charles O. Jones, *The Trusteeship Presidency: Jimmy Carter and the United States Congress* (Baton Rouge: Louisiana State University Press, 1988). There have also been several dissertations of special significance. Robert L. Lester, "Developments in Presidential-Congressional Relations: FDR–JFK" (Ph.D. diss., Woodrow Wilson Department of Government and Foreign Affairs, University of Virginia, 1969); Eric L. Davis, "Building Presidential Coalitions in Congress: Legislative Liaison in the Johnson White House" (Ph.D. diss., Stanford University, 1978); and Joseph A. Pika, "The White House Office of Congressional Relations: Exploring Institutionalization" (Ph.D. diss., University of Wisconsin-Madison, 1979).

11. Wayne, *The Legislative Presidency;* and George C. Edwards III, *Presidential Influence in Congress* (San Francisco: W. H. Freeman and Company, 1980).

12. George C. Edwards III, *At the Margins: Presidential Leadership of Congress* (New Haven: Yale University Press, 1989), 7.

13. Jon Bond and Richard Fleisher, *The President in the Legislative Arena* (Chicago: University of Chicago Press, 1990), 4.

14. Jon Healey, "Clinton Success Rate Declined to a Record Low in 1995," *Congressional Quarterly Weekly,* January 27, 1996, 193.

15. Bryce N. Harlow, Oral History OH 402, Dwight D. Eisenhower Library, 4.

16. Richard Reeves, *President Kennedy: Profile of Power* (New York: Simon and Schuster, 1993), 431.

17. Wayne, *The Legislative Presidency,* 171.

18. Bryce N. Harlow, Oral History OH 402, Dwight D. Eisenhower Library, 8.

19. Clifford Krauss, "Clinton's Woes on Capitol Hill Spur Sharp Criticism of His Top Lobbyist," *New York Times,* May 25, 1993, A7.

20. Cary R. Covington, "Congressional Support for the President: The View from the Kennedy/Johnson White House," *Journal of Politics* 48 (August 1986): 721–22; and Barbara Kellerman, *The Political Presidency: The Practice of Leadership from Kennedy Through Reagan* (New York: Oxford University Press, 1984), 49–50.

21. Bond and Fleisher, *The President in the Legislative Arena.*

22. Covington, "Congressional Support for the President," 717–28; and Terry Sullivan, "Headcounts, Expectations, and Presidential Coalitions in Congress," *American Journal of Political Science* 32 (1988): 657–89.

23. See also Wayne, *The Legislative Presidency,* 32.

24. "The Surtax Revolt," *Newsweek,* July 14, 1969, 22.

25. For a more extensive discussion of the different approaches to the use of roll call votes, see Edwards, *At the Margins,* chapter 2.

26. James MacGregor Burns, *The Deadlock of Democracy: Four-Party Politics in America* (Englewood Cliffs, N.J.: Prentice Hall, 1963); Edward S. Corwin, *The President: Office and Powers* (New York: New York University Press, 1940); Thomas E. Cronin, *The State of the Presidency,* 2d ed. (Boston: Little, Brown, 1980); Samuel P. Huntington, "Congressional Responses to the Twentieth Century," in *Congress and America's Future,* ed. David B. Truman (Englewood Cliffs, N.J.: Prentice Hall, 1965); Kellerman, *The Political Presidency;* Harold J. Laski, *The American Presidency, An Interpretation* (New York: Harper and Brothers, 1940); and Clinton Rossiter, *The American Presidency* (Baltimore: The Johns Hopkins University Press, 1987).

27. Neustadt, *Presidential Power and the Modern President.*

28. Jeffrey Tulis, *The Rhetorical Presidency* (Princeton: Princeton University Press, 1987), 9.

29. Bond and Fleisher, *The President in the Legislative Arena,* chapter 2.

30. Edwards, *At the Margins,* 4.

31. James McGregor Burns, "The 1994 Solution," *The American Prospect* 14 (summer 1993): 16.

32. Mark Peterson, *Legislating Together: The White House and Capitol Hill from Eisenhower to Reagan* (Cambridge: Harvard University Press, 1990), 7–8.

33. Ibid., 8–9.

34. Walter F. Mondale, "Two Views from Pennsylvania Ave.," *The American Prospect* 14 (summer 1993): 14.

35. Charles O. Jones, *The Presidency in a Separated System* (Washington, D.C.: The Brookings Institution, 1994), 16.

36. Dom Bonafede, "White House Report: Administration Realigns Hill Liaison to Gain Tighter Grip on Federal Policy," *National Journal,* January 13, 1973, 36.

37. Robert Luce, *Congress: An Explanation* (Cambridge: Harvard University Press, 1926), 110–11.

38. Jones, *The Presidency in a Separated System,* 18.

39. Neustadt, *Presidential Power and the Modern President,* 29.

40. This discussion owes much to Mark Peterson's discussion of the "pure" and "malleable" context. Peterson, *Legislating Together,* chapter 4.

41. Bond and Fleisher, *The President in the Legislative Arena*, 12.

42. Ken Collier and Terry Sullivan, "Presidential Support vs. Influence: An Exploration" (paper presented at the American Political Science Association Meetings, New Orleans, Louisiana, August 1985).

43. Peterson, *Legislating Together*, 118–41. See also Mark Peterson, "The President and Congress," in *The Presidency in the Political System*, ed. Michael Nelson, 4th ed. (Washington, D.C.: Congressional Quarterly Press, 1995), 440–67.

44. David R. Mayhew, *Congress: The Electoral Connection* (New Haven: Yale University Press, 1974).

45. Stephen E. Ambrose, *Eisenhower: The President* (New York: Simon and Schuster, 1984), 381.

46. Richard Reeves, *President Kennedy: Profile of Power* (New York: Simon and Schuster, 1993), 261.

47. Edwards, *At the Margins*, 10–11.

48. William E. Leuchtenburg, *In the Shadow of FDR: From Harry Truman to Bill Clinton*, 2d ed. (Ithaca: Cornell University Press, 1993).

49. Fred I. Greenstein, *The Hidden-Hand Presidency: Eisenhower as Leader* (New York: Basic Books, 1982).

50. Paul Charles Light, *The President's Agenda: Domestic Policy Choice from Kennedy to Carter* (Baltimore: The Johns Hopkins University Press, 1982), 2.

51. For different discussions of year-to-year variations in congressional elections and the electoral insecurity of Congress, see Melissa P. Collie, "Incumbency, Electoral Safety, and Turnover in the House of Representatives," *American Political Science Review* 75 (1981): 119–31; R. Douglas Arnold, *The Logic of Congressional Action* (New Haven: Yale University Press, 1990), 68; Gary C. Jacobson, "The Marginals Never Vanished: Incumbency and Competition in Elections to the U.S. House of Representatives, 1952–1982," *American Journal of Political Science* 31 (1987): 126–41; and John R. Wright, *Interest Groups and Congress: Lobbying, Contributions, and Influence* (Boston: Allyn and Bacon, 1996), 83–85.

52. Richard F. Fenno, Jr., *Home Style: House Members in Their Districts* (Boston: Little, Brown, 1978), 14.

53. Samuel Kernell, *Going Public: New Strategies of Presidential Leadership*, 2d ed. (Washington, D.C.: Congressional Quarterly Press, 1993), chapter 2.

54. Dick Kirschten, "A Crowded Stage," *National Journal*, March 18, 1989, 642.

55. Daniel Patrick Moynihan, *Counting Our Blessings: Reflections on the Future of America* (Boston: Little, Brown, 1980), 119.

56. Joseph A. Pika, "White House Boundary Roles: Marginal Men Amidst the Palace Guard," *Presidential Studies Quarterly* 16 (fall 1986): 700–715.

57. Curt Suplee, "The Capitol Connection," *Washington Post*, June 29, 1981, C1.

58. Kernell, *Going Public*, 10–12.

59. Ken Collier, "Eisenhower and Congress: The Autopilot Presidency," *Presidential Studies Quarterly* 24 (spring 1994): 309–25.

60. Greenstein, *The Hidden-Hand Presidency*, 51–52.

61. John Manley, "Presidential Power and White House Lobbying," *Political Science Quarterly* 93 (summer 1978): 253–66.

62. This term is borrowed from Neustadt's discussion of the president and the public (Neustadt, *Presidential Power and the Modern President*, 83).

63. See Jeffrey Cohen, "Presidential Rhetoric and the Public Agenda," *American Journal of Political Science* 39 (February 1995): 87–107.

64. Neustadt, *Presidential Power and the Modern President,* chapter 5.

65. David E. Rosenbaum, "Clinton's Plan for Economy May Hinge on His Popularity," *New York Times,* April 29, 1993, A1.

66. Light, *The President's Agenda,* 27.

67. This term is borrowed from Richard Neustadt's discussion of the president and the public (Neustadt, *Presidential Power and the Modern President,* 77).

2. THE EISENHOWER ADMINISTRATION

1. Ambrose, *Eisenhower: The President,* 18.

2. Dwight D. Eisenhower, *Waging Peace, 1956–1961* (Garden City, N.Y.: Doubleday and Company, 1965).

3. Emmet John Hughes, *The Ordeal of Power: A Political Memoir of the Eisenhower Years* (New York: Antheneum, 1963), 66.

4. General Wilton Persons, Oral History OH 334, Dwight D. Eisenhower Library, 29.

5. Jack Z. Anderson, Oral History OH 321, Dwight D. Eisenhower Library, 17.

6. Ambrose, *Eisenhower: The President,* 45.

7. John Hart, "Staffing the Presidency: Kennedy and the Office of Congressional Relations," *Presidential Studies Quarterly* 13 (winter 1983): 106.

8. It is also interesting to note that despite Adams's legendary terse manner, he created few problems with his dealings with members of Congress. This is a remarkable contrast to the congressional response to future chiefs of staff like Donald Regan and John Sununu.

9. Greenstein, *The Hidden-Hand Presidency,* 106.

10. Staff Meeting Notes, September 28, 1953, in "ACW Diary Aug., Sept.–Oct. 1953 (3)" in Ann Whitman Diary Series, Box 1, Dwight D. Eisenhower Library.

11. Dwight D. Eisenhower, *The White House Years: Mandate for Change* (Garden City, N.Y.: Doubleday and Company, 1963), 194.

12. Dwight Eisenhower, Oral History OH 11, Oral History Collection of Columbia University, 72.

13. In one case it did draw a request to have a letter retyped to correct a typographical error that put a member in the first rather than the second district.

14. General Wilton Persons, Oral History OH 334, Dwight D. Eisenhower Library, 41.

15. Gerald Morgan, Oral History OH 223, Dwight D. Eisenhower Library, 78.

16. Bryce N. Harlow, Oral History OH 214, Dwight D. Eisenhower Library, 57–58.

17. Hughes, *The Ordeal of Power,* 128.

18. Ken Collier, "Eisenhower and Congress: The Autopilot Presidency," *Presidential Studies Quarterly* 24 (spring 1994): 309–25.

19. Additional discussion of Eisenhower's view of delegation can be found in Fred I. Greenstein, "Dwight D. Eisenhower: Leadership Theorist in the White House," in *Leadership in the Modern Presidency,* ed. Fred I. Greenstein (Cambridge: Harvard University Press, 1988).

20. Memorandum for Sherman Adams from President Eisenhower, September 29, 1953, in "ACW Diary Aug.-Sept.-Oct. 1953," Ann Whitman Diary Series, Box 1, Dwight D. Eisenhower Library.

21. Notes from staff meeting, September 28, 1953, in "ACW Diary Aug.-Sept.-Oct. 1953," Ann Whitman Diary Series, Box 1, Dwight D. Eisenhower Library.

22. Bryce N. Harlow, Oral History OH 214, Dwight D. Eisenhower Library, 21.

23. Dwight D. Eisenhower, *The White House Years,* 323–24.

24. Handwritten notes of Arthur Minnich from "Legislative Meeting, January 25, 1954," in

L-9 (4) Legislative Meeting Series, Box 1, Office of the Staff Secretary, Dwight D. Eisenhower Library, 142.

25. "Legislative Leadership Meeting, Supplemental Notes, June 5, 1958" in "Legislative Meetings—1958 (3)," Legislative Meeting Series, Box 3, Ann Whitman File, Dwight D. Eisenhower Library; and Jack Z. Anderson, Oral History OH 321, Dwight D. Eisenhower Library, 36–39.

26. Duane Tananbaum, *The Bricker Amendment Controversy: A Test of Eisenhower's Political Leadership* (Ithaca: Cornell University Press, 1988), 78–79, 217–18. Senate Joint Resolution 1, introduced by Senator John Bricker, with the cosponsorship of sixty-two other senators (including forty-four of the forty-seven Senate Republicans) was the most serious of congressional efforts to limit presidential power and expand congressional authority. The Bricker Amendment was designed to limit the president's ability to enter into agreements with other nations.

27. Hughes, *The Ordeal of Power,* 126.

28. Memorandum for General Persons from Ed McCabe, May 8, 1957, in "Leadership (Congressional Meetings—Misc.)" in Bryce Harlow Files, Box 12, Dwight D. Eisenhower Library.

29. Draft letter to Charlie Halleck from Eisenhower, July 15, 1953, in "Drafts 1953 (4)," Ann Whitman File, Diary Series, Box 1, Dwight D. Eisenhower Library.

30. Thomas B. Curtis, Oral History OH 176, Oral History Collection of Columbia University, 20–21.

31. Diary Entry, March 31, 1954, Ann Whitman File, DDE Diary Series, Box 9, Dwight D. Eisenhower Library.

32. Greenstein, *The Hidden-Hand Presidency,* 79.

33. Charles Halleck, Oral History OH 489, Dwight D. Eisenhower Library, 18–19; also Memorandum for Mrs. Whitman, March 9, 1959, in "Memorandum re White House Meetings," Jack Anderson Papers, Box 1, Dwight D. Eisenhower Library.

34. Ed McCabe, Oral History OH 41, Oral History Collection of Columbia University, 93, 104.

35. Eisenhower, *The White House Years,* 194.

36. Memorandum for the president from Bryce Harlow, January 19, 1959, in "Legislative Leaders Conference Reports," Gerald Morgan Records, Box 18, Dwight D. Eisenhower Library.

37. Bryce Harlow, Oral History II, Lyndon B. Johnson Library, 3, 13.

38. Eisenhower, *The White House Years,* 192.

39. Ibid., 195.

40. Sherman Adams, *First Hand Report: The Story of the Eisenhower Administration* (New York: Harper and Brothers, 1961), 166.

41. Adams, *First Hand Report,* 166.

42. Ambrose, *Eisenhower: The President,* 218.

43. Ibid., 294.

44. Letter to Thomas Dewey, October 8, 1954, in Thomas E. Dewey, Administration Series, Box 11, Ann Whitman File, Dwight D. Eisenhower Library.

45. Memorandum for Mrs. Whitman, March 9, 1959, in "Memorandum re White House Meetings," Jack Anderson Papers, Box 1, Dwight D. Eisenhower Library.

46. Letter to Thomas Dewey, October 8, 1954, in "Dewey, Thomas E.," Administration Series, Box 11, Ann Whitman File, Dwight D. Eisenhower Library.

47. Hagerty Diary, May 21, 1954, Box 1, James C. Hagerty Papers, Dwight D. Eisenhower Library.

48. Charles A. Halleck, Oral History, Lyndon B. Johnson Library, 27.

49. Letter to Swede Hazlett, December 8, 1954, in "DDE Diary December 1954 (2)," DDE Diary Series, Box 8, Dwight D. Eisenhower Library, 3.

50. Adams, *First Hand Report*, 58.

51. "Legislative Leadership Meeting Supplemental Notes, January 11, 1954," in "Legislative Meetings—1954 (1)" Legislative Meeting Series, Box 1, Ann Whitman File, Dwight D. Eisenhower Library.

52. Ambrose, *Eisenhower: The President*, 222.

53. Holtzman, *Legislative Liaison*, 240.

54. Letter to Homer Gruenther from L. Mendel Rivers, November 11, 1958, in "1958 Election—Outgoing Letters to Winners and Losers #2," Homer Gruenther Records, Box 1, Dwight D. Eisenhower Library.

55. Bryce Harlow, Oral History, Lyndon B. Johnson Library, 54.

56. Ibid., 53.

57. Neustadt, *Presidential Power and the Modern Presidents*, 78.

58. Greenstein, *The Hidden-Hand Presidency*, 58–59.

59. Ibid., 59–60.

60. See the discussion of the "cuffing hand" in Greenstein, "Dwight D. Eisenhower: Leadership Theorist," 95–98.

61. Eisenhower vetoed 181 bills (73 regular vetoes and 108 pocket vetoes) and was overridden on only two, both of which were minor.

62. Joseph G. Feeney, Oral History, Harry S. Truman Library, 26.

63. Jacob Javits, Oral History OH 74, Oral History Collection of Columbia University, 14.

64. Hughes, *The Ordeal of Power*, 129–31.

65. Gerald Morgan, Oral History OH 223, Dwight D. Eisenhower Library, 84.

66. Hughes, *The Ordeal of Power*, 129.

67. Ibid., 131.

68. Ibid., 131–32.

69. Charles Halleck, Oral History OH 489, Dwight D. Eisenhower Library, 4, 17.

70. Staff memo from the president, no date, Ann Whitman Diary Series, Box 1, Ann Whitman File, Eisenhower Library.

71. Letter to Emmet Hughes from the president, December 10, 1953, in "Hughes, Emmet J., 1953–54," Administration Series, Box 1, Ann Whitman File, Eisenhower Library, 6.

72. Letter to Milton Eisenhower from the president, no date, in "Drafts (Illegal Possessions) 1953 (3)," Draft Series, Box 1, Ann Whitman File, Dwight D. Eisenhower Library, 1–2.

73. Handwritten note, in DDE Diary Dec. 1953 (1), DDE Diary Series, Box 4, Ann Whitman File, Dwight D. Eisenhower Library.

74. Diary entry, January 18, 1954, in "DDE Personal Diary January–November 1954, DDE Diary Series, Box 4, Ann Whitman File, Eisenhower Library, 7.

75. Letter to Emmet Hughes from the president, December 10, 1953, in "Hughes, Emmet J., 1953–54," Administration Series, Box 1, Ann Whitman File, Dwight D. Eisenhower Library, 4.

76. Adams, *First Hand Report*, 460.

77. Wilfred E. Binkley, *President and Congress*, 3d ed. (New York: Vintage Books, 1962), 45.

78. G. Russell Pipe, "Congressional Liaison: The Executive Branch Consolidates Its Relations with Congress," *Public Administration Review* 36 (March/April 1966): 14.

79. Stephen Horn, *The Cabinet and Congress* (New York: Columbia University Press, 1960), 180.

80. Wilton Persons, Oral History OH 334, Dwight D. Eisenhower Library, 32–33.

81. Sidney L. Gardner, "Congressional Liaison in the Military Establishment," *Public and International Affairs* 3 (spring 1965): 6.

82. Eisenhower, *The White House Years,* 194.

83. Memorandum for the president from Wilton Persons, October 29, 1957, in "Legislation (Misc. A–H)" in Bryce Harlow Files, Box 12, Dwight D. Eisenhower Library.

84. Memorandum for Bryce Harlow from Earl Chesney, May 31, 1955, in "Housing #3," Bryce Harlow, Box 11, Dwight D. Eisenhower Library.

85. Bryce Harlow, Oral History OH 402, Dwight D. Eisenhower Library, 5.

86. John Hart, "Staffing the Presidency: Kennedy and the Office of Congressional Relations," *Presidential Studies Quarterly* 13 (winter 1983): 102.

87. Bryce Harlow, Oral History OH 402, Dwight D. Eisenhower Library, 5.

88. John D. Eisenhower, *Strictly Personal* (Garden City, N.Y.: Doubleday and Company, 1964), 328.

89. Adams, *First Hand Report,* 460.

90. Hart, "Staffing the Presidency: Kennedy and the Office of Congressional Relations," 107. Also see Stephen Hess, *Organizing the Presidency,* 2d ed. (Washington, D.C.: The Brookings Institution, 1988), 66.

3. THE KENNEDY ADMINISTRATION

1. Arthur M. Schlesinger, Jr., *A Thousand Days: John F. Kennedy in the White House* (Boston: Houghton Mifflin Company, 1965), 708.

2. Lawrence F. O'Brien, Oral History XII, Lyndon B. Johnson Library, 4.

3. Edward P. Morgan, "O'Brien Presses on with the 'Four P's,'" *New York Times Magazine,* March 25, 1962, 28.

4. Nigel Bowles, *The White House and Capitol Hill: The Politics of Persuasion* (Oxford: Clarendon Press, 1987), 18.

5. Lawrence F. O'Brien, Oral History I, Lyndon B. Johnson Library, 39.

6. Ibid., 39, 110.

7. Lawrence F. O'Brien, Oral History I, 108; also Oral History V, Lyndon B. Johnson Library, 56.

8. Lawrence F. O'Brien, Oral History XIV, Lyndon B. Johnson Library, 25.

9. Lawrence F. O'Brien, Oral History I, Lyndon B. Johnson Library, 36.

10. Ibid., 41; Lawrence F. O'Brien, *No Final Victories* (Garden City, N.Y.: Doubleday and Company, 1974), 107–108.

11. Bryce Harlow, Oral History II, Lyndon B. Johnson Library, 50–52.

12. O'Brien, *No Final Victories,* 101. For a discussion of the issue of experience in the recruitment of liaison staff, see Pika, "White House Boundary Roles," 701–703. Also see Holtzman, *Legislative Liaison,* chapter 4.

13. For example, see Meg Greenfield, "Why Are You Calling Me, Son?" *The Reporter,* August 16, 1962, 29–31; and James N. Giglio, *The Presidency of John F. Kennedy* (Lawrence: University of Kansas Press, 1991), 98, 109.

14. "What They Say About Congress," *U.S. News and World Report,* August 13, 1962, 36.

15. Greenfield, "Why Are You Calling Me, Son?" 30.

16. Ibid., 31.

17. Lawrence F. O'Brien, Oral History I, Lyndon B. Johnson Library, 71.

18. O'Brien, *No Final Victories,* 167; also Lawrence F. O'Brien, Oral History I, Lyndon B. Johnson Library, 65. O'Brien believed that Johnson was very disappointed by his loss of clout in the

Senate and may not have accepted the vice presidency had he anticipated the Senate's reaction (Lawrence F. O'Brien, Oral History III, Johnson Library, 13).

19. "Lyndon's Lobbyists: How They Get What He Wants," *Nation's Business* (spring 1965): 38.

20. Bryce Harlow, Oral History OH 402, Dwight D. Eisenhower Library, 42.

21. Claude J. Desautels, Oral History, Lyndon B. Johnson Library, 6–7.

22. "The Administration: The Man on the Hill," *Time* magazine, September 1, 1961, 10.

23. For example, see "Kennedy's Liaison Man: Lawrence Francis O'Brien," *New York Times*, January 10, 1963, A10; "The Administration: The Man on the Hill," 10; or Morgan, "O'Brien Presses on with the 'Four P's,'" 28.

24. Morgan, "O'Brien Presses on with the 'Four P's,'" 116.

25. Neil MacNeil, *Forge of Democracy: The House of Representatives* (New York: David McKay Company, Inc., 1963), 260.

26. O'Brien, Oral History I, Lyndon B. Johnson Library, 57. This principle is often repeated throughout O'Brien's oral histories and was repeated to a reporter in 1962. Morgan, "O'Brien Presses On With the 'Four P's,'" 118.

27. O'Brien, Oral History I, Lyndon B. Johnson Library, 57.

28. O'Brien, Oral History II, Lyndon B. Johnson Library, 66, 66.

29. O'Brien, Oral History IV, Lyndon B. Johnson Library, 71–72.

30. O'Brien, Oral History IV, Lyndon B. Johnson Library, 72–73.

31. A discussion of the history of the Rules Committee and its role in the legislative process can be found in Robert L. Peabody, "The Enlarged Rules Committee," in *New Perspectives on the House of Representatives,* ed. Robert L. Peabody and Nelson W. Polsby (Chicago: Rand McNally and Company, 1963), 129–64.

32. O'Brien, Oral History I, Lyndon B. Johnson Library, 109–10.

33. Ibid., 39–41.

34. O'Brien, Oral History I, Lyndon B. Johnson Library, 44; O'Brien, *No Final Victories,* 106–07.

35. Neustadt, *Presidential Power and the Modern President,* 254–55.

36. O'Brien, Oral History I, Lyndon B. Johnson Library, 44.

37. Memorandum from Henry Hall Wilson to Lawrence F. O'Brien, no date, "Presidential," Box 5, Office Files of Henry Hall Wilson, Lyndon B. Johnson Library.

38. O'Brien, Oral History IV, Lyndon B. Johnson Library, 4.

39. Giglio, *The Presidency of John F. Kennedy,* 38–39.

40. Schlesinger, *A Thousand Days,* 710.

41. O'Brien, Oral History VI, 1.

42. Schlesinger, *A Thousand Days,* 710.

43. O'Brien, *No Final Victories,* 113.

44. The role of "educating" the president and the White House more generally is discussed in detail in the Carter chapter.

45. "What They Say About Congress," 36.

46. O'Brien, *No Final Victories,* 115.

47. O'Brien, Oral History V, Lyndon B. Johnson Library, 48–50.

48. "What They Say About Congress," 36.

49. Schlesinger, *A Thousand Days,* 721. A hippodrome was the open-air stadium for horse and chariot races in ancient Greece.

50. O'Brien, Oral History I, Lyndon B. Johnson Library, 104.

51. Rowland Evans, Jr., and Robert D. Novak, *Nixon in the White House: The Frustration of Power* (New York: Vintage Books, 1971), 105.

52. "The Administration: The Man on the Hill," 10.

53. "From White House to Capitol . . . How Things Get Done: Interview with Lawrence F. O'Brien, Newest Member of the Cabinet," *U.S. News and World Report,* September 20, 1965, 69.

54. O'Brien, Oral History I, Lyndon B. Johnson Library, 60–61.

55. Dwight Eisenhower, Oral History OH 11, Oral History Collection of Columbia University, 72.

56. O'Brien, Oral History I, Lyndon B. Johnson Library, 56.

57. Claude J. Desautels, Oral History, Lyndon B. Johnson Library, 19.

58. O'Brien, *No Final Victories,* 111; O'Brien, Oral History I, 48. O'Brien sent his own birthday greetings to every member.

59. O'Brien, Oral History I, Lyndon B. Johnson Library, 54.

60. O'Brien, *No Final Victories,* 149.

61. Ibid., Lawrence F. O'Brien, Oral History I, Lyndon B. Johnson Library, 49. Desautels also calls the *Sequoia* "the best tool we had." Claude J. Desautels, Oral History, Lyndon B. Johnson Library, 20.

62. Morgan, "O'Brien Presses on with the 'Four P's,'" 29.

63. Claude J. Desautels, Oral History, Lyndon B. Johnson Library, 12–13.

64. O'Brien, *No Final Victories,* 120. Also O'Brien, Oral History I, Lyndon B. Johnson Library, 94–95.

65. "Arm twisting" refers to the use of personal or political pressure to persuade or to gain support.

66. O'Brien, Oral History IV, Lyndon B. Johnson Library, 14.

67. Schlesinger, *A Thousand Days,* 711.

68. O'Brien, *No Final Victories,* 112. Also, O'Brien, Oral History VI, Lyndon B. Johnson Library, 2.

69. O'Brien, Oral History I, Lyndon B. Johnson Library, 66–67.

70. "White House 'Lobby' Operates on Capitol Hill," *Congressional Quarterly Weekly,* June 30, 1961, 1181.

71. "The Administration: The Man on the Hill," 10.

72. O'Brien, Oral History II, Lyndon B. Johnson Library, 34–35.

73. O'Brien, Oral History I, Lyndon B. Johnson Library, 54.

74. O'Brien, Oral History I, Lyndon B. Johnson Library, 54.

75. Morgan, "O'Brien Presses on with the 'Four P's,'" 29.

76. Claude J. Desautels, Oral History, Lyndon B. Johnson Library, 15.

77. O'Brien, Oral History III, Lyndon B. Johnson Library, 62.

78. O'Brien, Oral History II, Lyndon B. Johnson Library, 30–31. Also, Patrick Anderson, *The President's Men* (Garden City, N.Y.: Doubleday and Company, 1969), 308.

79. "The Administration: The Man on the Hill," 11. See also, O'Brien, Oral History V, Lyndon B. Johnson Library, 31.

80. O'Brien, Oral History I, Lyndon B. Johnson Library, 43, 61, 122.

81. O'Brien, Oral History IV, Lyndon B. Johnson Library, 5–9. According to Mike Manatos, Mansfield's warning was, "Mike, get those goddamned guys off the Hill. We're going to lose this bill." Mike Manatos, Oral History I, Lyndon B. Johnson Library, 53.

82. John Hart, "Staffing the Presidency: Kennedy and the Office of Congressional Relations," *Presidential Studies Quarterly* 23 (winter 1983): 101–10. Also see Stephen Hess, *Organizing the Presidency,* 66.

83. Bryce Harlow, Oral History OH 402, Dwight D. Eisenhower Library, 42.

84. "The Administration: The Man on the Hill," 10.

85. Richard Reeves, *President Kennedy: Profile of Power* (New York: Simon and Schuster, 1993); and Robert J. Williams and David A. Kershaw, "Kennedy and Congress: The Struggle for the New Frontier," *Political Studies* 27 (1979): 390–404.

4. THE JOHNSON ADMINISTRATION

1. Light, *The President's Agenda*, 10.

2. Joseph A. Califano, Jr., *A Presidential Nation* (New York: W. W. Norton and Company, 1975), 72.

3. "The 89th: LBJ's Do-Plenty Congress," *Newsweek*, February 15, 1965, 21.

4. Charles A. Halleck, Oral History, Lyndon B. Johnson Library, 2, 18.

5. O'Brien, *No Final Victories*, 163; Patrick Anderson, "He Delivered the Votes, Now O'Brien Delivers the Mail," *New York Times Magazine*, November 14, 1965, 150–51.

6. "From White House to Capitol . . . How Things Get Done," 73; Lawrence F. O'Brien, Oral History XI, Lyndon B. Johnson Library, 29.

7. "Larry O'Brien Discusses White House Contacts with Capitol Hill," *Congressional Quarterly Weekly*, July 23, 1965, 1434.

8. Lawrence F. O'Brien, Oral History VI, Lyndon B. Johnson Library, 90.

9. There is consensus on this point from the Oral Histories of O'Brien, Manatos, Desautels, and Wilson.

10. Mike Manatos, Oral History I, Lyndon B. Johnson Library, 13.

11. Mike Manatos, Oral History I, Lyndon B. Johnson Library, 42.

12. Barefoot Sanders, "Congressional-Executive Relations During the 1960s," in *The Presidency and the Congress: A Shifting Balance of Power?*, ed. William S. Livingston, Lawrence C. Dodd, and Richard L. Schott (Austin: Lyndon B. Johnson School of Public Affairs, 1979), 292.

13. O'Brien, *No Final Victories*, 182.

14. Anderson, "He Delivered the Votes, Now O'Brien Delivers the Mail," 54.

15. Claude J. Desautels, Oral History, Lyndon B. Johnson Library, 11.

16. Nigel Bowles, *The White House and Capitol Hill: The Politics of Persuasion* (Oxford: Clarendon Press, 1987), chapter 6.

17. Memorandum from Barefoot Sanders to the president, "Congressional Liaison Aides," Box 19, Papers of Harold Barefoot Sanders, Lyndon B. Johnson Library.

18. Bowles, *The White House and Capitol Hill*, 45.

19. O'Brien, *No Final Victories*, 182.

20. O'Brien, Oral History II, Lyndon B. Johnson Library, 22.

21. O'Brien, *No Final Victories*, 170.

22. O'Brien, Oral History VI, Lyndon B. Johnson Library, 9.

23. Lawrence F. O'Brien, Oral History II, Lyndon B. Johnson Library, 18–19. This story is also recounted in *No Final Victories*, 170.

24. John Connally with Mickey Herskowitz, *In History's Shadow: An American Odyssey* (New York, Hyperion, 1993), 78. One Democrat who had voted against Johnson commented that often Johnson didn't really need a phone: "If he had opened the window of his office, I could have heard him without any telephone" (Jack Bell, *The Johnson Treatment: How Lyndon B. Johnson Took Over the Presidency and Made it His Own* [New York: Harper and Row, 1965], 94).

25. Claude J. Desautels, Oral History, Lyndon B. Johnson Library, 7.

26. Connally, *In History's Shadow*, 209.

27. O'Brien, Oral History II, Lyndon B. Johnson Library, 18, 25.

28. Claude J. Desautels, Oral History, Lyndon B. Johnson Library, 37.

29. Memoranda from Henry Hall Wilson to Lawrence F. O'Brien, January 10, 1964, "Presidential," Box 5, Office Files of Henry Hall Wilson, Lyndon B. Johnson Library.

30. O'Brien, Oral History VI, Lyndon B. Johnson Library, 4.

31. Memoranda from Barefoot Sanders to the president, August 1, 1967, "August 1967 (Notes . . .)," Box 23, Handwriting File, Lyndon B. Johnson Library.

32. "The Politics of Power: Portrait of a Master," *Newsweek*, August 2, 1965, 22.

33. O'Brien, *No Final Victories*, 171.

34. O'Brien, Oral History VI, Lyndon B. Johnson Library, 4.

35. Charles A. Halleck, Oral History, Lyndon B. Johnson Library, 9–11.

36. "The Politics of Power: Portrait of a Master," *Newsweek*, August 2, 1965, 22.

37. O'Brien, Oral History XI, Lyndon B. Johnson Library, 49.

38. Neil Sheehan, "Congress Hailed by Johnson Aides," *New York Times*, October 23, 1966, 27.

39. "The 89th: LBJ's Do-Plenty Congress," *Newsweek*, February 15, 1965, 20.

40. "The Politics of Power: Portrait of a Master," *Newsweek*, August 2, 1965, 22.

41. "Draft Remarks to Congressional Reception, February 9, 1965," in "FG 400 The Legislative Branch, 1/29/65–2/23/65," White House Central File: FG, Box 321, Lyndon B. Johnson Library.

42. "Memorandum for the Secretaries of the Army, Navy and Air Force, March 25, 1964," in "FG 400 The Legislative Branch, 11/22/64–6/14/64," White House Central Files, FG, Box 321, Lyndon B. Johnson Library.

43. Larry Temple, Oral History V, Lyndon B. Johnson Library, 4–5.

44. Mike Manatos, Oral History I, Lyndon B. Johnson Library, 30.

45. Louis Harris, "Concerns of the Nation—1965," *Newsweek*, January 11, 1965, 20.

46. Harold Barefoot Sanders, Oral History III, Lyndon B. Johnson Library, 7.

47. "An Interview with LBJ," *Newsweek*, August 2, 1965, 21.

48. Harry McPherson, *A Political Education: A Washington Memoir* (Boston: Houghton Mifflin Company, 1988), 268.

49. "The State of the Union," *Newsweek*, January 11, 1965, 15.

50. Robert A. Caro, *The Years of Lyndon Johnson: The Path to Power* (New York: Alfred A. Knopf, 1982), 606–64.

51. Memo from Hubert H. Humphrey to the president, August 23, 1965, "FG 400: US Congress 6/15/65–12/28/65," Box 322, White House Central Files, FG, Lyndon B. Johnson Library.

52. Memo from Henry Wilson to Mike Manatos, March 12, 1965, "FG 400: US Congress 3/3/65–5/28/65," Box 322, White House Central Files, FG, Lyndon B. Johnson Library.

53. Memo to Mike Manatos from Sidney Spector, April 23, 1966, "Rent Supplement," Box 9, Office Files of Mike Manatos, Lyndon B. Johnson Library.

54. Memo from Irv Sprague to Barefoot Sanders, September 18, 1968, "Sanders, Barefoot, Memos for," Box 7, White House Aides files, Irv Sprague, Lyndon B. Johnson Library.

55. Memorandum from Harry McPherson to the president, December 30, 1966, "December 1966 (Notes . . .) 2 of 2," Box 19, Handwriting File, Lyndon B. Johnson Library.

56. "Every day, every hour, it was drive, drive, drive—to use the basketball term, a full court press" (O'Brien, *No Final Victories*, 181).

57. O'Brien, Oral History VI, Lyndon B. Johnson Library, 3.

58. Sanders, "Congressional-Executive Relations During the 1960s," 288.

59. Ibid., 287.

60. January Birthdays of Members of Congress, 1966, "Legislative General 1965, July—December," Box 1, Mike Manatos, Lyndon B. Johnson Library.

61. O'Brien, Oral History XI, Lyndon B. Johnson Library, 12. Also O'Brien, Oral History V, Lyndon B. Johnson Library, 48–50.

62. Bowles, *The White House and Capitol Hill,* 100–101.

63. Memorandum from Jean Lew to Henry Wilson, February 24, 1967, "Congressional Receptions," Box 11, Henry Hall Wilson, Lyndon B. Johnson Library.

64. Memorandum from Jack Valenti to the president, January 4, 1965, "FG 400 The Legislative Branch, 12/25/64–1/28/65," White House Central File, FG Box 321, Lyndon B. Johnson Library.

65. O'Brien, Oral History III, Lyndon B. Johnson Library, 26–27.

66. O'Brien, *No Final Victories,* 171.

67. Ibid.

68. Sanders, "Congressional-Executive Relations During the 1960s," 291.

69. "Lyndon's Lobbyists: How They Get What He Wants," 38.

70. Ibid.

71. Sanders, "Congressional-Executive Relations During the 1960s," 291.

72. "Lyndon's Lobbyists: How They Get What He Wants," 8.

73. Lyndon Baines Johnson, *The Vantage Point* (New York: Rinehart and Winston, 1971), 450.

74. Transcript of telephone conversation between Vice President Johnson and Theodore Sorensen, June 3, 1963, Lyndon B. Johnson Library, 2.

75. O'Brien, Oral History V, Lyndon B. Johnson Library, 3.

76. Sanders, "Congressional-Executive Relations During the 1960s," 288.

77. Transcript of telephone conversation between Vice President Johnson and Theodore Sorensen, June 3, 1963, Lyndon B. Johnson Library, 19.

78. Johnson, *The Vantage Point,* 164.

79. *Congressional Record,* Volume 111, Part 4, 5058–61.

80. Letter to President Johnson from Senator Edmund Muskie, March 19, 1965, Aides Files: Busby, Box 3, File: "Voting Rights 3-15-65," Lyndon B. Johnson Library.

81. Telegram to the president from Senator Thomas Dodd, Legislative Background: Voting Rights Act, File: "Voting Rights Legislation," Lyndon B. Johnson Library.

82. Various telegrams, Aides Files: Busby, Box 3, File: "Voting Rights 3-15-65," Lyndon B. Johnson Library.

83. "A Barrier Falls: The U.S. Negro Moves to Vote," *Newsweek,* August 16, 1965, 15. Johnson used one hundred different pens to sign the bill.

84. Memorandum for the president, August 4, 1965, "Jan. 64–Aug. 66—Voting Rights Legislation," Box: Voting Rights Act, Legislative Background Files, Lyndon B. Johnson Library.

85. O'Brien, Oral History V, Lyndon B. Johnson Library, 25–29.

86. Memorandum from Bob Hardesty to the president, January 19, 1968, "Congressional Liaison Meetings," Box 335, Office Files of Fred Panzer, Lyndon B. Johnson Library.

87. O'Brien, Oral History XIX, Lyndon B. Johnson Library, 9–14. The extent of this can been seen in the story that one member received two copies of the speech stapled together and ended up giving the speech twice.

88. O'Brien, Oral History XIX, Lyndon B. Johnson Library, 15–16.

89. Memorandum to All White House Congressional Staff, March 21, 1968, "Congressional Liaison Aides," Box 19, Papers of Harold Barefoot Sanders, Jr., Lyndon B. Johnson Library.

90. Memorandum from Barefoot Sanders to the president, July 30, 1968, "Memos to the President," Box 25, Papers of Harold Barefoot Sanders, Jr., Lyndon B. Johnson Library.

91. Memorandum for the president from Orville Freeman, February 20, 1965, in "May 1–May 15 1965 1 of 2," Box 7, Handwriting File, Lyndon B. Johnson Library.

92. Johnson, *The Vantage Point,* 451.

93. Memorandum from Charles A. Horsky, December 22, 1964, "Congressmen 89th," Box 96, File of Charles A. Horsky, Lyndon B. Johnson Library. This folder also contains several earlier and later drafts of this list.

94. Memorandum of Meeting with Cong. George W. Grider, no date, "Congressmen 89th," Box 96, File of Charles A. Horsky, Lyndon B. Johnson Library.

95. A discharge petition requires that a majority of the House sign a petition forcing the committee to report the bill.

96. Memorandum for Henry Wilson from Charles A. Horsky, September 21, 1965, "Home Rule (2 of 30)," Box 96, Files of Charles A. Horksy, Lyndon B. Johnson Library. Also Lawrence F. O'Brien, Oral History XII, Lyndon B. Johnson Library, 1.

97. Charles A. Halleck, Oral History, Lyndon B. Johnson Library, 4.

98. Memorandum for Bill Moyer from Henry Hall Wilson, March 23, 1964, "[1963–64 Congressional Files] S," Box 19, Office Files of White House Aides, Henry Hall Wilson, Lyndon B. Johnson Library.

99. Memorandum for Barefoot Sanders from John Gonella, January 20, 1968, in "Congressional Liaison Aides," Box 19, Papers of Harold Barefoot Sanders, Lyndon B. Johnson Library.

100. O'Brien, Oral History I, Lyndon B. Johnson Library, 96.

101. O'Brien, Oral History XVIII, Lyndon B. Johnson Library, 7–8.

102. Memo from Jack Valenti to the president, July 28, 1965, "July 20–31, 1965, 2 of 2," Box 9, Handwriting File, Lyndon B. Johnson Library.

103. Memorandum for Orren Beaty from Henry Hall Wilson, May 2, 1964, "[1963–64 Congressional Files] E," Box 18, Office Files of White House Aides, Henry Hall Wilson, Lyndon B. Johnson Library.

104. Dirksen, Senator Everett McKinley (R-IL), "Favors—Congressmen D," Box 7, Office Files of Larry O'Brien, Lyndon B. Johnson Library. The sets of numbers and letters separated by dashes are the number of photo negatives from rolls of film taken by the White House photographer.

105. Memo from Charles Roche to Larry O'Brien, June 14, 1965, "DNC, Chuck Roche (2 of 2)," Box 23, Office Files of Larry O'Brien, Lyndon B. Johnson Library.

106. "Congressional Social File 1968," Box 20, Papers of Harold Barefoot Sanders, Lyndon B. Johnson Library.

107. Barefoot Sanders to the president, 1/2/68, "Congressional Liaison Aides," Box 19, Papers of Harold Barefoot Sanders, Lyndon B. Johnson Library.

108. O'Brien, Oral History XVIII, Lyndon B. Johnson Library, 3.

109. O'Brien, *No Final Victories,* 183–84.

110. Letter from John Gonella to Brig. General James Lawrence, December 27, 1967, "Congressional II (folder 1 of 2)," Box 10, Papers of Harold Barefoot Sanders, Lyndon B. Johnson Library.

111. Memorandum from Hubert Gallager to Barefoot Sanders, May 7, 1968, "May 68 Tax Canvass $4 Billion Reduction," Box 24, Papers of Harold Barefoot Sanders, Lyndon B. Johnson Library.

112. R. W. Apple, Jr., "An Excess of the Pulpit and Not Enough Bully?" *New York Times,* August 5, 1993, A10.

113. Wilson to Desautels, 1/10/64, "White House Staff," White House Aides Files: Henry H. Wilson Box 6, Lyndon B. Johnson Library.

114. O'Brien, Oral History XI, Lyndon B. Johnson Library, 38.

115. Claude J. Desautels, Oral History, Lyndon B. Johnson Library, 16–17.

116. Memo from Bill Moyers to Henry Wilson, April 27, 1964, "Perkins, Rep. Carl D.," Box 18, White House Aides Files: Lawrence F. O'Brien, Lyndon B. Johnson Library.

117. O'Brien, Oral History I, Lyndon B. Johnson Library, 97–98.

118. O'Brien, Oral History XVIII, Lyndon B. Johnson Library, 3–4.

119. Claude J. Desautels, Oral History, Lyndon B. Johnson Library, 44–45.

120. Wilson to Macy, 3/6/65, "O'Brien, Lawrence," Box 340, Files of John Macy, Lyndon B. Johnson Library.

121. Bowles, *The White House and Capitol Hill,* 113.

122. Apple, "An Excess of the Pulpit and Not Enough Bully?," A10.

123. Sanders, "Congressional-Executive Relations During the 1960s," 295. For an example of these scores, see Memo for the Congressional Liaison Staff from Barefoot Sanders (with attachments), January 12, 1968, "Congressional Liaison Meetings," Box 335, Office Files of Fred Panzer, Johnson Library.

124. Barefoot Sanders to Bruce Thomas, January 20, 1968, "Congressional II (folder 1 of 2)," Box 10, Papers of Harold Barefoot Sanders, Lyndon B. Johnson Library.

125. James Cannon, *Time and Chance: Gerald Ford's Appointment with History* (New York: HarperCollins Publisher, 1994), 87.

5. THE NIXON ADMINISTRATION

1. Dom Bonafede and Andrew J. Glass, "White House Report: Nixon Deals Cautiously with Hostile Congress," *National Journal,* June 27, 1970, 1353.

2. Rowland Evans, Jr., and Robert D. Novak, *Nixon in the White House: The Frustration of Power* (New York, Vintage Books, 1971), 104.

3. Mike Manatos, Oral History, Lyndon B. Johnson Library, 34.

4. "The New Crisis in Leadership," *Newsweek,* July 14, 1969, 22.

5. Richard J. Ellis, *Presidential Lightning Rods: The Politics of Blame Avoidance* (Lawrence: University Press of Kansas, 1994).

6. "The New Crisis in Leadership," *Newsweek,* July 14, 1969, 20–21.

7. Bonafede and Glass, "White House Report: Nixon Deals Cautiously with Hostile Congress," 1365.

8. Interview with Richard Cook, September 16, 1977, A. James Reichley Research Interviews, Gerald R. Ford Presidential Library, 2.

9. Evans and Novak, *Nixon in the White House,* 105.

10. Bonafede and Glass, "White House Report: Nixon Deals Cautiously with Hostile Congress," 1365.

11. Bryce Harlow, Oral History OH 402, Dwight D. Eisenhower Library, 39.

12. Dom Bonafede, "President Still Seeks to Restore Staff Efficiency, Morale," *National Journal,* January 5, 1974, 5.

13. Bonafede and Glass, "White House Report: Nixon Deals Cautiously with Hostile Congress," 1365.

14. "The White House Persuaders: Timmons and his Team," *Congressional Quarterly Weekly,* December 1, 1973, 3124.

15. "Box Score on Reform," *Time* magazine, September 28, 1970, 11.

16. Interview with Fred Weber, October 17, 1977, A. James Reichley Research Interviews, Gerald R. Ford Presidential Library, 3.

17. Evans and Novak, *Nixon in the White House,* 108–10.

18. H. R. Haldeman, *The Haldeman Diaries: Inside the Nixon White House* (New York: G. P. Putnam's Sons, 1994), 66.

19. Interview with Eugene Cowen, October 5, 1977, A. James Reichley Research Interviews, Gerald R. Ford Presidential Library, 1–2. Cowen, during a staff meeting, asked Ehrlichman, "Why are you treating the people of the Republic of China better than you are treating the Congress?" See also, Interview with Fred Weber, October 17, 1977, A. James Reichley Research Interviews, Gerald R. Ford Presidential Library, 3.

20. Bonafede and Glass, "White House Report: Nixon Deals Cautiously with Hostile Congress," 1353. Also, Dom Bonafede, "White House Report: Ford's Lobbyists Expect Democrats to Revise Tactics," *National Journal,* June 21, 1975, 925.

21. Donald Smith, "New Life for White House Liaison with Congress," *Congressional Quarterly Weekly,* January 30, 1975, 1.

22. Pika, "White House Boundary Roles," 700–715; also, Pika, "The White House Office of Congressional Relations."

23. Pika, "White House Boundary Roles," 707.

24. "New White House Attitude: 'I Care About Congress,'" *Congressional Quarterly Weekly,* May 28, 1971, 1151.

25. "Nixon's Campaign Chief: Clark MacGregor," *New York Times,* July 3, 1972, A15.

26. Bonafede, "President Still Seeks to Restore Staff Efficiency, Morale," 4. One testament to the importance of Bryce Harlow is that many of Ford's advisors were concerned that Ford was expected to fill the vacuum left by Harlow's departure.

27. Bonafede, "President Still Seeks to Restore Staff Efficiency, Morale," 4.

28. Ibid., 5.

29. At one point, George Bush was briefly considered for a similar role. Haldeman, *The Haldeman Diaries,* 217.

30. Evans and Novak, *Nixon in the White House,* 378–79.

31. "New White House Attitude: 'I Care About Congress,'" 1153.

32. The role of "educating" the White House staff is discussed in more depth in the chapter on the Carter administration.

33. Harlow, "Text of Harlow Keynote Address at Nashville Symposium," 7.

34. Bonafede and Glass, "White House Report: Nixon Deals Cautiously with Hostile Congress," 1365.

35. Ibid., 1355.

36. Interview with Bryce Harlow, July 27, 1985, William A. Syers Interviews, Gerald R. Ford Presidential Library, 3.

37. Memo from the president to Bob Haldeman, December 1, 1969, HRH 229, quoted in Bruce Oudes, *Richard Nixon's Secret Files* (New York: Harper and Row, 1989), 74.

38. Connally, *In History's Shadow,* 256.

39. Haldeman, *The Haldeman Diaries,* 98.

40. Memo from the president to Mr. Stephen Bull, March 10, 1973, PPF 4—w/RN from HRH 230, quoted in Oudes, *Richard Nixon's Secret Files,* 582.

41. Haldeman, *The Haldeman Diaries,* 188.

42. Cannon, *Time and Chance,* 98.

43. Haldeman, *The Haldeman Diaries,* 190.

44. Cannon, *Time and Chance,* 99.

45. "The Surtax Revolt," *Newsweek,* July 14, 1969, 22.

46. Bonafede, "White House Report: Ford's Lobbyists Expect Democrats to Revise Tactics," 925.

47. Some of this misunderstanding likely resulted from a misreading of Bryce Harlow's philosophy that the head of the operation should not spend too much time on the Hill. The rest of the staff, however, maintained a strong presence on the Hill. One staff member considered a presence essential: "To not be seen in that job is to be dead."

48. Memo from the president to Bob Haldeman, John Ehrlichman, Bryce Harlow, and Henry Kissinger, November 24, 1969, HRH 229, quoted in Oudes, *Richard Nixon's Secret Files*, 69–70.

49. Evans and Novak, *Nixon in the White House*, 108.

50. See, for example, Charles Goodel and Richard Schweiker Interviews, A. James Reichley Research Interviews, Gerald R. Ford Presidential Library.

51. Memorandum from the president to Bryce Harlow, July 1, 1969, "Presidential Handwriting July 1969," Presidential Office Files, Box 2, White House Subject File, Nixon Project, National Archives.

52. Smith, "New Life for White House Liaison with Congress," 1. By this time Congress had been able to read transcripts of Oval Office conversations in which members were referred to as "clowns."

53. Interview with Bryce Harlow, July 27, 1985, William A. Syers Interviews, Gerald R. Ford Presidential Library, 3.

54. Memo from the president to Bob Haldeman, December 1, 1969, HRH 138, 229, quoted in Oudes, *Richard Nixon's Secret Files*, 74–75.

55. Memo from the president to Mr. Haldeman, December 4, 1970, HRH 164—w/RN from HRH 138, 139, 229 and 164, quoted in Oudes, *Richard Nixon's Secret Files*, 182.

56. Memo from the president to Chuck Colson, May 19, 1972, PPF 4; HRH 162, 230, quoted in Oudes, *Richard Nixon's Secret Files*, 451.

57. Interview with Senator Bob Dole, September 9, 1977, A. James Reichley Research Interviews, Gerald R. Ford Presidential Library, 1–2.

58. Haldeman, *The Haldeman Diaries*, 288.

59. Haldeman, *The Haldeman Diaries*, 584.

60. Somewhat defensive of the term *enemies*, this source pointed out that "even paranoids have real enemies."

61. Lyn Nofziger, *Nofziger* (Washington, D.C.: Regnery Gateway, 1992), 112.

62. Memo from the president to Bob Haldeman and John Ehrlichman, April 14, 1969, PPF 1; HRH 229, quoted in Oudes, *Richard Nixon's Secret Files*, 23.

63. Memo from the president to Bob Haldeman, March 10, 1970, HRH 138, 164, 229, quoted in Oudes, *Richard Nixon's Secret Files*, 107.

64. Memo from Bill Timmons to the Staff Secretary, February 19, 1970, "Presidential Handwriting February 16–28, 1970," Presidential Office Files, Box 5, White House Subject File, Nixon Project, National Archives.

65. Richard Nixon, *In the Arena: A Memoir of Victory, Defeat and Renewal* (New York: Simon and Schuster, 1990), 208.

66. Haldeman, *The Haldeman Diaries*, 586.

67. Ibid., 113.

68. Stephen E. Ambrose, *Nixon Volume Two: The Triumph of a Politician 1962–1972* (New York: Simon and Schuster, 1989), 287.

69. Haldeman, *The Haldeman Diaries*, 532.

70. Ibid., 562.

71. Cannon, *Time and Chance*, xiv.

72. Haldeman, *The Haldeman Diaries*, 70.

73. Interview with Tom Korologos, August 31, 1977, A. James Reichley Research Interviews, Gerald R. Ford Presidential Library, 3.

74. Cannon, *Time and Chance*, 98.

75. Haldeman, *The Haldeman Diaries*, 91.

76. Ibid., 323.

77. Gary King and Lyn Ragsdale, *The Elusive Executive: Discovering Statistical Patterns in the Presidency* (Washington, D.C.: Congressional Quarterly Press, 1990), 302.

78. Memorandum for the president from William E. Timmons, December 31, 1973, "Executive-Legislative Relations-93rd Congress, 1st Session," William E. Timmons Files, Box 3, Gerald R. Ford Library, 3.

79. Don Bonafede, "White House Report: Executive Office in Transitional Stage, According to President's Senior Aides," *National Journal*, August 25, 1973, 1244. Timmons made a similar case to the president in his year-end summary of the 93rd Congress (Memorandum for the president from William E. Timmons, December 31, 1973, folder: "Executive-Legislative Relations-93rd Congress, 1st Session," William E. Timmons Files, Box 3, Gerald R. Ford Library, 3).

80. Don Bonafede, "Presidential Focus: Two Hill Defeats . . . and Puncturing a Balloon," *National Journal*, May 24, 1974, 788.

81. Charles O. Jones, *The Presidency in a Separated System* (Washington, D.C.: The Brookings Institution, 1994), 135.

82. One casualty of Watergate was departmental liaison offices, which became neglected as the White House became more and more involved in the battles surrounding Watergate. In a 1975 memorandum, Vern Loen noted that "During the past years the agency types often felt cut off from the White House. Watergate preoccupation led to a sort of malaise among the [cabinet department] liaison teams." (Memorandum from Vern Loen to Max L. Friedersdorf, January 1975 Folder, "Loen Chronological File: January 1975," Vernon Loen and Charles Leppert Files, Box 33, Gerald R. Ford Presidential Library.)

83. William Chapman, "Nixon Lobbyists Say His Woes Didn't Affect Legislation," *Washington Post*, January 2, 1975, A28.

84. Kernell, *Going Public*, 2.

85. Jon Bond and Richard Fleisher, "The Limits of Presidential Popularity as a Source of Influence in the US House," *Legislative Studies Quarterly* 5 (1980): 69–78.

86. Bond and Fleisher, *The President in the Legislative Arena*.

87. Edwards, *At the Margins;* Peterson, *Legislating Together;* and Ken Collier and Terry Sullivan, "New Evidence Undercutting the Linkage of Approval with Presidential Support and Influence," *Journal of Politics* 57 (February 1995): 197–209.

88. Charles W. Ostrom, Jr., and Dennis M. Simon, "Promise and Performance: A Dynamic Model of Presidential Popularity," *American Political Science Review* 79 (June 1985): 349.

89. Douglas Rivers and Nancy L. Rose, "Passing the President's Program: Public Opinion and Presidential Influence in Congress," *American Journal of Political Science* 29 (May 1985): 183–96.

90. Paul Brace and Barbara Hinckley, *Follow the Leader: Opinion Polls and the Modern Presidents* (New York: Basic Books, 1992), 81.

91. Rivers and Rose, "Passing the President's Program," 187.

92. Jones, *The Presidency in a Separated System*, 120.

93. Ibid.

94. Bond and Fleisher, *The President in the Legislative Arena*, 194.

95. Jones, *The Presidency in a Separated System*, 119. Also, Rivers and Rose, "Passing the President's Program," 187.

96. One example of their success in attracting top people is Ken Duberstein, who served in the General Services Administration and Labor Department during the Nixon administration. Duberstein later served as head of White House Legislative Affairs and as chief of staff under Ronald Reagan and currently heads a successful public relations firm. Timmons also recruited John Marsh, who would serve as the counselor to President Ford responsible for overseeing legislative and public liaison. He later served for eight years as secretary of the army under Reagan.

97. Memorandum for Secretary Peter Brennan from William E. Timmons, October 28, 1974, Folder: "White House Staff, Miscellaneous-Memoranda," William E. Timmons Files, Box 12, Gerald R. Ford Presidential Library.

6. THE FORD ADMINISTRATION

1. Robert Dahl, "Myth of the Presidential Mandate" *Political Science Quarterly* 105 (fall 1990): 355–72.

2. "Strategic Options Available to the President in His Relations to the Congress," no date, folder: "Congressional Relations—General," James E. Connor Files, Box 9, Gerald R. Ford Presidential Library, 2–3.

3. Ibid., 6.

4. Text of an Address by the President to a Joint Session of the Congress, August 12, 1974, "State of the Union Address," William E. Timmons Files, Box 11, Gerald R. Ford Presidential Library.

5. Don Hill, "The President's Man from the Shenandoah Valley," *Virginian-Pilot,* September 1, 1974. Marsh went on to serve as secretary of the army for all eight years of the Reagan administration.

6. Interview with Max L. Friedersdorf, April 30, 1976, A. James F. C. Hyde, Jr., and Stephen J. Wayne Interviews, Gerald R. Ford Presidential Library, 5–6.

7. Bonafede, "White House Report: Ford's Lobbyists Expect Democrats to Revise Tactics," 926.

8. Smith, "New Life for White House Liaison with Congress," 1.

9. Minutes of Cabinet Meeting, January 8, 1975, 1975/01/08 Cabinet Meeting, James E. Connor Files, Box 3, Gerald R. Ford Presidential Library, 7.

10. Interview with Max L. Friedersdorf, April 30, 1976, A. James F. C. Hyde, Jr., and Stephen J. Wayne Interviews, Gerald R. Ford Presidential Library, 13.

11. Bonafede, "White House Report: Ford's Lobbyists Expect Democrats to Revise Tactics," 926.

12. Memorandum from Vern Loen to Max Friedersdorf and Jack Marsh, January 9, 1976, "General Subject File: Legislative Report for 1976," Robert K. Wolthuis Files, Box 2, Gerald R. Ford Presidential Library.

13. Bonafede, "White House Report: Ford's Lobbyists Expect Democrats to Revise Tactics," 926.

14. Interview with Joe Jenckes, August 8, 1985, William A. Syers Interviews, Gerald R. Ford Presidential Library, 2.

15. Bonafede, "White House Report: Ford's Lobbyists Expect Democrats to Revise Tactics," 926.

16. Interview with Max L. Friedersdorf, April 30, 1976, A. James F. C. Hyde, Jr., and Stephen J. Wayne Interviews, Gerald R. Ford Presidential Library, 15.

17. Bonafede, "White House Report: Administration Realigns Hill Liaison to Gain Tighter Grip on Federal Policy," 40.

18. Rowland Evans and Robert Novak, "'Brass Knuckle' Tactics in the White House," *Washington Post*, January 7, 1976.

19. Interview with Max Friedersdorf, October 27, 1977, A. James Reichley Research Interviews, Gerald R. Ford Presidential Library, 6.

20. Interview with Charles Leppert, July 10, 1985, William A. Syers Interviews, Gerald R. Ford Presidential Library, 3.

21. Interview with John Anderson, September 21, 1977, A. James Reichley Research Interviews, Gerald R. Ford Presidential Library, 1–2.

22. Bonafede, "President Still Seeks to Restore Staff Efficiency, Morale," 4.

23. Interview with Max Friedersdorf, October 27, 1977, A. James Reichley Research Interviews, Gerald R. Ford Presidential Library, 3.

24. John Manley, "Presidential Power and White House Lobbying," *Political Science Quarterly* 93 (summer 1978): 262.

25. Manley, "Presidential Power and White House Lobbying," 262.

26. Memorandum for Max L. Friedersdorf from William T. Kendall, April 19, 1976, "Memo Chronological Files, Max L. Friedersdorf Files, Box 2, Gerald R. Ford Presidential Library (emphasis in the original).

27. Elizabeth Wehr, "Reagan's Team on the Hill Getting Member's Praise for Hard Work, Experience," *Congressional Quarterly Weekly*, May 2, 1981, 748.

28. Interview with Pat O'Donnell, September 27, 1985, William A. Syers Interviews, Gerald R. Ford Presidential Library, 6.

29. Memorandum for Doug Bennett from Max Friedersdorf, July 21, 1975, "Memo Chronological Files July 1975," Max L. Friedersdorf Files, Box 1, Gerald R. Ford Presidential Library.

30. John Manley, "Presidential Power and White House Lobbying," *Political Science Quarterly* 93 (summer 1978): 262.

31. Dwight Eisenhower, Oral History OH 11, Oral History Collection of Columbia University, 72.

32. O'Brien, *No Final Victories*, 118.

33. Lawrence F. O'Brien, Oral History I, Lyndon B. Johnson Library, 74.

34. Connecting the Eisenhower, Nixon, and Ford administrations is Bryce Harlow. While Harlow did not serve in the Ford White House in an official capacity, he consulted with Ford frequently. Further, Timmons, Friedersdorf, and others in the Congressional Relations staffs of Ford and Reagan had been influenced by Harlow.

35. Eric L. Davis, "Legislative Liaison in the Carter Administration," *Political Science Quarterly* 94, no. 2 (summer 1979): 289.

36. Wehr, "Reagan's Team on the Hill Getting Member's Praise for Hard Work, Experience," 748.

37. Eric M. Uslaner, *The Decline of Comity in Congress* (Ann Arbor: University of Michigan Press, 1993).

38. Lawrence F. O'Brien, Oral History I, Lyndon B. Johnson Library, 49.

39. Memoranda from Charles Leppert to Max Friedersdorf through Vern Loen, January 14, 1975, "General Subject File: Congressional Relations Office," Vernon Leon and Charles Leppert Files, Box 5, Gerald R. Ford Presidential Library.

40. Minutes of Cabinet Meeting, January 8, 1975, "1975/01/08 Cabinet Meeting," James E. Connor Files, Box 3, Gerald R. Ford Presidential Library, 6.

41. Ibid., 10.

42. Interview with Richard Cook, September 16, 1977, A. James Reichley Research Interviews, Gerald R. Ford Presidential Library, 1.

43. Minutes of Cabinet Meeting, January 8, 1975, "1975/01/08 Cabinet Meeting," James E. Connor Files, Box 3, Gerald R. Ford Presidential Library, 9.

44. Interview with Joe Jenckes, August 8, 1985, William A. Syers Interviews, Gerald R. Ford Presidential Library, 5.

45. Memoranda from Vern Loen to Jack Marsh through Max Friedersdorf, January 6, 1976, "General Subject File: Legislative Report for 1976," Robert K. Wolthuis Files, Box 2, Gerald R. Ford Presidential Library.

46. A. James Reichley, *Conservatives in an Age of Change: The Nixon and Ford Administrations* (Washington, D.C.: The Brookings Institution, 1981), 326.

47. Barefoot Sanders to the president, 1/2/68, "Congressional Liaison Aides," Box 19, Papers of Harold Barefoot Sanders, Lyndon B. Johnson Library.

48. Memoranda from William E. Timmons to Ronald H. Nessen, October 14, 1974, "Messages to Congress, 11/17/74," William E. Timmons Files, Box 6, Gerald R. Ford Presidential Library.

49. Memorandum from Tom Korologos to William Timmons, August 19, 1974, "Subject File: Congressional Relations Memoranda, 8/74," Patrick O'Donnell and Joseph Jenckes Files, Box 2, Gerald R. Ford Presidential Library.

50. Mike Manatos, Oral History I, Lyndon B. Johnson Library, 46.

51. Memoranda from Charlie Leppert to Jack Marsh and Max Friedersdorf, February 3, 1975, "General Subject File: Congressional Relations Office," Vernon Loen and Charles Leppert Files, Box 5, Gerald R. Ford Presidential Library. (Emphasis in the original.)

52. Interview with William Kendall, June 26, 1985, William A. Syers Interviews, Gerald R. Ford Presidential Library, 6.

53. Note to Bud McFarlane from Tom Korologos, August 26, 1974, "General Subject File: Korologos Notes, 9/74 (1)," William T. Kendall Files, Box 13, Gerald R. Ford Presidential Library (emphasis in the original).

54. Memorandum from Tom Korologos to William Timmons, September 27, 1974, "Memoranda—Timmons to the president—September 1974 (2)," William E. Timmons Files, Box 5, Gerald R. Ford Presidential Library.

55. Memorandum for Jim Lynn and Jim Cannon from Max Friedersdorf, October 18, 1975, "Memo Chronological Files October 17–31, 1975," Max L. Friedersdorf Files, Box 2; and Memorandum for Todd Hullin from Tom Korologos, September 18, 1974, "Subject File: Congressional Relations Memoranda, 9/12–30/74," Patrick O'Donnell and Joseph Jenckes Files, Box 2, Gerald R. Ford Presidential Library.

56. Memorandum for Max Friedersdorf from Patrick O'Donnell, September 3, 1975, "Subject File: Congressional Relations Memoranda, 9/75," Patrick O'Donnell and Joseph Jenckes Files, Box 2, Gerald R. Ford Presidential Library.

57. Bonafede, "White House Report: Ford's Lobbyists Expect Democrats to Revise Tactics," 926.

58. Schlesinger, *The Imperial Presidency,* 409–10.

59. "Strategic Options Available to the President in His Relations to the Congress," no date, folder: "Congressional Relations—General," James E. Connor Files, Box 9, Gerald R. Ford Presidential Library, 1.

60. Schlesinger, *The Imperial Presidency,* 409–10.

61. Christopher Madison, "A Man of the House," *National Journal,* March 18, 1989, 646.

62. Interview with William Kendall, June 26, 1985, William A. Syers Interviews, Gerald R. Ford Presidential Library, 3.

63. Califano, *A Presidential Nation,* 72.

64. Comments made at a conference in Chicago sponsored by Time, Inc., on the role of Congress, December 5, 1972. Quoted in Charles O. Jones, *The Trusteeship Presidency* (Baton Rouge: Louisiana State University Press, 1988), 64.

65. Norman J. Ornstein, Thomas E. Mann, and Michael J. Malbin, eds., *Vital Statistics on Congress, 1991–1992* (Washington, D.C.: Congressional Quarterly Press, 1992), 127.

66. Interview with Vernon C. Loen, November 18, 1976, James F. C. Hyde, Jr., and Stephen J. Wayne, Oral History Collection, Gerald R. Ford Presidential Library, 22.

67. Interview with Richard Cook, September 16, 1977, A. James Reichley Research Interviews, Gerald R. Ford Presidential Library, 4.

68. Hedrick Smith, *The Power Game: How Washington Works* (New York: Ballantine Books, 1988), 147.

69. Morris Fiorina, "The Presidency and the Contemporary Electoral System," in *The Presidency and the Political System,* ed. Michael Nelson (Washington, D.C.: Congressional Quarterly Press, 1984), 204–26.

70. Haynes B. Johnson, *In the Absence of Power: Governing America* (New York: Viking Press, 1980), 168.

71. Leroy N. Rieselbach, *Congressional Reform* (Washington, D.C.: Congressional Quarterly Press, 1986), 50–52.

72. Madison, "A Man of the House," 646.

73. Reichley, *Conservatives in an Age of Change,* 326.

74. Congressional Record, February 10, 1976, E-572, from "White House Memoranda: Friedersdorf, Max—2/76," John O. Marsh Files, Box 79, Gerald R. Ford Presidential Library. Loen's apology according to Pressler resolved the issue. However, Loen left the White House within two months to take a job as a public affairs assistant at the National Aeronautics and Space Administration. Loen's departure, while not linked to his confrontation with Pressler, was likely predicated on his public battle with Pressler and derogatory comments in the press about freshman members. On one occasion he reportedly said, "Listen, I've been around Washington for a long time, I don't have to take any —— from a freshman." Jack Anderson with Les Whitten, "Ford's Lobbyist Loses Cool: Losing Friends for the President," *Detroit Free Press,* May 9, 1975.

75. Memorandum from Max Friedersdorf to Vern Loen, Charlie Leppert, and Tom Loeffler, Folder, "Memo Chronological File December 1975," Max L. Friedersdorf Files, Box 2, Gerald R. Ford Presidential Library.

76. Memorandum from Vern Loen to Max Friedersdorf and Jack Marsh, January 9, 1976, Folder, "General Subject File: Legislative Report for 1976," Robert K. Wolthuis Files, Box 2, Gerald R. Ford Presidential Library.

77. Memorandum for the president from William Timmons, December 10, 1974, "Memoranda—Timmons to the president—December 1974," William E. Timmons Files, Box 6, Gerald R. Ford Presidential Library.

78. Interview with William Kendall, June 26, 1985, William A. Syers Interviews, Gerald R. Ford Presidential Library, 5.

79. Interview with Richard Cook, September 16, 1977, A. James Reichley Research Interviews, Gerald R. Ford Presidential Library, 3.

80. Lawrence F. O'Brien, Oral History V, Lyndon B. Johnson Library, 43.

81. "Strategic Options Available to the President in His Relations to the Congress," no date, folder: "Congressional Relations—General," James E. Connor Files, Box 9, Gerald R. Ford Presidential Library, 3.

82. Light, *The President's Agenda,* 12.

83. James L. Sundquist, *The Decline and Resurgence of Congress* (Washington, D.C.: The Brookings Institution, 1981).

84. Reichley, *Conservatives in an Age of Change*, 335.

85. "Strategic Options Available to the President in His Relations to the Congress," no date, folder: "Congressional Relations—General," James E. Connor Files, Box 9, Gerald R. Ford Presidential Library, 5.

86. Memorandum to the president from Frank Moore, Dan Tate, and Bill Cable, July 19, 1977, "Congress/President," Chief of Staff: Hamilton Jordan, Box 34, Jimmy Carter Presidential Library, 2.

87. Text of an Address by the President to a Joint Session of the Congress, August 12, 1974, Folder, "State of the Union Address," William E. Timmons Files, Box 11, Gerald R. Ford Presidential Library.

88. "Ford Rides His Congress," *Economist*, June 21, 1975, 45.

89. Memorandum from Vern Loen to Max Friedersdorf and Jack Marsh, January 9, 1976, "General Subject File: Legislative Report for 1976," Robert K. Wolthuis Files, Box 2, Gerald R. Ford Presidential Library.

90. An extensive exploration of the veto power can be found in Louis Fisher, *Constitutional Conflicts Between Congress and the President*, 3d ed. (Lawrence: University Press of Kansas, 1991).

91. Memorandum from Vern Loen to Max Friedersdorf and Jack Marsh, January 9, 1976 Folder, "General Subject File: Legislative Report for 1976," Robert K. Wolthuis Files, Box 2, Gerald R. Ford Presidential Library.

92. Memorandum from Vern Loen to Max Friedersdorf, January 7, 1975, Folder, "Loen Chronological Files," Vernon Loen and Charles Leppert Files, Box 3, Gerald R. Ford Presidential Library.

93. Background, Participants and Press Plan, Cabinet Meeting, May 7, 1975, 1975/05/07 Cabinet Meeting, James E. Connor Files, Box 4, Gerald R. Ford Presidential Library, 1.

94. Interview with William Kendall, June 26, 1985, William A. Syers Interviews, Gerald R. Ford Presidential Library, 5.

95. Phone message for Tom Korologos, Folder, "General Subject File: Korologos Notes, 9/74 (1)," White House Memoranda Files, Box 79, Gerald R. Ford Presidential Library.

96. Memorandum from William E. Timmons to Donald Rumsfeld, Folder, "White House Operations—Memoranda," William E. Timmons Files Box 12, Gerald R. Ford Presidential Library.

97. Cannon, *Time and Chance*, 338.

7. THE CARTER ADMINISTRATION

1. Donald J. Balz, "Carter's Honeymoon on the Hill—How Long Can It Last?" *National Journal*, November 11, 1977, 1618.

2. Jones, *The Trusteeship Presidency*.

3. Memorandum to Frank Moore From Al McDonald and Hugh Carter, February 26, 1980, "Congressional Relations," Staff Office: Hugh Carter Box 16, Jimmy Carter Presidential Library.

4. Dom Bonafede, "Carter and Congress—It Seems That 'If Something Can Go Wrong, It Will,'" *National Journal*, November 12, 1977, 1756. Harlow also conceded that Eisenhower had gotten off to a rough start. Dom Bonafede, "Carter's Relationship with Congress—Making a Mountain Out of a 'Moorehill,'" *National Journal*, March 26, 1977, 456.

5. James A. Barnes, "Poor Stroking by Bush Political Crew," *National Journal*, July 22, 1989, 1878.

6. Bonafede, "Carter's Relationship with Congress," 456.

7. "Frank Moore: Carter's Chief Arm-Twister," *U.S. News and World Report*, September 18, 1978, 22.

8. Ibid.

9. Bonafede, "Carter's Relationship with Congress," 456.

10. Balz, "Carter's Honeymoon on the Hill," 1621.

11. Mercer Cross, "Carter and Congress: Fragile Friendship," *Congressional Quarterly Weekly*, February 23, 1977, 1.

12. For example: Letter from Representative Jim Wright to President Carter, February 21, 1977, and Letter from Representative Sam B. Hall, Jr., July 26, 1979, FG6-1-1/Moore, Frank, White House Central Files, Jimmy Carter Presidential Library.

13. This story came from an interview with Les Francis, who had worked in Mineta's office before serving in the White House. Because the source for this story would be clear to anyone who knew him he agreed to have the story attributed to him.

14. Memorandum to the president from Frank Moore, Dan Tate, and Bill Cable, July 19, 1977, "Congress/President," Chief of Staff: Hamilton Jordan Box 34, Jimmy Carter Presidential Library, 4.

15. Memorandum for the president from Frank Moore, April 3, 1978, "Congressional Liaison—1978 [2]," Staff Office—Administration: Hugh Carter Box 16, Jimmy Carter Presidential Library, 4.

16. Memorandum to the president from Frank Moore, Dan Tate, and Bill Cable, July 19, 1977, "Congress/President," Chief of Staff: Hamilton Jordan, Box 34, Jimmy Carter Presidential Library, 4–7.

17. Memorandum for the president from Frank Moore, April 3, 1978, "Congressional Liaison—1978 [2]," Staff Office—Administration: Hugh Carter, Box 16, Jimmy Carter Presidential Library, 3–4.

18. Interview with Vernon C. Loen, November 18, 1976, James F. C. Hyde, Jr., and Stephen J. Wayne, Oral History Collection, Gerald R. Ford Presidential Library, 27.

19. Bryce Harlow, Oral History OH 402, Dwight D. Eisenhower Library, 8.

20. Davis, "Legislative Liaison in the Carter Administration," 289.

21. For example, see Mike Manatos, Oral History I, Lyndon B. Johnson Library, 21. This was also mentioned to the author by lobbyists from several administrations.

22. Paul C. Light, *Vice-Presidential Power: Advice and Influence in the White House* (Baltimore: The Johns Hopkins University Press, 1984). Also, Joel K. Goldstein, *The Modern American Vice Presidency: The Transformation of a Political Institution* (Princeton: Princeton University Press, 1982).

23. Letter from Garner to FDR, November 11, 1934, in Hyde Park Files. Quoted in Lester, "Developments in Presidential-Congressional Relations: FDR–JFK," 44–45.

24. Memorandum for the president from the vice president, September 6, 1977, "Vice President," Chief of Staff: Hamilton Jordan, Box 37, Jimmy Carter Presidential Library, 7.

25. Memorandum for the president from Frank Moore, February 3, 1979, "Legislative Reports," Chief of Staff: Hamilton Jordan, Box 48, Jimmy Carter Presidential Library, 24.

26. Private sector lobbyists perform a similar function for their clients. Several veterans of the congressional relations staff reported that they often did much the same thing after going to work for interest groups or corporations.

27. Pika, "White House Boundary Roles," 700–715. See also Pika, "The White House Office of Congressional Relations."

28. Interview with Eugene Cowen, October 5, 1977, A. James Reichley Research Interviews, Gerald R. Ford Presidential Library, 1–2.

29. Jones, *The Trusteeship Presidency*, 120.

30. Memoranda from Max Friedersdorf to Jack Marsh, September 8, 1975, "Memo Chronological Files," Max L. Friedersdorf Files, Box 1, Gerald R. Ford Presidential Library.

31. Memorandum from William E. Timmons to Donald Rumsfeld, "White House Operations—Memoranda," William E. Timmons Files, Box 12, Gerald R. Ford Presidential Library.

32. Jones, *The Trusteeship Presidency*, 84.

33. Ibid.

34. Smith, *The Power Game*, 454.

35. Memorandum from Hamilton Jordan to the president, September 1, 1978, "Energy Bill, 1978," Chief of Staff: Hamilton Jordan, Box 44, Jimmy Carter Presidential Library.

36. Memorandum for the president from Frank Moore, April 30, 1978, "Legislative Reports," Chief of Staff: Hamilton Jordan, Box 48, Jimmy Carter Presidential Library, 10.

37. Burton I. Kaufman, *The Presidency of James Earl Carter, Jr.* (Lawrence: University of Kansas Press, 1993), 178.

38. Kernell, *Going Public*, 23.

39. Califano, *A Presidential Nation*, 142.

40. Hedrick Smith, "Congress and Carter: An Uneasy Adjustment," *New York Times*, February 18, 1977, B16.

41. Ibid.

42. Jimmy Carter, *Keeping Faith: Memoirs of a President* (New York: Bantam Books, 1982), 7.

43. David S. Broder, "Mending an Estranged Alliance," *Washington Post*, February 27, 1978, A6.

44. Balz, "Carter's Honeymoon on the Hill" 1618.

45. Broder, "Mending an Estranged Alliance," A6.

46. Congressional Leadership Breakfast [Briefing Paper], September 18, 1978, "9/19/78," Office of Staff Secretary: Handwriting File, Box 101, Jimmy Carter Presidential Library, 3–4; and Memorandum for the president from Frank Moore, October 31, 1978, "11/8/78 [2]," Office of Staff Secretary: Handwriting File, Box 108, Jimmy Carter Presidential Library, 2.

47. Broder, "Mending an Estranged Alliance," A6.

48. Reichley, *Conservatives in an Age of Change*, 327.

49. Broder, "Mending an Estranged Alliance," A6.

50. Memorandum for the president from Frank Moore, April 30, 1978, "Legislative Reports," Chief of Staff: Hamilton Jordan, Box 48, Jimmy Carter Presidential Library, 10.

51. Edwards, *At the Margins*, 35.

52. Talking Points for the Russell Long Meeting, [September 17, 1980], "9/17/80 [2]," Office of Staff Secretary: Handwriting File, Box 205, Jimmy Carter Presidential Library.

53. Neustadt, *Presidential Power and the Modern President*, 235.

54. Memorandum for the president from Frank Moore, April 3, 1978, "Congressional Liaison—1978 [2]," Staff Office—Administration: Hugh Carter, Box 16, Jimmy Carter Presidential Library, 2.

55. Joseph A. Pika, "Opening Doors for Kindred Souls: The White House Office of Public Liaison," in *Interest Group Politics*, ed. Allan J. Cigler and Burdett A. Loomis (Washington, D.C.: Congressional Quarterly Press, 1991), 277–98.

56. Smith, "Congress and Carter: An Uneasy Adjustment," B16.

57. This term is borrowed from Neustadt's discussion of the president and the public. Neustadt, *Presidential Power and the Modern President*, 77.

58. Neustadt, *Presidential Power and the Modern President,* 255. Anne Wexler's skill at grassroots lobbying was sufficiently admired that she could open the Wexler Group, her own very successful firm, after her service in the Carter White House.

59. Dom Bonafede, "To Anne Wexler, All the World Is a Potential Lobbyist," *National Journal,* September 9, 1979, 1476.

60. Kenneth M. Duberstein, "Commentary: On Interest Groups and Lobbying," in *Making Government Work: From White House to Congress,* ed. Robert E. Hunter, Wayne L. Berman, and John F. Kennedy (Boulder, Colo.: Westview Press, 1986), 246.

61. Memorandum from Hamilton Jordan to the president, September 1, 1978, "Energy Bill, 1978," Chief of Staff: Hamilton Jordan, Box 44, Jimmy Carter Presidential Library, 2.

62. Bonafede, "To Anne Wexler, All the World is a Potential Lobbyist," 1476.

63. Jones, *The Trusteeship Presidency,* 107.

64. Judith Miller, "Reagan's Liaison Chief on Capitol Hill To Focus on Harmony as His Priority," *New York Times,* January 6, 1981, B8.

65. Haynes B. Johnson, *In the Absence of Power: Governing America* (New York: Viking Press, 1980), 165.

66. Jones, *The Trusteeship Presidency,* 67.

67. Jack McWethy, "Report from the White House: What Carter's Aides Really Think of Congress," *U.S. News and World Report,* August 14, 1978, 15.

8. THE REAGAN ADMINISTRATION

1. The most often cited examples of this perspective include James L. Sundquist, "The Crisis of Competence in Government," in *Setting National Priorities: Agenda for the 1980s,* ed. Joseph A. Pechman (Washington, D.C.: The Brookings Institution, 1980), 531; and Lloyd N. Cutler, "To Form a Government," *Foreign Affairs,* fall 1980, 126–43.

2. Gerald R. Ford, "Imperiled, Not Imperial," *Time* magazine, November 10, 1980, 30; and Joseph Kraft, "The Post-Imperial Presidency," *New York Times Magazine,* November 23, 1980, 31.

3. James Pfiffner, "The Carter-Reagan Transition: Hitting the Ground Running," *Presidential Studies Quarterly* 13 (fall 1983): 627.

4. Eight years in the White House compounded by a high turnover rate on the liaison staff make going into the background of each member of the liaison staff cumbersome. I instead focus on those who headed the operation or who played a special role.

5. Elizabeth Wehr, "Reagan's Team on the Hill Getting Members' Praise for Hard Work, Experience," *Congressional Quarterly Weekly,* May 2, 1981, 750.

6. Suplee, "The Capitol Connection," C3.

7. Wehr, "Reagan's Team on the Hill Getting Members' Praise for Hard Work, Experience," 748.

8. Friedersdorf's philosophy was mentioned by several people who worked with Friedersdorf over the years. See also Helen Dewar and Lee Lescaze, "Reagan Hill Team Gets Rave Reviews," *Washington Post,* March 17, 1981, A8.

9. Suplee, "The Capitol Connection," C3.

10. After serving in the Reagan White House, Duberstein opened Duberstein and Company, an influential Washington lobbying firm. He has since served as an advisor to House Speaker Newt Gingrich and potential presidential candidate Colin Powell.

11. Steven Pressman, "White House Lobbyists Find Congress is Less Supportive," *Congressional Quarterly Weekly,* June 16, 1984, 1430–31.

12. Dick Kirschten, "Second-Term Legislative Strategy Shifts to Foreign Policy and Defense Issues," *National Journal,* March 30, 1985, 696. Ogelsby had experienced some health problems

and wanted to accept a lucrative offer in the private sector in order to escape the heavy work-load in the White House. The president persuaded him to stay, saying that they couldn't do without him, and then brought Friedersdorf back into the White House.

13. The Carter liaison staff was roughly the same size but had a larger support staff.

14. Stephen J. Wayne, "Congressional Liaison in the Reagan White House: A Preliminary Assessment of the First Year," in *President and Congress: Assessing Reagan's First Year,* ed. Norman J. Ornstein (Washington, D.C.: American Enterprise Institute for Public Policy Research, 1982), 51.

15. Miller, "Reagan's Liaison Chief on Capitol Hill To Focus on Harmony as His Priority," B8.

16. Dewar and Lescaze, "Reagan Hill Team Gets Rave Reviews," A8.

17. Wehr, "Reagan's Team on the Hill Getting Members' Praise for Hard Work, Experience," 749.

18. Miller, "Reagan's Liaison Chief on Capitol Hill To Focus on Harmony as His Priority," B8.

19. Ibid.

20. Wayne, "Congressional Liaison in the Reagan White House," 61.

21. The "Troika" or "rule by three" was composed of Reagan's three top advisors: James Baker, Michael Deaver, and Ed Meese. These three advisors worked together to make decisions about strategy.

22. Larry Speakes with Robert Pack, *Speaking Out: The Reagan Presidency from Inside the White House* (New York: Charles Scribner's Sons, 1988), 70.

23. Duberstein, "Commentary: On Interest Groups and Lobbying," 246–47.

24. William J. Gribbin, "The President and the Congress: The Office of Legislative Affairs," *Mandate for Leadership III: Political Strategies for the 1990s,* ed. Charles L. Heatherly and Burton Yale Pines (Washington, D.C.: The Heritage Foundation, 1989), 45.

25. Pika, "White House Boundary Roles," 700–715.

26. Speakes, *Speaking Out,* 87.

27. Smith, *The Power Game,* 340.

28. Ibid., 464.

29. Richard E. Cohen and Dick Kirschten, "An Era of Deadlock?" *National Journal,* January 18, 1986, 129.

30. Ibid., 127.

31. Jane Mayer and Doyle McManus, *Landslide: The Unmaking of the President, 1984–1988* (Boston: Houghton Mifflin Company, 1988), 41.

32. Dick Kirschten, "Damage Control Team," *National Journal,* January 18, 1986, 133.

33. Ibid., 132–33.

34. Ronald Reagan, *An American Life* (New York: Simon and Schuster, 1990), 234.

35. Carter told Speaker O'Neill, "I'll handle them [Congress] just as I handled the Georgia legislature. Whenever I had problems with the Georgia legislature I took the problems to the people of Georgia." Recounted in Haynes Johnson, *The Absence of Power* (New York: Viking Press, 1980), 159–61.

36. This term is borrowed from Neustadt's discussion of the president and the public. Neustadt, *Presidential Power and the Modern President,* 83.

37. For a detailed discussion of Reagan's appeals on behalf of his first three budgets, see Kernell, *Going Public,* chapter 5.

38. Reagan, *An American Life,* 285.

39. Kernell, *Going Public,* 19.

40. Ibid., 2.

41. Ibid., 4.

42. Neustadt, *Presidential Power and the Modern President.*

43. This two-way effect is discussed by Charles W. Ostrom, Jr., and Dennis M. Simon, "Promise and Performance: A Dynamic Model of Presidential Popularity," *American Political Science Review* 79 (June 1985): 349. See also Paul Brace and Barbara Hinckley, *Follow the Leader: Opinion Polls and the Modern President* (New York: Basic Books, 1992).

44. Norman Ornstein, "Assessing Reagan's First Year," *President and Congress: Assessing Reagan's First Year,* ed. Norman J. Ornstein (Washington, D.C.: American Enterprise Institute for Public Policy Research, 1982), 95.

45. Michael J. Malbin, "House Democratic Reforms Cut Both Ways," *National Journal,* August 29, 1981, 1540.

46. Kernell, *Going Public,* 3.

47. Dick Kirschten, "They'll Take All the Help They Can Get," *National Journal,* March 7, 1981, 387.

48. Jeffrey Tulis, *The Rhetorical Presidency* (Princeton: Princeton University Press, 1987), 189.

49. Mondale, "Two Views from Pennsylvania Ave.," 14.

50. Kernell, *Going Public,* 31.

51. Smith, "Congress and Carter: An Uneasy Adjustment," B16.

52. Barefoot Sanders, "Congressional-Executive Relations During the 1960s," in *The Presidency and the Congress: A Shifting Balance of Power?,* ed. William S. Livingston, Lawrence C. Dodd, and Richard L. Schott (Austin: Lyndon B. Johnson School of Public Affairs, 1979), 299.

53. Kernell, *Going Public,* chapter 2.

54. Smith, *The Power Game,* 14.

55. A similar point is made in Kernell, *Going Public,* chap. 2. See also Steven V. Roberts, "President's Coalition," *New York Times,* October 27, 1982, 13.

56. Ornstein, "Assessing Reagan's First Year," 92.

57. Smith, *The Power Game,* 450.

58. Richard E. Cohen, "The 'Revolution' on Capitol Hill: Is It Just a Temporary Coup?" *National Journal,* August 29, 1981, 1538.

59. Ibid.

60. George C. Edwards III, *Presidential Influence in Congress* (San Francisco: W. H. Freeman and Company, 1980), 37.

61. David A. Stockman, *The Triumph of Politics: How the Reagan Revolution Failed* (New York, Harper and Row, 1986), 257.

62. Apple, "An Excess of the Pulpit and Not Enough Bully?" A10.

63. Smith, *The Power Game,* 469–70.

64. Kirschten, "They'll Take All the Help They Can Get," 387.

65. Wayne, "Congressional Liaison in the Reagan White House," 54–55.

66. Tip O'Neill with William Novak, *Man of the House: The Life and Political Memoirs of Speaker Tip O'Neill* (New York: Random House, 1987), 342.

67. Stockman, *The Triumph of Politics,* 214.

68. Smith, *The Power Game,* 458.

69. Stockman, *The Triumph of Politics,* 234.

70. Smith, *The Power Game,* 456.

71. Lyn Nofziger, *Nofziger* (Washington, D.C.: Regnery Gateway, 1992), 138.

72. Greenstein, *The Hidden-Hand Presidency.*

73. Fred I. Greenstein, "Ronald Reagan—Another Hidden-Hand Ike?" *PS* 23 (March 1990): 12.

74. Jonathan Alter, "The Discipline Gap," *Newsweek,* August 22, 1994, 19.

75. David Rapp, "Reagan Added Luster but Little Clout to Office," *Congressional Quarterly Weekly,* January 7, 1989, 3.

76. Ronald D. Elving, "Dealing with the Hill Critical for Success," *Congressional Quarterly Weekly,* September 10, 1988, 2515.

77. Rapp, "Reagan Added Luster but Little Clout to Office," 3.

9. THE BUSH ADMINISTRATION

1. Robin Toner, "Congress Still Purring as Bush Applies the Right Strokes," *New York Times,* January 31, 1989, A20.

2. Elizabeth Neuffer, "Bush Seen Adding to Gridlock on the Hill; Hands-off Style, Vetoes Are Cited," *Boston Globe,* August 6, 1992, 1.

3. *Inaugural Addresses of the Presidents of the United States, Bicentennial Edition* (Washington, D.C.: United States Government Printing Office, 1989), 349.

4. Michael Duffy and Dan Goodgame, *Marching in Place: The Status Quo Presidency of George Bush* (New York: Simon and Schuster, 1992), 16.

5. Duffy and Goodgame, *Marching in Place,* 47.

6. Dan Balz, "The Guardian of Bipartisanship," *Washington Post,* February 9, 1989, 17.

7. Burt Solomon, "George Bush's Congressional Crew Has an Oar or Two Out of Sync," *National Journal,* June 24, 1989, 1651.

8. Balz, "The Guardian of Bipartisanship," 17.

9. Burt Solomon, "The People Who Keep the White House Going," *National Journal,* July 7, 1990, 1646.

10. During his hiatus from the Bush White House, Calio joined the Duberstein Group, a prestigious political consulting firm headed by Ken Duberstein who had served as head of congressional relations and later chief of staff during the Reagan administration. After leaving the White House at the end of the Bush administration, Calio opened up a lobbying firm with Larry O'Brien, Jr., the son of Kennedy and Johnson's chief lobbyist.

11. Burt Solomon, "Doubts Linger on Whether Lessons of Tower Affair Have Been Learned," *National Journal,* March 25, 1989, 755.

12. James A. Barnes, "Poor Stroking by Bush Political Crew," *National Journal,* July 22, 1989, 1878. Also, Solomon, "George Bush's Congressional Crew has an Oar or Two Out of Sync," 1651.

13. Solomon, "George Bush's Congressional Crew has an Oar or Two Out of Sync," 1650.

14. Ibid., 1651. Also, Solomon, "The People Who Keep the White House Going," 1646.

15. Solomon, "George Bush's Congressional Crew Has an Oar or Two Out of Sync," 1651.

16. Burt Solomon, "No-Nonsense Sununu," *National Journal,* September 16, 1989, 2252.

17. Richard L. Berke, "Loyalty is Rewarded at White House," *New York Times,* April 15, 1993, A9.

18. Burt Solomon, "Sununu Has 'a Constituency of One,'" *National Journal,* September 16, 1989, 2250.

19. Solomon, "The People Who Keep the White House Going," 1646.

20. Burt Solomon, "Send in the Clones," *National Journal,* March 21, 1992, 678.

21. Richard Darman not only brought the clout of his role as director of the Office of Management and Budget and as a close advisor to Bush, he also had the experience of being one of the founding members of the Reagan LSG.

22. Solomon, "Doubts Linger on Whether Lessons of Tower Affair Have Been Learned," 755.

23. Burt Solomon, "In Bush's White House Planning Seems to Be for the Short Term," *National Journal,* October 21, 1989, 2595.

24. Dan Balz, "The Guardian of Bipartisanship," *Washington Post,* February 9, 1989, 17.

25. Solomon, "Doubts Linger on Whether Lessons of Tower Affair Have Been Learned," 754.

26. Susan Page, "A Saga of Misjudgments, Miscues and Mistakes," *Newsday,* March 10, 1989, 5.

27. Maureen Dowd, "Kindness Is Foundation as Bush Builds Bridges," *New York Times,* February 6, 1980, A1.

28. Richard Cohen, "The Gloves Are Off," *National Journal,* October 14, 1989, 2509.

29. Robin Toner, "Congress Still Purring as Bush Applies the Right Strokes," *The New York Times,* January 31, 1989, A20.

30. Toner, "Congress Still Purring as Bush Applies the Right Strokes," A20.

31. Maureen Dowd, "Kindness Is Foundation as Bush Builds Bridges," *The New York Times,* February 6, 1980, A8.

32. Toner, "Congress Still Purring as Bush Applies the Right Strokes," A20.

33. Burt Solomon, "Clinton Tries a Reagan-Style Pitch but with Just a Bush-sized Bench," *National Journal,* February 2, 1993, 533.

34. Toner, "Congress Still Purring as Bush Applies the Right Strokes," A20.

35. Neuffer, "Bush Seen Adding to Gridlock on the Hill," 1.

36. Jack W. Germond and Jules Witcover, "Memories of Harsh '88 Race May Haunt Bush," *National Journal,* March 11, 1989, 606.

37. Burt Solomon, "Bush's Disdain for Image Making May Come to Plague His Tenure," *National Journal,* May 11, 1989, 603.

38. Neuffer, "Bush Seen Adding to Gridlock on the Hill," 1.

39. Solomon, "In Bush's White House Planning Seems to Be for the Short Term," 2595.

40. Neuffer, "Bush Seen Adding to Gridlock on the Hill," 1.

41. Robin Toner, "For Bush and Congress, Some Spirited Battles but No Full-Scale War," *New York Times,* August 9, 1989, B6.

42. Cohen, "The Gloves Are Off," 2511.

43. Jack W. Germond and Jules Witcover, "It's Only February and the Honeymoon's Over," *National Journal,* February 18, 1989, 426.

44. Drawn from the comments of several lawmakers interviewed. See also Janet Hooks, "Avalanche of Veto Threats Divides Bush, Congress," *Congressional Quarterly Weekly,* September 22, 1980, 2991; and Duffy and Goodgame, *Marching in Place,* 78.

45. Duffy and Goodgame, *Marching in Place,* 78.

46. Hooks, "Avalanche of Veto Threats Divides Bush, Congress," 2991.

47. Janet Hooks, "Bush Gets Reputation of Mr. Veto from Hill," *Washington Times,* September 28, 1980, A4.

48. Neuffer, "Bush Seen Adding to Gridlock on the Hill," 1.

49. Executive Office of the President, "Statement of Administration Policy, H.R. 3040—Unemployment Insurance Reform Act of 1991," September 12, 1991.

50. Of the forty-six vetoes carried out by Bush, fifteen were pocket vetoes not subject to congressional override because Congress was no longer in session. Of the remaining thirty-one vetoes, only one, on cable deregulation, was overridden.

51. Lawrence F. O'Brien, Oral History I, Lyndon B. Johnson Library, 105.

52. O'Brien, Oral History I, Lyndon B. Johnson Library, 101–102. Also O'Brien, Oral History V, 47.

53. Greenstein, *The Hidden-Hand Presidency.*

54. Memorandum to the president from Frank Moore, Dan Tate, and Bill Cable, July 19, 1977, "Congress/President," Chief of Staff: Hamilton Jordan, Box 34, Jimmy Carter Presidential Library, 4.

55. Memorandum for the president from Stu Eizenstat, December 27, 1977, FG-1, White House Central File, Jimmy Carter Presidential Library, 4.

56. Minutes of Cabinet Meeting, January 8, 1975, folder: 1975/01/08 Cabinet Meeting, James E. Connor Files, Box 3, Gerald R. Ford Presidential Library, 10.

57. Bryce Harlow, Oral History II, Lyndon B. Johnson Library, 8, 11.

58. Richard Fenno, *The President's Cabinet: An Analysis in the Period from Wilson to Eisenhower* (Cambridge: Harvard University Press, 1959), 207.

59. Fenno, *The President's Cabinet,* 197.

60. Herring, *Presidential Leadership,* 100.

61. Greenfield, "Why Are You Calling Me, Son?" 30.

62. Mike Manatos, Oral History I, Lyndon B. Johnson Library, 53–54.

63. For a more detailed discussion of the legal barriers to executive branch lobbying, see chapter 3.

64. Memorandum from Bob Bonitati to Max Friedersdorf, December 17, 1974, Folder: "General Subject File: Congressional Relations Office—General (1)," John O. Marsh Files, Box 10, Gerald R. Ford Presidential Library.

65. The Bureau of the Budget was reorganized and renamed the Office of Management and Budget in the middle of Nixon's first term.

66. Bryce Harlow, Oral History OH 402, Dwight D. Eisenhower Library, 11.

67. Interview with Max L. Friedersdorf, April 30, 1976, A. James F. C. Hyde, Jr., and Stephen J. Wayne Interviews, Gerald R. Ford Presidential Library, 13.

68. Memorandum for Bill Walker from Max Friedersdorf, March 27, 1975, "White House Memoranda: Friedersdorf, Max—2/75–4/75," John O. Marsh Files, Box 78, Gerald Ford Presidential Library.

69. Duffy and Goodgame, *Marching in Place,* 85, 102–108.

70. Solomon, "Clinton Tries a Reagan-Style Pitch with a Bush-sized Bench," 533.

10. THE CLINTON ADMINISTRATION

1. Richard E. Cohen, "What Coattails?" *National Journal,* May 29, 1993, 1285.

2. Helen Dewar, "On Hill, Clinton Will Find Neither Gridlock Nor Compliance: Next President's Diplomatic Skill To Be Put to Test," *Washington Post,* November 5, 1992, A25.

3. Richard M. Valelly, "In Search of a Governing Party," *The American Prospect* 14 (summer 1993): 18.

4. Richard E. Cohen, "Doing Business," *National Journal,* June 12, 1993, 1395.

5. Bob Woodward, *The Agenda: Inside the Clinton White House* (New York: Simon and Schuster, 1994), 129.

6. Ann Devroy, "Taking Leave of the White House," *Washington Post Weekly Edition,* November 29–December 5, 1993, 12.

7. Clifford Krauss, "Clinton's Woes on Capitol Hill Spur Sharp Criticism of His Top Lobbyist," *New York Times,* May 25, 1993, A7; Richard E. Cohen, "The White House Isn't K Street, Mr. Paster," *National Journal,* June 12, 1993, 1396; and Cohen, "Doing Business," 1397.

8. Woodward, *The Agenda,* 324.

9. Press Release, "Press Secretary Statement on Pat Griffin Resignation 1.4.96." The White House, January 4, 1996.

10. Pika, "White House Boundary Roles," 700–715.

11. Elizabeth Drew, *On the Edge: The Clinton Presidency* (New York: Simon and Schuster, 1994), 108.

12. Clifford Krauss, "Clinton's Woes on Capitol Hill Spur Sharp Criticism of His Top Lobbyist," *New York Times*, May 25, 1993, A7.

13. Cohen, "The White House Isn't K Street, Mr. Paster," 1396.

14. Richard E. Cohen, "For Clinton, A Congressional Baptism," *National Journal*, April 17, 1993, 942.

15. Cohen, "For Clinton, A Congressional Baptism," 942.

16. Lloyd Grove, "Replacing the Carrot with a Stick," *Washington Post Weekly Edition*, April 12–18, 1993, 13. Gore was especially irritated by Shelby's treatment because he had been working throughout the budget process to try to help Shelby protect the space station project that was considered important to Shelby's home state. Shelby would switch parties before the next election.

17. Grove, "Replacing the Carrot with a Stick," 13.

18. See, for example, Gwen Ifill, "Clinton Goes to the Capitol Seeking Democrats' Favor," *New York Times*, April 30, 1992, A1, and Adam Clymer, "Clinton Returns to Capitol, and Bouquets All Around," *New York Times*, December 9, 1992, A13.

19. Woodward, *The Agenda*, 205.

20. Richard L. Berke, "G.O.P. Serves Clinton Familiar Doubts," *New York Times*, March 3, 1993, A10; and Richard E. Cohen, "Can Clinton Keep Ignoring the GOP?" *National Journal*, June 12, 1993, 1424.

21. Woodward, *The Agenda*, 297.

22. Cohen, "Doing Business," 1395.

23. Drew, *On the Edge*, 107.

24. Burt Solomon, "Clinton's Roller-Coaster Presidency, *National Journal*, December 11, 1993, 2960.

25. Kevin Merida, "Running Away from Bill Clinton," *Washington Post Weekly Edition*, September 26–October 2, 1994, 12.

26. Woodward, *The Agenda*, 141.

27. Thomas T. Connally and Alfred Steinberg. *My Name is Tom Connally* (New York: Thomas Y. Crowell Company, 1954), 189.

28. Dan Balz, "Mistakes Were Made—and How: The Clinton Administration has 20-20 Hindsight on How it Sold the Economic Package," *Washington Post Weekly Edition*, August 16–22, 1993, 12.

29. Steven Waldman, *The Bill: How the Adventures of Clinton's National Service Bill Reveal What is Corrupt, Comic, Cynical—and Noble—About Washington* (New York: Viking Press, 1995), 71–72.

30. Gwen Ifill, "56 Long Days of Coordinated Persuasion," *New York Times*, November 19, 1993, A11.

31. David Van Biema, "Gored But Not Gone," *Time* magazine, November 22, 1993, 40.

32. Sidney Blumenthal, "The Making of a Machine," *New Yorker*, November 29, 1992, 92.

33. Adam Clymer, "Presidential Health Show Travels to a Friendly Spot," *New York Times*, April 19, 1994, A10.

34. Joe Klein, "Bungee-Jumping," *Newsweek*, March 1, 1993, 29.

35. Chuck McCutcheon, "Dems Not Distancing Themselves From Clinton: Those Seeking Re-Election Support President," *Congressional Quarterly Fax Report*, February 1, 1996.

36. James G. Gimpel, *Fulfilling the Contract: The First 100 Days* (Boston: Allyn and Bacon, 1996), 2–12.

37. B. Drummon Ayres, Jr., "Cooperate, Dole Tells Clinton, Or Face Brawl with Congress," *New York Times,* September 6, 1995, A12.

38. Bill Turque and Evan Thomas, "Missing the Moment," *Newsweek,* November 27, 1995, 26.

39. Jim Abrams, "Clinton Budget Rejected: Republicans Threaten to Shut Off Programs They Don't Want to Fund," *Kansas City Star,* January 8, 1996, A1.

40. Elaine Sciolino, "Awaiting Call, Helms Put Foreign Policy on Hold," *New York Times,* September 24, 1995, A1.

41. Guy Gugliotta, "'They Flat Do Not Care': For Many of the GOP Freshman, a Balanced Budget Outstrips the Prospects of Reelection," *Washington Post Weekly Edition,* January 1–7, 1996, 13.

42. Ironically, just as the second budget shutdown ended, a snowstorm closed federal offices in Washington for several days.

43. The Christian Coalition spent $1.4 million to oppose the Clinton health care plan. Robin Toner, "First Lady Opens Fire on Health Care Plan Critics," *New York Times,* February 16, 1994, A12.

44. Peter H. Stone, "Follow the Leaders," *National Journal,* June 24, 1995, 1640–44.

45. George Archibald, "Generational Lapses," *Washington Times,* March 7, 1993.

46. Ron Raucheux, "The Grassroots Explosion," *Campaigns and Elections,* December-January, 21.

47. Jonathan Alter, "The Discipline Gap," *Newsweek,* August 22, 1994, 20.

48. Waldman, *The Bill,* 54–55, 141–42.

49. Jon R. Bond and Richard Fleisher, "Clinton and Congress: A First Year Assessment," *American Politics Quarterly,* July 1995, 355–72. Jon Healey, "Clinton Success Rate Declined to a Record Low in 1995," *Congressional Quarterly Weekly,* January 27, 1996, 193.

50. Healey, "Clinton Success Rate Declined to a Record Low in 1995," 193.

51. Burns, "The 1994 Solution," 16.

11. CONCLUSION

1. Moynihan, *Counting Our Blessings,* 128.

2. Neustadt, *Presidential Power and the Modern President,* 210–12. See also Edwards, *At the Margins,* 9–10.

3. Richard L. Berke, "White House Tries to Rescue Lawmakers from Labor Revenge," *New York Times,* March 15, 1994, A9.

4. Haynes B. Johnson, *In the Absence of Power: Governing America* (New York: Viking Press, 1980), 168.

5. William S. White, "Truman and the Congress: Another 'Cold' War," *New York Times,* June 15, 1952, 6E.

6. Ken Duberstein, "Commentary," in *Beyond Gridlock? Prospects for Governance in the Clinton Years—and After Washington,* ed. James L. Sundquist (Washington, D.C.: The Brookings Institution, 1993), 20.

7. Dick Kirschten, "The Pennsylvania Ave. Connection—Making Peace on Capitol Hill," *National Journal,* March 7, 1981, 384.

8. Pika, "White House Boundary Roles, 700–715.

9. Suplee, "The Capitol Connection," C1.

10. Kirschten, "The Pennsylvania Ave. Connection," 386.

11. Steven Pressman, "Two GOP Freshmen in the House Rate the White House Lobbying Effort," *National Journal,* June 16, 1984, 1431.

12. Mondale, "Two Views from Pennsylvania Ave.," 14.

13. Norman Ornstein, "Too Many 'Lone Rangers,'" *Washington Post Weekly Edition,* September 12–18, 1994, 28.

14. David S. Broder and Michael Weissdopf, "Back to Gridlock as Usual," *Washington Post Weekly Edition,* June 21–27, 1993, 12.

15. Neustadt, *Presidential Power and the Modern President,* 185.

16. Apple, "An Excess of the Pulpit and Not Enough Bully?" A10.

17. Light, *The President's Agenda,* 6.

18. Broder and Weissdopf, "Back to Gridlock as Usual," 12.

19. Paul Taylor, "Getting What We Asked For: The 'Train Wreck,' Believe It or Not, Is a Sign That the System Is Working," *Washington Post Weekly Edition,* November 27–December 3, 1995, 11.

20. Duberstein, "Commentary: On Interest Groups and Lobbying," 242.

21. Moynihan, *Counting Our Blessings,* 119.

22. Harlow, "Text of Harlow Keynote Address at Nashville Symposium," 7.

INDEX

Adams, Sherman, 32, 50, 55
AFL-CIO, 19
Agnew, Spiro, 117, 138
Air Force One, 105
Albert, Carl, 80, 122
Ambrose, Stephen, 42
Anderson, I. Jack, 31, 32, 36–37
Anderson, John, 141
Anderson, Robert, 44
Andres, Gary, 233
Arend, Les, 105
Arm Twisting, 73–74
At the Margins, 9
Autopilot approach, 16–17, 30: definition of, 48–51

Baker, Howard, 143, 150, 198, 205–06, 219
Baker, James, 201, 205
Ball, William A., 200
Beckel, Bob, 165, 172
BeLieu, Kenneth, 117
Bentsen, Lloyd, 266
Between the branches, 15, 281–84
Bill-signing ceremonies, 94–95
Boggs, J. Caleb, 88
Bonatati, Bob, 254–55
Bond, Jon R., 4, 9, 11, 133, 134, 188, 277
Boundary role persons, 116, 175, 282
Bowles, Nigel, 82
Brace, Paul, 134
Breaux, John, 238
Broder, David, 186
Brophy, Susan, 262
BTU tax, 228–29
Buchanan, Pat, 115, 177, 204
Budget and Impoundment Act, 25, 151, 152, 159
Burns, James McGregor, 8, 9, 278
Bush, George, 5, 22, 27, 166, 217, 231–59: and Gulf War popularity 240; and Veto

threats, 241–43; compared to Ford, 237; compared to Reagan, 228, 231; congressional relations staff of, 232–37; and departmental liaison, 244–55; and friendships with lawmakers, 231–32; and John Tower nomination, 237; relation of with members of Congress, 237–41; and underutilization of the presidency, 232; and use of hidden-hand leadership, 243–44; and use of public relations, 239, 257, 258
Byrd, Harry, 57, 72, 106
Byrd, Robert C., 185–86, 203, 217

Cabinet secretaries, 250–53
Cable, William, 164–65, 172
Califano, Joe, 81, 152–53, 184
Calio, Nicholas, 233, 276
Cannon, James, 130
Carpenter, Liz, 91
Carter, Jimmy, 22, 25–26, 148, 159, 163–97, 201, 207, 219, 260–61; anti-Washington campaign of, 163, 170–71, 179–80; compared to Ford, 178, 180; compared to Johnson, 178, 180; compared to Nixon, 193; compared to Reagan, 190, 224; and congressional honeymoon, 163; congressional relations staff of, 164–66, 170–173; early mistakes of, 165–66, 167–70; and favors, 148; and interest in details, 181–82; and pork barrel projects, 163, 183; problems of with congressional Democrats, 164, 185–87; relations with members of Congress, 179–84; trusteeship presidency of, 164; use of Office of Public Liaison, 164, 189–95, 196
Cheney, Richard B., 219
Chesney, Earl D., 31, 32
chief of staff (role of), 205–07
Civil Rights Act, 90
Clinton, Bill, 5, 27, 217, 228–29: and health

Clinton, Bill, *(cont.)*
  care reform, 275; and new Republican
    majority, 270–74; and public relations,
    266–70; battles of with interest groups,
    274–77; compared to Carter 274–75; con-
    gressional relations staff of, 261–65; early
    problems of, 263–65; legislative victories,
    261, 277–78; and relations with members
    of Congress, 265–66; stimulus package of,
    268–69
Clinton, Hillary Rodham, 270
CNN, 214, 215
Colson, Chuck, 115, 129, 177, 193
Conable, Barber B., 101, 115, 125, 140
Congress-centered perspective, 8–9
Congressional Budget Office, 20, 25, 151,
    152, 286
Congressional Research Service, 153
Connally, John, 84, 121
Connally, Tom, 268
Constituent mail, congressional use of, 154
Contract with America, 272
Cook, Richard, 10
Corwin, Edward S., 8
Covington, Cary, 6
Cowen, Eugene, 113
Cronin, Thomas, 8
C-SPAN, 26, 213, 214, 215, 286
Cycle of decreasing influence, 79

Daly, Charles, 60
Darman, Richard, 201, 224, 235
D.C. home rule bill, 97–99
Deaver, Michael, 202
Decentralization of congressional power, 25,
    154, 155, 159–60, 189
DeLay, Tom, 271
Departmental relations, 2, 19–20, 25, 51–52,
    244–55: under Bush, 244–55; under
    Carter, 245; under Eisenhower, 52–55;
    248; under Johnson, 91–92; under
    Kennedy, 61–62; under Nixon, 135–36.
    See also Cabinet secretaries
Derrick, Butler, 221–22
Desautels, Claude, 60, 62, 104
Dewey, Thomas, 45
Dingell, John, 264
Dirksen, Everett, 39, 69, 75, 84, 90, 101–02,
    127
Discharge petition, 98
Dodd, Thomas, 94

Dole, Robert, 122, 126, 128, 150, 237, 260,
    271
Donahue, Richard, 60
Drew, Elizabeth, 266
Duberstein, Kenneth, 199, 200–01, 205, 276,
    281, 283, 284, 286
Dyer, James W., 233

Earmarking, 152, 286
Edwards, George, 3–4, 13, 134, 188, 219–20
Ehrlichman, John, 114, 115, 118, 122, 124,
    130, 131
Eisenhower, Dwight, 5, 12, 13, 14, 17, 22, 23,
    29–56, 72, 170: and Alaskan statehood,
    36–37, 48; and Bricker amendment, 37,
    42; and hardball politics, 46–47; and Re-
    publican National Committee, 44, 45; atti-
    tude of toward separation of powers
    29–30, 34, 39, 77; autopiolot approach of,
    30, 34–51, 55–56; compared to Lyndon
    Johnson, 34, 78; compared to Richard
    Nixon, 126–27; congressional relations
    staff of, 30–34; departmental relations
    under, 51–55, 248; and doubts about
    GOP leadership, 38, 42; hidden-hand
    leadership of, 17, 22, 44–47; and meet-
    ings with Sam Rayburn and Lyndon John-
    son, 19, 41, 70, 127; on leadership, 49–50,
    55; on maintaining relations with lawmak-
    ers, 33, 71, 144; partisanship of, 41–44,
    46; and Republican leadership meetings,
    40–41; and use of delegation, 30, 31–32,
    35–37, 47, 50–51, 53, 55–56; and use of
    party leaders, 39–40, 47; and use of public
    relations, 47–48
Eizenstat, Stuart, 191, 193
Electoral Connection, The, 12
Electoral expectations theory, 12–13, 22, 198,
    229
Emulation, 2, 15, 286
Evans and Novak, 112, 141

Farley, Jim, 74
Favors, granting or trading of, 18, 24,
    99–107. *See also* Maintaining favor
Fenno, Richard, 250–51
Fiorina, Morris, 154
First one hundred days, 279–80
Fleisher, Richard, 4, 9, 11, 133, 134, 188, 277
Floating coalitions, 146
Foley, Tom, 143

Ford, Gerald, 5, 25, 27, 138–62, 163, 187, 197, 231, 237: and "hardball" politics, 141; as congressional leader, 69, 85, 122, 126, 146; as vice-president, 116–17; compared to Nixon, 145–46, 147, 150; congressional experience of, 141–42; congressional relations staff of, 139–40; floating coalition strategy of, 146–47; and maintaining favor, 142–51; relationship of with members of Congress, 141–42; use of veto by, 161–62

Free, James C., 165, 171

Freeman, Orville, 97

Friedersdorf, Max, 15, 112, 140, 143, 147–48, 150, 155, 156, 175, 195–96, 198, 199, 201, 206, 219, 256, 282

Garner, John Nance, 173

General Accounting Office, 153

Gephardt, Dick, 188

Gergen, David, 202, 205, 211

Germond, Jack, 240–41

Giglio, James, 67

Gingrich, Newt, 28, 206, 271, 272, 274, 286

Going public, 20, 93–97, 107, 209, 211. *See also* Merchandising; Prestige

Goldwater, Barry, 43

Gore, Al, 269, 280

Graham, Katharine, 98

Gramm-Latta, 225

Greenstein, Fred I., 13, 17, 23, 39, 45, 229, 267

Grider, George W., 98

Griffin, Patrick, 263

Gruenther, Homer, 31, 44

Hagerty, Kenneth, 257

Haldeman, H. R., 110, 114, 115, 118, 124, 130

Halleck, Charles, 37–38, 39, 43, 69, 80, 83, 85, 90

Hamilton, Alexander, 51

Hardesty, Bob, 96

Harlow, Bryce, 1, 5, 6, 30–31, 32, 33, 34, 35, 44, 52, 54, 59, 62, 74, 77, 110–11, 112, 113, 115, 116, 119, 120, 124, 125, 130, 132, 155, 166, 170, 171, 174, 175, 176

Harsha, William, Jr., 90

Hatch, Orin, 166

Hays, Wayne, 84

Helms, Jesse, 272

Herring, Pendleton, 1, 251

Hidden-hand leadership, 17–18, 22, 23, 239: use of by Bush, 243–44; use of by Truman, 47

Hilley, John, 263

Hinckley, Barbara, 134

Hollingsworth, E. Boyd, 233

Horsky, Charles, 98

Humphrey, Hubert, 68, 88, 154, 173, 281

Huntington, Samuel, 8

Hymel, Gary, 155

Imperial presidency, 151, 197, 212

Individualized pluralism, 14, 20–22, 160, 184, 196

Influence, 4–8

Institutionalized pluralism, 14, 16–20, 27, 69, 137, 232, 258

Interviews, 291

Intrabranch lobby, 244–50

Jacobson, Jack, 96

Johnson, Lady Bird, 91

Johnson, Lyndon, x, 1, 19, 24, 79–108, 109, 141, 197, 244: and congressional elections, 88–89; compared to Eisenhower, 34; compared to Kennedy, 83; compared to Nixon, 87, 110, 111, 129–30; concern for overuse of, 84; congressional relations staff of, 80–83; departmental liaison under, 91–92; and full court press, 89–90; impact of 1964 election on, 87, 88, 107; impact of 1966 election on, 89; and the "Johnson treatment," 83–87; policy development of, 89–90; and public relations, 93–97; relation of with members of Congress, 83–87; relationship of with Larry O'Brien, 80–81; as Senate Democratic leader, 19, 29, 40, 41, 46, 248, 272; and use of going public, 93–97, 107; as vice-president, 62, 93

Johnson, Nancy, 283

Jones, Charles, 5, 10, 132, 134, 164, 180

Jordan, Hamilton, 174, 175, 177, 193, 206

Kaufman, Burton, 182–83

Kellerman, Barbara, 6, 8

Kemp, Jack, 248, 253

Kendall, Bill, 140

Kennedy, John F., 5, 13, 23, 57–78, 79, 95, 165, 244–44: arm-twisting of, 67, 73–74, 77; compared to Johnson, 78; compared

Kennedy, John F. *(cont.)*
to Eisenhower, 70; congressional experience of, 57, 63, 68; and congressional favors, 101; congressional relations staff of, 58–65; and Democratic National Committee, 76; and expansion of Rules Commitee, 58, 65–67; and the "Friendly Lobbies," 70–71; and Medicare, 69; and 1960 election, 57, 77–78; patronage of, 74–76; relationship of with Larry O'Brien, 63–65; relationship of with members of Congress, 67–68, 73–74; reliance of on party leaders, 68–69; and tensions with Speaker McCormack, 68–69; and Trade Expansion Act of 1962, 76; and Tuesday morning meeting with leadership, 65; use of Democratic National Committee by, 76; use of interest group lobbyists by, 76–77; use of public appeals by, 69
Kennedy, Ted, 69
Kernell, Samuel, 14, 16, 20, 133, 209, 211, 212–13, 215
Kerrey, Bob, 267–68
Kissinger, Henry, 114
Korologos, Tom, 103, 113, 114, 130–31, 132, 149–50, 198, 200, 264–65
Kranowitz, Alan, 200

Laird, Melvin, 116
Laski, Harold, 8
Legislative Presidency, The, 3
Legislating Together, 9
Legislative Strategy Group, 26, 198, 201–05, 207, 211, 224, 230
Legislators, electoral concerns of, ix, 11–12, 16, 18, 22, 64, 70, 88–89, 147, 192, 195, 198, 217–21
Leppert, Charlie, 149
Leuchtenburg, William, 13
Levitas, Elliot, 186
Lewis, Jean, 60
Light, Paul, 13, 79, 158, 285
Lobbying: interest group, 19, 23, 76–77; vice-president's role in, 62, 173–74. *See also* Intrabranch lobby; White House, lobbyists
Loen, Vern, 140, 156
Long, Clarence, 103
Long, Russell, 189
Lott, Trent, 220
Luce, Robert, 10

Madison, James, 287

Maher, Robert, 165
Maintaining favor, 18, 25, 142–50: contrasted to "trading favors," 142–43; Eisenhower on, 33, 144
Manatos, Mike, 60, 68, 81, 86
Manley, John, 142
Mansfield, Mike, 68, 77, 84, 102, 105, 122
Marsh, John, 139, 158, 175
Martin, Jack, 31, 32
Martin, Joesph, 36, 38, 39
Mayhew, David, 12
McCabe, Ed, 31, 32, 37, 44
McClure, Frederick, 232–37
McCormack, John, 68
McCurdy, Dave, 267
McGregor, Clark, 116, 117
McIntyre, Thomas, 88
McLarty, Mack, 262
McNamara, Robert, 106
McNeil, Neil, 63
McPherson, Harry, 87
Meese, Ed, 202
Merchandising, 20–21, 24, 207–16
Merrill, Rich, 165, 171
Michel, Bob, 220
Miller, George, 261
Miller, Lorraine, 262
Mills, Wilbur, 69, 89, 104, 158
Mineta, Norm, 168
Molinari, Guy, 234
Mondale, Walter, 10, 153, 169, 173–74, 182, 197, 212, 284
Moore, Frank, 164, 166, 167–68, 176, 177, 178, 182, 189, 200, 264, 280
Moore, Powell, 199, 283
Moore, W. Henson, 235
Morgan, Gerald T., 31, 32
Moyers, Bill, 105
Moynihan, Daniel Patrick, 15, 286
Muskie, Edmund, 94, 169

National Emergencies Act, 152
Neustadt, Richard, 1, 2, 279
Nickles, Don, 238
Nixon, Richard, x, 2, 7, 14, 21, 24–25, 109–37, 138, 147, 197; and antiballistic missile treaty, 123, 124, 129, 130; compared to Eisenhower 121, 126–27; compared to Johnson, 110, 111, 121, 129–30, 87; compared to Kennedy, 121; compared to Reagan, 116, 135; congressional relations staff of, 110–20, 123, 136; decline in

Nixon, Richard, *(cont.)*
  popularity of, 131–33; dislike of for members of Congress, 125–27; emphasis of on public relations, 127–35; hoarding of campaign funds by, 125, 126; impact of 1968 election on, 109; relationship of with members of Congress, 120–27, 144; and role of personality in congressional relations, 124; and staff tension, 115–16; use of departmental liaison by, 135–36; use of interest groups by, 129; as vice-president, 173
Nofziger, Lyn, 128
Nominations, 236–37
North American Free Trade Agreement, 269–70
Nunn, Sam, 237

O'Brien, Larry, 23, 32, 57, 62, 80–82, 119, 120, 135, 140, 144, 157, 165–66, 285; and "full court press," 89–90; and lack of Washington experience, 58–59, 77
O'Brien, Larry, III, 285
Office of Communications, 202
Office of Intergovernmental Affairs, 202
Office of Legislative Affairs. *See* White House Office of Legislative Affairs
Office of Management and Budget (OMB), 2, 25, 140, 136, 191, 242, 254, 256–57
Office of Political Affairs, 202
Office of Public Liaison (OPL), 26, 164, 189–95, 196, 202
Office of Technology Assessment, 153, 286
Ogelsby, M. B., 199
O'Neill, Tip, 85, 86, 144, 160, 166, 185–86, 197, 213, 272
Ornstein, Norman, 218, 284
Ostrom, Charles, 134

Panama Canal treaties, 172, 183
Pashayan, Charles, 238
Paster, Howard, 6, 261–62, 263, 264, 265, 276
Patronage, 74–76
Perkins, Carl, 81, 105
Perot, Ross, 269
Persons, Wilton B., 1, 30, 31, 32, 33, 52
Peterson, Howard C., 76
Peterson, Mark, 9, 11, 12
Pika, Joseph, 15, 21, 116, 175, 264
Pinson, Valerie, 165, 171
Pipes, G. Russell, 51
Powell, Jody, 175

Presidency-centered perspective, 8–9
President as party leader, 184–89
Prestige, 21–22, 24, 133–35, 136: compared to merchandising, 21, 116, 209–10
Price, Melvin, 90

Quayle, Dan, 188, 235

Rayburn, Sam, 19, 29, 40, 41, 65–66, 68
Reagan, Ronald, 1, 5, 13, 14, 15, 22, 26–27, 94, 197–230: compared to Bush, 228, 231; compared to Carter, 224, 227; compared to Franklin Roosevelt, 208; compared to Nixon, 208–09, 228; compared to other presidents, 227; congressional relations staff of, 198–201; emphasis of on legislative victories, 201, 210; impact of assassination attempt on, 224, 225; perceived electoral clout of, 216–21, 229; relationship of with members of Congress, 197, 222–29; staff tension of, 203–05; use of Legislative Strategy Group, 26, 198, 201–05, 207, 211, 224, 230; use of public appeals by, 207–16, 229–30; use of "special publics" by, 221–22; work of with outside groups, 222
Reeves, Richard, 5, 13, 78
Regan, Donald, 205, 206
Reineck, Edwin, 90
Ribicoff, Abraham, 86
Ricchetti, Steve, 262
Rivers, Douglas, 134
Rivers, Mendel L., 44
Roche, Chuck, 82
Rockefeller, Nelson, 148
Roosevelt, Franklin, 13, 29, 170, 279
Rose, Nancy, 134
Rossiter, Clinton, 8
Russell, Richard, 84
Russo, Marty, 188

Sanders, Barefoot, 81, 82, 92, 93, 101–02, 106, 214–15
Saund, D. S., 72
Schlesinger, Arthur, 57, 68, 151
Scott, Hugh, 148, 150
Sequoia, 71–72, 144, 145
Shelby, Richard, 264
Shivers, Allen, 17
Simon, Dennis, 134
Simpson, Dick, 43
Skinner, Samuel, 235

Smith, Hedrick, 216, 224
Solomon, Gerald, 234
Sorensen, Ted, 93
Sources, ix
Speakes, Larry, 202, 204
Special publics, 22–23, 189–95, 221–22: compared to hidden-hand leadership, 22
Statement of Administration Policy, 242–43
Stennis, John, 149
Stephanopoulos, George, 263
Stockman, David, 202, 207, 220, 223, 224
Straub, Terrence, 165
Success measures, 4–8
Sullivan, Terry, 134
Sununu, John, 234–35

Taft, Robert, 29, 38
Talking notes, 123
Tananbaum, Duane, 37
Tandem institution perspective, 9–10, 12
Tate, Dan C., 165
Taylor, Paul, 285
Teeter, Robert, 235
Thompson, Robert, 165
Thurmond, Strom, 104
Timmons, William (Bill), 112–14, 119, 124, 135–36, 140, 156, 162, 166, 179, 198
Trade Expansion Act of 1962, 76–77
Trading favors. See Favors, granting or trading of
Truman, Harry, 29, 42, 47, 170

Trusteeship presidency, 164
Tulis, Jeffrey, 8, 212
Turner, Pamela J., 199

Valenti, Jack, 91, 100, 102
Veto threats, 27, 161, 241–43, 258
Vetoes, 5, 27, 139, 160–61
Voting Rights Act, 90, 94–95

War Powers Resolution, 151, 152, 159
Wayne, Stephen, 3, 6, 201
Wexler, Anne, 129, 164, 190–95
Weyrich, Paul, 239
White, William S., 281
White House: "education" of, 26, 174–79, 203–04; lobbyists, 118–20
White House Office of Legislative Affairs, 15–16, 22, 26: access and credibility of, 118–20; as "boundary role persons," 116, 175, 282; creation of, 30–32; organization of, 33–34, 61, 170–73, 201; role of, 174–79
Wick, Charles Z., 222
Will, George, 257–58
Wilson, Henry Hall, Jr., 60, 67, 81, 84, 106
Wilson, William A., 222
Wirthlin, Dick, 202
Witcover, Jules, 240–41
Woodward, Bob, 262
Wright, Jim, 181, 240

Yeutter, Clayton, 235